the**TOP10**
of everything

the TOP10
of everything

Russell Ash

hamlyn

Contents

Produced for Hamlyn by
Palazzo Editions Ltd
15 Gay Street, Bath, BA1 2PH

Publishing director: Colin Webb
Art director: Bernard Higton
Project editor: Sonya Newland
Editor: Marion Dent
Picture researcher: David Penrose
Indexer: Michael Dent

First published in Great Britain in 2006 by
Hamlyn, a division of
Octopus Publishing Group Ltd
2–4 Heron Quays, London E14 4JP

Copyright © Octopus Publishing Group Ltd
2006
Text copyright © Russell Ash 2006

ISBN-13: 978-0-600-61630-6
ISBN-10: 0-600-61630-4

A CIP catalogue record for this book is
available from the British Library

Printed and bound in China

10 9 8 7 6 5 4 3 2 1

Introduction

Coming of Age

Like my elder son, *The Top 10 of Everything* has reached its age of majority, having been published annually for 18 years. To those of you who have loyally bought it every year, I would like to extend my thanks. You now have nearly 5,000 pages of Top 10 lists and have filled 50 cm (20 inches) of shelving.

Top 10 – the Ground Rules

The Top 10 of Everything is a book of definitive, quantifiable Top 10 lists. It is not a book of 'bests', except those that are measurably bestsellers, while 'worsts' such as disasters are similarly ranked by cost or the number of victims. All the lists are all-time and global unless a year or territory is stated. Film lists are based on cumulative global earnings, irrespective of production or marketing budgets, and inflation – that eternal bugbear of those who compile such lists – is not taken into account. Figures for country and city populations are based on the latest available census, with estimates for increases where officially available, while in most instances 'countries' should be taken as meaning 'countries, colonies and dependent territories'. The only detours from strict Top 10-ism are found in occasional 'asides', Amazing Fact features on everything from giant squids to extraordinary names, the most-married man to the first airmail letter.

Why Lists?

We are constantly assailed with lists. Newspapers and TV programmes present rankings based on market research and polls, lists of the best places to live, the greatest films, the bestselling books, the worst crime rates and so on. Ranked lists have become a journalistic shorthand overview of what might otherwise be a daunting mass of facts and figures. The Top 10 of Everything provides a unique collection of lists in a diverse array of categories.

The Rate of Change

In my work in compiling *The Top 10 of Everything*, I am constantly aware of just how much the world is changing and how the rate and scale of change seems inexorably to accelerate. For example, not many more than 40 films have ever earned over $1/2 billion worldwide, but 25 of them have done so since 2000. In 2006 a single photograph was sold at auction for £1.7 million ($2.9 million) and the world's largest passenger ship, *Freedom of the Seas*, was launched. It was predicted that the US population will top 300 million as this book is published and that 2007 will mark the year in which the balance of the world's population tips from predominantly rural to a majority of urban dwellers.

Caught in the Web

In 2006 world Internet usage topped 1 billion and, for the first time, music tracks reached No. 1 in the chart based solely on downloads, rather than physical record sales. As is often stated, the Internet is both a blessing and a curse. Information that was previously unavailable or not released until often years later, now becomes accessible almost instantaneously, so, for example, my film database which was once updated as and when figures were released can now be updated almost daily – and because it can be, I do.

Source Material

My sources encompass international organizations, commercial companies and research bodies, specialized publications and, especially, a network of individuals around the world who have shared their knowledge of everything from snakes and skyscrapers to ships and skateboarding. As ever, I gladly acknowledge their invaluable contribution (see page 255 for a full list of credits), as well as the many people who have been involved with the book at all stages of its development.

Want to be in the Book?

★ Become an actor and get nominated for at least six Oscars (you will be in two lists if you win one before your 21st birthday).

★ Make at least 20 films, such as the James Bond series, that earn over $3.7 billion worldwide.

★ Be worth more than $18 billion, or earn more than $7 million a year after your death.

★ Drive a car at more than 1,228 km/h (763 mph).

★ Become a monarch and rule for over 59 years, or serve as a president for more than 22 years.

★ Record a single that sells at least 8 million copies, or if you are a female singer, have more than 12 Top 10 hits.

★ Win more than eight Olympic medals if you are a woman or 11 if you are a man, or run 100 m in under 9.86 seconds.

★ Score more than 14 goals in soccer World Cup matches. This will probably also guarantee you a transfer fee of £28 million-plus, and a place in yet another Top 10 list.

Contact Me

Your comments, corrections and suggestions for new lists are always welcome. Please contact me via the publishers or visit my website:

http://www.top10ofeverything.com

Russell Ash

THE UNIVERSE & THE EARTH

1

Space Bodies

top10 **LARGEST BODIES** IN THE SOLAR SYSTEM

	BODY	MAXIMUM DIAMETER KM	MILES	SIZE COMPARED WITH EARTH
1	Sun	1,392,140	865,036	109.136
2	Jupiter	142,984	88,846	11.209
3	Saturn	120,536	74,898	9.449
4	Uranus	51,118	31,763	4.007
5	Neptune	49,528	30,775	3.883
6	Earth	12,756	7,926	1.000
7	Venus	12,104	7,521	0.949
8	Mars	6,805	4,228	0.533
9	Ganymede	5,262	3,270	0.413
10	Titan	5,150	3,200	0.404

Along with Mercury, with a diameter of 4,879 km (3,032 miles), most of the planets are visible with the naked eye. The exceptions are Uranus and Neptune and, outside the Top 10, Pluto. Its diameter is approximately 2,390 km (1,485 miles), but its status as a planet is argued. A newly discovered body known as 2003 UB313 is larger at some 2,700 km (1,678 miles) and is described by some astronomers as the '10th planet'.

top10 **STARS** NEAREST TO THE EARTH

	STAR*	LIGHT YEARS	DISTANCE KM (MILLIONS)	MILES (MILLIONS)
1	Proxima Centauri	4.22	39,923,310	24,792,500
2	Alpha Centauri	4.39	41,531,595	25,791,250
3	Barnard's Star	5.94	56,195,370	34,897,500
4	Wolf 359	7.78	73,602,690	45,707,500
5	Lalande 21185	8.31	78,616,755	48,821,250
6	Sirius	8.60	81,360,300	50,525,000
7	Luyten 726-8	8.72	82,495,560	51,230,000
8	Ross 154	9.69	91,672,245	56,928,750
9	Ross 248	10.32	97,632,360	60,630,000
10	Epsilon Eridani	10.49	99,240,645	61,628,750

* Excluding the Sun

Source: Peter Bond, Royal Astronomical Society

A spaceship travelling at 40,237 km/h (25,000 mph) – faster than any human has yet reached in space – would take over 113,200 years to reach the Earth's closest star, Proxima Centauri. Even stars within the Milky Way are as much as 2,500 light years from us, while our own galaxy may span 100,000 light years end to end, with the Sun some 25,000 to 30,000 light years from its centre.

top10 **LONGEST YEARS** IN THE SOLAR SYSTEM

	BODY*	LENGTH OF YEAR# YEARS	DAYS
1	Pluto	247	256
2	Neptune	164	298
3	Uranus	84	4
4	Saturn	29	168
5	Jupiter	11	314
6	Mars		687
7	Earth		365
8	Venus		225
9	Mercury		88
10	Sun		0

* Excludes satellites
\# Period of orbit round the Sun, in Earth years/days

⬆ Ceres launches series
The first and largest asteroid was discovered by Italian astronomer Giuseppe Piazzi and called Ceres after the patron goddess of Sicily, the location of Palermo Observatory. The element cerium, identified in Sweden two years later, was named after it.

top10 LARGEST **ASTEROIDS**

	NAME	NO.	DISCOVERED	MAXIMUM DIAMETER* KM	MILES
1	Ceres	1	1 Jan 1801	940	584
2	Vesta	4	29 Mar 1807	576	357
3	Pallas	2	28 Mar 1802	538	334
4	Hygeia	10	12 Apr 1849	430	267
5	Interamnia	704	2 Oct 1910	338	210
6	Davida	511	30 May 1903	324	201
7	Cybele	65	8 Mar 1861	308	191
8	Europa	52	4 Feb 1858	292	181
9	Sylvia	87	16 May 1866	282	175
10	Patienta	451	4 Dec 1899	280	173

* Most asteroids are irregular in shape

Asteroids, sometimes known as 'minor planets', are fragments of rock orbiting between Mars and Jupiter. Up to 16 November 2005, some 305,624 had been found: 120,437 with orbits calculated and assigned numbers and 12,712 named. Each of the four Beatles has an asteroid named after him, as do Walt Disney, Frank Zappa, James Bond and the members of the Monty Python team.

top10 LARGEST PLANETARY **MOONS**

MOON	PLANET	DIAMETER KM	MILES
Ganymede	Jupiter	5,262.4	3,269.9

1 Discovered by Galileo on 11 January 1610, Ganymede – one of Jupiter's 63 known satellites and the largest moon in the Solar System – is thought to have a surface of ice about 97 km (60 miles) thick.

Titan	Saturn	5,150.0	3,200.1

2 Titan is the largest of Saturn's 49 moons and is larger than two of the planets in the Solar System, Mercury and Pluto. We have no idea what its surface looks like because it has a dense atmosphere containing nitrogen, ethane and other gases which shroud its surface – not unlike that of the Earth four billion years ago.

Callisto	Jupiter	4,820.6	2,995.4

3 Possessing a similar composition to Ganymede, Callisto is heavily pitted with craters, perhaps more so than any other body in the Solar System.

Io	Jupiter	3,642.6	2,263.4

4 Most of what we know about Io was reported back by the 1979 *Voyager 1* probe, which revealed a crust of solid sulphur with massive volcanic eruptions in progress, hurling sulphurous material 300 km (186 miles) into space.

Moon	Earth	3,476.2	2,160.0

5 Our own satellite is a quarter of the size of the Earth, the fifth largest in the Solar System and, to date, the only one to have been explored by Man.

Europa	Jupiter	3,121.6	1,939.7

6 Although Europa's ice-covered surface is apparently smooth and crater-free, it is covered with mysterious black lines, with some of them 64 km (40 miles) wide and resembling canals.

Triton	Neptune	2,706.8	1,681.9

7 Discovered on 10 October 1846 by British brewer and amateur astronomer William Lassell, 17 days after German astronomer Johann Galle had discovered Neptune itself, Triton is the only known satellite in the Solar System that revolves around its planet in the opposite direction to the planet's rotation.

Titania	Uranus	1,577.8	980.4

8 The largest of Uranus's 27 moons, Titania was discovered by William Herschel (who had discovered the planet six years earlier) in 1787 and has a snowball-like surface of ice.

Rhea	Saturn	1,528.0	947.6

9 Saturn's second-largest moon was discovered in 1672. *Voyager 1*, which flew past Rhea in November 1980, confirmed that its icy surface is pitted with craters, one of them 225 km (140 miles) in diameter.

Oberon	Uranus	1,522.8	946.2

10 Oberon was discovered by Herschel and given the name of the fairy king husband of Queen Titania, both characters in Shakespeare's *A Midsummer Night's Dream*.

⬆ *Mighty moons*
Our own Moon (shown immediately above) is smaller than the other natural satellites Ganymede, Callisto and Io (top to bottom), as well as Saturn's Titan, whose appearance is shrouded by a dense layer of gases.

⬆ **Roving reporter**
NASA's Mars Exploration Rovers are the latest planetary probes.

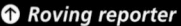

➡ **Moon Ranger**
Ranger 7 was one of several successful US lunar launches.

top10 FIRST **PLANETARY PROBES**

PROBE/COUNTRY*	PLANET	ARRIVAL#
1 Venera 4	Venus	18 Oct 1967
2 Venera 5	Venus	16 May 1969
3 Venera 6	Venus	17 May 1969
4 Venera 7	Venus	15 Dec 1970
5 Mariner 9, USA	Mars	13 Nov 1971
6 Mars 2	Mars	27 Nov 1971
7 Mars 3	Mars	2 Dec 1971
8 Venera 8	Venus	22 Jul 1972
9 Venera 9	Venus	22 Oct 1975
10 Venera 10	Venus	25 Oct 1975

* USSR unless otherwise stated
\# Successfully entered orbit or landed

This list excludes 'fly-bys' – probes that passed by but did not land on the surface of another planet. The USA's *Pioneer 10*, for example, launched on 2 March 1972, flew past Jupiter on 3 December 1973, but did not land. *Venera 4* was the first unmanned probe to land on a planet, and *Venera 9* the first to transmit pictures from a planet's surface. *Mariner 9* was the first to orbit another planet and transmit photographs.

top10 FIRST UNMANNED **MOON LANDINGS**

NAME	COUNTRY	DATE (LAUNCH/IMPACT)
1 Luna 2	USSR	12/13 Sep 1959
2 Ranger 4	USA	23/26 Apr 1962
3 Ranger 6	USA	30 Jan/2 Feb 1964
4 Ranger 7	USA	28/31 Jul 1964
5 Ranger 8	USA	17/20 Feb 1965
6 Ranger 9	USA	21/24 Mar 1965
7 Luna 5	USSR	9/12 May 1965
8 Luna 7	USSR	4/8 Oct 1965
9 Luna 8	USSR	3/7 Dec 1965
10 Luna 9	USSR	31 Jan/3 Feb 1966

The first nine on this list were the first successful Moon landings – but all impacted at speed and were destroyed. *Luna 9* was the first to make a soft landing and transmit photographic images back to Earth. Among subsequent US landings were seven *Surveyors* (1966–68) and five *Lunar Orbiters* (1966–67). Before crashing onto the Moon, the 380-kg (838-lb) *Orbiters* relayed detailed photographic images of the surface, mapping suitable sites for the manned *Apollo* landings that followed.

the 10 FIRST **PLANETARY MOONS** TO BE DISCOVERED

	MOON	PLANET	DISCOVERER	YEAR
1	Moon	Earth	—	Ancient
2	=Io	Jupiter	Galileo Galilei, Italy	1610
	=Europa	Jupiter	Galileo Galilei	1610
	=Ganymede	Jupiter	Galileo Galilei	1610
	=Callisto	Jupiter	Galileo Galilei	1610
6	Titan	Saturn	Christian Huygens, Netherlands	1655
7	Iapetus	Saturn	Giovanni Cassini, Italy/France	1671
8	Rhea	Saturn	Giovanni Cassini	1672
9	=Tethys	Saturn	Giovanni Cassini	1684
	=Dione	Saturn	Giovanni Cassini	1684

While the Earth's Moon has been observed since ancient times, it was not until the development of the telescope that Galileo was able to discover (on 7 January 1610) the first moons of another planet. These, which are Jupiter's four largest, were named by German astronomer Simon Marius and are known as the Galileans.

❯ Mirror image
Comprising 91 hexagonal mirrors, the internationally funded SALT (South African Large Telescope) is so powerful that it is capable of detecting light from distant stars a billion times fainter than the human eye can see.

the 10 FIRST **ASTEROIDS** TO BE DISCOVERED

	ASTEROID / DISCOVERER / COUNTRY	DISCOVERED
1	Ceres Giuseppe Piazzi, Italy	1 Jan 1801
2	Pallas Heinrich Olbers, Germany	28 Mar 1802
3	Juno Karl Ludwig Harding, Germany	1 Sep 1804
4	Vesta Heinrich Olbers, Germany	29 Mar 1807
5	Astraea Karl Ludwig Hencke, Germany	8 Dec 1845
6	Hebe Karl Ludwig Hencke, Germany	1 Jul 1847
7	Iris John Russell Hind, UK	13 Aug 1847
8	Flora John Russell Hind, UK	18 Oct 1847
9	Metis Andrew Graham, UK	25 Apr 1848
10	Hygeia Annibale de Gasparis, Italy	12 Apr 1849

top 10 LARGEST REFLECTING **TELESCOPES**

	TELESCOPE NAME (YEAR BUILT)	LOCATION	APERTURE M	FT
1	Southern African Large Telescope (2005)	Sutherland, South Africa	11.0	36.1
2	Gran Telescopio Canarias (2005)	La Palma, Canary Islands, Spain	10.4	34.1
3	=Keck I Telescope* (1993)	Mauna Kea, Hawaii, USA	9.8	32.2
	=Keck II Telescope* (1996)	Mauna Kea, Hawaii, USA	9.8	32.2
5	Hobby-Eberly Telescope (1997)	Mt Fowlkes, Texas, USA	9.2	30.2
6	Large Binocular Telescope* (2004)	Mt Graham, Arizona, USA	8.4	27.6
7	Subaru Telescope (1999)	Mauna Kea, Hawaii, USA	8.3	27.2
8	=Antu Telescope# (1998)	Cerro Paranal, Chile	8.2	26.9
	=Kueyen Telescope# (1999)	Cerro Paranal, Chile	8.2	26.9
	=Melipal Telescope# (2000)	Cerro Paranal, Chile	8.2	26.9
	=Yepun Telescope# (2001)	Cerro Paranal, Chile	8.2	26.9

* Twin
# Combine to form VLT (Very Large Telescope)

Based on a c.1670 design by Sir Isaac Newton, reflecting telescopes are optical telescopes with mirrors, offering greater power and accuracy than the lenses of refractors. Recent technology has enabled progressive increases in the size of the world's research reflectors.

Space Explorers

top10 LONGEST **SPACE SHUTTLE** FLIGHTS*

FLIGHT	DATES	DAYS	DURATION HRS	MINS	SECS
1 STS-80 Columbia	19 Nov–7 Dec 1996	17	8	53	18
2 STS-78 Columbia	20 Jun–7 Jul 1996	16	21	48	30
3 STS-67 Endeavour	2–18 Mar 1995	16	15	9	46
4 STS-107 Columbia#	16 Jan–1 Feb 2003	15	22	20	32
5 STS-73 Columbia	20 Oct–5 Nov 1995	15	21	53	16
6 STS-90 Columbia	17 Apr–3 May 1998	15	21	15	58
7 STS-75 Columbia	22 Feb–9 Mar 1996	15	17	41	25
8 STS-94 Columbia	1–17 Jul 1997	15	16	46	1
9 STS-87 Atlantis	25 Sep–6 Oct 1997	15	16	35	1
10 STS-65 Columbia	8–23 Jul 1994	14	17	55	0

* To 1 Jan 2006
\# Destroyed on re-entry

➔ Monkey around
*Named for USAF's School of
Aviation Medicine, Miss Sam
orbited in a Mercury capsule.*

top10 FIRST **ANIMALS** IN SPACE

NAME / ANIMAL / STATUS	COUNTRY	DATE
1 Laika (name used by Western press: actually the name of the breed to which the dog named Kudryavka, a female Samoyed husky, belonged). *Died in space*	USSR	3 November 1957
2 = Laska and Benjy (mice) *Re-entered Earth's atmosphere, but not recovered*	USA	13 December 1958
4 = Able and Baker (female rhesus monkey/female squirrel monkey). *Successfully returned to Earth*	USA	28 May 1959
6 = Otvazhnaya (female Samoyed husky) and an unnamed rabbit. *Recovered*	USSR	2 July 1959
8 Sam (male rhesus monkey). *Recovered*	USA	4 December 1959
9 Miss Sam (female rhesus monkey). *Recovered*	USA	21 January 1960
10 = Belka and Strelka (female Samoyed huskies), plus 40 mice and two rats. *First to orbit and return safely*	USSR	19 August 1960

top10 COUNTRIES WITH THE **MOST** **SPACEFLIGHT** EXPERIENCE

COUNTRY	ASTRONAUTS	TOTAL DURATION OF MISSIONS* DAYS	HRS	MINS	SECS
1 USSR/Russia	97	16,858	17	8	24
2 USA	275	9,380	10	4	48
3 France	9	384	23	38	0
4 Kazakhstan	2	349	14	59	3
5 Germany	10	309	17	8	56
6 Canada	8	122	13	30	58
7 Japan	5	88	6	0	40
8 Italy	4	76	6	34	9
9 Switzerland	1	42	12	5	32
10 South Africa	1	24	22	28	22
UK	*1*	*7*	*21*	*13*	*45*

* To 24 Oct 2004 landing of Soyuz TMA-4

The long-duration stays of its cosmonauts on board the *Mir* Space Station have given the USSR (now Russia) its lead. The USA has had many more astronauts in space but its missions were shorter.

USA's first EVA
During the USA's 8th space mission, astronaut Edward H. White makes his country's first-ever spacewalk above the Gulf of Mexico, tethered to the Gemini 4 capsule and using a hand-held oxygen-jet gun to manoeuvre.

Seas & Lakes

top10 DEEPEST DEEP-SEA TRENCHES

	TRENCH*	DEEPEST POINT M	FT
10	Yap	8,527	27,973
9	Puerto Rico	8,605	28,229

Each of the eight deepest ocean trenches would be deep enough to submerge Mount Everest, which is 8,850 m (29,035 ft) above sea level.

	TRENCH*	DEEPEST POINT M	FT
8	Izu	9,695	31,805
7	Kuril	9,750	31,985
6	New Britain	9,940	32,609
5	Bonin	9,994	32,786
4	Kermadec#	10,047	32,960
3	Philippine	10,497	34,436

top10 DEEPEST OCEANS AND SEAS

	SEA / OCEAN	AVERAGE DEPTH M	FT
1	Pacific Ocean	3,939	12,925
2	Indian Ocean	3,840	12,598
3	Atlantic Ocean	3,575	11,730
4	Caribbean Sea, Atlantic Ocean	2,575	8,448
5	Sea of Japan, Pacific Ocean	1,666	5,468
6	Gulf of Mexico, Atlantic Ocean	1,614	5,297
7	Mediterranean Sea, Atlantic Ocean	1,501	4,926
8	Bering Sea, Pacific Ocean	1,491	4,893
9	South China Sea, Pacific Ocean	1,463	4,802
10	Black Sea, Atlantic Ocean	1,190	3,906

top10 LARGEST OCEANS AND SEAS

	SEA / OCEAN	APPROXIMATE AREA* SQ KM	SQ MILES
1	Pacific Ocean	166,242,500	64,186,600
2	Atlantic Ocean	86,557,800	33,420,160
3	Indian Ocean	73,427,800	28,350,640
4	Arctic Ocean	13,223,800	5,105,740

top 10 SHALLOWEST OCEANS AND SEAS

SEA* / OCEAN	AVERAGE DEPTH M	FT
1 Yellow Sea, Pacific Ocean	36.8	121
2 Baltic Sea, Atlantic Ocean	54.8	180
3 Hudson Bay, Atlantic Ocean	92.9	305
4 North Sea, Atlantic Ocean	93.8	308
5 Persian Gulf, Indian Ocean	99.9	328
6 East China Sea, Indian Ocean	188.9	620
7 Red Sea, Indian Ocean	537.6	1,764
8 Gulf of California, Pacific Ocean	723.9	2,375
9 Sea of Okhotsk, Pacific Ocean	972.9	3,192
10 Arctic Ocean	1,038.4	3,407

* Excludes landlocked seas

The Yellow Sea, or Huang Hai, an arm of the Pacific Ocean, north of the China Sea between China and Korea, is so-called for the colour of mineral deposits from the rivers that discharge into it. With a maximum depth of 152 m (500 ft), ice fields form during the winter and shifting sandbanks make it treacherous to shipping. It has been predicted that environmental changes in the next few millenia will result in its total disappearance.

top 10 LARGEST LAKES

LAKE / LOCATION	APPROX. AREA SQ KM	SQ MILES
1 Caspian Sea, Azerbaijan/Iran/ Kazakhstan/Russia/Turkmenistan	371,000	143,000
2 Michigan/Huron*, Canada/USA	117,436	45,342
3 Superior, Canada/USA	82,103	31,700
4 Victoria, Kenya/Tanzania/Uganda	69,485	26,828
5 Tanganyika, Burundi/Tanzania/ Dem. Rep. of Congo/Zambia	32,893	12,700
6 Baikal, Russia	31,500	12,162
7 Great Bear, Canada	31,328	12,096
8 Malawi (Nyasa), Tanzania/Malawi/ Mozambique	28,880	11,150
9 Great Slave, Canada	28,568	11,030
10 Lake Erie, Canada/USA	25,667	9,910

* Now considered two lobes of the same lake

Lake Michigan/Huron is the world's largest freshwater lake. As recently as 1960, the Aral Sea (Kazakhstan/Uzbekistan), which has an area (including several lake islands) of some 68,300 sq km (26,371 sq miles) was the fourth largest lake in the world, but as a result of the diverting of rivers for irrigation, it has dropped to 17,158 sq km (6,625 sq miles) and thus fallen out of the Top 10.

↓ Scratching the surface
An ice hockey game on Siberia's frozen Baikal, the world's deepest lake.

top 10 DEEPEST LAKES

	LAKE / LOCATION	GREATEST DEPTH M	FT
10	Hornindals Norway	514	1,686
9	Toba Sumatra, Indonesia	529	1,736
8	Crater Oregon, USA	589	1,932
7	Matana Sulawesi, Indonesia	590	1,936
6	Great Slave Canada	614	2,015
5	Issyk-kul Kyrgyzstan	668	2,191
4	Malawi Malawi/Mozambique/ Tanzania	706	2,316
3	Caspian Sea Azerbaijan/Iran/Kazakhstan/ Russia/Turkmenistan	1,025	3,363
2	Tanganyika Burundi/Tanzania/Dem. Rep. of Congo/Zambia	1,471	4,825
1	Baikal Russia	1,741	5,712

Rivers & Waterfalls

top10 **LONGEST** RIVERS

RIVER / LOCATION	APPROXIMATE LENGTH KM	MILES
1 Nile, Burundi/Dem. Rep. of Congo/ Egypt/Eritrea/Ethiopia/Kenya/ Rwanda/Sudan/Tanzania/Uganda	6,695	4,160
2 Amazon, Peru/Brazil	6,448	4,007
3 Yangtze (Chang Jiang), China	6,378	3,964
4 Huang He (Yellow), China	5,464	3,395
5 Amur, China/Russia	4,415	2,744
6 Lena, Russia	4,400	2,734
7 Congo, Angola/Dem. Rep. of Congo	4,373	2,718
8 Irtysh, China/Kazkhakstan/Mongolia/Russia	4,248	2,640
9 Mackenzie, Canada	4,241	2,635
10 Mekong, Tibet/China/Myanmar/Laos/ Thailand/Cambodia/Vietnam	4,183	2,600

➊ Egyptian enigma
Its precise length the subject of debate among geographers, the River Nile flows through Egypt and nine other countries.

The source of the Nile was discovered in 1858 when British explorer John Hanning Speke reached Lake Victoria Nyanza, in what is now Burundi. The river is today generally accepted to be the world's longest, with an overall length of 6,695 km (4,160 miles). It was not until almost 100 years later, in 1953, that the source of the Amazon was identified as a stream called Huarco flowing from the Misuie glacier in the Peruvian Andes mountains. After following a series of feeders, it joins the Amazon's main tributary at Ucayali, Peru, giving a total length of 6,448 km (4,007 miles). By following the Amazon from its source and up the Rio Pará, it is possible to sail for some 6,750 km (4,195 miles), which is a greater distance than the length of the Nile, but because experts do not regard this entire route as part of the Amazon basin, the Nile is still considered the world's longest river.

top10 **LONGEST** RIVERS IN THE UK

RIVER	LENGTH KM	MILES
1 Severn	354	220
2 Thames	346	215
3 Trent	297	185
4 Aire	259	161
5 Great Ouse	230	143
6 Wye	215	135
7 Tay	188	117
8 Spey	172	107
9 Nene	161	100
10 Clyde	158	98

top10 **WIDEST** WATERFALLS

WATERFALL / RIVER / COUNTRY	WIDTH M	FT
1 Chutes de Khône, Mekong River, Laos	10,783	35,376
2 Salto Pará, Rio Caura, Venezuela	5,608	18,400
3 = Salto del Guaíra, Rio Paraná, Brazil	4,828	15,840
= Chutes de Livingstone, Congo River, Congo	4,828	15,840
5 Celilo Falls, Columbia River, USA	3,219	10,560
6 Kongou Falls, Ivindo River, Gabon	3,200	10,500
7 Salto de Iguaçu, Rio Iguaçu, Argentina/Brazil	2,700	8,858
8 = Saltos dos Patos e Maribondo, Rio Grande, Brazil	2,012	6,600
= Salto do Urubupungá, Rio Paraná, Brazil	2,012	6,600
10 Victoria Falls, Zambezi River, Zimbabwe/Zambia	1,737	5,700

top10 **HIGHEST** WATERFALLS

WATERFALL RIVER / LOCATION	TOTAL DROP M	FT
1 Angel Carrao, Venezuela	979	3,212*
2 Tugela Tugela, South Africa	850	2,800
3 Utigård Jostedal Glacier, Nesdale, Norway	800	2,625
4 Mongefossen Monge, Mongebekk, Norway	774	2,540
5 Mutarazi Mutarazi River, Zimbabwe	762	2,499
6 Yosemite Yosemite Creek, California, USA	739	2,425
7 Østre Mardøla Foss Mardals, Eikisdal, Norway	656	2,152
8 Tyssestrengane Tysso, Hardanger, Norway	646	2,120
9 Cuquenán Arabopo, Venezuela	610	2,000
10 Sutherland Arthur, South Island, New Zealand	580	1,904

* Longest single drop 807 m (2,648 ft)

Although earlier explorers may have seen it, American adventurer James Crawford Angel (1899–1956) first sighted the Angel Falls, Venezuela, from the air on 16 November 1933, noting in his logbook, 'I found myself a waterfall'. When Angel's report was investigated, the falls on the River Churún were confirmed as the world's highest and named Salto Angel (Angel Falls) in his honour.

top10 **HIGHEST** WATERFALLS IN THE UK

WATERFALL / LOCATION	TOTAL DROP M	FT
1 Eas a' Chàul Aluinn, Scotland	201	658
2 Cautley Spout, England	198	650
3 Pystill Gwyn, Wales	152	500
4 Barvick Falls, Scotland	150	492
5 Falls of Buchan Burn, Scotland	135	443
6 = Rhaeadr y Cwm, Wales	122	400
= Rhaeadr Myherin, Wales	122	400
8 An Steall Ban, Scotland	120	395
9 Falls of Glomach, Scotland	113	370
10 Pistyll Blaen y Cwm, Wales	107	350

Angel Falls
These dramatic falls are over 10 times the height of the Statue of Liberty.

The Lie of the Land

top10 DEEPEST **CAVES**

The world's deepest cave is a comparatively recent discovery: in January 2001 a team of Ukrainian cave explorers in the Arabikskaja system in the western Caucasus mountains of the Georgian Republic found a branch of the Voronja, or 'Crow's Cave', and established that its depth of 1,710 m (5,610 ft) far exceeded anything previously known. Progressively deeper penetrations have taken its extent to more than seven times the height of the Eiffel Tower.

CAVE SYSTEM / LOCATION	DEPTH M	FT
10 Sistema Huautla, Mexico	1,475	4,839
9 Sistema Cheve (Cuicateco), Mexico	1,484	4,869
8 Shakta Vjacheslav Pantjukhina, Georgia	1,508	4,948
7 Cehi 2, Slovenia	1,533	5,033
6 Sarma, Georgia	1,543	5,062
5 Torca del Cerro del Cuevon/ Torca de las Saxifragas, Spain	1,589	5,213
4 Réseau Jean Bernard, France	1,602	5,256
3 Gouffre Mirolda, France	1,626	5,335
2 Lamprechtsofen Vogelschacht Weg Schacht, Austria	1,632	5,354
1 Krubera (Voronja), Georgia	2,140	7,021

top10 LARGEST **METEORITE CRATERS**

	CRATER / LOCATION	DIAMETER KM	MILES
1	Vredefort, South Africa	300	186
2	Sudbury, Ontario, Canada	250	155
3	Chicxulub, Yucatán, Mexico	170	107
4	=Manicougan, Quebec, Canada	100	62
	=Popigai, Russia	100	62
6	=Acraman, Australia	90	56
	=Chesapeake Bay, Virginia, USA	90	56
8	Puchezh-Katunki, Russia	80	50
9	Morokweng, South Africa	70	43
10	Kara, Russia	65	40

Source: Earth Impact Database, Planetary and Space Science Centre, University of New Brunswick

Unlike on the Solar System's other planets and moons, many astroblemes (collision sites) on Earth have been weathered over time and obscured, and debate continues as to whether certain crater-like structures are of meteoric origin or the remnants of long-extinct volcanoes. The Vredefort Ring, once thought to be meteoric, was declared in 1963 to be volcanic, but has since been claimed as a definite meteor crater, as are all the giant meteorite craters in the Top 10, as listed by the International Union of Geological Sciences Commission on Comparative Planetology.

top10 LARGEST **ISLANDS**

	ISLAND / LOCATION	AREA* SQ KM	SQ MILES
1	Greenland (Kalaatdlit Nunaat), North Atlantic	2,175,600	840,004
2	New Guinea, Southwest Pacific	785,753	303,381
3	Borneo, West mid-Pacific	748,168	288,869
4	Madagascar, Indian Ocean	587,713	226,917
5	Baffin Island, North Atlantic	503,944	194,574
6	Sumatra, Northeast Indian Ocean	443,065	171,068
7	Great Britain, off coast of Northwest Europe	229,957	88,787
8	Honshu, Sea of Japan	227,413	87,805
9	Victoria Island, Arctic Ocean	217,292	83,897
10	Ellesmere Island, Arctic Ocean	196,236	75,767

* Mainlands, including areas of inland water, but excluding offshore islands

Australia is regarded as a continental land mass rather than an island; otherwise it would rank first, at 7,618,493 sq km (2,941,517 sq miles), or 35 times the size of Great Britain.

top10 HIGHEST **MOUNTAINS**

	MOUNTAIN / LOCATION	FIRST ASCENT	TEAM NATIONALITY	HEIGHT* M	HEIGHT* FT
1	Everest, Nepal/China	29 May 1953	British/New Zealand	8,850	29,035
2	K2 (Chogori), Pakistan/China	31 July 1954	Italian	8,607	28,238
3	Kangchenjunga, Nepal/India	25 May 1955	British	8,598	28,208
4	Lhotse, Nepal/China	18 May 1956	Swiss	8,511	27,923
5	Makalu I, Nepal/China	15 May 1955	French	8,481	27,824
6	Lhotse Shar II, Nepal/China	12 May 1970	Austrian	8,383	27,504
7	Dhaulagiri I, Nepal	13 May 1960	Swiss/Austrian	8,172	26,810
8	Manaslu I (Kutang I), Nepal	9 May 1956	Japanese	8,156	26,760
9	Cho Oyu, Nepal	19 Oct 1954	Austrian	8,153	26,750
10	Nanga Parbat (Diamir), Kashmir	3 July 1953	German/Austrian	8,126	26,660

* Height of principal peak; lower peaks of the same mountain are excluded

When the results of the 19th-century Great Trigonometrical Survey of India were studied, it was first realized that Everest was Earth's tallest mountain. Its height originally was computed as 8,840 m (29,002 ft), adjusted in 1955 to 8,848 m (29,029 ft) and in 1993 to 8,848 m (29,028 ft). In 1999 an analysis of data beamed from sensors on Everest's summit to GPS (Global Positioning System) satellites established a new height of 8,850 m (29,035 ft), which is now accepted as the current 'official' figure.

top10 LARGEST **DESERTS**

	DESERT / LOCATION	APPROX. AREA SQ KM	APPROX. AREA SQ MILES
1	Sahara, Northern Africa	9,100,000	3,500,000
2	Australian, Australia*	3,400,000	1,300,000
3	Arabian Peninsula, Southwest Asia#	2,600,000	1,000,000
4	Turkestan, Central Asia†	1,900,000	750,000
5 =	Gobi, Central Asia	1,300,000	500,000
=	North American Desert, US/Mexico☆	1,300,000	500,000
7	Patagonia, Southern Argentina	670,000	260,000
8	Thar, Northwest India/Pakistan	600,000	230,000
9	Kalahari, Southwestern Africa	570,000	220,000
10	Takla Makan, Northwestern China	480,000	185,000

* Includes Gibson, Great Sandy, Great Victoria and Simpson
# Includes an-Nafud and Rub al-Khali
† Includes Kara-Kum and Kyzylkum
☆ Includes Great Basin, Mojave, Sonorah and Chihuahuan

top10 COUNTRIES WITH THE **LOWEST ELEVATIONS**

	COUNTRY*	HIGHEST POINT	ELEVATION M	ELEVATION FT
1	Maldives	Unnamed on Wilingili Island in the Addu Atoll	2.4	7.8
2	Tuvalu	Unnamed	5	16.4
3	Marshall Islands	Unnamed on Likiep	10	32.8
4	The Gambia	Unnamed	53	173.9
5	Nauru	Unnamed on plateau rim	61	200.1
6	The Bahamas	Mount Alvernia on Cat Island	63	206.7
7	Vatican City	Unnamed	75	246.1
8	Kiribati	Unnamed on Banaba	81	265.7
9	Qatar	Qurayn Abu al Bawl	103	337.9
10	Singapore	Bukit Timah	166	544.6

* Excludes overseas possessions, territories and dependencies

Source: CIA, 'The World Factbook 2005'

Weather

WEATHER STATION / LOCATION	HEIGHT (M)	AVERAGE ANNUAL TEMPERATURE* °C	°F
1 Cairngorm Summit, Scottish Highlands	1,245	0.5	32.9
2 Aonach Mor, Scottish Highlands	1,130	1.2	34.1
3 Cairnwell, Scottish Highlands	933	2.3	36.1
4 Great Dun Fell (No. 2), Lake District	847	3.6	38.5
5 Faelar Lodge, Scottish Highlands	560	4.8	40.6
6 Bealach Na Ba (No. 2), Scottish Highlands	773	5.1	41.2
7 Lowther Hill, Dumfries and Galloway, Scotland	754	5.2	41.3
8 = Cairngorm Chairlift, Scottish Highlands	663	5.3	41.5
= Glen Ogle, Scottish Highlands	564	5.3	41.5
= Moor House, Cumbria	556	5.3	41.5

* Based on The Meteorological Office's 30-year averages for the period 1971–2000

Source: The Met Office

top10 COLDEST **YEARS** IN THE UK

YEAR	AVERAGE TEMPERATURE* °C	°F
1 = 1740	6.86	44.35
2 = 1695	7.29	45.12
3 1879	7.44	45.39
4 = 1694	7.67	45.81
= 1698	7.67	45.81
6 1692	7.73	45.91
7 1814	7.78	46.00
8 1784	7.85	46.13
9 1688	7.86	46.15
10 1675	7.88	46.18

* Since 1659, based on Central England averages

Source: The Met Office

top10 **WETTEST** PLACES IN THE UK

WEATHER STATION
LOCATION
AVERAGE ANNUAL RAINFALL* MM/IN

5 Beinn Ime,
Ben Lomond, Scotland
4,000.2 / 157.5

7 Strath Cluanie,
Scottish Highlands
3,728.3 / 146.8

9

2 Styhead,
Lake District, England
4,392.1 / 172.9

4 Hallival,
Isle of Rhum, Scottish Highlands
4,110.1 / 161.8

Allt Uaine,
Southern Grampians, Scotla
3,664.5 / 144.3

6 Llydaw Intake,
Snowdonia
3,835.4 / 150.9

3 Delta,
Snowdonia
4,311.2 / 169.7

8 Pen-Y-Pass,
Snowdonia
3,684.8 / 145.1

10

1 Crib Goch,
Snowdonia, Wales
4,472.3 / 176.0

Glenshiel Forest
Scottish Highland
3,588.8 / 141.3

* Based on The Meteorological Office's 30-year averages for the period 1971–2000

Source: The Met Office

the 10 DRIEST PLACES IN GREAT BRITAIN

	LOCATION	AVERAGE ANNUAL RAINFALL*	
		MM	IN
1	St Osyth, Essex	507	19.96
2	Shoeburyness and Southend-on-Sea, Essex	509	20.04
3	Burnham-on-Crouch, Essex	518	20.39
4 =	Languard Point, Suffolk	524	20.63
=	Peterborough, Cambridgeshire	524	20.63
6	Ely, Cambridgeshire	526	20.71
7 =	Tilbury and Grays area, Essex	530	20.87
=	Thamesmead, East London	530	20.87
9	Huntingdon, Cambridgeshire	531	20.91
10	Walton-on-the-Naze, Essex	534	21.02

* Based on The Meteorological Office's 30-year averages for the period 1961–90

Source: The Met Office

top 10 WARMEST PLACES IN THE UK*

1 12.1 / 53.8
St Helier Harbour, Jersey

2 11.9 / 53.4
St Mary's Airport, Isles of Scilly

3 11.8 / 53.2
= St Helier, Jersey
= Lancresse, Guernsey

5 11.7 / 53.
= Central London
= Round Island, Isles of Scilly

7 11.6 / 52.9
St Mary's, Isles of Scilly

8 11.4 / 52.5
= Pendennis Point, Cornwall
= St James's Park, London

10 11.3 / 52.3
= Greenwich, London
= Isle of Grain, Kent
= Penlee Gardens, Penzance
= Portland, Dorset
= Ryde, Isle of Wight
= St Ives, Cornwall
= Southsea, Hampshire

* Based on The Meteorological Office's 30-year averages for the period 1971–2000: first temperature is Celsius, second Fahrenheit

Source: The Met Office

top 10 WARMEST YEARS IN THE UK

	YEAR	AVERAGE TEMPERATURE*	
		°C	°F
1 =	1990	10.63	51.13
=	1999	10.63	51.13
3	1949	10.62	51.12
4	2002	10.60	51.08
5	1997	10.53	50.95
6	1995	10.52	50.94
7	2003	10.51	50.92
8	1989	10.50	50.90
9	1959	10.48	50.86
10 =	1733	10.47	50.85
=	1834	10.47	50.85
=	1921	10.47	50.85

* Since 1659, based on Central England averages

Source: The Met Office

Natural Disasters

LOCATION / DATE / ESTIMATED NO. KILLED

Tambora, Indonesia
5–12 Apr 1815, 92,000

Krakatoa, Sumatra/Java
26–27 Aug 1883, 36,380

Mont Pelée, Martinique
8 May 1902, 27,000

Nevado del Ruiz, Colombia
13 Nov 1985, 22,940

Mt Etna, Sicily
11 Mar 1669, up to 20,000

Mt Etna, Sicily
1169, over 15,000

Unzen, Japan
1 April 1792, 14,300

Laki, Iceland
Jan–Jun 1783, 9,350

Kelut, Indonesia
19 May 1919, 5,110

Galunggung, Indonesia
8 Oct 1882, 4,011

The eruption of Tambora on the island of Sumbawa killed about 10,000 islanders immediately, with a further 82,000 dying subsequently (38,000 on Sumbawa, 44,000 on neighbouring Lombok) from disease and famine resulting from crops being destroyed.

the 10 WORST EARTHQUAKES

LOCATION / DATE / ESTIMATED NO. KILLED

Near East/Mediterranean
20 May 1202, 1,100,000

Shenshi, China
2 Feb 1556, 820,000

Calcutta, India
11 Oct 1737, 300,000

Antioch, Syria
20 May 526, 250,000

Tangshan, China
28 Jul 1976, 242,419

Nan Shan, China
22 May 1927, 200,000

Yeddo, Japan
30 Dec 1703, 190,000

Kansu, China
16 Dec 1920, 180,000

Messina, Italy
28 Dec 1908, 160,000

Tokyo/Yokohama, Japan
1 Sept 1923, 142,807

There are some discrepancies between the 'official' death tolls in many of the world's worst earthquakes. For example, 750,000 is sometimes quoted for the Tangshan earthquake of 1976, and totals of 58,000– 250,000 are given for the quake that devastated Messina in 1908.

the 10 WORST TSUNAMIS

LOCATION / DATE / ESTIMATED NO. KILLED

Southeast Asia,
26 Dec 2004, 287,534

Krakatoa, Sumatra/Java*,
27 Aug 1883, 36,380

Sanriku, Japan,
15 Jun 1896, 28,000

Agadir, Morocco#,
29 Feb 1960, 12,000

Lisbon, Portugal,
1 Nov 1755, 10,000

Papua New Guinea,
18 Jul 1998, 8,000

Chile/Pacific islands/Japan,
22 May 1960, 5,700

Philippines,
17 Aug 1976, 5,000

Hyuga to Izu, Japan,
28 Oct 1707, 4,900

Sanriku, Japan,
3 Mar 1933, 3,000

Often mistakenly called tidal waves, tsunamis (from the Japanese *tsu*, port, and *nami*, wave) are powerful waves caused by undersea disturbances, such as earthquakes or volcanic eruptions, often resulting in massive devastation of low-lying coastal settlements.

*Combined effect of volcanic eruption and tsunamis
#Combined effect of earthquake and tsunamis

the 10 WORST HURRICANES, TYPHOONS AND CYCLONES

LOCATION / DATE / ESTIMATED NO. KILLED

East Pakistan (Bangladesh)
13 Nov 1970, 500,000–1,000,000

Bengal, India
7 Oct 1737, >300,000

Haiphong, Vietnam
8 Oct 1881, 300,000

Bengal, India
31 Oct 1876, 200,000

Bangladesh
29 Apr 1991, 138,000

Bombay, India
6 June 1882, >100,000

Southern Japan
23 Aug 1281, 68,000

Northeast China
2–3 Aug 1922, 60,000

Calcutta, India
5 Oct 1864, 50,000–70,000

Bengal, India
15–16 Oct 1942, 40,000

The cyclone of 1970 hit the Bay of Bengal with winds of over 190 km/h (120 mph). Loss of life was worst in the Bhola region, so it is often known as the Bhola cyclone. The cyclone that struck India in 1737 churned the sea into a 12-m (40-ft) storm surge, flooding land and destroying ships.

LIFE ON EARTH

Dinosaurs

top 10 DINOSAUR **DISCOVERERS**

	DISCOVERER / COUNTRY	PERIOD	DINOSAURS NAMED*
1	Friedrich von Huene (Germany)	1902–61	46
2	Othniel Charles Marsh (USA)	1870–94	39
3	Dong Zhiming (China)	1973–2003	35
4	= Edward Drinker Cope (USA)	1866–92	30
	= Harry Govier Seeley (UK)	1869–98	30
6	José Fernando Bonaparte (Argentina)	1969–2000	28
7	Richard Owen (UK)	1841–84	23
8	= Barnum Brown (USA)	1873–1963	17
	= Henry Fairfield Osborn (USA)	1902–24	17
	= Yang Zhong-Jian ('C.C. Young') (China)	1937–82	17

* Including joint namings

top 10 **LONGEST** DINOSAURS EVER DISCOVERED

This Top 10 is based on the most reliable recent evidence of dinosaur lengths and indicates the probable ranges. As more information is assembled, these are undergoing constant revision. To compare the sizes of these dinosaurs with living animals, note that the largest recorded crocodile measured 6.2 m (20 ft 4 in) and the largest elephant 10.7 m (35 ft) from trunk to tail and weighed about 12 tonnes.

NAME
ESTIMATED WEIGHT (TONNES) / LENGTH (M)

1 Argentinosaurus huinculensis
80–100 / 35–45
An Argentinian farmer discovered a 1.8-m (6-ft) bone in 1988. It was found to be the shinbone of a previously unknown dinosaur, which was given the name *Argentinosaurus*.

⊙ *African elephants at approximately same scale.*

2 Seismosaurus
50–80 / 33
A skeleton of this colossal plant-eater was excavated in 1985 near Albuquerque, New Mexico, by US palaeontologist David Gillette and given a name that means 'earth-shaking lizard'.

3 Paralititan stromeri
70 / 25–30
Remains discovered in 2001 in the Sahara Desert in Egypt suggest that it was a giant plant-eater. Its name means 'Stromer's tidal giant', and commemorates the site's discoverer, Bavarian geologist Ernst Stromer von Reichenbach.

4 Sauroposeidon
50–60 / 30
From vertebrae discovered in 1994, it has been estimated that this creature was probably the tallest ever to walk on Earth, able to extend its neck to 18 m (60 ft). Its name means 'earthquake lizard-god'.

5 Supersaurus vivianae
50 / 24–30
The remains of *Supersaurus* were found in Colorado in 1972. Some scientists have suggested a length of up to 42 m (138 ft) and a weight of perhaps 75–100 tonnes.

Gentle giants
Two Brachiosaurus *graze on tree tops. Although of fearsome size, they were docile vegetarians.*

the 10 **FIRST** DINOSAURS TO BE NAMED

	NAME	MEANING	NAMED BY	YEAR
1	Megalosaurus	Great lizard	William Buckland	1824
2	Iguanodon	Iguana tooth	Gideon Mantell	1825
3	Hylaeosaurus	Woodland lizard	Gideon Mantell	1833
4	Macrodontophion	Large tooth snake	A. Zborzewski	1834
5	= Palaeosaurus	Ancient lizard	Henry Riley and Samuel Stutchbury	1836
6	= Thecodontosaurus	Socket-toothed lizard	Henry Riley and Samuel Stutchbury	1836
7	Plateosaurus	Flat lizard	Hermann von Meyer	1837
8	Poekilopleuron	Varying side	Jacques Armand Eudes-Deslongchamps	1838
9	= Cetiosaurus	Whale lizard	Richard Owen	1841
	Cladeiodon	Branch tooth	Richard Owen	1841

The 10 first dinosaurs were all identified and named within a quarter of a century – although subsequent research has since cast doubt on the authenticity of certain specimens. The name *Megalosaurus*, the first to be given to a dinosaur, was proposed by William Buckland (1784–1856), an English geologist, in an article published in 1824 in the *Transactions of the Geological Society of London*. Then the *Iguanodon* was identified by Gideon Algernon Mantell (1790–1852) in 1825. A doctor in his home town of Lewes in Sussex, he devoted much of his life to the study of geology. Mantell (or, according to some authorities, his wife Mary) found the first *Iguanodon* teeth in 1822 in a pile of stones being used for road repairs. After much detailed study, he concluded that they resembled an enormous version of the teeth of the Central American iguana lizard, and hence he suggested the name *Iguanodon*.

top 10 **SMALLEST** DINOSAURS

	DINOSAUR	MAX. SIZE CM	IN
1	Micropachycephalosaurus	50	20
2	= Saltopus	60	23
	= Yandangornis	60	23
4	Microraptor	77	30
5	= Lesothosaurus	90	35
	= Nanosaurus	90	35
7	= Bambiraptor	91	36
	= Sinosauropteryx	91	36
9	Wannanosaurus	99	39
10	Procompsognathus	120	47

AMAZING FACT

The Name of the Beasts
A number of dinosaurs had been named before the word 'dinosaur' itself was invented. 'Dinosauria', or 'terrible lizards', was proposed in April 1842 by British anatomist Richard Owen (1804–92) in a report for the British Association for the Advancement of Science.

6 Andesaurus delgadoi
12.5 / 18–30
Found in Argentina and named in 1991 by Calvo and José Bonaparte, its vertebrae alone measure 0.6 m (2 ft).

7 Giraffatitan brancai
Uncertain / 25–30
This lightly built but long dinosaur was found in Tanzania and named by Gregory S. Paul in 1988.

8 Diplodocus
10–18 / 27
As it was long and thin, *Diplodocus* was a relative lightweight in the dinosaur world. It was also probably one of the most stupid dinosaurs, having the smallest brain in relation to its body size.

9 Barosaurus
40 / 20–27
Barosaurus (meaning 'heavy lizard', so named by Othniel C. Marsh in 1890) has been found in both North America and Africa, thus proving the existence of a land link in Jurassic times (205–140 million years ago).

10 Brachiosaurus
30–80 / 26
Its name (given by US palaeontologist Elmer S. Riggs in 1903) means 'arm lizard'. A mounted skeleton of the dinosaur in the Humboldt Museum, Berlin, is the largest in the world.

Nature's Heavyweights

top10 HEAVIEST BIRDS

BIRD* / SCIENTIFIC NAME	HEIGHT CM	HEIGHT IN	WEIGHT KG	WEIGHT LB
1 Ostrich (male) (*Struthio camelus*)	255	100.4	156.0	343
2 Northern cassowary (*Casuarius unappendiculatus*)	150	59.1	58.0	127
3 Emu (female) (*Dromaius novaehollandiae*)	155	61.0	55.0	121
4 Emperor penguin (female) (*Aptenodytes forsteri*)	115	45.3	46.0	101
5 Greater rhea (*Rhea americana*)	140	55.1	25.0	55
6 Mute swan# (*Cygnus olor*)	238	93.7	22.5	49
7 Kori bustard# (*Ardeotis kori*)	270	106.3	19.0	41
8 = Andean condor# (*Vultur gryphus*)	320	126.0	15.0	33
= Great white pelican# (*Pelecanus onocrotalus*)	360	141.7	15.0	33
10 European black vulture# (Old World) (*Aegypius monachus*)	295	116.1	12.5	27

* By species
# Flighted, all others are flightless

Source: Chris Mead

top10 LAND ANIMALS WITH THE BIGGEST BRAINS

ANIMAL SPECIES	AVERAGE BRAIN WEIGHT GM	LB	OZ
1 Elephants (genus *Elephantidae*)	6,000	13	4
2 Adult human (*Homo sapiens*)	1,350	3	0
3 Camels (*Camelus* species)	762	1	11
4 Giraffe (*Giraffa camelopardalis*)	680	1	8
5 Hippopotamus (*Hippopotamus amphibius*)	582	1	4
6 Horses (*Equus* species)	532	1	3
7 Gorilla (*Gorilla gorilla gorilla*)	500	1	1
8 Polar bear (*Ursus maritimus*)	498	1	1
9 Cows (*Bos* species)	445	0	15
10 Chimpanzee (*Pan troglodytes*)	420	0	15

The sperm whale has the heaviest brain of all animals, weighing in at a massive 7.8 kg (17 lb 3 oz).

top10 HEAVIEST TERRESTRIAL MAMMALS

MAMMAL* / SCIENTIFIC NAME
LENGTH M/FT / WEIGHT KG/LB

African elephant
(*Loxodonta africana*)
7.5 / 24.6   7,500 / 16,534

Hippopotamus
(*Hippopotamus amphibius*)
5.0 / 16.4   4,500 / 9,920

White rhinoceros
(*Ceratotherium simum*)
4.2 / 13.7   3,600 / 7,937

Giraffe
(*Giraffa camelopardalis*)
4.7 / 15.4   1,930 / 4,255

American buffalo
(*Bison bison*)
3.5 / 11.4   1,000 / 2,205

Moose (*Alces alces*)
3.1 / 10.1   825 / 1,820

Brown (grizzly) bear
(*Ursus arctos*)
3.0 / 9.8   780 / 1,720

Arabian camel (dromedary)
(*Camelus dromedarius*)
3.45 / 11.3   690 / 1,521

Siberian tiger
(*Panthera tigris altaica*)
3.3 / 10.8   360 / 793

Gorilla
(*Gorilla gorilla gorilla*)
2.0 / 6.5   275 / 606

* Heaviest species per genus

The list excludes domesticated cattle and horses, focusing on the heavyweight champions within distinctive large mammal groups or megafauna. Chief among them, the elephant, is 357,000 times as heavy as the smallest mammal, the pygmy shrew.

top10 LARGEST SPECIES OF **FRESHWATER FISH** CAUGHT

SPECIES	ANGLER / LOCATION/DATE	KG	GM	LB	OZ
1 Mekong giant catfish (*Pangasianodon gigas*)	Team of five anglers, Mekong River, Thailand, 1 May 2005	293	0	646	0
2 White sturgeon (*Acipenser transmontanus*)	Joey Pallotta III, Benicia, California, USA, 9 Jul 1983	212	28	468	0
3 Alligator gar (*Atractosteus spatula*)	Bill Valverde, Rio Grande, Texas, USA, 2 Dec 1951	126	55	279	0
4 Nile perch (*Lates niloticus*)	William Toth, Lake Nasser, Egypt, 20 Dec 2000	104	32	230	0
5 Beluga sturgeon (*Huso huso*)	Ms Merete Lehne, Guryev, Kazakhstan, 3 May 1993	102	0	224	13
6 Flathead catfish (*Pylodictis olivaris*)	Ken Paulie, Withlacoochee River, Florida, USA, 14 May 1998	55	79	123	9
7 Blue catfish (*Ictalurus furcatus*)	William P. McKinley, Wheeler Reservoir, Tennessee, USA, 5 Jul 1996	50	35	111	0
8 Redtailed catfish (*Phractocephalus hemioliopteru*)	Gilberto Fernandes, Amazon River, Brazil, 16 July 1988	44	20	97	7
9 Chinook salmon (*Oncorhynchus tshawytscha*)	Les Anderson, Kenai River, Alaska, USA, 17 May 1985	44	11	97	4
10 Giant tigerfish (*Hydrocynus goliath*)	Raymond Houtmans, Zaïre River, Kinshasa, Zaïre, 9 Jul 1988	44	0	97	0

Source: International Game Fish Association, 'World Record Game Fishes, 2005'

⊙ Big babies

While carnivores produce relatively large offspring, tiger cubs are only 40 per cent of the weight of a newborn human.

top10 CARNIVORES WITH THE **HEAVIEST NEWBORN**

MAMMAL / SCIENTIFIC NAME	BIRTH WEIGHT GM	LB	OZ
1 African lion (*Panthera leo*)	1,650	3	10
2 Spotted hyena (*Crocuta crocuta*)	1,500	3	5
3 Tiger (*Panthera tigris*)	1,255	2	11
4 Brown (grizzly) bear (*Ursus arctos*)	1,000	2	3
5 Jaguar (*Panthera onca*)	816	1	13
6 Polar bear (*Ursus maritimus*)	641	1	7
7 Leopard (*Panthera pardus*)	549	1	3
8 Snow leopard (*Panthera uncia*)	442	1	0
9 Grey wolf (*Canis lupus*)	425	0	15
10 Mountain lion (*Puma concolor*)	400	0	14

The ratio in size between a tiny, new-born kangaroo (under 2.5 cm/1 inch long) and an adult is the greatest of all mammals.

Great Lengths

top10 LARGEST BUTTERFLIES AND MOTHS

	BUTTERFLY / MOTH (SCIENTIFIC NAME)	APPROX. WINGSPAN MM	IN
● 1	Atlas moth (*Attacus atlas*)	300	11.8
● 2	Owlet moth (*Thysania agrippina*)*	290	11.4
○ 3	Queen Alexandra's birdwing (*Ornithoptera alexandrae*)	280	11.0
● 4	Chickweed geometer (*Haematopis grataria*)	260	10.2
○ 5	African giant swallowtail (*Papilio antimachus*)	230	9.1
○ 6 =	Goliath birdwing (*Ornithoptera goliath*)	210	8.3
● =	Hercules emperor moth (*Coscinocera hercules*)	210	8.3
○ 8 =	Buru opalescent birdwing (*Troides prattorum*)	200	7.9
○ =	Birdwing (*Trogonoptera trojana*)	200	7.9
○ =	Birdwing (*Troides hypolitus*)	200	7.9

* Exceptional specimen measured at 308 mm (12.2 in)

○ Butterfly ● Moth

top10 MAMMALS WITH THE LONGEST GESTATION PERIODS

	MAMMAL	AVERAGE GESTATION (DAYS)
1	African elephant (*Loxodonta africana*)	660
2	Asiatic elephant (*Elephas maximus*)	600
3	Baird's beaked whale (*Berardius bairdii*)	520
4	White rhinoceros (*Ceratotherium simum*)	490
5	Walrus (*Odobenus rosmarus*)	480
6	Giraffe (*Giraffa camelopardalis*)	460
7	Tapir (*Tapirus*)	400
8	Arabian camel (dromedary) (*Camelus dromedarius*)	390
9	Fin whale (*Balaenoptera physalus*)	370
10	Llama (*Lama glama*)	360

The 480-day gestation of the walrus includes a delay of up to five months while the fertilized embryo is held as a blastocyst (a sphere of cells), but it is not implanted until later in the wall of the uterus. This option enables offspring to be produced at a more favourable time of the year. Other mammals capable of this 'delayed implantation' trick include the roe deer and the badger.

top10 BIRDS WITH THE LARGEST WINGSPANS

	BIRD*	MAXIMUM WINGSPAN CM	IN
1	Great white pelican (*Pelecanus onocrotalus*)	360	141
2	Wandering albatross# (*Diomedea exulans*)	351	138
3	Andean condor (*Vultur gryphus*)	320	126
4	Himalayan griffon (vulture) (*Gyps himalayensis*)	310	122
5	Black vulture (Old World) (*Coragyps atratus*)	295	116
6	Marabou stork (*Leptoptilos crumeniferus*)	287	113
7	Lammergeier (*Gypaetus barbatus*)	282	111
8	Sarus crane (*Grus antigone*)	280	110
9	Kori bustard (*Ardeotis kori*)	270	106
10	Steller's sea eagle (*Haliaeetus pelagicus*)	265	104

* By species
# Royal albatross, a close relative, is the same size

Source: Chris Mead

The measurements are, as far as can be ascertained, for wingtip to wingtip of live birds measured in a natural position. Much bigger wingspans have been claimed for many species, but dead specimens may be stretched by 15 to 20 per cent.

top10 LONGEST LAND ANIMALS

	ANIMAL*	MAXIMUM LENGTH M	FT
1	Reticulated (royal) python (*Python regius*)	10.7	35
2	Tapeworm (*Cestoda* class)	10.0	33
3	African elephant (*Loxodonta africana*)	7.3	24
4	Estuarine crocodile (*Crocodylus porosus*)	5.9	19
5	Giraffe (*Giraffa camelopardalis*)	5.8	19
6	White rhinoceros (*Ceratotherium simum*)	4.2	14
7	Hippopotamus (*Hippopotamus amphibius*)	4.0	13
8	American bison (*Bison bison*)	3.9	13
9	Arabian camel (dromedary) (*Camelus dromedarius*)	3.5	12
10	Siberian tiger (*Panthera tigris altaica*)	3.3	11

* Longest representative of each species

⊙ *How the animals measure up: comparative lengths at the same scale.*

➔ *Atlas Moth, shown actual size.*

wingspan of great white pelican

African elephant

top10 LONGEST **SNAKES**

SNAKE / SCIENTIFIC NAME / MAXIMUM LENGTH M/FT

Although the South American anaconda is sometimes claimed to be the longest snake, this has never been authenticated: reports of monsters up to 36.5 m (120 ft) have been published, but without material evidence. Former US President and hunting enthusiast Theodore Roosevelt once offered $5,000 to anyone who could produce the skin or vertebra of an anaconda of over 9 m (30 ft), but the prize was never won.

1 Reticulated (royal) python (*Python regius*) 10.7 / 35 **2** Anaconda (*Eunectes murinus*) 8.5 / 28

3 Indian python (*Python molurus molurus*) 7.6 / 25 **4** Diamond python (*Morelia spilota spilota*) 6.4 / 21

5 King cobra (*Opiophagus hannah*) 5.8 / 19 **6** Boa constrictor (*Boa constrictor*) 4.9 / 16

7 Bushmaster (*Lachesis muta*) 3.7 / 12 **8** Giant brown snake (*Oxyuranus scutellatus*) 3.4 / 11

9 Diamondback rattlesnake (*Crotalus atrox*) 2.7 / 9 **10** Indigo or gopher snake (*Drymarchon corais*) 2.4 / 8

top10 LONGEST **MOLLUSCS***

MOLLUSC / SCIENTIFIC NAME	CLASS	LENGTH MM	IN
1 Giant squid (*Architeuthis* sp.)	Cephalopod	16,764	660#
2 Giant clam (*Tridacna gigas*)	Marine bivalve	1,300	51
3 Australian trumpet (*Syrinx aruanus*)	Marine snail	770	30
4 Sea slug (*Hexabranchus sanguineus*)	Sea slug	520	20
5 Heteropod (*Carinaria cristata*)	Heteropod	500	19
6 Steller's Coat of Mail shell (*Cryptochiton stelleri*)	Chiton	470	18
7 Freshwater mussel (*Cristaria plicata*)	Freshwater bivalve	300	11
8 Giant African snail (*Achatina achatina*)	Land snail	200	7
9 Tusk shell (*Dentalium vernedi*)	Scaphopod	138	5
10 Apple snail (*Pila werneri*)	Freshwater snail	125	4

* Largest species within each class # Estimated; actual length unknown

AMAZING FACT

Monster of the Deep

Although the giant squid heads the list of longest molluscs, the Norwegian legend of the monstrous kraken and tales told by sailors in Jules Verne's *Twenty Thousand Leagues Under the Sea* have given rise to the myth of creatures of vast size capable of dragging ships to the bottom. However, even the graphically named Colossal Squid seldom exceeds 14 m (46 ft), and such stories should be taken with a pinch of sea salt.

At the same scale, The Blue Whale is twice this length

reticulated python

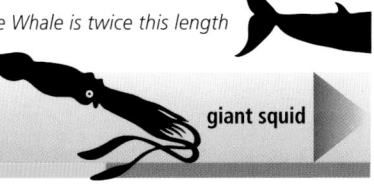

giant squid

Animal Speed

ANIMAL / SCIENTIFIC NAME*
MAXIMUM RECORDED SPEED KM/H / MPH

top10 FASTEST **BIRDS**

Recent research reveals that, contrary to popular belief, swifts are not fast fliers, but efficient with long, thin, glider-like wings and low wing-loading. Fast fliers generally have a combination of high wing-loading and fast wing beats.

1 Common eider
(*Somateria mollissima*)
76 / 47

2 Bewick's swan
(*Cygnus columbianus*)
72 / 44

3 = Barnacle goose
(*Branta leucopsis*)
68 / 42

= Common crane
(*Grus grus*)
68 / 42

top10 FASTEST **MAMMALS***

The cheetah can deliver its astonishing maximum speed over only relatively short distances. For comparison, the human male 100-m record (Asafa Powell, Jamaica, 2005) stands at 9.77 seconds, equivalent to a speed of 37 km/h (23 mph),

1 Cheetah
(*Acinonyx jubatus*)
114 / 71

2 Pronghorn antelope
(*Antilocapra americana*)
95 / 57

3 = Blue wildebeest
(brindled gnu)
(*Connochaetes taurinus*)
80 / 50

= Lion
(*Panthera leo*)
80 / 50

top10 FASTEST **FISH**

Flying fish are excluded: they have a top speed in the water of only 37 km/h (23 mph), but airborne they can reach 56 km/h (35 mph). Many sharks qualify for this list, but only two (the blue and the tiger) are given here to prevent the list becoming overly shark-infested.

1 Sailfish
(*Istiophorus platypterus*)
112 / 69

2 Striped marlin
(*Tetrapturus audax*)
80 / 50

3 Wahoo
(peto, jack mackerel)
(*Acanthocybium solandri*) 77 / 48

4 Southern bluefin tu
(*Thunnus maccoyii*)
76 / 47

top10 SLOWEST **MAMMALS**

	MAMMAL / SCIENTIFIC NAME*	AVERAGE SPEED KM/H	MPH
1	Three-toed sloth (*Bradypus variegatus*)	0.1–0.3	0.06–0.19
2	Short-tailed (giant mole) shrew (*Blarina brevicauda*)	2.2	1.4
3	= Pine vole (*Pitymys pinetorum*)	4.2	2.6
	= Red-backed vole (*Clethrionomys gapperi*)	4.2	2.6
5	Opossum (genus *Didelphis*)	4.4	2.7
6	Deer mouse (genus *Peromyscus*)	4.5	2.8
7	Woodland jumping mouse (*Napaeozapus insignis*)	5.3	3.3
8	Meadow jumping mouse (*Zapus hudsonius*)	5.5	3.4
9	Meadow mouse or meadow vole (*Microtus pennsylvanicus*)	6.6	4.1
10	White-footed mouse (*Peromyscus leucopus*)	6.8	4.2

* Of those species for which data available

top10 HIBERNATING MAMMALS WITH THE **SLOWEST HEARTBEATS***

	SPECIES	HEARTBEATS PER MINUTE NON-HIBERNATING	HIBERNATING
1	Franklin's ground squirrel (*Spermophilus franklinii*)	n/a	2–4
2	Olympic marmot (*Marmota olympus*)	130–140	4
3	Syrian (golden) hamster (*Mesocricetus auratus*)	500–600	6
4	American black bear# (*Ursus americanus*)	40–50	8
5	Hedgehog (*Erinaceus europaeus*)	190	20
6	Garden dormouse (*Eliomys quercinus*)	n/a	25
7	Eastern pigmy possum (dormouse possum, possum mouse) (*Cercartetus nanus*)	300–650	28–80
8	Birch mouse (*Sicista betulina*)	550–600	30
9	Big brown bat (*Eptesicus fuscus*)	450	34
10	Edible dormouse (*Glis glis*)	450	35

* Of those species for which data are available; one species per genus listed
# Not considered true hibernators by some experts – the heartbeat drops although body temperature is not significantly lowered

34 LIFE ON EARTH

5 =6 =6 8 =9 9

Mallard
(*Anas platyrhynchos*)
65 / 40

= Red-throated diver
(*Gavia stellata*)
61 / 38

= Wood pigeon
(*Columba palumbus*)
61 / 38

Oystercatcher
(*Haematopus ostralegus*)
58 / 36

= Ring-necked pheasant
(*Phasianus colchichus*)
54 / 33

= White-fronted goose
(*Anser albifrons*)
54 / 33

Source: Chris Mead

=6 =6 =8 =8 10

= Springbok
(*Antidorcas marsupialis*)
80 / 50

= Brown hare
(*Lepus capensis*)
77 / 48

= Red fox
(*Vulpes vulpes*)
77 / 48

= Grant's gazelle
(*Gazella granti*)
76 / 47

= Thomson's gazelle
(*Gazella thomsonii*)
76 / 47

Horse
(*Equus caballus*)
72 / 45

* Of those species for which data available

5 6 =7 =7 9 10

Yellowfin tuna
(*Thunnus albacares*)
74 / 46

Blue shark
(*Prionace glauca*)
69 / 43

= Bonefish
(*Albula vulpes*)
64 / 40

= Swordfish
(*Xiphias gladius*)
64 / 40

Tarpon (ox-eye herring)
(*Megalops cyprinoides*)
56 / 35

Tiger shark
(*Galeocerdo cuvier*)
53 / 33

Source: Lucy T. Verma

➔ Flying fins
As many anglers have discovered to their cost, the marlin is one of the fastest and most powerful of all fish.

Nature by Numbers

top10 WILD MAMMALS WITH THE LARGEST LITTERS

	MAMMAL / SCIENTIFIC NAME	AVERAGE LITTER
1	Common tenrec (*Tenrec ecaudatus*)	25
2	Virginia (common) opossum (*Didelphis virginiana*)	21
3	Southern (black-eared) opossum (*Didelphis marsupialis*)	10
4	= Ermine (*Mustela erminea*)	9
	= Prairie vole (*Microtus ochrogaster*)	9
	= Syrian (golden) hamster (*Mesocricetus auratus*)	9
7	African hunting dog (*Lycaon pictus*)	8.8
8	= Dhole (Indian wild dog) (*Cuon alpinus*)	8
	= Pygmy opossum (*Marmosa robinsoni*)	8
	= South American mouse opossum (*Gracilinanus agilis*)	8

The prairie vole probably holds the world record for most offspring produced in a season. It has up to 17 litters in rapid succession, bringing up to 150 young into the world. Rabbits, despite their reputation as fast breeders, fail to make the list with an average litter size of six. All the numbers in the list are averages: the tiny tenrec can produce as many as 31 in a single litter, and instances of domestic pigs producing 30 or more piglets at one go are not uncommon. Despite these prodigious reproductive peaks, mammalian litter sizes appear minute when compared with those of other animal groups. Many fish, for instance, can lay over 10,000 eggs at a time and many amphibians over 1,000.

◉ *A pot of gold*
Although its average litter size is about nine, extreme instances of golden hamsters producing as many as 26 have been recorded. In theory, a single pair could produce up to 100,000 descendants in a single year.

the10 RAREST NATIVE MAMMALS IN THE UK

	MAMMAL	ESTIMATED NUMBER
1	Grey long-eared bat (*Plecotus austriacus*)	1,000
2	Bechstein's bat (*Myotis bechsteinii*)	1,500
3	Wildcat (*Felis sylvestris*)	3,500
4	Pine marten (*Martes martes*)	3,650
5	Greater horseshoe bat (*Rhinophalus ferrumequinum*)	6,600
6	Skomer vole (*Clethrionomys glarebus skomerensis*)	7,000
7	Otter (*Lutra lutra*)	9,465
8	Barbastelle bat (*Barbastella barbastellus*)	10,000
9	Sertotine bat (*Eptesicus serotinus*)	15,000
10	Nathuslus pipistrelle bat (*Pipistrelle nathuslii*)	16,000

Source: UK Mammals: Species Status and Population Trends, JNCC/Tracking Mammals Partnership 2005

The black or ship rat (*Rattus rattus*) is rare, its population being put at the low hundreds, but it is an alien species that first appeared in Britain in the Middle Ages.

top10 MOST COMMON MAMMALS IN THE UK

	MAMMAL	ESTIMATED NO.
1	Common rat (*Rattus norvegicus*)	76,790,000
2	House mouse (*Mus domesticus*)	75,192,000
3	Field vole (*Mictotus agrestis*)	75,000,000
4	Common shrew (*Sorex araneus*)	41,700,000
5	Wood mouse (*Apodemus sylvaticus*)	38,000,000
6	Rabbit (*Oryctolagus cuniculus*)	37,500,000
7	Mole (*Talpa europaea*)	31,000,000
8	Bank vole (*Clethrionomys glareolus*)	23,000,000
9	Pygmy shrew (*Sorex minutus*)	8,600,000
10	Grey squirrel (*Sciurus carolinensis*)	2,520,000

Source: UK Mammals: Species Status and Population Trends, JNCC/Tracking Mammals Partnership 2005

The populations of only the first three mammals in the list exceed the human population of the UK, and purists may argue that *Homo sapiens* should appear as No. 4.

top10 MOST ENDANGERED **BIRDS** IN THE UK*

BIRD

1 Red-backed shrike (*Lanius collurio*)

2 Wryneck (*Jynx torquilla*)

3 Common crane (*Grus grus*)

4 Savi's warbler (*Locustella luscinioides*)

5 White-tailed eagle (*Haliaeetus albicilla*)

6 Spotted crake (*Porzana porzana*)

7 Montagu's harrier (*Circus pygargus*)

8 Bittern (*Botaurus stellaris*)

9 Red-necked phalarope (*Phalaropus lobatus*)

10 Marsh warbler (*Acrocephalus palustris*)

*List based on such factors as relative degrees of threat and declines in habitat, not on populations

Source: Chris Mead, 'The State of the Nation's Birds'

➲ ***A plague of locusts***
Individual swarms containing an estimated 12.5 trillion locusts provide a pointer to the sheer numbers of insect species.

top10 LARGEST **ENTOMOLOGICAL COLLECTIONS**

COLLECTION* / COUNTRY	APPROX. NO. OF SPECIMENS
1 = Muséum d'Histoire Naturelle Paris, France	30,000,000
= Smithsonian Institution Washington, D.C., USA	30,000,000
3 Natural History Museum London, UK	28,000,000
4 Zoologische Staatssammlung Munich, Germany	16,566,000
5 American Museum of Natural History New York, USA	16,204,000
6 Canadian National Collection Ottawa, Canada	15,000,000
7 Zoologisches Forschungsinstitut & Museum Alexander König, Bonn, Germany	14,000,000
8 Bernice P. Bishop Museum Honolulu, Hawaii, USA	13,250,000
9 Musée Royal de l'Afrique Centrale Tervuren, Belgium	10,510,000
10 = Australian National Insect Collection Canberra, Australia	10,000,000
= Museum für Naturkunde der Humboldt-Universität Berlin, Germany	10,000,000

* Excluding Russian collections, for which data not available at time of collection

top10 MOST COMMON **INSECTS***

ORDER / SCIENTIFIC NAME	APPROXIMATE NO. OF KNOWN SPECIES
1 Beetles (*Coleoptera*)	400,000
2 Butterflies and moths (*Lepidoptera*)	165,000
3 Ants, bees and wasps (*Hymenoptera*)	140,000
4 True flies (*Diptera*)	120,000
5 Bugs (*Hemiptera*)	90,000
6 Crickets, grasshoppers and locusts (*Orthoptera*)	20,000
7 Caddisflies (*Trichoptera*)	10,000
8 Lice (*Phthiraptera/Psocoptera*)	7,000
9 Dragonflies and damselflies (*Odonata*)	5,500
10 Lacewings (*Neuroptera*)	4,700

* By number of known species

This list includes only species that have been discovered and named: it is surmised that many thousands of species still await discovery. It takes no account of the absolute numbers of each species, which are truly colossal, if speculative, one authority suggesting that there are 5,000,000,000,000,000 (5,000 trillion) individuals, or 770,000 for every one of the Earth's 6.5 billion humans, which together would weigh at least 12 times as much as the human race and at least three times more than the combined weight of all other living animals.

Deadly Creatures

top10 **DEADLIEST** SPIDERS

SPIDER / SCIENTIFIC NAME	RANGE
1 Banana spider (*Phonenutria fera*)	Central and South America
2 Sydney funnel web (*Atrax robustus*)	Australia
3 Wolf spider (*Lycosa raptoria/ erythrognatha*)	Central and South America
4 Black widow (*Latrodectus* species)	Widespread
5 Violin spider/Recluse spider (*Loxesceles reclusa*)	Widespread
6 Sac spider (*Cheiracanthium punctorium*)	Central Europe
7 Tarantula (*Eurypelma rubropilosum*)	Neotropics
8 Tarantula (*Acanthoscurria atrox*)	Neotropics
9 Tarantula (*Lasiodora klugi*)	Neotropics
10 Tarantula (*Pamphobetus* species)	Neotropics

This list ranks spiders according to their 'lethal potential' – their venom yield divided by their venom potency. The banana spider, for example, yields 6 mg of venom, with 1 mg being the estimated lethal dose for humans. However, the venom yield of most is low compared with that of the most dangerous snakes: the tarantula, for example, produces 1.5 mg of venom, but its lethal dose for an adult human is 12 mg.

top10 SNAKES WITH THE **DEADLIEST BITES**

SNAKE / LATIN NAME	EST. LETHAL DOSE FOR HUMANS (MG)	AVE. VENOM PER BITE (MG)	POTENTIA HUMAN KILLE PER BIT
1 Coastal taipan (*Oxyuranus scutellatus*)	1	120	12
2 Common krait (*Bungarus caeruleus*)	0.5	42	84
3 Philippine cobra (*Naja naja philippinensis*)	2	120	60
4 = King cobra (*Ophiophagus hannah*)	20	1,000	50
= Russell's viper (*Daboia russelli*)	3	150	50
6 Black mamba (*Dendroaspis polyepis*)	3	135	45
7 Yellow-jawed tommygoff (*Bothrops asper*)	25	1,000	40
8 = Multibanded krait (*Bungarus multicinctus*)	0.8	28	35
= Tiger snake (*Notechis scutatus*)	1	35	35
10 Jararacussu (*Bothrops jararacussu*)	25	800	32

Source: Russell E. Gough

In comparing the danger posed by poisonous snakes, this takes account of such factors as venom strength – hence its lethality – and the amount injected per bite (most snakes inject about 15 per cent of their venom per bite).

the10 TYPES OF SHARK THAT HAVE **KILLED THE MOST** HUMANS

SHARK SPECIES	UNPROVOKED ATTACKS* (TOTAL)	(FATALITIES#)
1 Great white (*Carcharodon carcharias*)	212	61
2 Tiger (*Galeocerdo cuvieri*)	83	28
3 Bull (*Carcharhinus leucas*)	68	21
4 Requiem (family *Carcharhinidae*)	33	7
5 Blue (*Prionace glauca*)	12	4
6 = Sand tiger (*Carcharias taurus*)	31	2
= Shortfin mako (*Isurus* species)	8	2
8 = Dusky (*Carcharhinus obscurus*)	3	1
= Galápagos (*Carcharhinus galapagensis*)	1	1
= Ganges (*Glyphis gangeticus*)	1	1
= Oceanic whitetip (*Carcharhinus longimanus*)	5	1

* 1580–2004
\# Where fatalities are equal, entries are ranked by total attacks

Source: International Shark Attack File, Florida Museum of Natural History

These are the only species of shark that are on record for having actually killed humans, although there have been a total of 32 species involved in attacks that have not proved fatal.

the 10 BODY PARTS **MOST OFTEN INJURED** IN SHARK ATTACKS ON DIVERS

BODY PART INJURED / % OF ATTACKS

 Calf/knee 35.6

 Arm 28.9

 Thigh 23.5

 Foot 22.1

 Hand 12.8

 Abdomen/stomach 9.4

 Chest 8.7

 = Buttocks 7.4

= Shoulder 7.4

10 Back 6.7

Source: International Shark Attack File, Florida Museum of Natural History

the 10 **PLACES** WHERE MOST PEOPLE ARE **ATTACKED** BY SHARKS

LOCATION	FATAL ATTACKS	LAST FATAL ATTACK	TOTAL ATTACKS*
1 USA (excluding Hawaii)	39	2004	761
2 Australia	134	2004	294
3 South Africa	41	2004	204
4 Hawaii	15	2004	100
5 Brazil	20	2004	85
6 Papua New Guinea	25	2000	48
7 New Zealand	9	1968	45
8 Mexico	20	1997	35
9 Iran	8	1985	23
10 The Bahamas	1	1968	22

* Confirmed unprovoked attacks, including non-fatal

Source: International Shark Attack File/American Elasmobranch Society/Florida Museum of Natural History

The International Shark Attack File monitors worldwide incidents, a total of almost 2,000 of which have been recorded since the 16th century. The 1990s had 514 attacks, the most of any decade. This upward trend is believed to reflect the increase in the numbers of people engaging in aquatic activities, rather than an increase in the

The Truth about Cats & Dogs

top10 MOST INTELLIGENT DOG BREEDS

1 Border collie
2 Poodle
3 German shepherd (Alsatian)
4 Golden retriever
5 Doberman pinscher
6 Shetland sheepdog
7 Labrador retriever
8 Papillon
9 Rottweiler
10 Australian cattle dog

Source: Stanley Coren, 'The Intelligence of Dogs' (Scribner, 1994)

American psychology professor and pet trainer Stanley Coren devised a ranking of 133 breeds of dogs after studying their responses to a range of IQ tests, as well as the opinions of judges in dog obedience tests. Dog owners who have criticized the results (especially those whose own pets scored badly) maintain that dogs are bred for specialized abilities, such as speed or ferocity, and that obedience to their human masters is only one feature of their 'intelligence'.

the10 LEAST INTELLIGENT DOG BREEDS

1 Afghan hound
2 Basenji
3 Bulldog
4 Chow Chow
5 Borzoi
6 Bloodhound
7 Pekinese
8 Beagle
= Mastiff
10 Basset Hound

Source: Stanley Coren, 'The Intelligence of Dogs' (Scribner, 1994)

Canine IQ
The clever collie and the intellectually challenged Afghan exemplify the spectrum of dog intelligence as ranked after an in-depth study of an extensive range of breeds.

top10 DOG BREEDS IN THE UK

	BREED	NO. REGISTERED BY KENNEL CLUB 2005
1	Labrador retriever	45,779
2	Cocker spaniel	17,468
3	English springer spaniel	15,180
4	German shepherd (Alsatian)	13,165
5	Staffordshire bull terrier	13,070
6	Cavalier King Charles spaniel	11,165
7	Golden retriever	10,165
8	West Highland white terrier	9,775
9	Boxer	9,542
10	Border terrier	6,447

Source: The Kennel Club

There are perhaps 500 dog breeds in the world and The Kennel Club currently recognizes 201 in seven groups: gundog, hound, pastoral, terrier, toy, utility and working.

top10 **PEDIGREE** CAT BREEDS IN THE UK

BREED	NO. REGISTERED BY CAT FANCY, 2005
1 British short hair	6,761
2 Siamese	4,049
3 Persian	3,178
4 Bengal	3,113
5 Burmese	2,488
6 Maine coon	2,145
7 Birman	1,838
8 Ragdoll	1,734
9 Norwegian forest	1,157
10 Oriental short hair	1,030

Source: The Governing Council of the Cat Fancy

This Top 10 is based on a total of 32,649 cats registered in 2005.

◐ *Feline favourite*
Although unknown in the West until 1884, the Siamese cat has become one of the most popular of all pedigree breeds.

LUCY!

the10 **LATEST WINNERS** OF 'BEST IN SHOW' AT CRUFTS

YEAR / BREED / NAME

2006 Australian shepherd
Caitland Isle Take a Chance

2005 Norfolk terrier
Cracknoe Cause Celebre

2004 Whippet
Cobyco Call the Tune

2003 Pekingese
Yakee A Dangerous Liaison

2002 Standard poodle
Nordic Champion
Topscore Contradiction

2001 Basenji hound
Jethard Cidevant

2000 Kerry blue terrier
Torums Scarf Michael

1999 Irish setter
Caspians Intrepid

1998 Welsh terrier
Saredon Forever Young

1997 Yorkshire terrier
Ozmilion Mystification

top10 **CATS'** NAMES IN THE UK

CHARLIE!

GIRLS		BOYS
Lucy	**1**	Charlie
Poppy	**2**	Sammy
Cleo	**3**	Billy
Holly	**4**	Oscar
Daisy	**5**	Oliver
Molly	**6**	Ben
Tabitha	**7**	Smokie
Misty	**8**	Tigger
Amber	**9**	Sooty
Chloe	**10**	Leo

Source: Feline Advisory Bureau/Felix

The traditional Puss and Tiddles of yesteryear have been consigned to the cat litter of history: today's cats receive human names to an even greater extent than dogs – three-quarters of the 20 most common cats names are also found in the Top 20 British babies' names.

top10 **DOGS'** NAMES IN THE UK

MOLLY!

FEMALE		MALE
Molly	**1**	Max
Holly	**2**	Charlie
Rosie	**3**	Ben
Poppy	**4**	Jake
Lucy	**5**	Barney
Ellie	**6**	Jack
Tess	**7**	Buster
Meg	**8**	Toby
Bonnie	**9**	Jasper
Daisy	**10**	Oscar

Source: Argos Insurance Services

Recent surveys of dogs' names in the UK have produced slightly differing results, but they all indicate the trend for giving them names that could equally be those of humans. One possible explanation may be that, in many instances, pets are substitutes for babies, regarded as family members and named accordingly.

Plants

top10 POT PLANTS GROWN IN THE UK

1 Primroses (*Primula vulgaris*) and polyanthus (*Primula polyanthus*)
2 Chrysanthemums (*Chrysanthemum* species)
3 Cyclamen (*Cyclamen hederifolium*)
4 Begonias (*Begonia* species)
5 Poinsettias (*Euphorbia pulcherrima*)
6 New Guinea impatiens (*Impatiens* x *hawkeri*)
7 Hedera (*Hedera* species)
8 Planted arrangements (multiple species)
9 Cape daisy (*Osteospermum* species)
10 Ferns (*Pteridophyta*)

Source: Department for Environment, Food and Rural Affairs

top10 FLOWERS GROWN FROM BULBS IN THE UK

1 Narcissus (*Narcissus* species)
2 Tulip (*Tulipa* species)
3 Crocus (*Crocus* species)
4 Hyacinth (*Hyacinthus* species)
5 Dahlia (*Dahlia* species)
6 Gladioli (*Gladiolus* species)
7 Begonia (*Begonia* species)
8 Snowdrop (*Galanthus* species)
9 Anemone (*Anemone* species)
10 Scilla (*Scilla* species)

Source: Suttons Seeds

top10 FLOWERS SENT BY INTERFLORA IN THE UK

1 Lilies (*Lilium* species)
2 Freesias (*Freesia* species)
3 Roses (*Rosa* species)
4 Sweet peas (*Lathyrus odoratus*)
5 Gerbera (*Gerbera* species)
6 Carnations (*Dianthus caryophyllus*)
7 Alstroemeria (*Alstroemeria* species)
8 Delphinums (*Delphinium* species)
9 Tulips (*Tulipa* species)
10 Orchids (*Orchis* species)

Source: Interflora

Top 10 FLOWERS GROWN FROM SEED IN THE UK

1 Sweet pea (*Lathyrus odoratus*)
2 Night-scented stock (*Matthiola* species)
3 Lobelia (*Lobelia* species)
4 Nasturtium (*Tropaeolum* species)
5 French marigold (*Tagetes* species)
6 Alyssum (*Alyssum* species)
7 Godetia (*Clarkia* species)
8 Impatiens (Busy Lizzie) (*Impatiens* species)
9 Sunflower (*Eriophyllum, Helianthus, Tithonia* species)
10 Geranium (*Geranium* species)

Source: Suttons Seeds

top10 COUNTRIES REGISTERING THE **MOST NEW PLANT** VARIETIES

COUNTRY / VARIETIES REGISTERED*

* As recorded by World Intellectual Property Organization, 2002

| 1 USA 1,510 | 2 Japan 1,321 | 3 Russia 479 | 4 Australia 286 |

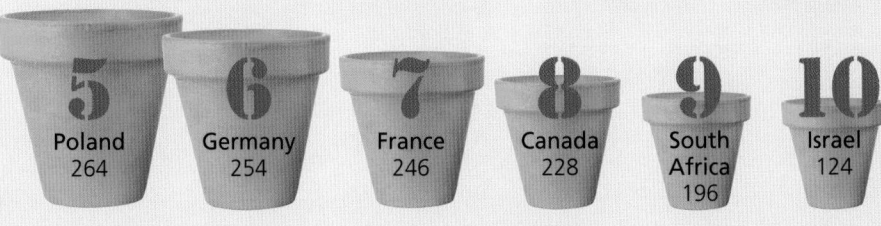

| 5 Poland 264 | 6 Germany 254 | 7 France 246 | 8 Canada 228 | 9 South Africa 196 | 10 Israel 124 |

the10 OLDEST **BOTANIC GARDENS** IN THE UK

GARDEN	FOUNDED
1 Oxford University Botanic Garden, Oxford	1621
2 Royal Botanic Garden, Edinburgh	1670
3 Chelsea Physic Garden, London	1673
4 Royal Botanic Gardens, Kew	1759
5 Cambridge University Botanic Garden, Cambridge	1762*
6 Bath Botanical Gardens, Bath	1779
7 Glasgow Botanic Gardens, Glasgow	1817
8 York Museum Gardens, York	1827
9 Belfast Botanic Garden, Belfast	1828
10 Birmingham Botanical Gardens, Birmingham	1829

* Moved to present site 1846

The first botanic gardens for the study of plants date from the medieval era. Plants were then widely used in the preparation of remedies, so gardens were often attached to medical schools, such as that at the first European medical school at Salerno, Italy, dating from 1309, which became the model for gardens set up in Venice, Pisa and Padua. Other European universities, such as Leiden, Leipzig and Heidelberg followed suit, with the University of Oxford creating the first in the British Isles. In the 18th century botanic gardens were set up in various parts of the world, including Pamplemousses, Mauritius (1735), Sibpur, India (1787) and the Dublin National Botanic Gardens, Glasnevin (1795).

the10 COUNTRIES WITH THE **MOST THREATENED** PLANT SPECIES

COUNTRY / TOTAL NO. OF THREATENED PLANTS

#	Country	Total
1	Ecuador	1,815
2	Malaysia	683
3	China	443
4	Indonesia	383
5	Brazil	381
6	Cameroon	334
7	Sri Lanka	280
8	Madagascar	276
9	Peru	274
10	Mexico	261

UK 13

Source: 2004 IUCN Red List of Threatened Species

Of 11,824 species of plants evaluated by the IUCN in 2004 (out of a total 287,655 known), some 8,321, or 70 per cent of the total, were considered threatened. Of these, the most threatened are flowering plants belonging to the class *Magnoliopsida*, of which 7,025 were so-categorized.

Trees & Forests

top10 LARGEST FORESTS IN THE UK

FOREST*	AREA SQ KM	SQ MILES
1 Galloway Forest Park, Dumfries and Galloway	770	297
2 Kielder Forest Park, Northumberland	610	235
3 New Forest, Hampshire	270	104
4 Dornoch Forest, Sutherland	260	100
5 Argyll Forest Park, Argyll	210	81
6 Queen Elizabeth Forest Park, Stirling	200	77
7 Thetford Forest Park, Norfolk/Suffolk	190	73
8 Affric Forest, (Fort Augustus), Inverness-shire	180	69
9 Tay Forest Park, Perthshire	170	65
10 Glengarry Forest, (Lochaber Forest District), Inverness-shire	165	63

* Forestry Commission forests, including areas designated as Forest Parks, which can include areas not covered by woodland

Source: Forestry Commission

top10 COUNTRIES WITH THE LARGEST AREAS OF TROPICAL FOREST

COUNTRY	AREA SQ KM	SQ MILES
1 Brazil	3,012,730	1,163,222
2 Dem. Rep. of Congo	1,350,710	521,512
3 Indonesia	887,440	343,029
4 Peru	756,360	292,032
5 Bolivia	686,380	265,012
6 Venezuela	556,150	214,730
7 Columbia	531,860	205,352
8 Mexico	457,650	176,700
9 India	444,500	171,622
10 Angola	375,640	145,035

Source: Food and Agriculture Organization of the United Nations, 'State of the World's Forests, 2005'

top10 MOST COMMON TREES IN THE UK

TREE / PERCENTAGE OF TOTAL FOREST AREA

1 Sitka spruce (*Picea sitchensis*) 29

2 Scots pine (*Pinus sylvestris*) 10

3 Oak (*Quercus robur*) 9

4 Birch (*Betula pubescens*) 7

5 Lodgepole pine (*Pinus contorta latifolia*) 6

6 = Ash (*Fraxinus excelsior*) 5

= Japanese/hybrid larch (*Larix kempferi/Larix x eurolepis*) 5

8 Beech (*Fagus sylvatica*) 4

9 = Norway spruce (*Picea abies*) 3

= Sycamore (*Acer pseudoplatanus*) 3

Source: Forestry Commission

Seven per cent of the UK's forested areas is classified as mixed broadleaves and one per cent as mixed conifers, a large proportion of which grows in forests managed by the Forestry Commission. The Commission came into existence as a result of the Forestry Act of 1919, planting its first trees at Eggesford Forest, Devon, on 8 December 1919.

top10 COUNTRIES WITH THE LARGEST AREAS OF FOREST

COUNTRY /
AREA SQ KM/
SQ MILES

The world's forests occupy 29.6 per cent of the total land area of the planet. Just under half of Russia is forested, a total area that is almost the size of the whole of Brazil.

1 Russia 8,513,920/ 3,287,243

2 Brazil 5,439,905/ 2,100,359

3 Canada 2,445,710/ 944,294

4 USA 2,259,930/ 872,564

5 China 1,634,800/ 631,200

6 Australia 1,545,390/ 596,678

7 Dem. Rep. of Congo 1,352,070/ 522,037

8 Indonesia 1,049,860/ 405,353

9 Angola 697,560/ 269,329

10 Peru 652,7/ 251,7

Source: Food and Agriculture Organization of the United Nations, 'State of the World's Forests, 2005'

⬇ Clinging on
Even the extensive forest cover of Surinam is dwindling, threatening the natural habitats of creatures such as the red-bellied tree frog.

top10 **MOST FORESTED** COUNTRIES

COUNTRY	PERCENTAGE FOREST COVER
1 Surinam	90.5
2 Solomon Islands	88.8
3 Gabon	84.7
4 Brunei	83.9
5 Guyana	78.5
6 Palau	76.1
7 Finland	72.0
8 North Korea	68.2
9 Papua New Guinea	67.6
10 Seychelles	66.7
UK	*11.6*

Source: Food and Agriculture Organization of the United Nations, 'State of the World's Forests, 2005'

These are the 10 countries with the greatest area of forest and woodland as a percentage of their total land area. With increasing deforestation, the world average has fallen from about 32 per cent in 1972 to its present 29.6 per cent. The least forested large countries in the world are the desert lands of the Middle East and North Africa, such as Oman, which has none, and Egypt and Qatar, each with just 0.1 per cent.

top10 **DEFORESTING** COUNTRIES

COUNTRY	ANNUAL FOREST COVER LOSS 1990-2000 SQ KM	SQ MILES
1 Brazil	23,090	8,915
2 Indonesia	13,120	5,065
3 Sudan	9,590	3,702
4 Zambia	8,510	3,286
5 Mexico	6,310	2,436
6 Dem. Rep. of Congo	5,320	2,054
7 Myanmar	5,170	1,996
8 Nigeria	3,980	1,537
9 Zimbabwe	3,200	1,235
10 Argentina	2,850	1,100

Source: Food and Agriculture Organization of the United Nations, 'State of the World's Forests, 2005'

THE HUMAN WORLD

Healthcare

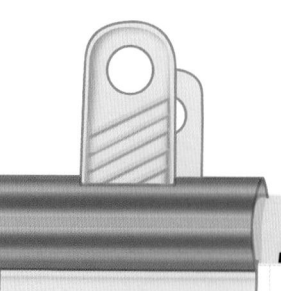

the 10 LEAST HEALTHY COUNTRIES

	COUNTRY	HEALTHY LIFE EXPECTANCY AT BIRTH*
1	Sierra Leone	28.6
2	Lesotho	31.4
3	Angola	33.4
4	Zimbabwe	33.6
5	Swaziland	34.2
6 =	Malawi	34.9
=	Zambia	34.9
8	Burundi	35.1
9	Liberia	35.3
10 =	Afghanistan	35.5
=	Niger	35.5

* Average number of years expected to be spent in good health

Source: World Health Organization

top 10 HEALTHIEST COUNTRIES

	COUNTRY	HEALTHY LIFE EXPECTANCY AT BIRTH*
1	Japan	75.0
2	San Marino	73.4
3	Sweden	73.3
4	Switzerland	73.2
5	Monaco	72.9
6	Iceland	72.8
7	Italy	72.7
8 =	Australia	72.6
=	Spain	72.6
10 =	Canada	72.0
=	France	72.0
=	Norway	72.0
	UK	70.6

* Average number of years expected to be spent in good health

Source: World Health Organization

HALE (Health Adjusted Life Expectancy) differs from life expectancy in that an adjustment is made for years spent in ill health as a result of poor diet, disease, lack of health care and other factors. It is the method used by the World Health Organization to compare the state of health of nations and graphically illustrates the contrast between the HALEs of Western countries – more than double those of developing countries, especially sub-Saharan Africa.

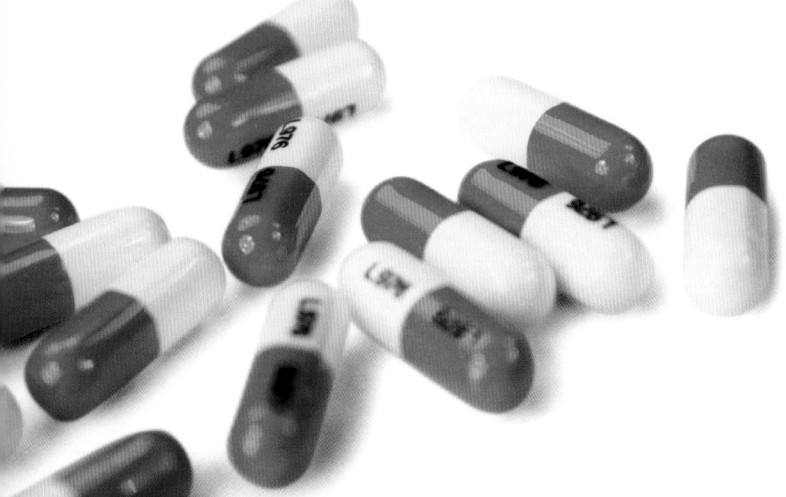

AMAZING FACT

Life Expectancy

Average life expectancy at birth in prehistoric times was about 20 years. During the Greek and Roman era it increased to 28 and in the Medieval period to 33. By the end of the 19th century it was 37, steadily rising during the 20th century to the present-day figure of about 65 years and predicted to reach 75 by 2050. Today, the greatest disparity is between the 80 years of many developed countries to under 50 in others.

the10 COUNTRIES SPENDING THE LEAST ON HEALTH CARE

	COUNTRY	HEALTH SPENDING PER CAPITA IN 2002 ($)
1	North Korea	0.3
2	Burundi	3
3	=Dem. Rep. of Congo	4
	=Liberia	4
5	=Ethiopia	5
	=Madagascar	5
7	=Sierra Leone	6
	=Somalia [2001]	6
	=Tajikistan	6
10	Niger	7

Source: World Health Organization

top10 COUNTRIES THAT SPEND THE MOST ON HEALTH CARE

	COUNTRY	HEALTH SPENDING PER CAPITA IN 2002 ($)
1	USA	5,274
2	Switzerland	4,219
3	Norway	4,033
4	Monaco	3,656
5	Luxembourg	2,951
6	Iceland	2,916
7	Denmark	2,835
8	Germany	2,631
9	Sweden	2,489
10	Japan	2,476
	UK	*2,031*

Source: World Health Organization

top10 COUNTRIES WITH THE FEWEST PATIENTS PER DOCTOR

	COUNTRY	PATIENTS PER DOCTOR
1	Italy	162
2	Cuba	165
3	Georgia	206
4	Greece	220
5	Belgium	223
6	Russia	235
7	Lithuania	252
8	Uruguay	256
9	Israel	272
10	Kazakhstan	273
	UK	*469*

Source: World Health Organization

top10 MOST COMMON REASONS FOR VISITS TO THE DOCTOR IN THE UK

	COMPLAINT	RATE*
1	Blood pressure disorders	946
2	Dermatitis and eczema	897
3	Skin disorders	884
4	Acute upper respiratory infections	802
5	Disorders of the eye	792
6	Disorders of the ear and mastoid process	731
7	Other accute lower respiratory infections	716
8	Chronic lower respiratory diseases	696
9	Dorsopathies (back problems)	640
10	Non-inflamatory female disorders	543

* Patients consulting per 10,000

Source: Office of Health Economics, 'Compendium of Health Statistics', 17th edn, 2005–2006

top10 OVER-THE-COUNTER HEALTH-CARE PRODUCTS IN THE UK

	PRODUCT	ANNUAL SALES, 2004 (£)
1	Cough, cold and allergy (hay fever) remedies	570,200,000
2	Analgesics (painkillers)	499,000,000
3	Vitamins and dietary supplements	441,900,000
4	Medicated skin care	395,300,000
5	Digestive remedies	285,800,000
6	Smoking-cessation aids	83,900,000
7	Eye care	58,200,000
8	Wound treatments	34,500,000
9	Adult mouthcare	33,700,000
10	Calming and sleeping products	25,400,000
	Total (including products not in Top 10)	*2,473,700,000*

Source: Euromonitor

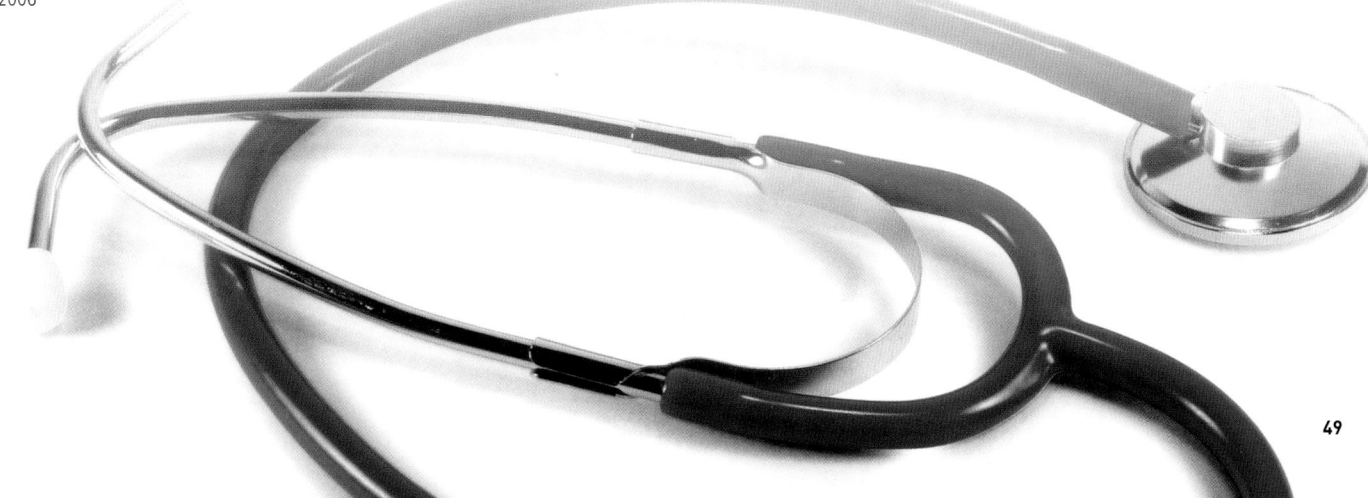

Healthy Living

top10 **FAT** CONSUMERS

	COUNTRY	AVERAGE DAILY FAT CONSUMPTION PER CAPITA, 2002 GMS	OZ
1	France	170.8	6.02
2	Belgium	159.6	5.62
3	Austria	158.2	5.58
4	Italy	158.1	5.57
5	USA	156.5	5.52
6	Switzerland	156.2	5.51
7	Greece	152.7	5.38
8	Spain	150.9	5.32
9	Hungary	147.2	5.19
10	Germany	146.4	5.16
	World average	*77.5*	*2.73*
	UK	*138.9*	*4.89*

Source: Food and Agricultural Organization of the United Nations

top10 **PROTEIN** CONSUMERS

	COUNTRY	AVERAGE DAILY PROTEIN CONSUMPTION PER CAPITA, 2002 GMS	OZ
1	Israel	128.6	4.53
2	Iceland	124.4	4.38
3	France	119.2	4.20
4	Malta	118.9	4.19
5	Portugal	118.4	4.17
6	Greece	115.7	4.08
7	Ireland	114.2	4.03
8	USA	114.0	4.02
9	Italy	113.1	3.98
10	Spain	111.7	3.94
	World average	*75.3*	*2.65*
	UK	*102.4*	*3.61*

top10 **CALORIE** CONSUMERS

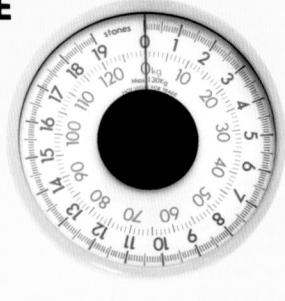

	COUNTRY	AVERAGE DAILY CALORIE CONSUMPTION PER CAPITA, 2002
1	USA	3,774.1
2	Portugal	3,740.9
3	Greece	3,721.1
4	Austria	3,673.3
5	Italy	3,670.6
6	Israel	3,666.1
7	Ireland	3,656.4
8	France	3,653.9
9	Canada	3,589.3
10	Malta	3,586.9
	World average	*2,804.4*
	UK	*3,412.2*

Source: Food and Agriculture Organization of the United Nations

The Calorie requirement of the average man is 2,700 and of a woman 2,500. Inactive people need less, while those engaged in heavy labour require more. The countries in the Top 10, as well as many others, are consuming over 30 per cent more than they need – hence the rise of obesity and related medical problems. However, the Calorie consumption of over 10 of the poorest African nations falls below 2,000, with Eritrea's average of 1,512.8 standing at just 40 per cent of the figure for the USA.

the10 MOST **OBESE** COUNTRIES

	COUNTRY	PERCENTAGE OF OBESE ADULTS* MEN	WOMEN		COUNTRY	PERCENTAGE OF OBESE ADULTS* MEN	WOMEN
1	Nauru	80.2	78.6	6	Qatar	34.6	45.3
2	Tonga	46.6	70.3	7	French Polynesia	36.3	44.3
3	Samoa	32.9	63.0	8	Saudi Arabia	26.4	44.0
4	Jordan#	32.7	59.8	9	Palestine	23.9	42.5
5	Nieue	15.0	46.0	10	United Arab Emirates	25.9	39.9
					England	*22.2*	*23.0*
					Scotland	*19.0*	*22.0*
					Wales	*17.0*	*18.0*

* Ranked by percentage of obese women (those with a BMI greater than 30) in those countries and latest year for which data available
# Urban population only

Source: International Obesity Task Force (IOTF)

top10 COUNTRIES WITH THE **HEAVIEST** SMOKERS

	COUNTRY	AVERAGE ANNUAL CIGARETTE CONSUMPTION PER ADULT, 1992–2000*
1	Greece	3,230
2	Bulgaria	3,222
3	Japan	2,950
4	Switzerland	2,880
5	Spain	2,826
6	Netherlands	2,775
7	Slovenia	2,742
8	Hungary	2,697
9	Russia	2,691
10	South Korea	2,686
	UK	1,553

* Smokers aged over 15, in those countries for which data available

Source: World Health Organization

top10 VITAMIN AND DIETARY **SUPPLEMENT** CONSUMERS

	COUNTRY	£ PER CAPITA PER ANNUM, 2004
1	Japan	49.31
2	USA	28.15
3	Norway	27.32
4	Taiwan	22.57
5	South Korea	16.74
6	Australia	16.32
7	Singapore	14.06
8	Belgium	13.59
9	Sweden	13.02
10	Italy	12.33
	UK	7.41

Source: Euromonitor

the10 MOST **EFFECTIVE** KEEP-FIT ACTIVITIES

1 Swimming
2 Cycling
3 Rowing
4 Gymnastics
5 Judo
6 Dancing
7 Football
8 Jogging
9 Walking (briskly!)
10 Squash

Source: Sports Council (now Sport England)

These are the sports and activities recommended by keep-fit experts as the best means of acquiring all-round fitness, building stamina and strength and increasing suppleness.

Disease & Illness

the10 WORST **DISEASE BURDENS**

	DISEASE, ETC	% OF DALYS*
1	HIV/AIDS	7.4
2	Coronary heart disease	6.8
3	Stroke	5.0
4	Depression	4.8
5	Road traffic injuries	4.3
6	Tuberculosis	4.2
7	Alcohol abuse	3.4
8	Violence	3.3
9	Obstructive pulmonary disease	3.1
10	Hearing loss	2.7

* Percentage of people's healthy lifespans that are lost as a result of these diseases, among men aged over 15

Source: World Health Organization

DALYs – Disability-adjusted Life Years – are potential healthy years of life that are lost as a result of contracting diseases or as a result of an injury or other disability. This is used as a measure of the 'burden of disease' that affects not only the individual sufferer but also has an effect on the cost of the provision of health services and consequent loss to a country's economy. These are world averages, but there are variations from country to country, with 10 per cent of DALYs lost as a result of cardiovascular disease in low- and middle-income countries, but as much as 18 per cent in high-income countries.

the10 MOST **COMMON CAUSES** OF ILLNESS

CAUSE	NEW CASES ANNUALLY
1 Diarrhoea (including dysentery)	4,002,000,000
2 Malaria	up to 500,000,000
3 Acute lower respiratory infections	395,000,000
4 Occupational injuries	350,000,000
5 Occupational diseases	217,000,000
6 Trichomoniasis	170,000,000
7 Mood (affective) disorders	122,865,000
8 Chlamydial infections	89,000,000
9 Alcohol-dependence syndrome	75,000,000
10 Gonococcal (bacterial) infections	62,000,000

Source: World Health Organization

AMAZING FACT

History's Worst Disease

Malaria has killed more people than any other disease. Its cause – a mosquito-borne parasite – was unknown until discovered by Charles Laveran (1845–1922), for which he received the 1907 Nobel Prize. Malaria remains a major killer and in 2005 the Bill & Melinda Gates Foundation pledged $258.3 million to fund research in combating it through prevention, drugs and a vaccine.

the10 COUNTRIES WITH THE
MOST CASES OF MALARIA

	COUNTRY	MALARIA CASES PER 100,000 PEOPLE*, 2000
1	Guinea	75,386
2	Botswana	48,704
3	Burundi	48,098
4	Zambia	34,204
5	Malawi	25,948
6	Mozambique	18,115
7	Gambia	17,340
8	Ghana	15,344
9	Solomon Islands	15,172
10	Yemen	15,160

* Data refer to malaria cases reported to the World Health Organization (WHO) and may represent only a fraction of the true number in a country

Source: United Nations, 'Human Development Report 2005'

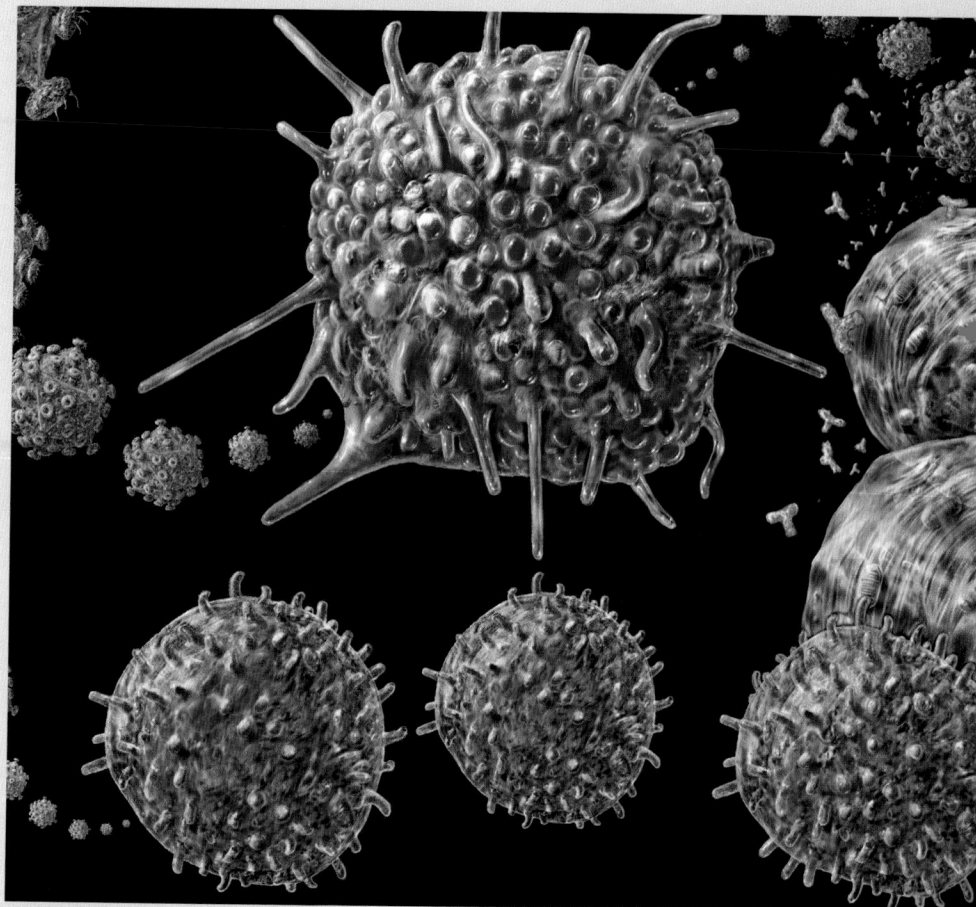

the10 COUNTRIES WITH THE
MOST CASES OF TUBERCULOSIS

	COUNTRY	TUBERCULOSIS CASES PER 100,000 PEOPLE*, 2000
1	Djibouti	1,161
2	Swaziland	769
3	Cambodia	734
4	Mali	695
5	Togo	688
6	Ivory Coast	634
7	Sierra Leone	628
8	Indonesia	609
9	Rwanda	598
10	Dem Rep of Congo	594
	World average	*257*
	UK	*12*

* Data refer to the prevalence of all forms of tuberculosis

Source: United Nations, 'Human Development Report 2004'

the10 COUNTRIES WITH THE **MOST CASES OF AIDS**

	COUNTRY	DEATHS, 2003	EST. NO. OF CASES
1	South Africa	370,000	5,300,000
2	India	N/A	5,100,000
3	Nigeria	310,000	3,600,000
4	Zimbabwe	170,000	1,800,000
5	Ethiopia	120,000	1,500,000
6	Tanzania	160,000	1,400,000
7	Mozambique	110,000	1,300,000
8	= Kenya	150,000	1,200,000
	= Zambia	170,000	1,200,000
10	Dem. Rep. of Congo	100,000	950,000
	World	*3,000,000*	*37,800,000*
	UK	*460*	*39,000*

Source: UNAIDS, '2004 Report on the Global AIDS Epidemic'

First identified in 1981, AIDS has killed over 25 million and affected the social and economic fabric of many African countries by orphaning children, decimating labour forces and stretching medical resources to their limit.

⬆ *Deadly virus*
The HIV (Human Immunodeficiency Virus) that causes AIDs (Acquired Immunodeficiency Syndrome) attacks healthy cells. Worldwide, some five million people become infected with AIDS every year.

Birth to Death

the10 COUNTRIES WITH THE MOST BIRTHS

COUNTRY	EST. BIRTHS, 2007
1 India	24,073,392
2 China	17,778,908
3 Nigeria	5,428,253
4 Indonesia	4,960,256
5 Pakistan	4,919,004
6 Bangladesh	4,417,163
7 USA	4,264,142
8 Brazil	3,097,174
9 Ethiopia	2,860,779
10 Dem. Rep. of Congo	2,798,765
World	*131,698,130*
UK	*648,482*

Source: US Census Bureau, International Data Base

As India's birth rate is maintained and China's is subject to curbs, the population of India is set to overtake that of China by 2030.

the10 COUNTRIES WITH THE HIGHEST BIRTH RATE

COUNTRY	ESTIMATED BIRTH RATE (LIVE BIRTHS PER 1,000, 2007)
1 Niger	50.16
2 Mali	49.57
3 Uganda	47.32
4 Afghanistan	46.61
5 Sierra Leone	45.51
6 Chad	45.30
7 Burkina Faso	45.28
8 Angola	44.61
9 Somalia	44.60
10 Liberia	43.73
World	*20.00*
UK	*10.67*

Source: US Census Bureau, International Data Base

The countries with the highest birth rates are amongst the poorest countries in the world. In these countries, people often deliberately have large families, so that the children can help earn income for the family when they are older. The 10 countries with the highest birth rate therefore corresponds very closely with the list of countries with the highest fertility rate – the average number of children born to each woman in the country.

the10 COUNTRIES WITH THE LOWEST BIRTH RATE

COUNTRY	ESTIMATED BIRTH RATE (LIVE BIRTHS PER 1,000, 2007)
1 Hong Kong	7.34
2 Andorra	8.45
3 Italy	8.54
4 Germany	8.65
5 Austria	8.69
6 Bosnia and Herzegovina	8.80
7 Lithuania	8.87
8 Czech Republic	8.96
9 Slovenia	9.00
10 Monaco	9.12

Source: US Census Bureau, International Data Base

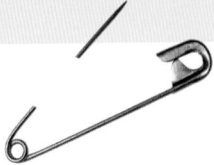

the10 YEARS WITH MOST BIRTHS IN THE UK

YEAR	BIRTHS
1 **1920**	1,194,068
2 **1903**	1,183,627
3 **1904**	1,181,770
4 **1902**	1,174,639
5 **1908**	1,173,759
6 **1906**	1,170,622
7 **1905**	1,163,535
8 **1899**	1,163,279
9 **1901**	1,162,975
10 **1900**	1,159,922

The total number of births in the UK more than doubled in the 19th century. High figures were also experienced in the early years of the 20th century, with an all-time peak in 1920, the so-called post-First World War 'bulge'. This was paralleled in 1947 by a post-Second World War surge to 1,025,000 (in 1941 the figure had been just 703,858). The 20th-century low was 657,000 in 1977. Since 1972, no year has had over 800,000 births. The 2004 total was 714,139.

the10 COUNTRIES WITH THE **HIGHEST** DEATH RATE

	COUNTRY	ESTIMATED DEATH RATE (DEATHS PER 1,000, 2007)
1	Swaziland	30.35
2	Botswana	29.43
3	Lesotho	28.57
4	Angola	23.90
5	Sierra Leone	22.64
6	South Africa	22.45
7	Liberia	22.26
8	Zimbabwe	21.76
9	Mozambique	21.68
10	Niger	20.59
	World average	*8.60*
	UK	*10.09*

Source: US Census Bureau, International Data Base

All 10 of the countries with the highest death rates are in sub-Saharan Africa. A decade ago, South Africa had a rate of 10.7, but the AIDS toll has changed its demographic profile as a high proportion of young people have fallen victim.

the10 COUNTRIES WITH THE **LOWEST** DEATH RATE

	COUNTRY	ESTIMATED DEATH RATE (DEATHS PER 1,000, 2007)
1	Kuwait	2.39
2	Saudi Arabia	2.55
3	Jordan	2.68
4	Libya	3.47
5	Brunei	3.49
6	Oman	3.78
7	Solomon Islands	3.87
8	=Bahrain	4.21
	=Ecuador	4.21
10	Costa Rica	4.39

Source: US Census Bureau, International Data Base

The crude death rate is derived by dividing the total number of deaths in a given year by the total population and multiplying by 1,000. Because countries with young populations appear to have low death rates and older populations high rates, statisticians also use age-standardized death rates, which factor in the age structure for a more accurate assessment.

the10 COUNTRIES WITH THE **MOST** CREMATIONS

	COUNTRY	PERCENTAGE OF DEATHS	CREMATIONS*
1	China	52.70	4,349,000
2	Japan	99.61	1,072,977
3	USA	28.63	693,742
4	UK	70.83	424,956
5	Germany	40.10	338,469
6	France	21.80	120,037
7	Canada	47.30	107,673
8	Czech Republic	76.54	85,180
9	Netherlands	50.90	71,815
10	Sweden	72.12	67,040

* In latest year for which data available

Source: The Cremation Society of Great Britain

Cremation is least practised in traditionally Roman Catholic countries, such as Italy (7.49 per cent), and the Republic of Ireland (6.78 per cent), whereas land shortages for burial and cultural factors have led to cremation being the dominant means of disposal of the dead in Japan.

the10 MOST **COMMON** CAUSES OF DEATH IN THE UK

		DEATHS, 2003			
	CAUSE	ENGLAND & WALES	SCOTLAND	NORTHERN IRELAND	UK TOTAL
1	Diseases of the circulatory system	205,508	22,102	5,448	233,058
2	Cancer and other neoplasms	139,360	15,412	3,882	158,654
3	Diseases of the respiratory system	75,138	7,454	2,082	84,674
4	Diseases of the digestive system	24,948	3,215	587	28,750
5	External causes (accidents, etc.)	16,693	2,311	550	19,554
6	Diseases of the nervous system and sense organs	15,793	1,303	481	17,877
7	Mental disorders	14,846	2,637	341	17,824
8	Diseases of the genito-urinary system	9,120	1,056	327	10,503
9	Endocrine, nutritional and metabolic diseases and immunity disorders	8,016	958	246	9,220
10	Infectious and parasitic diseases	4,763	660	157	5,580
	Total deaths from all causes (including some that do not appear in the Top 10)	*538,254*	*58,472*	*14,462*	*611,188*

Names

top10 MOST COMMON **MALE NAMES** IN ENGLAND & WALES

	NAME	NUMBER
1	David Jones	15,763
2	David Smith	14,341
3	John Smith	12,793
4	David Williams	11,392
5	Michael Smith	10,516
6	John Jones	10,021
7	John Williams	8,738
8	=Paul Smith	8,348
	=Peter Smith	8,348
10	David Evans	8,103

Source: Office for National Statistics

The Office for National Statistics' survey of the most common combinations of first names and surnames, based on the National Health Service Register, revealed that there are 24 different surnames in the male top 100, but only 11 different female surnames. Smith appears 44 times in the male list, but only 22 times in the female version. Although John is the most common first name overall, its 18 occurrences in the top 100 is less than that of David (22), since it appears with less frequency in combination with the most common surnames.

top10 MOST COMMON **FEMALE NAMES** IN ENGLAND & WALES

	NAME	NUMBER
1	Margaret Smith	7,640
2	Margaret Jones	7,068
3	Susan Smith	6,531
4	Susan Jones	5,108
5	Mary Smith	5,049
6	Patricia Smith	4,743
7	Margaret Williams	4,636
8	Elizabeth Jones	4,604
9	Mary Jones	4,522
10	Sarah Jones	4,359

Source: Office for National Statistics

In contrast to the male version of this list, the female one contains a greater number of different first names: David, the most common male name appears 22 times in the top 100, while Margaret, the most common female first name, has only 11 entries.

top10 **SURNAMES** IN THE UK

	SURNAME	NUMBER
1	Smith	652,56
2	Jones	538,87
3	Williams	380,37
4	Taylor	306,29
5	Brown	291,87
6	Davies*	279,64
7	Evans	225,58
8	Thomas	202,77
9	Wilson	201,22
10	Johnson	193,26

* There are also 97,349 people bearing the surname Davis

This survey of British surnames is based on an analysis of names appearing in the England and Wales electoral rolls. Some 12 people out of every thousand are called Smith, a decline in part due to the diluting effect of immigrant names – 137,088 people (or 2.52 per 1,000) now bear the name Patel, for example.

top10 **SURNAMES** IN SCOTLAND

	SURNAME	FREQUENCY* (1999-2001)
1	Smith	4,291
2	Brown	3,030
3	Wilson	2,876
4	Campbell	2,657
5	Stewart	2,626
6	Thomson	2,616
7	Robertson	2,536
8	Anderson	2,297
9	Macdonald	1,844
10	Scott	1,839

* Based on a survey of names appearing on birth and death registers, and both names on marriage registers

top10 **FIRST NAMES** IN ENGLAND & WALES, 2005

GIRLS		BOYS
Jessica +1	1	Jack
Emily −1	2	Joshua
Sophie +1	3	Thomas
Olivia +3	4	James
Chloe	5	Oliver +2
Ellie −4	6	Daniel −1
Grace +4	7	Samuel −1
Lucy −3	8	William
Charlotte −1	9	Harry +2
Katie −1	10	Joseph

+ Indicates rise in popularity since previous year
− Indicates decline in popularity since previous year

Source: Office for National Statistics

top10 **GIRLS' AND BOYS' NAMES** IN THE UK 100 YEARS AGO

GIRLS		BOYS
Mary	1	William
Florence	2	John
Doris	3	George
Edith	4	Thomas
Dorothy	5	Arthur
Annie	6	James
Margaret	7	Charles
Alice	8	Frederick
Elizabeth	9	Albert
Elsie	10	Ernest

AMADING FACT

Curious Cornish Names

A 2005 survey of names in birth, marriage and death documents in the Cornwall Record Office revealed the county's exceptional history of bizarre but genuine personal names. Its selection of over 1,000, mostly dating from the 17th to 19th centuries, includes Philadelphia Bunnyface, Agrippa Wadge, Boadicea Basher, Elizabeth Poo, Hugh Glues, Freak Ustick, Elizabeth Disco, Noah Flood, Priscilla Quiller, Thomas Tramplepleasure, Gentle Fudge and Levi Jeans.

Marriage & Divorce

top10 COUNTRIES WITH THE MOST MARRIAGES

	COUNTRY	MARRIAGES PER ANNUM*
1	USA	2,254,000
2	Bangladesh	1,181,000
3	Russia	1,001,589
4	Vietnam	964,701
5	Japan	757,331
6	Brazil	710,120
7	Iran	650,960
8	Ethiopia	630,290
9	Mexico	570,060
10	Egypt	525,412
	UK	*305,912*

* In those countries/latest year for which data available

Source: United Nations

↩ Chinese wedding belle
Exotic costumes are typical of weddings in China, the country that has the world's highest marriage rate.

top10 COUNTRIES WITH THE HIGHEST MARRIAGE RATE

	COUNTRY	MARRIAGES PER 1,000 PER ANNUM*
1	China	35.9
2	Cook Islands	32.8
3	Barbados	13.1
4	Cyprus	12.9
5	Vietnam	12.1
6	Seychelles	10.7
7	Jamaica	10.4
8	Ethiopia	10.2
9	Fiji	10.1
10	Iran	9.9
	UK	*5.1*

* In those countries/latest year for which data available

Source: United Nations

the10 COUNTRIES WITH THE LOWEST MARRIAGE RATE

	COUNTRY	MARRIAGES PER 1,000 PER ANNUM*
1	Peru	2.4
2	United Arab Emirates	2.5
3	Georgia	2.7
4	Andorra	2.8
5	Dominican Republic	2.9
6	French Guiana	3.0
7	= Argentina	3.2
	= Armenia	3.2
	= Saudi Arabia	3.2
10	Venezuela	3.3

* In those countries/latest year for which data available

Source: United Nations

AMAZING FACT

Till Death Us Do Part

On 20 June 1996 America's most married man, Baptist minister Glynn 'Scotty' Wolfe (born 1908) of Blythe, California, married America's most married woman, Linda Essex of Anderson, Indiana. It was the Rev Wolfe's 29th marriage since 1927 and Ms Essex's 23rd. Rumoured to be a publicity stunt, their wedding was filmed for a TV programme, but the couple separated shortly afterwards. Sadly, Glynn Wolfe died a year later – unmarried.

top10 MONTHS FOR MARRIAGES IN ENGLAND AND WALES

MONTH / MARRIAGES

AUGUST 43,957 — 1

JUNE 31,634 — 2

JULY 31,097 — 3

SEPTEMBER 30,617 — 4

MAY 24,385 — 5

OCTOBER 18,806 — 6

APRIL 15,105 — 7

NOVEMBER 14,283 — 8

MARCH 14,255 — 9

DECEMBER 13,819 — 10

Source: National Statistics

The figures are for 2002, when there were a total of 255,596 marriages in England and Wales. As Saturday is the favoured day for weddings, the apparent popularity of a particular month can be boosted if it has five Saturdays.

top10 COUNTRIES WITH THE **LOWEST** **DIVORCE** RATES

COUNTRY / DIVORCE RATE PER 1,000*

1 Guatemala 0.12
2 Belize 0.17
3 Mongolia 0.28
4 Libya 0.32
5 Georgia 0.40
6 Chile 0.42
7 St Vincent and the Grenadines 0.43
8 Jamaica 0.44
9 Armenia 0.47
10 Turkey 0.49

* In those countries/latest year for which data available

Source: United Nations

The countries that figure among those with the lowest rates represent a range of cultures and religions, which either condone or condemn divorce to varying extents, thus affecting its prevalence or otherwise. In some countries, legal and other obstacles make divorce difficult or costly, while in certain societies, such as Jamaica, where the marriage rate is also low, partners often separate without the formality of divorce.

the10 COUNTRIES WITH THE **HIGHEST** **DIVORCE** RATES

COUNTRY / DIVORCE RATE PER 1,000*

1 Russia 5.30
2 Aruba 5.27
3 USA 4.19
4 Ukraine 3.79
5 Belarus 3.77
6 Moldova 3.50
7 Cuba 3.16
8 Czech Republic 3.11
9 = Lithuania 3.05
= South Korea 3.05
UK 2.58

* In those countries/latest year for which data available

Source: United Nations

Religion

top10 RELIGIOUS **BELIEFS**

	RELIGION	FOLLOWERS
1	Christianity	2,135,784,198
2	Islam	1,313,983,654
3	Hinduism	870,047,346
4	Chinese folk-religions	404,922,244
5	Buddhism	378,809,103
6	Ethnic religions	256,340,652
7	New religions	108,131,713
8	Sikhism	25,373,879
9	Judaism	15,145,702
10	Spiritists	13,030,538

Source: World Christian Database

While some mainstream religious groups have experienced a decline in formal attendance, certain fringe religions have grown. Today, about one-third of the world's population are nominally, if not practicing, Christians and one-fifth are followers of Islam. At least 15 per cent of the world's population profess no religious beliefs of any kind.

top10 LARGEST **CHRISTIAN POPULATIONS**

	COUNTRY	CHRISTIANS
1	USA	252,394,312
2	Brazil	166,847,207
3	China	110,956,366
4	Mexico	102,011,835
5	Russia	84,494,596
6	Philippines	73,987,348
7	India	68,189,739
8	Germany	61,833,042
9	Nigeria	61,437,608
10	Dem. Rep. of Congo	53,370,662
	World total	*2,135,784,198*
	UK	*48,191,574*

Source: World Christian Database

Christian populations of these countries comprise almost half the world total. Christians exist in almost every country. Precise estimates of nominal membership (declared religious persuasion), rather than active participation (regular attendance at a place of worship), are inevitably vague.

top10 LARGEST **JEWISH POPULATIONS**

	COUNTRY	JEWS
1	USA	5,764,208
2	Israel	4,772,138
3	France	607,111
4	Argentina	520,130
6	Palestine	451,001
5	Canada	414,452
7	Brazil	383,837
8	UK	312,173
9	Russia	244,719
10	Germany	222,689
	World	*15,145,702*
	UK	*312,173*

Source: World Christian Database

The Diaspora or scattering of the Jewish people has established Jewish communities in almost every country in the world. In 1939 the estimated total Jewish population was 17 million, but six million fell victim to Nazi persecution, reducing the figure to about 11 million.

top10 LARGEST **MUSLIM POPULATIONS**

	COUNTRY	MUSLIMS
1	Pakistan	154,563,023
2	India	134,149,817
3	Bangladesh	132,868,312
4	Indonesia	121,606,358*
5	Turkey	71,322,513
6	Iran	67,724,004
7	Egypt	63,503,397
8	Nigeria	54,665,801
9	Algeria	31,858,555
10	Morocco	31,000,895
	World	*1,313,983,654*
	UK	*1,336,074*

* An additional 46 million people are considered Muslims by the Indonesian government but are more properly categorized as New Religionists (Islamicized syncretistic religions)

Source: World Christian Database

top10 LARGEST **HINDU POPULATIONS**

	COUNTRY	HINDUS
1	India	810,387,411
2	Nepal	19,020,312
3	Bangladesh	17,029,336
4	Indonesia	7,632,941
5	Sri Lanka	2,173,114
6	Pakistan	2,100,342
7	Malaysia	1,855,194
8	USA	1,143,864
9	South Africa	1,078,667
10	Myanmar	1,006,804
	World	*870,047,346*
	UK	*482,983*

Source: World Christian Database

top10 LARGEST **BUDDHIST POPULATIONS**

	COUNTRY	BUDDHISTS
1	China	111,358,666
2	Japan	70,722,505
3	Thailand	53,294,170
4	Vietnam	40,780,825
5	Myanmar	37,151,956
6	Sri Lanka	13,234,600
7	Cambodia	12,697,958
8	India	7,596,701
9	South Korea	7,281,110
10	Taiwan	4,823,361
	World	*378,809,103*
	UK	*166,430*

Source: World Christian Database

top10 **LONGEST-SERVING** POPES

	POPE	PERIOD IN OFFICE	DURATION		
			YRS	MTHS	DAYS
1	Pius IX	16 Jun 1846–7 Feb 1878	31	7	22
2	John Paul II	16 Oct 1978–2 Apr 2005	26	5	17
3	Leo XIII	20 Feb 1878–20 Jul 1903	25	5	0
4	Pius VI	15 Feb 1775–29 Aug 1799	24	6	14
5	Adrian I	1 Feb 772–25 Dec 795	23	10	24
6	Pius VII	14 Mar 1800–20 Aug 1823	23	5	6
7	Alexander III	7 Sep 1159–30 Aug 1181	21	11	23
8	Sylvester I	31 Jan 314–31 Dec 335	21	11	0
9	Leo I	29 Sep 440–10 Nov 461	21	1	12
10	Urban VIII	6 Aug 1623–29 Jul 1644	20	11	23

⬆ **John Paul II**
Among the 265 Popes, John Paul II's 26-year pontificate places him second among the longest-serving, with twice the 13-year average of incumbents of the office since 1700.

Popes are usually chosen from the ranks of cardinals, who are customarily men of mature years (Pope Benedict IX, elected in 1033, was said by some to have been as young as 12, but in all probability was in his twenties). As a result, it is unusual for a pope to remain in office for over 20 years. Although St Peter is regarded as the first pope, the historical accuracy of his reign and its dates are questionable. Pius IX, the longest-serving pope, was 85 years old at the time of his death. The longest-lived in the Top 10 was Leo XIII at 93. Although he served for less than two years, it is said, but with little evidence, that Pope Agatho was at least 100 when he was elected and died in 681 at the age of 106.

top10 RELIGIONS **100 YEARS AGO**

	RELIGION*	FOLLOWERS, 1900
1	Christians	558,130,722
2	Chinese universists#	380,006,038
3	Hindus	203,003,440
4	Muslims	199,913,833
5	Buddhists	127,076,771
6	Jews	12,292,210
7	Shintoists	6,720,000
8	Sikhs	2,962,300
9	Jains	1,323,280
10	Confucianists	640,050

* Excluding folk religions and miscellaneous groups
# Followers of traditional Chinese religion

Source: World Christian Database

top10 COUNTRIES WITH **MOST ATHEISTS**

	COUNTRY	ATHEISTS
1	China	104,076,894
2	Russia	7,107,848
3	Vietnam	5,777,868
4	Japan	3,672,367
5	North Korea	3,564,162
6	France	2,411,946
7	Italy	2,069,806
8	Ukraine	1,993,168
9	India	1,816,622
10	Germany	1,689,417
	World total	*768,598,424*
	UK	*854,465*

top10 RELIGIOUS **BELIEFS IN THE UK**

	RELIGION	FOLLOWERS
1	Christianity	48,191,574
2	Agnosticism	7,326,687
3	Islam	1,336,074
4	Atheism	854,465
5	Hinduism	482,983
6	Judaism	312,173
7	Sikhism	235,354
8	Buddhism	166,430
9	Zoroastrianism	89,498
10	Spiritism	69,700

Source: World Christian Database

Kings & Queens

top10 LARGEST MONARCHIES*

	COUNTRY	POPULATION
1	Japan	127,654,000
2	Britain#	124,522,000
3	Thailand	62,833,000
4	Spain	41,060,000
5	Morocco	30,566,000
6	Nepal	25,164,000
7	Malaysia	24,425,000
8	Saudi Arabia	24,217,000
9	Netherlands	16,149,000
10	Cambodia	14,144,000

* By population
# Commonwealth

The world's 29 monarchies rule over more than 540 million subjects, almost nine per cent of the population of the planet, with Monaco (pop. 32,000) the smallest.

top10 LONGEST-REIGNING LIVING MONARCHS*

	MONARCH	COUNTRY	DATE OF BIRTH	ACCESSION
1	Bhumibol Adulyadej	Thailand	5 Dec 1927	9 Jun 1946
2	Elizabeth II	UK	21 Apr 1926	6 Feb 1952
3	Malietoa Tanumafili II	Samoa	4 Jan 1913	1 Jan 1962#
4	Taufa'ahau Tupou IV	Tonga	4 Jul 1918	16 Dec 1965†
5	Haji Hassanal Bolkiah	Brunei	15 Jul 1946	5 Oct 1967
6	Sayyid Qaboos ibn Said al-Said	Oman	18 Nov 1942	23 Jul 1970
7	Margrethe II	Denmark	16 Apr 1940	14 Jan 1972
8	Jigme Singye Wangchuk	Bhutan	11 Nov 1955	24 Jul 1972
9	Carl XVI Gustaf	Sweden	30 Apr 1946	15 Sep 1973
10	Juan Carlos	Spain	5 Jan 1938	22 Nov 1975

* Including hereditary rulers of principalities, dukedoms, etc.
# Sole ruler since 15 Apr 1963
† Full sovereignty from 5 June 1970 when British protectorate ended

the10 LATEST COUNTRIES TO ABOLISH MONARCHIES

	COUNTRY	MONARCHY ABOLISHED
1	Iran	1979
2	Laos	1975
3	Ethiopia*	1974
4	= Afghanistan	1973
	= Greece#	1973
6	Cambodia†	1970
7	Libya	1969
8	Maldives	1968
9	Burundi	1966
10	Zanzibar☆	1964

* Emperor deposed 1974
# King exiled 1967
† Restored 1993
☆ Joined with Tanganyika to form Tanzania

the10 SHORTEST-REIGNING BRITISH MONARCHS

	MONARCH	REIGN	DURATION
1	Jane	1553	9 days
2	Edward V	1483	75 days
3	Edward VIII	1936	325 days
4	Richard III	1483–85	2 years
5	James II	1685–88	3 years
6	= Mary I	1553–58	5 years
	= Mary II	1689–94	5 years
8	Edward VI	1547–53	6 years
9	William IV	1830–37	7 years
10	Edward VII	1901–10	9 years

AMAZING FACT

The Kingdom of Hawaii

Hawaii is the only part of the USA that was once an independent monarchy. It ended when, within two years, its last king, Kalākaua, died in 1891 and was succeeded by his sister Queen Lili'uokalani. With the support of various businesses protecting sugar and other interests in the country, she was deposed in 1893 and the Republic of Hawaii declared, with the country becoming a US territory and, in 1959, the 50th state of the USA.

Victoria and Albert
Queen Victoria, the longest-reigning queen, on an inn sign; Prince Albert II of Monaco, one of the most recent incumbents among the world's 29 monarchies, is Queen Victoria's 8th cousin five times removed.

top 10 LONGEST-REIGNING MONARCHS

	MONARCH / COUNTRY	REIGN	AGE AT ACCESSION	REIGN YEARS
1	King Louis XIV, France	May 1643–Sep 1715	5	72
2	King John II, Liechtenstein	Nov 1858–Feb 1929	18	71
3	Emperor Franz-Josef Austria-Hungary	Dec 1848–Nov 1916	18	67
4	Queen Victoria, UK	Jun 1837–Jan 1901	18	63
5	Emperor Hirohito, Japan	Dec 1926–Jan 1989	25	62
6	Emperor K'ang Hsi, China	Feb 1661–Dec 1722	7	61
7	= King Sobhuza II*, Swaziland	Dec 1921–Aug 1982	22	60
	= Emperor Ch'ien Lung, China	Oct 1735–Feb 1796	25	60
9	= King Christian IV, Denmark	Apr 1588–Feb 1648	11	59
	= King George III, UK	Oct 1760–Jan 1820	22	59

* Paramount chief until 1967, when Great Britain recognized him as king with the granting of internal self-government

Although historically unsubstantiated, King Harald I of Norway is said to have ruled for 70 years from 870–940, while reigns of 95 years and 94 years, respectively, are claimed for King Mihti of Arakan (Myanmar), c.1279–1374, and Pharaoh Phiops (Pepi) II of Egypt (Neferkare), c.2269–2175 BC.

the 10 LATEST MONARCHS TO ASCEND THE THRONE

	TITLE/NAME	COUNTRY	ACCESSION
1	Emir Sabah al-Ahmad al-Saba	Kuwait	29 Jan 2006
2	Prince Abdullah	Saudi Arabia	1 Aug 2005
3	Prince Albert II	Monaco	6 Apr 2005
4	King Norodom Sihamoni	Cambodia	14 Oct 2004
5	Prince Alois	Liechtenstein	25 Aug 2004
6	Supreme Head of State Saiyid Sirajuddin ibni al-Marhum Saiyid Putra Jamalullail*	Malaysia	13 Dec 2001
7	King Gyanendra Bir Bikram Shah Deva	Nepal	4 Jun 2001
8	Grand Duke Henri	Luxembourg	7 Oct 2000
9	King Sayyidi Muhammad (VI) ibn al-Hasan	Morocco	23 Jul 1999
10	King (formerly Emir) Hamad ibn 'Isa al-Khalifah	Bahrain	6 Mar 1999

* Elected king

Malaysia has a unique system of 'revolving monarchy', which was established following Malaysia's independence from Britain in 1957. Each of the nine state sultans takes a five-year turn as king.

Politics

the10 **FIRST** FEMALE PRIME MINISTERS AND PRESIDENTS

	PRIME MINISTER / PRESIDENT	COUNTRY	FIRST PERIOD IN OFFICE
1	Sirimavo Bandaranaike (PM)	Sri Lanka	21 Jul 1960–27 Mar 1965
2	Indira Gandhi (PM)	India	19 Jan 1966–24 Mar 1977
3	Golda Meir (PM)	Israel	17 Mar 1969–3 Jun 1974
4	Maria Estela Perón (President)	Argentina	1 Jul 1974–24 Mar 1976
5	Elisabeth Domitien (PM)	Central African Republic	3 Jan 1975–7 Apr 1976
6	Margaret Thatcher (PM)	UK	4 May 1979–28 Nov 1990
7	Dr Maria Lurdes Pintasilgo (PM)	Portugal	1 Aug 1979–3 Jan 1980
8	Mary Eugenia Charles (PM)	Dominica	21 Jul 1980–14 Jun 1995
9	Vigdís Finnbogadóttir (President)	Iceland	1 Aug 1980–1 Aug 1996
10	Gro Harlem Brundtland (PM)	Norway	4 Feb–14 Oct 1981

Following the assassination of her husband Solomon West Ridgeway Dias Bandaranaike, Sirimavo Ratwatte Dias Bandaranaike (1916–2000) took over as leader of the Ceylon (later Sri Lanka) Freedom Party, won the election and became the world's first female prime minister. She served in this office three times (1960–65, 1970–77 and 1994–2000), while her daughter Chandrika Kumaratunga became the country's first female president in 1994.

← First lady
Margaret Thatcher became Britain and Europe's first female prime minister in 1979.

top10 PARLIAMENTS WITH THE **HIGHEST** PERCENTAGE OF WOMEN MEMBERS*

	PARLIAMENT (LATEST ELECTION)	WOMEN MEMBERS	TOTAL MEMBERS	PERCENTAGE WOMEN
1	Rwanda (2003)	39	80	48.8
2	Sweden (2002)	158	349	45.3
3	Norway (2005)	64	169	37.9
4	Finland (2003)	75	200	37.5
5	Denmark (2005)	66	179	36.9
6	Netherlands (2003)	55	150	36.7
7	= Cuba (2003)	219	609	36.0
	= Spain (2004)	126	350	36.0
9	Costa Rica (2006)	20	57	35.1
10	Argentina (2005)	90	257	35.0
	UK (2005)	*127*	*646*	*19.7*

* As at 27 Feb 2006

Source: Inter-Parliamentary Union

This list is based on the most recent general election results for all democratic countries, and based on the lower chamber where the parliament comprises two chambers. A total of 99 countries have at least 10 per cent female members of parliament, 40 countries over 20 per cent and 19 countries over 30 per cent.

AMAZING FACT

Votes for Women!

Women's suffrage – the right to vote in national elections – was extremely slow to be adopted. A few territories granted a limited form – only unmarried women and widows who owned property could vote in New Jersey in 1776, but this right was rescinded in 1807. New Zealand was first to grant this universal, unqualified right to women on 19 September 1893 – but they could not stand for election. The following year, in South Australia all women could vote and stand for parliament. It took until 1918 in Great Britain and Ireland (for women over 30) and 1920 in the USA before women could vote.

top10 LONGEST-SERVING PRESIDENTS TODAY

	PRESIDENT	COUNTRY	TOOK OFFICE
1	El Hadj Omar Bongo	Gabon	2 Dec 1967
2	Colonel Mu'ammar Gadhafi	Libya	*1 Sep 1969
3	Fidel Castro	Cuba	2 Nov 1976
4	Ali Abdullah Saleh	Yemen	17 Jul 1978
5	Maumoon Abdul Gayoom	Maldives	11 Nov 1978
6	Teodoro Obiang Nguema Mbasogo	Equatorial Guinea	3 Aug 1979
7	José Eduardo Dos Santos	Angola	21 Sep 1979
8	Hosni Mubarak	Egypt	6 Oct 1981
9	Paul Biya	Cameroon	7 Nov 1982
10	Lansana Conté	Guinea	3 Apr 1984

* Since a reorganization in 1979, Colonel Gadhafi has held no formal position, but continues to rule under the ceremonial title of 'Leader of the Revolution'

All the presidents in this list have been in power for over 20, some for almost 40 years. Fidel Castro became prime minister of Cuba as long ago as February 1959. As he was also chief of the army and there was no opposition party, he effectively ruled as dictator from then, but he was not technically president until the Cuban constitution was revised in 1976. Similarly, Robert Mugabe has ruled Zimbabwe since 18 April 1980, but only became president in 1987 (prior to this he held the title of prime minister).

William Pitt was by a wide margin the youngest prime minister ever. He had entered Cambridge University at 14 and Parliament at 22, becoming Chancellor of the Exchequer at 23. The title 'Prime Minister' was not officially used until 1878, so all those on this list except Tony Blair technically held the office as 'First Lord of the Treasury'.

the10 OLDEST SERVING BRITISH PRIME MINISTERS

	PRIME MINISTER	LEFT OFFICE	AGE ON LEAVING OFFICE		
			YEARS	MONTHS	DAYS
1	William E. Gladstone (1809–98)	1894	84	2	20
2	Viscount Palmerston (1784–1865)	1865*	80	11	28
3	Winston S. Churchill (1874–1965)	1955	80	4	6
4	Earl of Wilmington (c. 1674–1743)	1743*	c. 79		
5	Benjamin Disraeli (1804–81)	1880	75	4	0
6	Earl Russell (1792–1878)	1866	73	10	8
7	Marquess of Salisbury (1830–1903)	1902	72	5	8
8	Sir H. Campbell-Bannerman (1836–1908)	1908	71	6	29
9	Duke of Portland (1738–1809)	1809	71	5	20
10	Earl of Aberdeen (1784–1860)	1855	70	11	2

* Died in office # Precise birthdate unknown

top10 YOUNGEST BRITISH PRIME MINISTERS

	PRIME MINISTER	TOOK OFFICE*	AGE ON TAKING OFFICE		
			YEARS	MONTHS	DAYS
1	William Pitt (1759–1806)	1783	24	6	21
2	Duke of Grafton (1735–1811)	1768	33	0	16
3	Marquess of Rockingham (1730–82)	1765	35	2	0
4	Duke of Devonshire (c. 1720–64)	1756	c. 36#		–
5	Lord North (1732–92)	1770	37	9	15
6	Earl of Liverpool (1770–1828)	1812	42	0	1
7	Henry Addington (1757–1844)	1801	43	9	17
8	Tony Blair (b. 6 May 1953)	1997	43	11	26
9	Sir Robert Walpole (1676–1745)	1721	44	8	4
10	Viscount Goderich (1782–1859)	1827	44	10	1

* Where a prime minister served in more than one ministry, only the first is listed
# Precise birthdate unknown

Crime & Punishment

the 10 MOST **COMMON MURDER WEAPONS** & METHODS IN ENGLAND AND WALES

WEAPON / METHOD	VICTIMS, 2003–04		
	MEN	WOMEN	TOTAL
1 Sharp instrument	167	69	236
2 Hitting and kicking	111	13	124
3 Unknown	85	32	117
4 Shooting	66	11	77
5 Blunt instrument	44	17	61
6 Strangulation*	16	44	60
7 Burning	19	15	34
8 Poison or drugs	20	10	30
9 Motor vehicle#	16	4	20
10 Drowning	10	4	14
Other	*33*	*12*	*45*

* Including asphyxiation
# Excludes death by careless/dangerous driving and aggravated vehicle taking

Source: Home Office, 'Violent Crime Overview, Homicide and Gun Crime 2004–2005' (Supplementary Volume to 'Crime in England and Wales 2004–2005')

the 10 COUNTRIES WITH THE **HIGHEST MURDER RATES**

COUNTRY / MURDERS PER 100,000 POP.

1 Colombia 61.8		**6** Mexico 13.0
2 South Africa 49.6		**7** Estonia 10.7
3 Jamaica 32.4		**8** Latvia 10.4
4 Venezuela 31.6		**9** Lithuania 10.3
5 Russia 20.2		**10** Belarus 9.8

Source: United Nations

the 10 **WORST YEARS** FOR MURDER IN ENGLAND & WALES*

YEAR#	MURDER RATE PER MILLION POP.	TOTAL
1 2003	18.2	953
2 2005	15.5	820
3 2002	15.4	804
4 2004	15.0	793
5 2001	14.9	771
6 2000	13.0	674
7 1995	13.0	663
8 1999	12.5	646
9 1994	12.4	632
10 1991	12.3	623

* Since 1946; some offences initially recorded as homicide are later reclassified, so figures may reduce over time
# Prior to 1997, data relates to calendar year, from 1997 to financial year

Source: Home Office, 'Violent Crime Overview, Homicide and Gun Crime 2004–2005' (Supplementary Volume to 'Crime in England and Wales 2004–2005')

Murders in England and Wales were in the low hundreds throughout the 19th century. They topped 400 in 1952, 500 in 1974 and 600 in 1987. Since the 1960s, the number of murders per million population has more than doubled.

the10 COUNTRIES WITH THE
HIGHEST PRISON POPULATIONS

COUNTRY	PRISONERS PER 100,000 OF POP.	TOTAL PRISONERS*
1 USA	724	2,135,901
2 China	118	1,548,498
3 Russia	581	828,900
4 Brazil	183	336,358
5 India	31	322,357
6 Mexico	191	201,931
7 Ukraine	364	170,057
8 Thailand	264	168,264
9 South Africa	344	156,175
10 Iran	191	135,132
UK	*141*	*84,955*

* As at date of most recent data

Source: International Centre for Prison Studies,' World Prison Population List' (6th edition, 2005)

top10 LARGEST **PRISONS** IN THE UK

PRISON	CAPACITY*
1 Winson Green, Birmingham	1,450
2 Wandsworth, London	1,439
3 Walton, Liverpool	1,377
4 Strangeways, Manchester	1,269
5 Wormwood Scrubs, London	1,239
6 Pentonville, London	1,177
7 Armley, Leeds	1,150
8 Doncaster	1,120
9 Risley, Cheshire	1,073
10 Blakenhurst, Redditch	1,070

* As at Feb 2006

the last 10 MEN **HANGED** IN THE UK

	VICTIM	PRISON	HANGED
1	= Peter Anthony Allen	Liverpool	13 Aug 1964
	= John Robson Welby*	Manchester	13 Aug 1964
3	= Russell Pascoe	Bristol	17 Dec 1963
	= Dennis John Whitty	Winchester	17 Dec 1963
5	Henry John Burnett	Aberdeen	15 Aug 1963
6	James Smith	Manchester	28 Nov 1962
7	Oswald Augustus Grey	Birmingham	20 Nov 1962
8	James Hanratty	Bedford	4 Apr 1962
9	Robert Andrew McGladdery	Belfast	20 Dec 1961
10	Hendryk Niemasz	Wandsworth	8 Sep 1961

* Or Walby, aka Gwynne Owen Evans

Capital punishment was abolished in the UK on 9 November 1965. Welby and Allen, the last two men to be hanged, were executed on the same day but at different prisons, after being found guilty of stabbing John Alan West to death during a robbery.

the10 FIRST COUNTRIES TO
ABOLISH CAPITAL PUNISHMENT

COUNTRY	ABOLISHED
1 Russia	1826
2 Venezuela	1863
3 San Marino	1865
4 Portugal	1867
5 Costa Rica	1877
6 Brazil	1889
7 Panama	1903
8 Norway	1905
9 Ecuador	1906
10 Uruguay	1907
UK	*1965*

the10 COUNTRIES WITH THE
MOST EXECUTIONS

	COUNTRY	EXECUTIONS PER 100 MILLION POP.	EXECUTIONS, 2004
1	China	260	3,400
2	Iran	230	159
3	Vietnam	77	64
4	USA	20	59
5	Saudi Arabia	130	33
6	Pakistan	9	15
7	Kuwait	400	9
8	Bangladesh	5	7
9	= Egypt	8	6
	= Singapore	140	6
	= Yemen	30	6

Source: Amnesty International/Death Penalty Information Center

World World I

the 10 **LARGEST** ARMED FORCES OF WORLD WAR I

	COUNTRY	PERSONNEL*
1	Russia	12,000,000
2	Germany	11,000,000
3	British Empire	8,904,467
4	France	8,410,000
5	Austria-Hungary	7,800,000
6	Italy	5,615,000
7	USA	4,355,000
8	Turkey	2,850,000
9	Bulgaria	1,200,000
10	Japan	800,000

* Total at peak strength

the 10 **SMALLEST** ARMED FORCES OF WORLD WAR I

	COUNTRY	PERSONNEL*
1	Montenegro	50,000
2	Portugal	100,000
3	Greece	230,000
4	Belgium	267,000
5	Serbia	707,343
6	Romania	750,000
7	Japan	800,000
8	Bulgaria	1,200,000
9	Turkey	2,850,000
10	USA	4,355,000

* Total at peak strength

the 10 COUNTRIES WITH THE **MOST PRISONERS** OF WAR, 1914–18

	COUNTRY	CAPTURED*
1	Russia	2,500,000
2	Austria-Hungary	2,200,000
3	Germany	1,152,800
4	Italy	600,000
5	France	537,000
6	Turkey	250,000
7	British Empire	191,652
8	Serbia	152,958
9	Romania	80,000
10	Belgium	34,659
	Total of all nations	*7,750,919*

* Nationals of each country held prisoner

Among the total of over 65 million combatants, Russia's forces were relatively small in relation to the country's population at some six per cent, compared with 17 per cent in Germany. Several small European nations had large forces in relation to their populations, Serbia's representing 14 per cent of its population.

the 10 COUNTRIES SUFFERING THE **GREATEST MILITARY LOSSES** IN WORLD WAR I

1 CROSS = 100,000 KILLED / COUNTRY / KILLED

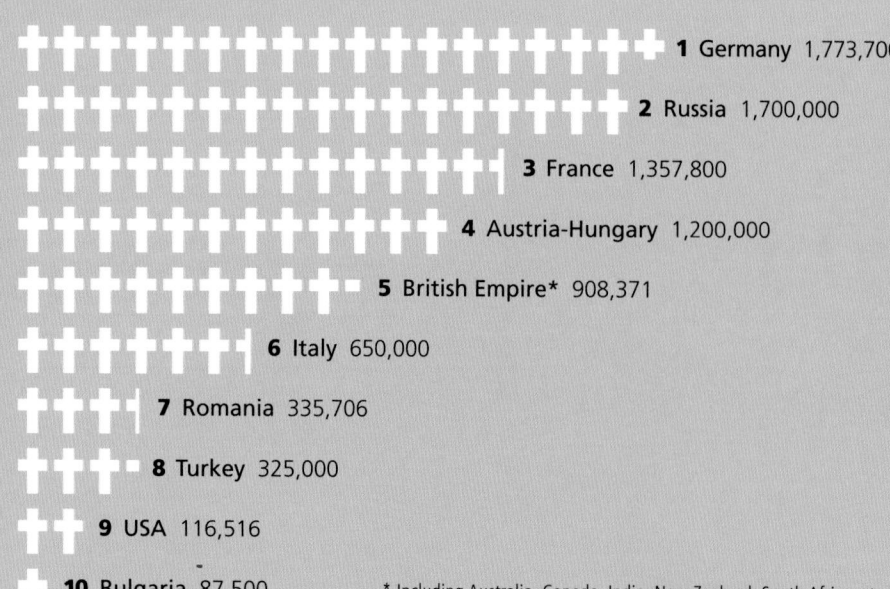

1 Germany 1,773,700
2 Russia 1,700,000
3 France 1,357,800
4 Austria-Hungary 1,200,000
5 British Empire* 908,371
6 Italy 650,000
7 Romania 335,706
8 Turkey 325,000
9 USA 116,516
10 Bulgaria 87,500

* Including Australia, Canada, India, New Zealand, South Africa, etc.

the 10 COUNTRIES WITH THE **GREATEST MERCHANT SHIPPING LOSSES** IN WORLD WAR I

	COUNTRY	VESSELS SUNK NUMBER	TONNAGE
1	UK	2,038	6,797,802
2	Italy	228	720,064
3	France	213	651,583
4	USA	93	372,892
5	Germany	188	319,552
6	Greece	115	304,992
7	Denmark	126	205,002
8	Netherlands	74	194,483
9	Sweden	124	192,807
10	Spain	70	160,383

→ The Red Baron
Seen here wearing his Pour le Mérite, *or 'Blue Max', medal (Germany's highest military award) and his Iron Cross, Manfred Albrecht Freiherr (Baron) von Richthofen (1892–1918) was the leading fighter pilot of World War I. With fellow fliers, including Nazi leader Herman Goering, he formed the Jasta 11 (11th Chasing Squadron), nicknamed the 'Flying Circus', with their aircraft (including 'Red Baron' Richthofen's Fokker triplane) flamboyantly painted crimson. Germany's foremost pilot was shot down on 21 April 1918, aged just 25.*

top10 **AIR ACES** OF WORLD WAR I

	PILOT ·	NATIONALITY	KILLS CLAIMED*
1	Rittmeister Manfred Albrecht Freiherr von Richthofen#	German	80
2	Capitaine René Paul Fonck	French	75
3	Maj William Avery Bishop	Canadian	72
4	Maj Edward Corringham 'Mick' Mannock#	British	68
5 =	Maj Raymond Collishaw	Canadian	62†
=	Oberleutnant Ernst Udet	German	62
7	Maj James Thomas Byford McCudden#	British	57
8 =	Capt Anthony Wetherby Beauchamp-Proctor	South African	54
=	Capt Donald Roderick MacLaren	Canadian	54
=	Capitaine George Marie Ludovic Jules Guynemer#	French	54

* Approximate – some kills disputed
# Killed in action
† Including two in Russian Civil War, 1919

The term 'ace' – or, more precisely, 'fighter ace' – was first used during World War I to describe a pilot who had brought down at least five enemy aircraft. The first-ever reference in print to an air 'ace' appeared in an article in *The Times* of 14 September 1917, which described Raoul Lufbery as 'the "ace" of the American Lafayette Flying Squadron'. The German equivalent was *Oberkanone*, which means 'top gun'. Although the definition varied from country to country and was never officially approved, it was used during both World Wars, with aces universally hailed as heroes.

World War II

the 10 LARGEST ARMED FORCES OF WORLD WAR II

1 SOLDIER=1,000,000 PERSONNEL / COUNTRY / PERSONNEL*

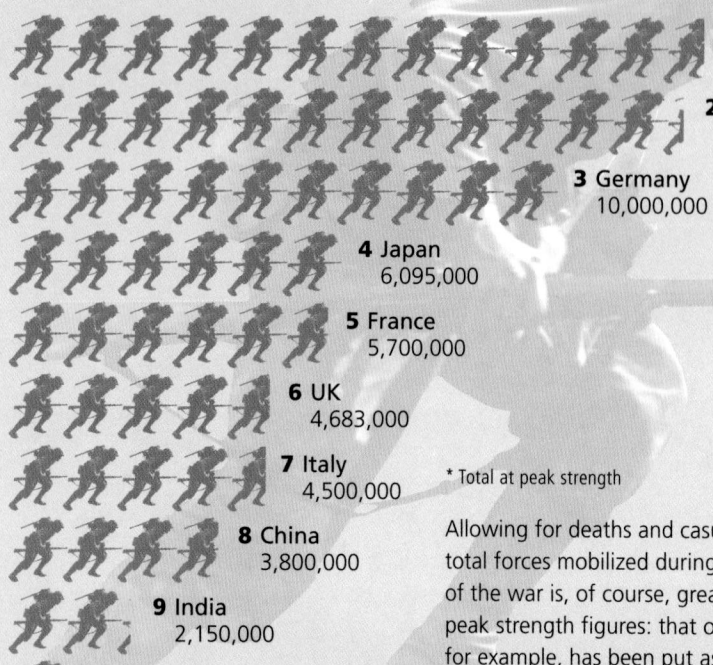

1 USSR
12,500,000

2 USA
12,364,000

3 Germany
10,000,000

4 Japan
6,095,000

5 France
5,700,000

6 UK
4,683,000

7 Italy
4,500,000

8 China
3,800,000

9 India
2,150,000

10 Poland
1,000,000

* Total at peak strength

Allowing for deaths and casualties, the total forces mobilized during the course of the war is, of course, greater than the peak strength figures: that of the USSR, for example, has been put as high as 20,000,000, the USA 16,354,000, Germany 17,900,000, Japan 9,100,000 and the UK 5,896,000.

the 10 SMALLEST ARMED FORCES OF WORLD WAR II

	COUNTRY	PERSONNEL*
1	Costa Rica	400
2	Liberia	1,000
3	= El Salvador	3,000
	= Honduras	3,000
	= Nicaragua	3,000
6	Haiti	3,500
7	Dominican Republic	4,000
8	Guatemala	5,000
9	= Bolivia	8,000
	= Paraguay	8,000
	= Uruguay	8,000

* Total at peak strength

The smallest European armed force was that of Denmark, with a maximum strength of 15,000, just 13 of whom were killed during the one-day German invasion of 9 April 1940. Several South American countries did not declare war until the closing stages, in order to become eligible to join the fledgling United Nations.

the 10 COUNTRIES SUFFERING THE GREATEST MILITARY LOSSES IN WORLD WAR II

	COUNTRY	KILLED
1	USSR	13,600,000*
2	Germany	3,300,000
3	China	1,324,516
4	Japan	1,140,429
5	British Empire# (UK 264,000)	357,116
6	Romania	350,000
7	Poland	320,000
8	Yugoslavia	305,000
9	USA	292,131
10	Italy	279,800

* Total, of which 7.8 million battlefield deaths
# Including Australia, Canada, India, New Zealand, etc.

The actual numbers killed in World War II have been the subject of intense argument for 60 years. The immense level of the military casualty rate of the USSR, in particular, is hard to comprehend. Most authorities now reckon that of the 30 million Soviets who bore arms, there were 13.6 million military deaths. This includes a battlefield deaths total of approximately 7.8 million, plus up to 2.5 million who died later of wounds received in battle and disease and, of the 5.8 million who were taken prisoner, as many as 3.3 million who died in captivity. It should also be borne in mind that these were military losses: to these should be added many untold millions of civilian war deaths, while recent estimates have suggested an additional figure of up to 25 million civilian deaths as a result of Stalinist purges, which began just before the outbreak of war.

the 10 COUNTRIES SUFFERING THE GREATEST CIVILIAN LOSSES IN WORLD WAR II

	COUNTRY	APPROX. NO. KILLED
1	China	8,000,000
2	USSR	6,500,000
3	Poland	5,300,000
4	Germany	2,350,000
5	Yugoslavia	1,500,000
6	France	470,000
7	Greece	415,000
8	Japan	393,400
9	Romania	340,000
10	Hungary	300,000

During World War II, many deaths among civilians, especially in China and the USSR, resulted from famine and internal purges.

the 10 WORST MILITARY SHIP LOSSES OF WORLD WAR II

	SHIP*	COUNTRY	DATE	APPROX. NO. KILLED
1	Wilhelm Gustloff	Germany	30 Jan 1945	7,800
2	Goya	Germany	16 Apr 1945	6,202
3	Cap Arcona	Germany	26 Apr 1945	6,000
4	Junyo Maru	Japan	18 Sep 1944	5,620
5	Toyama Maru	Japan	29 Jun 1944	5,400
6	Arcona	Germany	3 May 1945	5,000
7	Lancastria	Great Britain	17 Jun 1940	3,050
8	Steuben	Germany	9 Feb 1945	3,000
9	Thielbeck	Germany	3 May 1945	2,750
10	Yamato	Japan	7 Apr 1945	2,498

* Includes warships and passenger vessels used for troop and refugee transport

The German liner *Wilhelm Gustloff*, laden with civilian refugees and wounded German soldiers and sailors, was torpedoed off the coast of Poland by a Soviet submarine, S-13. Although imprecise, some sources even suggest a figure as high as 9,400, the probable death toll being some five times as great as that of the *Titanic*.

top 10 BRITISH AND COMMONWEALTH AIR ACES OF WORLD WAR II

	PILOT	NATIONALITY	KILLS CLAIMED
1	Sqd Ldr Marmaduke Thomas St John Pattle	South African	40+
2	Gp Capt James Edgar 'Johnny' Johnson	British	33.91
3	Wng Cdr Brendan 'Paddy' Finucane	Irish	32
4	Flt Lt George Frederick Beurling	Canadian	31.33
5	Wng Cdr John Randall Daniel Braham	British	29
6	Gp Capt Adolf Gysbert 'Sailor' Malan	South African	28.66
7	Wng Cdr Clive Robert Caldwell	Australian	28.5
8	Sqd Ldr James Harry 'Ginger' Lacey	British	28
9	Sqd Ldr Neville Frederick Duke	British	27.83
10	Wng Cdr Colin F. Gray	New Zealander	27.7

Uniquely to Western air forces in World War II, kills that are expressed as fractions refer to those that were shared with others, the number of fighters involved and the extent of each pilot's participation determining the proportion allocated to him.

🔙 *War at sea*
While many ship losses resulted from sea battles, some of the highest death tolls were caused by the bombing and torpedoing of vessels carrying refugees and other civilians.

Modern Conflict

top10 LARGEST ARMED FORCES

| COUNTRY | ARMY | ESTIMATED ACTIVE FORCES | | TOTAL |
		NAVY	AIR	
1 China	1,600,000	255,000	400,000	2,255,000
2 USA	502,000	376,750	379,500	1,473,960*
3 India	1,100,000	55,000	170,000	1,325,000
4 North Korea	1,106,000	46,000	110,000	1,262,000
5 Russia	395,000	142,000	170,000	1,037,000#
6 South Korea	560,000	63,000	64,700	687,700
7 Pakistan	550,000	24,000	45,000	619,000
8 Turkey	402,000	52,750	60,100	514,850
9 Vietnam	412,000	42,000	30,000	484,000
10 Egypt	340,000	18,500	30,000	468,500†
UK	*116,760*	*40,630*	*48,500*	*205,890*

* Includes 175,350 Marine Corps, 40,360 Coast Guard
\# Includes 80,000 Strategic Deterrent Forces, 250,000 Command and Support
† Includes 80,000 Air Defence Command

Source: The International Institute for Strategic Studies, 'The Military Balance 2005–2006'

Several countries also have substantial reserves on standby: South Korea's has been estimated at some 4.5 million plus 3.5 million Paramilitary, Vietnam's at 3 to 4 million and China's 800,000.

⬆ High rank
Indian troops in Kashmir celebrate Republic Day, 26 January. India's highly trained military forces are entirely voluntary, and rank third in the world in total size and ninth in defence budget. India is nuclear-capable and has a substantial armoury of conventional weapons.

the10 SMALLEST ARMED FORCES*

COUNTRY	ESTIMATED TOTAL ACTIVE FORCES
1 Antigua and Barbuda	170
2 Seychelles	450
3 Barbados	610
4 Gambia	800
5 Bahamas	860
6 Luxembourg	900
7 Belize	1,050
8 Guyana	1,100
9 East Timor	1,250
10 Cape Verde	1,200

* Includes only those countries that declare a defence budget

Source: The International Institute for Strategic Studies, 'The Military Balance 2005–2006'

A number of small countries maintain military forces for ceremonial purposes, national prestige or reasons other than national defence and would clearly be inadequate to resist an invasion by their much larger neighbours.

top 10 COUNTRIES WITH THE LARGEST DEFENCE BUDGETS

	COUNTRY	BUDGET ($)*
1	USA	465,000,000,000
2	China	62,500,000,000
3	Russia	61,900,000,000
4	France	51,600,000,000
5	UK	51,100,000,000
6	Japan	44,700,000,000
7	Italy	30,500,000,000
8	Germany	30,200,000,000
9	India	22,000,000,000
10	Saudi Arabia	21,300,000,000

* Estimated 2004 expenditure or 2005 budget

Source: The International Institute for Strategic Studies, 'The Military Balance 2005–2006'

the 10 COUNTRIES WITH THE SMALLEST DEFENCE BUDGETS

	COUNTRY*	BUDGET ($)#
1	Gambia	2,300,000
2	Antigua and Barbuda	4,810,000
3	Guyana	5,920,000
4	Cape Verde	6,800,000
5	Equatorial Guinea	7,300,000
6	Suriname	7,700,000
7	Guinea-Bissau	8,600,000
8	Moldova	9,200,000
9	Seychelles	12,600,000
10	Malawi	12,800,000

* Includes only those countries that declare defence budgets
# Estimated 2004 expenditure or 2005 budget

Source: The International Institute for Strategic Studies, 'The Military Balance 2005–2006'

top 10 NOBEL PEACE PRIZE-WINNING COUNTRIES

	COUNTRY	PEACE PRIZES
1	= International institutions	19
	= USA	19
3	UK	10
4	France	9
5	= Germany	5
	= Sweden	5
7	= Belgium	3
	= Israel	3
	= South Africa	3
	= Switzerland	3

Since 1901 it has been awarded for '...the most or best work for fraternity between the nations, for the abolition or reduction of standing armies and for the holding and promotion of peace congresses'.

top 10 ARMS EXPORTERS

	COUNTRY	EXPORTS, 2004 ($)
1	Russia	26,925,000,000
2	USA	25,930,000,000
3	France	6,358,000,000
4	Germany	4,878,000,000
5	UK	4,450,000,000
6	Ukraine	2,118,000,000
7	Canada	1,692,000,000
8	China	1,436,000,000
9	Sweden	1,290,000,000
10	Israel	1,258,000,000

Source: Stockholm International Peace Research Institute

top 10 ARMS IMPORTERS

	COUNTRY	IMPORTS, 2004 ($)
1	China	11,677,000,000
2	India	8,526,000,000
3	Greece	5,263,000,000
4	UK	3,395,000,000
5	Turkey	3,298,000,000
6	Egypt	3,103,000,000
7	South Korea	2,755,000,000
8	United Arab Emirates	2,581,000,000
9	Australia	2,177,000,000
10	Pakistan	2,018,000,000

Source: Stockholm International Peace Research Institute

top 10 COUNTRIES WITH THE HIGHEST MILITARY/CIVILIAN RATIO

	COUNTRY	RATIO*, 2004
1	North Korea	558
2	Israel	251
3	Quatar	199
4	Jordan	189
5	Syria	171
6	Oman	160
7	Bahrain	157
8	South Korea	144
9	Taiwan	128
10	United Arab Emirates	125
	UK	*35*

* Military personnel per 10,000 population

TOWN & COUNTRY

Countries of the World

top10 LARGEST COUNTRIES

	COUNTRY	AREA SQ KM	AREA SQ MILES	% OF WORLD TOTAL
1	Russia	17,075,200	6,592,772	11.5
2	Canada	9,984,670	3,855,103	6.7
3	China	9,634,057	3,719,731	6.5
4	USA	9,631,418	3,718,712	6.5
5	Brazil	8,511,965	3,286,488	5.7
6	Australia	7,686,850	2,967,910	5.2
7	India	3,287,590	1,269,346	2.2
8	Argentina	2,766,890	1,068,302	2.1
9	Kazakhstan	2,717,300	1,049,156	1.9
10	Sudan	2,505,810	967,499	1.7
	World total	*148,940,000*	*57,506,062*	*100.0*
	UK	*244,820*	*94,526*	*0.2*

Source: Central Intelligence Agency, 'The World Factbook 2005'

This list is based on the total area of a country within its borders, including offshore islands, inland water such as lakes, and rivers and reservoirs. It may thus differ from versions in which these are excluded. Antarctica has an approximate area of 13,200,000 sq km (5,096,549 sq miles) but is discounted, as it is not considered a country. The countries in the Top 10 collectively comprise 50 per cent of the total Earth's surface.

top10 LARGEST DIVIDED ISLANDS

	ISLAND	DIVIDED BETWEEN	AREA SQ KM	AREA SQ MILES
1	New Guinea	Indonesia/ Papua New Guinea	785,753	303,380
2	Borneo	Indonesia/Malaysia/ Brunei	748,168	288,869
3	Cuba	Cuba/USA (Guantánamo Bay)	110,861	42,803
4	Ireland	Ireland/United Kingdom	81,638	31,520
5	Hispaniola	Dominican Republic/ Haiti	73,929	28,544
6	Tierra del Fuego	Chile/Argentina	47,401	18,301
7	Timor	Indonesia/East Timor	28,418	10,972
8	Cyprus	Greece/Turkey	9,234	3,565
9	Sebatik Island	Indonesia/Malaysia	452	174
10	Usedom (Uznan)	Germany/Poland	445	172

Most islands are either countries or parts of larger (often, although not always, adjacent) countries, but some are divided between two or more countries. This may result from or remain the cause of political disputes, as with Ireland and Cyprus. Outside the Top 10, the island of St Martin is divided between Guadeloupe (a French overseas territory) and the Netherlands Antilles, while tiny Märket is split between Finnish-administered Åland and Sweden.

top10 SMALLEST COUNTRIES

	COUNTRY	AREA SQ KM	AREA SQ MILES
1	Vatican City	0.44	0.17
2	Monaco	1.95	0.75
3	Nauru	21.20	8.18
4	Tuvalu	25.63	9.89
5	San Marino	61.20	23.63
6	Liechtenstein	160.00	61.77
7	Marshall Islands	181.43	70.05
8	St Kitts and Nevis	269.40	104.01
9	Maldives	298.00	115.05
10	Malta	315.10	121.66

Although recognized as an independent state by a treaty of February 1929, the Vatican's 'country' status is questionable, since its government and other functions are intricately linked with those of Italy.

top10 COUNTRIES WITH THE LONGEST COASTLINES

	COUNTRY	TOTAL COASTLINE LENGTH KM	MILES
1	Canada	202,080	125,566
2	Indonesia	54,716	33,999
3	Russia	37,653	23,396
4	Philippines	36,289	22,559
5	Japan	29,751	18,486
6	Australia	25,760	16,007
7	Norway	25,148	15,626
8	USA	19,924	12,380
9	New Zealand	15,134	9,404
10	China	14,500	9,010

Including its islands, the coastline of Canada is over six times as long as the distance round the Equator (40,076 km/ 24,9012 miles). Greece and the UK fall just outside the Top 10.

the10 MOST RECENT INDEPENDENT COUNTRIES

	COUNTRY	INDEPENDENCE
1	East Timor	20 May 2002
2	Palau	1 Oct 1994
3	Eritrea	24 May 1993
4	= Czech Republic	1 Jan 1993
	= Slovakia	1 Jan 1993
6	Serbia and Montenegro	27 Apr 1992
7	Bosnia-Herzegovina	1 Mar 1992
8	Kazakhstan	16 Dec 1991
9	Turkmenistan	27 Oct 1991
10	Armenia	21 Sep 1991

Source: Central Intelligence Agency, 'The World Factbook 2005'

The break-up of the former Soviet Union was the main factor in the creation of some 28 new nation states since 1990.

⬆ *Remote region* Landlocked Kazakhstan is some 1,300 km (800 miles) from the nearest seaport.

top10 **LARGEST LANDLOCKED** COUNTRIES

COUNTRY / NEIGHBOURS	AREA SQ KM	SQ MILES
1 Kazakhstan China, Kyrgyzstan, Russia, Turkmenistan, Uzbekistan	2,717,300	1,049,156
2 Mongolia China, Russia	1,564,116	603,908
3 Niger Algeria, Benin, Burkina Faso, Chad, Libya, Mali, Nigeria	1,266,699	489,075
4 Chad Cameroon, Central African Republic, Libya, Niger, Nigeria, Sudan	1,259,201	486,180
5 Mali Algeria, Burkina Faso, Côte d'Ivoire, Guinea, Mauritania, Niger, Senegal	1,219,999	471,044
6 Ethiopia Djibouti, Eritrea, Kenya, Somalia, Sudan	1,127,127	435,186
7 Bolivia Argentina, Brazil, Chile, Paraguay, Peru	1,098,580	424,164
8 Zambia Angola, Dem. Rep. of Congo, Malawi, Mozambique, Namibia, Tanzania, Zimbabwe	752,614	290,585
9 Afghanistan China, Iran, Pakistan, Tajikistan, Turkmenistan, Uzbekistan	647,500	250,001
10 Central African Republic Cameroon, Chad, Congo, Dem. Rep. of Congo, Sudan	622,984	240,535

There are 42 landlocked countries in the world. Both Turkmenistan and Kazakhstan have coasts on the Caspian Sea (also landlocked).

top10 **SMALLEST LANDLOCKED** COUNTRIES

COUNTRY / NEIGHBOURS	AREA SQ KM	SQ MILES
1 Vatican City Italy	0.44	0.17
2 San Marino Italy	61.20	23.63
3 Liechtenstein Austria, Switzerland	160.00	61.77
4 Andorra France, Spain	468.00	180.70
5 Luxembourg Belgium, France, Germany	2,586	998
6 Swaziland Mozambique, South Africa	17,363	6,704
7 Macedonia Albania, Bulgaria, Greece, Yugoslavia	25,333	9,781
8 Rwanda Burundi, Dem. Rep. of Congo, Tanzania, Uganda	26,338	10,169
9 Burundi Dem. Rep.of Congo, Rwanda, Tanzania	27,830	10,745
10 Armenia Azerbaijan, Georgia, Iran, Turkey	29,800	11,506

Lacking direct access to the sea, landlocked countries rely on their neighbours for trade routes. At times of political conflict their geography may make them vulnerable to blockades.

Country Populations

⊕ *Rush hour, Bangladesh-style* A quarter of the country's densely packed population lives in the cities.

top10 MOST DENSELY POPULATED COUNTRIES

	COUNTRY	AREA (SQ KM)	POPULATION (2007 EST.)	POPULATION PER SQ KM
1	Macau	25	456,989	18,279.6
2	Monaco	1.95	32,671	16,754.4
3	Singapore	693	4,553,009	6,570.0
4	Hong Kong	1,092	6,980,412	6,392.3
5	Vatican City	0.44	921	2,093.2
6	Malta	315.10	401,880	1,275.4
7	Maldives	298.00	369,031	1,238.4
9	Bangladesh	133,911	150,448,339	1,123.5
8	Bahrain	665	708,573	1,065.5
10	Taiwan	35,980	23,174,294	644.1
	World	*148,940,000*	*6,600,115,810*	*44.3*
	UK	*244,820*	*60,776,238*	*248.25*

Source: US Census Bureau, International Data Base

Macau and Hong Kong are special Administrative Regions within China, but for the purposes of statistical comparison many agencies still consider them as countries.

top10 LEAST DENSELY POPULATED COUNTRIES

	COUNTRY	AREA (SQ KM)	POPULATION (2007 EST.)	POPULATION PER SQ KM
1	Mongolia	1,564,116	2,874,127	1.84
2	Namibia	825,418	2,055,080	2.49
3	Australia	7,686,850	20,434,176	2.66
4	Suriname	163,270	439,894	2.69
5	Botswana	600,370	1,639,131	2.73
6	Iceland	103,000	301,931	2.93
7	Mauritania	1,030,700	3,270,065	3.17
8	Canada	9,984,670	33,390,141	3.34
9	Libya	1,759,540	6,036,914	3.43
10	Guyana	214,970	769,095	3.58

Source: US Census Bureau, International Data Base

In marked contrast to the many countries that have population densities in the hundreds (and, in a few instances, thousands) per square kilometre, these sparsely populated countries of the world generally present environmental disadvantages that make human habitation challenging: some contain large tracts of mountain, desert or dense forest, or have extreme climates.

top10 COUNTRIES WITH LARGEST POPULATIONS

	COUNTRY	POPULATION (2007 EST.)
1	China	1,321,851,888
2	India	1,110,396,331
3	USA	301,139,947
4	Indonesia	248,883,917
5	Brazil	190,010,647
6	Pakistan	169,270,617
7	Bangladesh	150,448,339
8	Russia	142,369,485
9	Nigeria	135,031,164
10	Japan	127,467,972
	World	*6,600,115,810*
	UK	*60,776,238*

Source: US Census Bureau, International Data Base

top10 COUNTRIES WITH SMALLEST POPULATIONS

	COUNTRY	POPULATION (2007 EST.)
1	Vatican City	921
2	Tuvalu	11,992
3	Nauru	13,528
4	Palau	20,842
5	San Marino	28,615
6	Monaco	32,671
7	Liechtenstein	34,247
8	St Kitts and Nevis	39,349
9	Marshall Islands	61,782
10	Dominica	68,925

Source: US Census Bureau, International Data Base

⊙ City and country
Vatican City's power and world status contrast with its position as the world's smallest and least populated country.

The US Census Bureau projects that by 2034 India's population will reach 1,464,048,216, overtaking China's then 1,461,598,160 – and the USA's will be 375,273,474 – but the populations of many small countries, such as San Marino and Monaco, will barely alter.

top10 COUNTRIES WITH THE YOUNGEST POPULATIONS

	COUNTRY	PERCENTAGE UNDER 15 (2007 EST.)
1	Uganda	49.8
2	Mali	48.2
3	Chad	47.8
4 =	Dem. Rep. of Congo	47.3
=	São Tomé and Príncipe	47.3
6	Niger	46.9
7	Burkina Faso	46.7
8	Malawi	46.5
9 =	Burundi	46.3
=	Congo	46.3
=	Yemen	46.3
	World average	*27.2*
	UK	*17.2*

Source: US Census Bureau, International Data Base

Countries with high proportions of their population under the age of 15 are usually characterized by high birth rates and high death rates. Although not a country, in the Gaza strip almost one in two people (47.6 per cent) are aged under 15.

top10 COUNTRIES WITH THE OLDEST POPULATIONS

	COUNTRY	PERCENTAGE OVER 65 (2007 EST.)
1	Monaco	22.7
2	Japan	20.6
3	Italy	19.9
4	Germany	19.8
5	Greece	19.0
6	Sweden	17.9
7	Spain	17.8
8 =	Belgium	17.4
=	Bulgaria	17.4
10	Portugal	17.3
	World	*7.5*
	UK	*15.8*

Source: US Census Bureau, International Data Base

With lower death rates and a higher life expectancy than the rest of the world, nine of the 10 countries with the oldest populations are in Europe. On average, in Western Europe, 16.3 per cent of people are over 65, 4.8 per cent over 80 – Africa's average is only 3.3 per cent for over 65s.

top10 COUNTRIES THAT WILL DOUBLE THEIR POPULATIONS SOONEST

	COUNTRY	POPULATION DOUBLING TIME (YEARS)
1	Niger	20
2 =	Mali	21
=	Uganda	21
=	Yemen	21
5 =	Congo	22
=	Malawi	22
7 =	Comoros	23
=	Dem. Rep. of Congo	23
=	Guinea-Bissau	23
=	Marshall Islands	23
=	Mayotte	23

Source: Population Reference Bureau, '2005 World Population Data Sheet'

People on the Move

top10 COUNTRIES WITH THE **MOST REFUGEES**

COUNTRY	RATIO OF REFUGEE POP. TO TOTAL POP.	REFUGEE TOTAL
1 West Bank and Gaza	1:2	1,635,000
2 Iran	1:64	1,046,100
3 Pakistan	1:164	968,800
4 Syria	1:26	701,700
5 Tanzania	1:60	602,300
6 Thailand	1:38	460,000
7 China	1:3,257	401,500
8 India	1:2,763	393,300
9 Kenya	1:120	269,300
10 Lebanon	1:18	265,800
UK	*1:2,683*	*22,200*

Source: US Committee for Refugees and Immigrants

⬆ Hungry and homeless
Palestinian children are cared for in a refugee camp. Almost half the population of the West Bank and Gaza are refugees.

top10 COUNTRIES OF ORIGIN OF **UK IMMIGRANTS**

COUNTRY	TOTAL, 2004
1 India	11,100
2 Pakistan	10,025
3 Serbia and Montenegro	9,590
4 Philippines	8,200
5 South Africa	7,565
6 Turkey	6,060
7 Sri Lanka	4,875
8 Nigeria	4,620
9 USA	4,120
10 Somalia	3,825

Source: Home Office

These are the leading countries of origin of immigrants to the UK based on Home Office Grants of Settlement, of which a total of 139,260 were issued in 2004. The largest region of origin is Asia, with 53,115 immigrants, followed by Africa with 39,440, Europe 26,600 and the Americas 14,130.

top10 COUNTRIES OF ORIGIN FOR **REFUGEES AND ASYLUM SEEKERS***

COUNTRY	REFUGEES
1 Former Palestine	2,985,500
2 Afghanistan	2,088,200
3 Sudan	703,500
4 Myanmar	691,800
5 Burundi	482,200
6 Dem. Rep. of Congo	469,100
7 Iraq	366,100
8 Liberia	328,300
9 Somalia	324,900
10 Vietnam	310,300

* As of 1 January 2005

Source: US Committee for Refugees and Immigrants

top10 **ETHNIC GROUPS** IN THE UK

GROUP	POPULATION
1 White	55,153,898
2 Indian	1,053,411
3 Pakistani	747,285
4 Mixed	677,117
5 Black Caribbean	565,876
6 Black African	485,277
7 Bangladeshi	283,063
8 Other Asian	247,664
9 Chinese	247,403
10 Other ethnic groups	230,615

Source: Social Trends 36: 2006

Figures from National Statistics indicate something of the racial makeup of the British population – although they do not distinguish between those born in the country and immigrants. The category 'Other ethnic groups' comprises people identified as belonging to a variety of ethnic backgrounds, the larger of which could arguably qualify for 10th place in the list, while some 0.5 million individuals surveyed did not state affiliation with any ethnic group.

top10 COUNTRIES RECEIVING THE **MOST INCOME** FROM MIGRANTS*

	COUNTRY	RECEIPTS, 2004 ($)
1	India	21,700,000,000
2	China	21,300,000,000
3	Mexico	18,100,000,000
4	France	12,700,000,000
5	Philippines	11,600,000,000
6	Spain	6,900,000,000
7	Belgium	6,800,000,000
8	Germany	6,500,000,000
9	UK	6,400,000,000
10	Morocco	4,200,000,000

* Nationals working overseas

Source: International Monetary Fund/World Bank

AMAZING FACT

US Immigration

Emma Lazarus's poem, *The New Colossus*, inscribed on the Statue of Liberty, contains the lines, 'Give me your tired, your poor, Your huddled masses yearning to breathe free', and for many years the USA was the magnet that attracted vast numbers of immigrants. The first great immigration decade was 1901–10, when a total of 8,795,386 arrivals were recorded. The first year in which it topped a million was 1905, with 1,026,499, and a peak of 1,285,349 in 1907. This figure was not exceeded until 1990, when 1,536,483 were received, with 1991 the record year at 1,827,167 and a total of 9,095,417 for the decade 1990–2000. From 1820, when detailed records were first kept, until 2004, the total number of immigrants to the USA was 69,869,450.

⊕ *Fleeing to safety*
Refugees displaced within their own countries or fleeing to neighbouring territories have become an all-too familiar feature of the world's recent conflict zones.

Urban World

top10 LARGEST CAPITAL CITIES

CITY / COUNTRY	EST. POPULATION, 2006
1 Tokyo (including Yokohama and Kawasaki), Japan	34,200,000
2 Mexico City (including Nezahualcóyotl, Ecatepec and Naucalpan), Mexico	22,800,000
3 Seoul (including Bucheon, Goyang, Incheon, Seongnam and Suweon), South Korea	22,300,000
4 Delhi (including Faridabad and Ghaziabad), India	19,700,000
5 Jakarta (including Bekasi, Bogor, Depok and Tangerang), Indonesia	16,550,000
6 Cairo (including Al-Jizah and Shubra al-Khaymah), Egypt	15,600,000
7 Manila (including Kalookan and Quezon City), Philippines	14,950,000
8 Moscow, Russia	13,750,000
9 Buenos Aires (including San Justo and La Plata), Argentina	13,450,000
10 Dhaka, Bangladesh	13,250,000

Source: Th. Brinkhoff: The Principal Agglomerations of the World, http://www.citypopulation.de, 2006-01-28

top10 LARGEST CITIES IN THE UK

	AREA		POPULATION, 2004	
CITY	SQ KM	SQ MILES	DENSITY PER SQ KM	TOTAL POPULATION
1 London	1,572	606	4,726	7,429,200
2 Birmingham	268	103	3,703	992,400
3 Leeds	552	213	1,304	719,600
4 Glasgow	175	67	3,301	577,670
5 Sheffield	368	142	1,402	516,100
6 Bradford	366	141	1,314	481,100
7 Edinburgh	264	101	1,718	453,670
8 Liverpool	112	43	3,969	444,500
9 Manchester	116	45	3,762	437,000
10 Bristol	110	42	3,581	393,900

Source: Office for National Statistics/General Register Office for Scotland

top10 COUNTRIES WITH THE LARGEST URBAN POPULATIONS

COUNTRY	EST. TOTAL URBAN POPULATION, 2005*
1 China	535,958,000
2 India	312,887,000
3 USA	232,080,000
4 Brazil	151,925,000
5 Indonesia	104,048,000
6 Russia	102,731,000
7 Japan	101,831,000
8 Mexico	80,073,000
9 Germany	72,405,000
10 Nigeria	62,623,000
World	3,176,892,000
UK	53,842,000

* In those countries for which data available

Source: United Nations Population Division, 'World Urbanization Prospects: The 2003 Revision'

top10 CITIES WITH THE HIGHEST PROPORTION OF A COUNTRY'S POPULATION

CITY / COUNTRY	% OF TOTAL COUNTRY POPULATION
1 Singapore	100.0
2 San Juan, Puerto Rico	60.1
3 Beirut, Lebanon	49.1
4 Kuwait City, Kuwait	48.5
5 Tel Aviv, Israel	45.3
6 Montevideo, Uruguay	39.3
7 Tripoli, Libya	36.1
8 Yerevan, Armenia	35.3
9 Santiago, Chile	34.7
10 Buenos Aires, Argentina	34.0
London, UK	12.9

Source: United Nations Population Division, 'Urban Agglomerations 2003'

These are all capital cities (the United Nations and international law regard Tel Aviv as Israel's capital). If Puerto Rico were excluded as a dependency of the USA, Athens, Greece, with 29.3 per cent of the country's population, would enter the list.

top10 HIGHEST CITIES

CITY / COUNTRY	HEIGHT M	FT
1 Wenchuan, China	5,099	16,730
2 Potosí, Bolivia	3,976	13,045
3 Oruro, Bolivia	3,702	12,146
4 Lhasa, Tibet	3,684	12,087
5 La Paz, Bolivia	3,632	11,916
6 Cuzco, Peru	3,399	11,152
7 Huancayo, Peru	3,249	10,660
8 Sucre, Bolivia	2,835	9,301
9 Tunja, Colombia	2,820	9,252
10 Quito, Ecuador	2,819	9,249

Lhasa was formerly the highest capital city in the world, a role now occupied by La Paz, the capital of Bolivia. Wenchuan is situated at more than half the elevation of Everest, and even the towns and cities at the bottom of this list are more than one-third as high.

top10 **LARGEST** CITIES

CITY / COUNTRY	EST. POPULATION, 2006
1 Tokyo, Japan	34,200,000
2 Mexico City, Mexico	22,800,000
3 Seoul, South Korea	22,300,000
4 New York, USA	21,900,000
5 São Paulo, Brazil	20,200,000
6 Mumbai (Bombay), India	19,850,000
6 Delhi, India	19,700,000
8 Shanghai, China	18,150,000
9 Los Angeles, USA	18,000,000
10 Osaka, Japan	16,800,000

Source: Th. Brinkhoff: The Principal Agglomerations of the World, http://www.citypopulation.de, 2006-01-28

top10 LARGEST CITIES **100 YEARS AGO**

CITY / COUNTRY	POPULATION, 1907
1 London, UK	4,758,218
2 New York, USA	4,285,435
3 Paris, France	2,735,165
4 Tokyo, Japan	2,433,000
5 Chicago, USA	2,107,620
6 Berlin, Germany	2,096,318
7 Vienna, Austria	1,979,003
8 Osaka, Japan	1,765,000
9 St Petersburg, Russia	1,505,200
10 Philadelphia, USA	1,500,595

Censuses and population estimates conducted in or around 1907 indicated that these cities, plus a handful of others including Beijing (then spelled Peking), China; Buenos Aires, Argentina; Constantinople, Turkey; and Moscow, Russia, were the only ones with populations in excess of one million. Today, there are almost 440 world cities with million-plus populations.

⬆ Population centre
Tokyo replaced New York as the world's most populous city in 1965, a position it has maintained ever since.

⬇ New York, New York
Photographed in 1907 as the skyscraper age began, New York's population was then in second place after London's. Less than 20 years later, New York had overtaken it.

Place Names

> **Krung Thep Mahanakhon Amon Rattanakosin Mahi Burirom Udomratchaniwet Mahasathan Amon Piman**

top10 LONGEST PLACE NAMES*

NAME	LETTERS

1 Krung Thep Mahanakhon Amon Rattanakosin Mahinthara Ayuthaya Mahadilok Phop Noppharat Ratchathani Burirom Udomratchaniwet Mahasathan Amon Piman Awatan Sathit Sakkathattiya Witsanukam Prasit — **168**

It means 'The city of angels, the great city, the eternal jewel city, the impregnable city of God Indra, the grand capital of the world endowed with nine precious gems, the happy city, abounding in an enormous Royal Palace that resembles the heavenly abode where reigns the reincarnated god, a city given by Indra and built by Vishnukarn'. When the poetic name of Bangkok, capital of Thailand, is used, it is usually abbreviated to 'Krung Thep' (city of angels).

2 Taumatawhakatangihangakoauauotamateaturipukakapiki-maungahoronukupokaiwhenuakitanatahu — **85**

This is the longer version (the other has a mere 83 letters) of the Maori name of a hill in New Zealand. It translates as 'The place where Tamatea, the man with the big knees, who slid, climbed and swallowed mountains, known as land-eater, played on the flute to his loved one'.

3 Gorsafawddachaidraigddanheddogleddollônpenrhynareur-draethceredigion — **67**

A name contrived by the Fairbourne Steam Railway, Gwynedd, North Wales, for publicity purposes and in order to outdo its rival, No. 4. It means 'The Mawddach station and its dragon teeth at the Northern Penrhyn Road on the golden beach of Cardigan Bay'.

4 Llanfairpwllgwyngyllgogerychwyrndrobwllllantysiliogo-gogoch — **58**

This is the place in Gwynedd famed especially for the length of its railway tickets. It means 'St Mary's Church in the hollow of the white hazel near to the rapid whirlpool of the church of St Tysilio near the Red Cave'. Questions have been raised about its authenticity, since its official name comprises only the first 20 letters, and the full name appears to have been invented as a hoax in the 19th century by a local tailor.

5 El Pueblo de Nuestra Señora la Reina de los Ángeles de la Porciúncula — **57**

The site of a Franciscan mission and the full Spanish name of Los Angeles; it means 'The town of Our Lady the Queen of the Angels of the Little Portion'. Nowadays it is customarily known by its initial letters, 'LA', making it also one of the shortest-named cities in the world.

6 Chargoggagoggmanchaugagoggchaubunagungamaug — **43**

America's longest place name, a lake near Webster, Massachusetts. Its Indian name, loosely translated, is claimed to mean 'You fish on your side, I'll fish on mine, and no one fishes in the middle'. It is said to be pronounced 'Char-gogg-a-gogg (pause) man-chaugg-a-gog (pause) chau-bun-a-gung-a-maug'. It is, however, an invented extension of its real name (Chabunagungamaug, or 'boundary fishing place'), devised in the 1920s by Larry Daly, the editor of the *Webster Times*.

7 = Lower North Branch Little Southwest Miramichi — **40**

Canada's longest place name – a short river in New Brunswick.

= Villa Real de la Santa Fé de San Francisco de Asis — **40**

The full Spanish name of Santa Fe, New Mexico, translates as, 'Royal city of the holy faith of St Francis of Assisi'.

9 Te Whakatakanga-o-te-ngarehu-o-te-ahi-a-Tamatea — **38**

The Maori name of Hammer Springs, New Zealand; like the second name in this list, it refers to a legend of Tamatea, explaining how the springs were warmed by 'the falling of the cinders of the fire of Tamatea'. Its name is variously written either hyphenated or as a single word.

10 Meallan Liath Coire Mhic Dhubhghaill — **32**

The longest multiple name in Scotland, a place near Aultanrynie, Highland, alternatively spelled Meallan Liath Coire Mhic Dhughaill (30 letters).

* Including single-word, hyphenated and multiple names

Ayuthaya Mahadilok Phop Noppharat Ratchathani an Sathit Sakkathattiya Witsanukam Prasit (Bangkok)

top10 MOST COMMON **STREET NAMES** IN THE UK

1. High Street
2. Station Road
3. Main Street
4. Park Road
5. Church Road
6. Church Street
7. London Road
8. Victoria Road
9. Green Lane
10. Manor Road

top10 MOST COMMON **HOUSE NAMES** IN THE UK

1. The Cottage
2. Rose Cottage
3. The Bungalow
4. The Coach House
5. Orchard House
6. The Lodge
7. Woodlands
8. The Old School House
9. Ivy Cottage
10. The Willows

top10 MOST COMMON **PLACE NAMES** IN GREAT BRITAIN

NAME	NO. OF OCCURRENCES
1 Newton	150
2 Blackhill/Black Hill	136
3 Castlehill/Castle Hill	128
4 Mountpleasant/Mount Pleasant	126
5 Woodside/Wood Side	112
6 Newtown/New Town	110
9 Burnside	107
8 Greenhill/Green Hill	105
9 Woodend/Wood End	101
10 Beacon Hill	95

These entries include the names of towns, villages and other inhabited settlements, as well as woods, hills and other named locations, but exclude combinations of these names with others – Newton Abbot and Newton-le-Willows, for example, are not counted with the Newtons.

top10 LARGEST COUNTRIES THAT **CHANGED THEIR NAMES** IN THE PAST 100 YEARS

	FORMER NAME	CURRENT NAME	YEAR CHANGED	AREA SQ KM	SQ MILES
1	Zaïre	Dem. Rep. of Congo	1997	2,345,409	905,567
2	Persia	Iran	1935	1,633,188	630,577
3	Tanganyika/Zanzibar	Tanzania	1964	945,087	364,900
4	South West Africa	Namibia	1990	824,292	318,261
5	Northern Rhodesia	Zambia	1964	752,614	290,586
6	Burma	Myanmar	1989	676,552	261,218
7	Ubanghi Shari	Central African Republic	1960	622,984	240,535
8	Bechuanaland	Botswana	1966	581,730	224,607
9	Siam	Thailand	1939	513,115	198,115
10	Mesopotamia	Iraq	1921	438,317	169,235

Although not a country, Greenland (2,175,600 sq km/840,004 sq miles) has been officially known as Kalaallit Nunaat since 1979.

Skyscrapers

Although much debated by skyscraper experts, according to rules established by the Chicago-based Council on Tall Buildings and Urban Habitat, a building's height is measured from street level to its structural top. This includes spires, but not subterranean floors or non-structural additions, such as masts, antennae or flag poles. The CTBUH separately identifies such categories as highest occupied floor, top of roof and top of pinnacle or antenna.

BUILDING / LOCATION / YEAR COMPLETED

1 Burj Dubai, Dubai, UAR, 2008*
2 Taipei 101, Taipei, Taiwan, 2004
3 Busan Lotte Tower, Busan, South Korea, 2008*
4 Shanghai World Financial Center, Shanghai, China, 2007*
5 Al Bait Towers, Mecca, Saudi Arabia, 2009*
6 International Commerce Centre, Hong Kong, China, 2007*
7 Petronas Towers, Kuala Lumpur, Malaysia, 1998
8 Sears Tower, Chicago, USA, 1974
9 Jin Mao Building, Shanghai, China, 1998
10 Dailian International Trade Center, Dalian, China, 2007*

	1	2	3	4	5	6	7	8	9	10
STOREYS	160	101	107	101	76	118	88	108	88	78
HEIGHT M/FT	705/2,312	509/1,669	494/1,620	492/1,613	485/1591	484/1,587	452/1,482	442/1,450	421/1,381	420/137?

* Under construction, scheduled completion date

top10 TALLEST HABITABLE BUILDINGS DESTROYED

BUILDING / LOCATION (ALL USA) / YEAR COMPLETED	YEAR DESTROYED	STOREYS	HEIGHT M	FT
1 1 World Trade Center, New York, 1972	2001	110	417.0	1,368
2 2 World Trade Center, New York, 1973	2001	110	415.4	1,363
3 Singer Building, New York, 1908	1968	47	186.5	612
4 7 World Trade Center, New York, 1987	2001	47	173.7	570
5 Morrison Hotel, Chicago, 1926	1965	45	160.3	526
6 One Meridian Plaza, Philadelphia, 1972	1999	38	150.0	492
7 City Investing Building, New York, 1908	1968	33	148.1	486
8 Hudson's Department Store, Detroit, 1924	1998	26	133.8	439
9 National Bank Building, New York, 1928	1975	32	132.0	433
10 Savoy-Plaza Hotel, New York, 1930	1964	33	128.0	420

➜ **Broken record-holder**
New York's Singer Building, the world's tallest from 1908, was demolished in 1968 and replaced by the 225-m (743-ft) One Liberty Plaza in 1973.

top10 TALLEST **HOTELS**

→ Height of luxury
Modelled on the sail of an Arab dhow, the Burj al-Arab Hotel took the record as the world's tallest dedicated hotel structure.

	HOTEL* / LOCATION / YEAR	STOREYS	HEIGHT# M	FT
1	**Jin Mao Tower**, Shanghai, China, 1998 Grand Hyatt Hotel occupies floors 53 to 87	88	370	1,214
2	**Trump International Hotel & Tower** Chicago, USA, 2008†	92	357	1,171
3	**Shimao International Plaza**, Shanghai, China, 2005 48 floors of hotel occupancy	60	333	1,093
4	**Abbco Rotana Hotel**, Dubai, UAR, 2006†	72	315	1,033
5	**Baiyoke Tower 2**, Bangkok, Thailand, 1997 Baiyoke Sky Hotel occupies floors 22 to 74	89	309	1,013
6	**Burj Dubai Lake Hotel**, Dubai, UAR, 2007†	63	300	984
7	**Burj al-Arab**, Dubai, UAR, 1999	60	270	885
8	**Emirates Hotel Tower**, Dubai, UAR, 2000	54	261	856
9	**Thai Wah Tower II**, Bangkok, Thailand, 1996 Westin Banyan Tree Hotel occupies floors 33–60	60	260	853
10	**Mercure Grand Hotel Tower**, Dubai, UAR, 2008†	62	250	820

* Including mixed occupancy (hotel + residential/office) buildings
\# Excluding spire
† Under construction; scheduled completion date

top10 TALLEST **CYLINDRICAL** BUILDINGS

	BUILDING / LOCATION	YEAR COMPLETED	STOREYS	HEIGHT M / FT	
1	Treasury Building, Singapore	1986	52	235	770
2	Tun Abdul Prazak Building, Penang, Malaysia	1985	61	232	760
3	Westin Peachtree Plaza, Atlanta, USA	1973	71	220	721
4	Renaissance Center, Detroit, USA	1977	73	219	718
5	Hopewell Centre (Hong Kong, China)	1980	64	215	705
6	Marina City Apartments (twin towers),Chicago, USA	1969	61	179	588
7	Australia Square Tower, Sydney, Australia	1968	46	170	560
8	Amartapura Condominium 1, Tangerang, Indonesia	1996	54	163	535
9	Shenzen City Plaza, Shenzen, China	1996	37	150	490
10	Amartapura Condominium 2, Tangerang, Indonesia	1997	36	136	445

top10 CITIES WITH **MOST SKYSCRAPERS** *

	CITY/LOCATION	SKYSCRAPERS
1	Hong Kong, China	188
2	New York City, USA	183
3	Chicago, USA	87
4	Shanghai, China	68
5	Tokyo, Japan	61
6	Singapore City, Singapore	34
7	Houston, USA	29
8	Seoul, South Korea	26
9	= Sydney, Australia	24
10	= Kuala Lumpur, Malaysia	23
	London	8

* Habitable buildings of more than 152 m (500 ft)

Super Structures

top10 TALLEST PYRAMIDS

PYRAMID	BUILT	HEIGHT M	HEIGHT FT
1 Transamerica pyramid, San Francisco, USA	1972	260	853
2 Great Pyramid, Giza, Egypt	2530 BC	147	483
3 Chefren pyramid, Giza, Egypt	2500 BC	137	449
4 Luxor Hotel and Casino, Las Vegas, USA	1993	107	351
5 Red Pyramid of Sneferu, Dahsûr, Egypt	2600 BC	104	341
6 Bent pyramid, Dahsûr, Egypt	2605 BC	101	332
7 Great American Pyramid, Memphis, Tennessee, USA	1991	98	322
8 Meidum Pyramid, Meidum, Egypt	2610 BC	94	308
9 Pyramid of Mykerinos, Giza, Egypt	2480 BC	66	216
10 Pyramid of the Sun, Teotihuacán, Mexico	225	64	209

Some authorities have claimed that the so-called Great White Pyramid, Xian, China, is up to 300 m (984 ft high). However, this manmade earth mound may measure no more than 45 m (150 ft).

top10 TALLEST CHIMNEYS

CHIMNEY / LOCATION	HEIGHT M	HEIGHT FT
1 Ekibastuz power station, Kazakhstan	420	1,377
2 International Nickel Company, Copper Hill, Sudbury, Ontario, Canada	381	1,250
3 Homer City Generating Station Unit 3, Minersville, Pennsylvania, USA	371	1,216
4 Kennecott Copper Corporation, Magna, Utah, USA	370	1,215
5 Mitchel Power Plant, Moundsville, West Virginia, USA	368	1,206
6 Zasavje power station, Trbovlje, Slovenia	360	1,181
7 Endesa Termic, La Coruña, Spain	356	1,169
8 Syrdarya Power Plant Units 5–10, Syrdarya, Uzbekistan	350	1,148
9 Teruel Power Plant, Teruel, Spain	343	1,125
10 Plomin Power Plant, Plomin, Croatia	340	1,115

The chimney at the Ekibastuz power station, the world's largest coal-fired plant which was completed in 1991, tapers from 44 m (144 ft) at the base to 14 m (47 ft) at the top.

top10 TALLEST STRUCTURES ERECTED OVER 100 YEARS AGO

STRUCTURE / LOCATION	YEAR COMPLETED	HEIGHT M	HEIGHT FT
1 Eiffel Tower, Paris, France	1889	300	984
2 Washington Memorial, Washington, DC, USA	1885	169	555
3 Mole Antonelliana, Turin, Italy	1889	168	551
4 Philadelphia City Hall, Philadelphia, USA	1901	167	548
5 Ulm Cathedral, Ulm, Germany	1890	161	528
6 Lincoln Cathedral, Lincoln, England (destroyed 1548)	c.1307	160	525
7 Blackpool Tower, Blackpool, UK	1894	158	518
8 Cologne Cathedral, Cologne, Germany	1880	156.4	513
9 Rouen Cathedral I, Rouen, France (destroyed 1822)	1530	156	512
10 St Pierre Church, Beauvais, France (collapsed 1573)	1568	153	502

top10 TALLEST LIGHTHOUSES IN THE UK

LIGHTHOUSE / LOCATION	HEIGHT M	HEIGHT FT
1 = Bishop Rock, Scilly Isles	49.0	161
= Eddystone, English Channel	49.0	161
3 Skerryvore, Hebrides	48.2	158
4 Chicken Rock, Calf of Man	43.9	144
5 Dungeness, Kent (old)	43.6	143
6 Beachy Head, East Sussex	43.3	142
7 Dungeness, Kent (new)	43.0	141
8 North Ronaldsay, Orkney	42.1	138
9 = Smalls, Dyfed	41.1	135
= Tarbat Ness, Ross and Cromarty	41.1	135
= Wolf Rock, Cornwall	41.1	135

The Bishop Rock lighthouse off the Scilly Isles, built in 1858 is 49 m (161 ft) tall and surmounted by a helipad. The equally tall Eddystone lighthouse, off Plymouth, was originally made of wood. The one now standing, the fifth on the site, was opened in 1882.

⊕ *Superstructures compared: The Great Pyramid, Giza; The Eiffel Tower, Paris; Ekibastuz power station chimney, Kazakhstan; CN Tower, Toronto, Canada.*

top10 TALLEST **TELECOMMUNICATIONS TOWERS**

TOWER / LOCATION	YEAR COMPLETED	HEIGHT M	HEIGHT FT
1 Guangzhou TV & Sightseeing Tower, Guangzhou, China	2007*	610	2,001
2 CN Tower, Toronto, Canada	1975	555	1,821
3 Ostankino Tower#, Moscow, Russia	1967	537	1,762
4 Oriental Pearl Broadcasting Tower, Shanghai, China	1995	468	1,535
5 Borj-e Milad Telecommunications Tower, Tehran, Iran	2003	435	1,426
6 Menara Telecom Tower, Kuala Lumpur, Malaysia	1996	421	1,381
7 Tianjin TV and Radio Tower, Tianjin, China	1991	415	1,362
8 Central Radio and TV Tower, Beijing, China	1994	405	1,328
9 Kiev TV Tower, Kiev, Ukraine	1973	385	1,263
10 TV Tower, Tashkent, Uzbekistan	1983	375	1,230

* Under construction; scheduled completion
\# Severely damaged by fire, 27 August 2000, restored and reopened 2004

All the towers listed are self-supporting, rather than masts braced with guy wires. The completion of the Menara Telecom Tower meant that for the first time in 107 years the Eiffel Tower – which once headed the list – dropped out of the Top 10.

⊕ Towering achievement
Higher than the Eiffel Tower, Millau Viaduct, the world's tallest road bridge, has seven towers ranging in height from 175 m (574 ft) to 343 m (1,125 ft).

top10 TALLEST **BRIDGE TOWERS**

BRIDGE / LOCATION	YEAR COMPLETED	HEIGHT M	HEIGHT FT
1 Millau Viaduct, Millau, France	2004	343	1,125
2 Akashi-Kaikyo, Akashi, Japan	1998	298	978
3 East Bridge, Great Belt Fixed Link, Sprogø, Denmark	1997	254	833
4 Golden Gate, San Francisco, USA	1937	227	745
5 Tatara, Onomichi, Japan	1999	226	741
6 Jambatan Pulau Pinang, Penang Malaysia	1985	225	739
7 Le Ponte de Normandie, Le Havre, France	1994	215	705
8 Verrazano Narrows, New York City, USA	1964	211	692
9 Tsing Ma, Hong Kong, China	1997	206	675
10 Mezcala-Solidaridad, Cuilapan, Mexico	1993	205	673

The Forth Road Bridge, Queensferry, Scotland (completed 1964), has the UK's tallest towers at 156 m (512 ft). Scheduled for completion in 2012, the Strait of Messina Bridge between Sicily and mainland Italy will have two towers 383 m (1,256 ft) high.

CULTURE

World Languages

top10 LANGUAGES **MOST SPOKEN** IN THE UK

	LANGUAGE	APPROX. SPEAKERS*
1	English	58,190,000
2	Welsh	582,000
3	Eastern Panjabi	471,000
4 =	Bengali	400,000
=	Urdu	400,000
6 =	Chinese (Cantonese)	300,000
=	Sylheti	300,000
8 =	Greek	200,000
=	Italian	200,000
10	Caribbean Creole	170,000

* As primary language

top10 **MOST SPOKEN** LANGUAGES*

	LANGUAGE	SPEAKERS
1	Chinese (Mandarin)	873,014,298
2	Spanish	322,299,171
3	English	309,352,280
4	Hindi	180,764,791
5	Portuguese	177,457,180
6	Bengali	171,070,202
7	Russian	145,031,551
8	Japanese	122,433,899
9	German	95,392,978
10	Chinese (Wu)	77,175,000

* Primary speakers only

Source: Raymond G. Gordon, Jr. (ed.), 'Ethnologue: Languages of the World', 15th edition, 2005, Dallas, Texas: SIL International. Online version: http://www.ethnologue.com/

top10 COUNTRIES WITH THE **MOST ENGLISH LANGUAGE SPEAKERS**

	COUNTRY	APPROX. NO. OF SPEAKERS*
1	USA	215,423,557
2	UK	58,190,000
3	Canada	20,000,000
4	Australia	14,987,000
5	Ireland	3,750,000
6 =	New Zealand	3,700,000
=	South Africa	3,700,000
8	Jamaica#	2,600,000
9	Trinidad and Tobago#	1,145,000
10	Guyana#	650,000

* People for whom English is their mother tongue
# Includes English Creole

The Top 10 represents the countries with the greatest numbers of inhabitants who speak English as their mother tongue. After the 10th entry, the figures dive to around or under 260,000 in the case of the Bahamas, Barbados and Zimbabwe. In addition to these and others that make up a world total that is probably in excess of 500,000,000, there are perhaps as many as 1,000,000,000 who speak English as a second language: a large proportion of the population of the Philippines, for example, speaks English, and there are many countries, such as India, Nigeria and other former British colonies in Africa, where English is either an official language or is widely understood and used in conducting legal affairs, business and government.

top10 **MOST COMMON** WORDS IN ENGLISH

WRITTEN		SPOKEN
the	**1**	be
of	**2**	the
and	**3**	I
a	**4**	you
in	**5**	and
to	**6**	it
is	**7**	have
was	**8**	a
it	**9**	not
for	**10**	do

A survey of a wide range of texts containing a total of almost 90 million words indicated that, in written English, one word in every 16 is 'the'.

top10 **LANGUAGES INTO WHICH MOST BOOKS** ARE TRANSLATED

	LANGUAGE	TRANSLATIONS 1979–2002
1	German	247,631
2	Spanish	192,365
3	French	164,448
4	English	103,293
5	Japanese	90,803
6	Dutch	88,362
7	Portuguese	66,062
8	Russian	61,333
9	Polish	50,678
10	Danish	50,370

Source: UNESCO, 'Index Translationum (1979–2002)'

top10 **LANGUAGES FROM WHICH MOST BOOKS** ARE TRANSLATED

	LANGUAGE	TRANSLATIONS 1979–2002
1	English	860,139
2	French	161,826
3	German	146,176
4	Russian	89,860
5	Italian	48,240
6	Spanish	37,380
7	Swedish	27,089
8	Latin	14,797
9	Danish	13,916
10	Ancient Greek	12,993

Source: UNESCO, 'Index Translationum (1979–2002)'

top10 **ONLINE** LANGUAGES

	LANGUAGE	% OF ALL INTERNET USERS	INTERNET USERS*
1	English	30.6	311,241,881
2	Chinese	13.0	132,301,513
3	Japanese	8.5	86,300,000
4	Spanish	6.3	63,971,898
5	German	5.6	56,853,162
6	French	4.0	40,974,005
7	Korean	3.3	33,900,000
8	Portuguese	3.2	32,372,000
9	Italian	2.8	28,870,000
10	Russian	2.3	23,700,000
	Top 10 languages	*79.6*	*810,484,459*
	Rest of world languages	*20.4*	*207,572,930*
	World total	*100.0*	*1,018,057,389*

* As at 31 Dec 2005

Source: Internet World Stats http://www.internetworldstats.com/

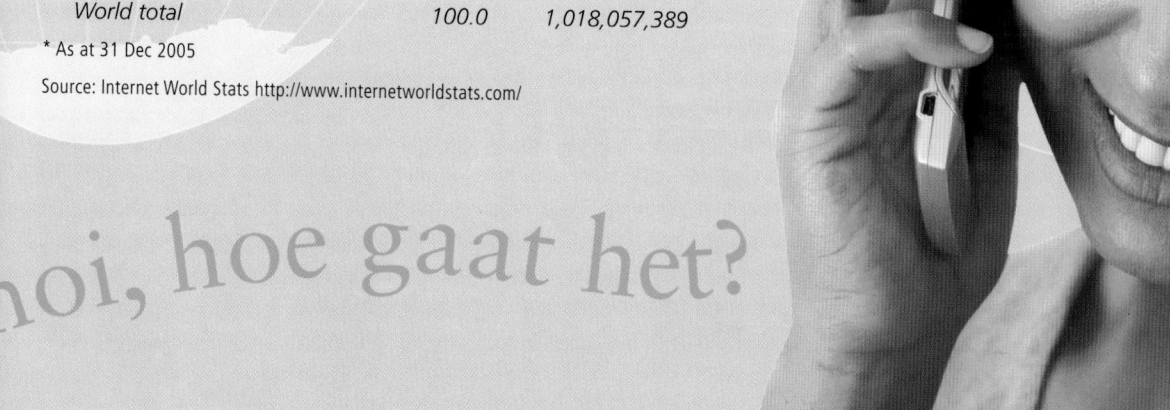

Education

top10 **LARGEST** UNIVERSITIES* **IN THE UK**

	UNIVERSITY	UNDERGRADUATES
1	University of London	82,732
2	University of Wales	51,512
3	Leeds Metropolitan University	41,660
4	University of Manchester	36,907
5	University of Leeds	35,963
6	Thames Valley University	34,000
7	London Metropolitan University	33,451
8	Manchester Metropolitan University	31,800
9	University of Nottingham	29,726
10	Anglia Ruskin University	28,154

* Excluding Open University (approx. 180,000 students)

top10 **OLDEST** UNIVERSITIES*

	UNIVERSITY	COUNTRY	FOUNDED
1	Parma	Italy	1064
2	Bologna	Italy	1088
3	Paris	France	1150
4	Oxford	England	1167
5	Modena	Italy	1175
6	Cambridge	England	1209
7	Salamanca	Spain	1218
8	Padua	Italy	1222
9	Naples	Italy	1224
10	Toulouse	France	1229

* Only those in continuous operation since founding

⊕ *Dreaming spires*
All Souls College, Oxford, was founded over 300 years into the university's 840-year history. Teaching began as early as 1096, but the university dates its origin to a decree by Henry II forbidding English students from attending the University of Paris. All Souls' Gothic spires were designed by Nicholas Hawksmoor in the early 18th century.

top10 OLDEST UNIVERSITIES **IN THE UK**

	UNIVERSITY	FOUNDED
1	Oxford	1167
2	Cambridge	1209
3	St Andrews	1411
4	Glasgow	1451
5	Aberdeen	1495
6	Edinburgh	1583
7	Dublin*	1592
8	Durham#	1832
9	London†	1836
10	Manchester	1851

* Ireland then part of England
# A short-lived Cromwellian establishment was set up in 1657
† Constituent colleges founded earlier: University College 1826, King's College 1828

top10 LARGEST UNIVERSITIES

	UNIVERSITY / COUNTRY	STUDENTS
1	Kameshwara Singh Darbhanga Sanskrit, India	515,000
2	Calicut, India	300,000
3	Paris, France	279,978
4	Mexico City, Mexico	269,000
5	Mumbai, India	262,350
6	Chhatrapati Shahuji Maharaj University, India	220,000
7	Utkal, India	200,000
8	Rome, Italy	189,000
9	Buenos Aires, Argentina	183,397
10	Guadalajara, Mexico	180,776

With 594,227 students, the Indira Gandhi National Open University, India, is the world's largest distance-learning establishment, while currently some 180,000 students are enrolled with the Open University in the UK.

the10 OLDEST SCHOOLS IN THE UK

	SCHOOL / LOCATION	FOUNDED
1	King's School, Canterbury	597
2	King's School, Rochester	604
3	St Peter's School, York	627
4	Warwick School	914
5	St Alban's School	948
6	King's School, Ely	970
7	Norwich School	1096
8	Abingdon School	1100
9	Thetford Grammar School	1119
10	High School of Glasgow	1124

top10 COUNTRIES WITH **MOST FOREIGN STUDENTS***

	COUNTRY	FOREIGN STUDENTS
1	USA	582,996
2	Germany	240,619
3	UK	227,273
4	France	221,567
5	Australia	179,619
6	Japan	74,892
7	Russia	68,602
8	Spain	53,639
9	Belgium	41,856
10	Canada	40,033

* In tertiary education

Source: UNESCO, 'Global Education Digest 2005'

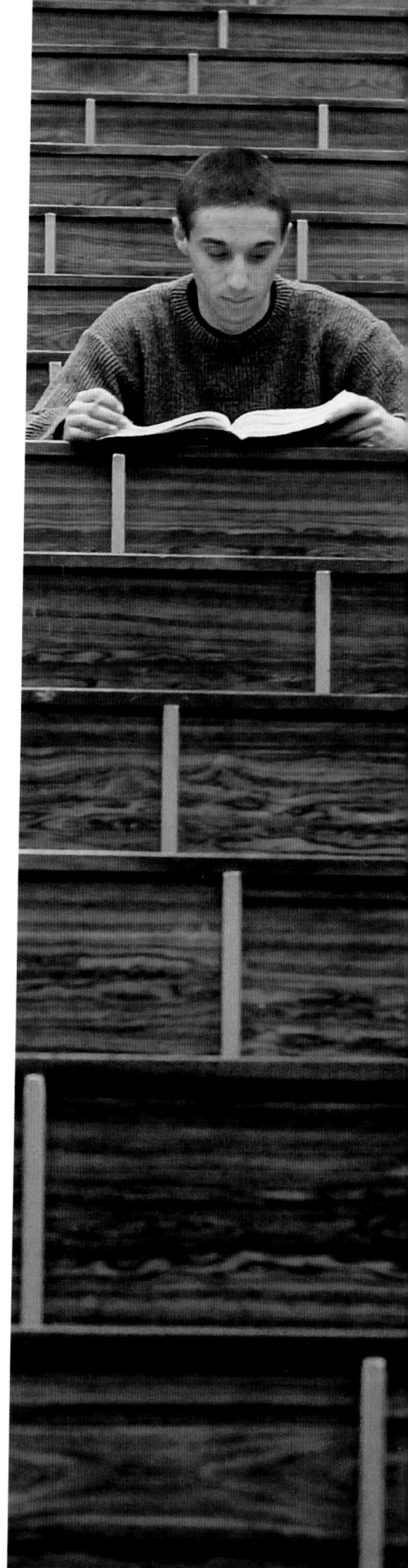

Books

top10 **NON-FICTION BESTSELLERS** IN THE UK, 2005

AUTHOR / TITLE	SALES IN 2005
1 Jeremy Clarkson, The World According to Clarkson	843,645
2 Jamie Oliver, Jamie's Italy	735,202
3 Sharon Osbourne, Sharon Osbourne Extreme: My Autobiography	608,966
4 Wayne Gould, The Times Su Doku Book 1	595,757
5 Gloria Hunniford, Next to You	446,229
6 Carol Vorderman, Carol Vorderman's How to do Sudoku	432,596
7 Guinness World Records 2006	420,249
8 Paul McKenna, I Can Make You Thin	375,015
9 Gillian McKeith, You Are What You Eat Cookbook	322,716
10 Michael Mepham, The Daily Telegraph Sudoku	307,020

Source: Nielsen BookScan

the10 LATEST **MAN BOOKER PRIZE WINNERS**

YEAR	AUTHOR / TITLE
2005	John Banville, The Sea
2004	Alan Hollinghurst, The Line of Beauty
2003	D.B.C. Pierre, Vernon God Little
2002	Yann Martel, Life of Pi
2001	Peter Carey, True History of the Kelly Gang
2000	Margaret Atwood, The Blind Assassin
1999	J.M. Coetzee, Disgrace
1998	Ian McEwan, Amsterdam
1997	Arundhati Roy, The God of Small Things
1996	Graham Swift, Last Orders

top10 **BESTSELLING** BOOKS

AUTHOR/BOOK / YEAR OF PUBLICATION / MINIMUM ESTIMATED SALES*

1
The Bible (c.1451–55)
6,000,000,000

2
Quotations from the Works of Mao Tse-tung (1966)
900,000,000

3 =
J.R.R. Tolkien, The Lord of the Rings trilogy (1954–55) 100,000,000

3 =
Noah Webster, American Spelling Book (1783) 100,000,000

5
William Holmes McGuffey, The McGuffey Readers (1836)
60,000,000

6
Benjamin Spock, The Common Sense Book of Baby and Child Care (1946)
50,000,000

7
Betty Crocker's Cookbook (1950)
45,000,000

8
Elbert Hubbard, A Message to Garcia (1899)
40,000,000

9 =
Rev Charles Monroe Sheldon, In His Steps: 'What Would Jesus Do?' (1896)
30,000,000

9 =
Jacqueline Susann, Valley of the Dolls (1966)
30,000,000

* Including translations; excluding annual publications and series

top10 COUNTRIES FOR **BOOK SALES**

	COUNTRY	FICTION	FORECAST BOOK SALES, 2007 NON-FICTION	TOTAL
1	China	628,838,000	7,856,761,000	8,485,599,000
2	USA	971,127,000	1,718,030,000	2,689,157,000
3	Japan	702,001,000	630,069,000	1,332,070,000
4	Russia	172,800,000	392,000,000	564,800,000
5	France	222,157,000	238,750,000	460,907,000
6	Germany	178,603,000	268,669,000	447,272,000
7	UK	150,098,000	223,768,000	373,866,000
8	Brazil	46,908,000	322,066,000	368,974,000
9	Spain	107,893,000	167,312,000	275,205,000
10	Italy	111,236,000	157,006,000	268,242,000

Source: Euromonitor

top10 **FICTION BESTSELLERS** IN THE UK, 2005

	AUTHOR / TITLE	SALES IN 2005
1	J.K. Rowling, Harry Potter and the Half-Blood Prince	3,538,482
2	Dan Brown, The Da Vinci Code	2,223,328
3	Dan Brown, Angels and Demons	1,464,729
4	Dan Brown, Digital Fortress	858,239
5	Audrey Niffenegger, The Time Traveler's Wife	652,015
6	Marian Keyes, The Other Side of the Story	488,058
7	John Grisham, The Broker	480,406
8	Maeve Binchy, Nights of Rain and Stars	455,313
9	Ian Caldwell and Dustin Thomason, The Rule of Four	451,747
10	Andrea Levy, Small Island	427,501

Source: Nielsen BookScan

top10 COUNTRIES FOR **ELECTRONIC BOOKS**

	COUNTRY	FORECAST ELECTRONIC BOOK SALES, 2007
1	USA	129,908,000
2	China	126,682,000
3	Italy	39,976,000
4	France	27,965,000
5	UK	15,019,000
6	Canada	7,904,000
7	Brazil	5,653,000
8	Belgium	3,932,000
9	Japan	3,368,000
10	Spain	3,347,000

Source: Euromonitor

Downloads of eBooks are predicted to increase dramatically as electronic readers and titles become widely available.

The Press

top10 NEWSPAPER-READING COUNTRIES

	COUNTRY	DAILY COPIES PER 1,000 PEOPLE, 2004
1	Iceland	705.9
2	Norway	684.0
3	Japan	646.9
4	Sweden	590.0
5	Finland	524.2
6	Bulgaria	472.7
7	Macau	448.9
8	Denmark	436.6
9	Switzerland	419.6
10	UK	393.4

Source: World Association of Newspapers, 'World Press Trends 2004', www.wan-press.org

top10 SUNDAY NEWSPAPERS IN THE UK

	NEWSPAPER	AVERAGE CIRCULATION*
1	News of the World	3,630,390
2	The Mail on Sunday	2,285,387
3	Sunday Mirror	1,451,834
4	The Sunday Times	1,371,545
5	The People	884,410
6	Sunday Express	862,987
7	The Sunday Telegraph	683,741
8	Sunday Mail (Scotland)	535,970
9	The Observer	484,357
10	Independent on Sunday	244,286

* Jan–Feb 2006

Source: Audit Bureau of Circulations Ltd

top10 DAILY NEWSPAPERS IN THE UK

	NEWSPAPER	AVERAGE NET CIRCULATION*
1	The Sun	3,145,433
2	The Daily Mail	2,439,142
3	The Mirror	1,656,655
4	The Daily Telegraph	901,123
5	Daily Express	827,905
6	Daily Star	791,900
7	The Times	669,691
8	Daily Record	450,302
9	Financial Times	440,837
10	The Guardian	382,931

* Jan–Feb 2006

Source: Audit Bureau of Circulations Ltd

top10 MAGAZINES IN THE UK

	TITLE	AVERAGE NET CIRCULATION, 2005
1	What's on TV	1,673,790
2	Saga Magazine	1,245,006
3	Take a Break	1,200,397
4	TV Choice	1,157,622
5	Radio Times	1,080,199
6	BBC Pre-School Magazines (Group)	929,452
7	Reader's Digest	776,902
8	Glamour	609,626
9	Chat	609,163
10	Now	591,795

Source: Periodical Publishers Association

AMAZING FACT

Heavyweight Press

The heaviest newspaper ever published was the Sunday edition of the *New York Times* of 14 September 1987. It contained 1,612 pages and tipped the scales at over 5.4 kg (12 lb), the total edition weighing over 6,000 tonnes. At this time, it was calculated that the newspaper consumed the equivalent of a forest of 75,000 trees every Sunday, but the progressive increase in the use of recycled paper, the planting of sustainable forest and the reduction in the page size have reduced this figure.

top10 OLDEST NATIONAL NEWSPAPERS
PUBLISHED IN THE UK

NEWSPAPER	FIRST PUBLISHED
1 The London Gazette	16 Nov 1665

Originally published in Oxford as the *Oxford Gazette*, while the royal court resided there during an outbreak of the plague. After 23 issues, it moved to London with the court and changed its name.

2 Lloyd's List	Apr 1734

Providing shipping news, originally on a weekly basis (as *Lloyd's News*), but since 1734 Britain's oldest daily.

3 The Times	1 Jan 1785

First published as the *Daily Universal Register*, it changed its name to *The Times* on 1 March 1788.

4 The Observer	4 Dec 1791

Britain's first Sunday newspaper was *Johnson's British Gazette and Sunday Monitor*, first published on 2 March 1780. It survived only until 1829, thus making *The Observer* the longest-running Sunday paper.

5 Morning Advertiser	8 Feb 1794

Britain's oldest trade newspaper (a daily established by the Licensed Victuallers Association to earn income for its charity), and the first national paper on Fleet Street, the *Morning Advertiser* changed its name to *The Licensee* and became a twice-weekly news magazine in 1994, at the time of its 200th anniversary, reverting to its original name in 2000.

6 The Scotsman	25 Jan 1817

Originally published weekly, the *Daily Scotsman* was published from July 1855 to December 1859 and re-titled *The Scotsman* in January 1860.

7 The Sunday Times	18 Feb 1821

Issued as the *New Observer* until March 1821 and the *Independent Observer* from April 1821 until 22 October 1822, when it changed its name to *The Sunday Times*. On 4 February 1962 it became the first British newspaper to issue a colour supplement.

8 The Guardian	5 May 1821

A weekly until 1855 (and called *The Manchester Guardian* until 1959).

9 News of the World	1 Oct 1843

The first issue of the national Sunday newspaper declared its aim as being 'To give to the poorer classes of society a paper that would suit their means, and to the middle, as well as the rich, a journal which, from its immense circulation, should command their attention.' This aspiration was achieved in April 1951, when sales peaked at 8,480,878 copies, the highest-ever circulation of any British newspaper.

10 The Daily Telegraph	29 Jun 1855

The first issues were published as *The Daily Telegraph and Courier*, but from 20 August 1855 *Courier* was dropped from the title.

top10 DAILY NEWSPAPERS

NEWSPAPER	COUNTRY	AVERAGE DAILY CIRCULATION, 2005
1 Yomiuri Shimbun	Japan	14,532,694
2 Asahi Shimbun	Japan	12,601,375
3 Sichuan Ribao	China	8,000,000
4 Mainichi Shimbun	Japan	5,845,857
5 Bild-Zeitung	Germany	5,674,400
6 Chunichi Shimbun	Japan	4,323,144
7 The Sun	UK	3,718,354
8 Renmin Ribao	China	3,000,000
9 Sankei Shimbun	Japan	2,890,835
10 Nihon Keizai Shimbun	Japan	2,705,877

Source: World Association of Newspapers

In 2005 *Yomiuri Shimbun*, Japan's and the world's bestselling daily newspaper, achieved a record sales average of 14,532,694 copies a day. Founded in 1874, the name *Yomiuri*, 'selling by reading', refers to the Japanese practice of vendors reading aloud from newssheets in the era before moveable type.

① Chinese whispers
The importance of the press in China is exemplified by the presence of two Chinese dailies among the world's Top 10.

Art on Show

top10 **BEST-ATTENDED** ART EXHIBITIONS **IN THE UK**, 2005

	EXHIBITION	VENUE / DATES	ATTENDANCE* DAILY	ATTENDANCE* TOTAL
1	Turner Whistler Monet	Tate Britain, 10 Feb–15 May	4,024	382,269
2	Frida Kahlo	Tate Modern, 6 June–9 Oct	3,002	369,249
3	Triumph of Painting Part I	Saatchi Gallery, 26 Jan–27 Jun	1,761	280,000
4	Turks, 600–1600 AD	Royal Academy of Arts, 22 Jan–12 Apr	3,358	272,000
5	Barbara Kruger	Gallery of Modern Art, Glasgow, 26 May–25 Nov	1,418	260,922
6	Caravaggio: The Final Years	National Gallery, 23 Feb–22 May	2,752	244,955
7	Triumph of Painting Part II	Saatchi Gallery, 5 Jul–26 Oct	2,239	206,000
8	Matisse: His Art and his Textiles	Royal Academy of Arts, 5 Mar–30 May	2,356	205,000
9	BP Portrait Award	National Portrait Gallery, 15 Jun–25 Nov	1,144	187,622
10	Glasgow's Art: Prints from the Collection	Gallery of Modern Art, Glasgow, 26 Jan–21 Aug	1,746	153,677

* Approximate totals provided by museums; excludes exhibitions that began in 2004

Source: 'The Art Newspaper'

top10 **BEST-ATTENDED** ART EXHIBITIONS, 2005

	EXHIBITION	VENUE / CITY / COUNTRY / DATES	ATTENDANCE* DAILY	ATTENDANCE* TOTAL
1	Tutankhamun and the Pharaohs	Los Angeles County Museum of Art, California, USA, 16 Jun–20 Nov	5,934	937,613
2	Tutankhamun, the Golden Beyond	Kunst der Bundesrepublik, Bonn, Germany, 4 Nov 2004–1 May 2005	5,644	866,812
3	Art Informel and Abstract Expressionism	Guggenheim Museum, Bilbao, Spain, 8 Mar–6 Nov	3,278	721,074
4	Pharaoh	Institut du Monde Arabe, Paris, France, 15 Oct 2004–12 Jun 2005	3,396	699,483
5	19th-century Masterpieces from the Louvre	Yokohama Museum of Art, Japan, 23 Feb–22 May	7,066	621,814
6	Van Gogh in Context	National Museum of Modern Art, Tokyo, Japan, 23 Feb–22 May	5,890	518,307
7	Turner Whistler Monet	Grand Palais, Paris, France, 13 Oct 2004–17 Jan 2005	6,043	501,601
8	Chanel	Metropolitan Museum of Art, New York, USA, 5 May–7 Aug	5,519	463,603
9	Vincent Van Gogh: The Drawings	Metropolitan Museum of Art, New York, USA, 18 Oct–31 Dec	6,571	459,972
10	Monet, the Seine and Water Lilies	Museum di Santa Giulia, Brescia, Italy, 23 Oct 2004–3 Apr 2005	3,150	440,564

* Approximate totals provided by museums

Source: 'The Art Newspaper'

⬆ *Head of his people*
Sioux warrior Crazy Horse (c.1837–77) is commemorated by this massive work in progress, carved out of a mountain in South Dakota and begun almost 60 years ago. The face alone took from 1987 to 1998 and stands 28.7 m (87.5 ft) high.

top10 TALLEST FREE-STANDING STATUES

STATUE / LOCATION	HEIGHT M	FT
1 Crazy Horse Memorial, Thunderhead Mountain, South Dakota, USA	172	563

Started in 1948 by Polish-American sculptor Korczak Ziolkowski and continued after his death in 1982 by his widow and eight of his children, this gigantic equestrian statue, even longer than it is high (195 m/641 ft), is not expected to be completed for several years.

2 Ushiku Amida Buddha, Joodo Teien Garden, Japan	120	394

This Japan-Taiwanese project, unveiled in 1993, took seven years to complete and weighs 1,000 tonnes.

3 The Indian Rope Trick, Riddersberg Säteri, Jönköping, Sweden	103	337

Sculptor Calle Örnemark's 144-tonne wooden sculpture stands in an open-air museum and depicts a long strand of 'rope' held by a fakir, while another figure ascends.

4 Peter the Great, Moscow, Russia	96	315

Georgian sculptor Zurab Tsereteli's statue of the Russian ruler on a galleon was moved from St Petersburg in 1997.

5 Motherland, Volgograd, Russia	82	270

This 1967 concrete statue of a woman with a raised sword, designed by Yevgeniy Vuchetich, commemorates the Soviet victory at the Battle of Stalingrad (1942–43).

6 Kannon, Sanukimachi, Tokyo Bay, Japan	56	184

The immense statue of the goddess of mercy was unveiled in 1961 in honour of the dead of World War II.

7 Statue of Liberty, New York, USA	46	151

Designed by Auguste Bartholdi and presented to the USA by the people of France, the statue was shipped in sections to Liberty (formerly Bedloes) Island where it was assembled, before being unveiled on 28 October 1886.

8 Christ the Redeemer, Rio de Janeiro, Brazil	38	125

The work of sculptor Paul Landowski and engineer Heitor da Silva Costa, the figure of Christ was unveiled in 1931.

9 Tian Tan (Temple of Heaven) Buddha, Po Lin Monastery, Lantau Island, Hong Kong, China	34	112

This was completed after 20 years' work and unveiled on 29 December 1993.

10 Quantum Cloud, Greenwich, London, UK	29	95

A gigantic steel human figure surrounded by a matrix of steel struts, it was created in 1999 by Antony Gormley, the sculptor of the similarly gigantic 20-m (66-ft) Angel of the North, Gateshead, UK.

top10 ART GALLERIES AND MUSEUMS IN THE UK

ATTRACTION / LOCATION	VISITORS, 2005
1 British Museum, London	4,536,064
2 National Gallery, London	4,202,020
3 Tate Modern, London	3,902,017
4 Natural History Museum, London	3,080,401
5 Science Museum, London	2,013,000
6 Victoria & Albert Museum, London	1,920,219
7 Tate Britain, London	1,733,120
8 National Portrait Gallery, London	1,539,766
9 National Maritime Museum, London	1,515,755
10 Royal Museum & Museum of Scotland, Edinburgh	828,367

Source: Association of Leading Visitor Attractions (ALVA)

Paintings at Auction

top10 MOST EXPENSIVE PAINTINGS

PAINTING / ARTIST	SALE	PRICE* (£)
1 Garçon à la Pipe, Pablo Picasso (Spanish, 1881–1973)	Sotheby's, New York, 5 May 2004	51,854,245 ($93,000,000)
2 Dora Maar With Cat, Pablo Picasso	Sotheby's, New York 3 May 2006	46,436,415 ($85,000,000)
3 Massacre of the Innocents, Sir Peter Paul Rubens (Flemish; 1577-1640)	Sotheby's, London, 10 Jul 2002	45,000,000
4 Portrait du Dr. Gachet, Vincent van Gogh (Dutch; 1853–90)	Christie's, New York, 15 May 1990	44,550,045 ($75,000,000)
5 Bal au Moulin de la Galette, Montmartre Pierre-Auguste Renoir (French; 1841–1919)	Sotheby's, New York, 17 May 1990	42,274,486 ($71,000,000)
6 Portrait de l'Artiste Sans Barbe, Vincent van Gogh	Christie's, New York, 19 Nov 1998	39,959,481 ($65,000,000)
7 Femme aux Bras Croises, Pablo Picasso	Christie's Rockefeller, New York, 8 Nov 2000	34,873,340 ($50,000,000)
8 Rideau, Cruchon et Compôtier, Paul Cézanne (French; 1839–1906)	Sotheby's, New York, 10 May 1999	33,808,705 ($55,000,000)
9 Les Noces de Pierrette, Pablo Picasso	Binoche et Godeau, Paris, 30 Nov 1989	33,075,627 (F.Fr315,000,000)
10 Femme Assise Dans un Jardin, Pablo Picasso	Sotheby's, New York, 10 Nov 1999	27,731,559 ($45,000,000)

* Excluding buyer's premium; converted at rate prevailing at time of sale

top10 MOST EXPENSIVE **OLD MASTER PAINTINGS**

PAINTING / ARTIST	SALE	PRICE (£)
1 Massacre of the Innocents, Sir Peter Paul Rubens	Sotheby's, London 10 Jul 2002	45,000,000
2 Portrait of Duke Cosimo I de Medici, Jacopo da Carucci (Pontormo)	Christie's, New York, 31 May 1989	20,545,746 ($32,000,000)
3 Giudecca, La Donna della Salute and San Giorgio, J.M.W. Turner	Christie's, New York, 6 Apr 2006	20,437,920 ($35,856,000)
4 Descent into Limbo, Andrea Mantegna	Sotheby's, New York, 23 Jan 2003	15,749,490 ($25,500,000)
5 Portrait of Omai, Standing in a Landscape, wearing Robes and a Head-dress, Sir Joshua Reynolds	Sotheby's, London, 29 Nov 2001	9,400,000
6 The Old Horse Guards, London, from St James's Park, Canaletto	Christie's, London, 15 Apr 1992	9,200,000
7 Vue de la Giudecca et du Zattere, à Venice, Francesco Guardi	Sotheby's, Monaco, 1 Dec 1989	8,933,075 (F.Fr85,000,000)
8 Portrait of a Bearded Man in a Red Doublet, Rembrandt	Christie's Rockefeller, New York, 26 Jan 2001	7,864,216 ($11,500,000)
9 Le Retour du Bucentaure le Jour de l'Ascension, Canaletto	Ader Tajan, Paris 15 Dec 1993	7,570,109 (F.Fr 66,000,000)
10 Tieleman Roosterman in Black Doublet, White Ruff, Frans Hals (elder)	Christie's, London, 8 Jul 1999	7,500,000

⊕ *Portrait du Dr. Gachet*
Van Gogh painted two versions of this portrait of the doctor who cared for him in 1890, in the last months of his life. One hangs in the Musée d'Orsay, Paris, while this took the then record as the world's most expensive painting in 1990 when it was sold to a Japanese businessman.

top10 MOST EXPENSIVE PAINTINGS **BY WOMEN ARTISTS**

	PAINTING / ARTIST	SALE	PRICE (£)
1	**Calla Lilies with Red Anemone,** Georgia O'Keeffe (American; 1887–1986)	Christie's Rockefeller, New York, 23 May 2001	3,923,492 ($5,600,000)
2	**Cache-cache,** Berthe Morisot (French; 1841–1895)	Sotheby's, New York, 9 Nov 2000	2,807,825 ($4,000,000)
3	**Marche au Minho,** Sonia Delaunay (French/Russian, 1885–1979)	Laurence Calmels, Paris, 14 Jun 2002	2,628,223 ($4,100,000)
4	**Black Cross with Stars and Blue,** Georgia O'Keeffe	Christie's Rockefeller, New York, 23 May 2001	2,592,307 ($3,700,000)
5	**In the Box,** Mary Cassatt (American; 1844–1926)	Christie's, New York, 23 May 1996	2,450,656 ($3,700,000)
6	**The Conversation,** Mary Cassatt	Christie's, New York, 11 May 1988	2,179,923 ($4,100,000)
7	**Cache-cache,** Berthe Morisot	Sotheby's, New York, 10 May 1999	2,151,463 ($3,500,000)
8	**Rams Head, Blue Morning Glory,** Georgia O'Keeffe	Christie's Rockefeller, New York, 25 Apr 2002	2,139,111 ($3,100,000)
9	**Mother, Sara and the Baby,** Mary Cassatt	Christie's, New York, 10 May 1989	2,108,434 ($3,500,000)
10	**From the Plains,** Georgia O'Keeffe	Sotheby's, New York, 3 Dec 1997	1,961,833 ($3,300,000)

top10 ARTISTS WITH MOST WORKS **SOLD FOR OVER £1 MILLION**

	ARTIST	TOTAL VALUE OF WORKS SOLD (£)	NO. OF WORKS SOLD FOR OVER £1 MILLION
1	**Pablo Picasso** (Spanish, 1881–1973)	1,384,883,089	237
2	**Claude Monet** (French, 1840–1926)	1,029,612,975	189
3	**Pierre Auguste Renoir** (French, 1841–1919)	592,987,984	122
4	**Edgar Degas** (French, 1834–1917)	354,127,353	74
5	**Henri Matisse** (French, 1869–1954)	338,458,023	69
6	**Paul Cézanne** (French, 1839–1906)	509,449,001	68
7	**Amedeo Modigliani** (Italian, 1884–1920)	313,953,418	59
8	**Andy Warhol** (American, 1928–87)	159,171,420	56
9	**Vincent van Gogh** (Dutch, 1853–90)	576,442,817	54
10	**Camille Pissarro** (French, 1830–1903)	113,373,094	45

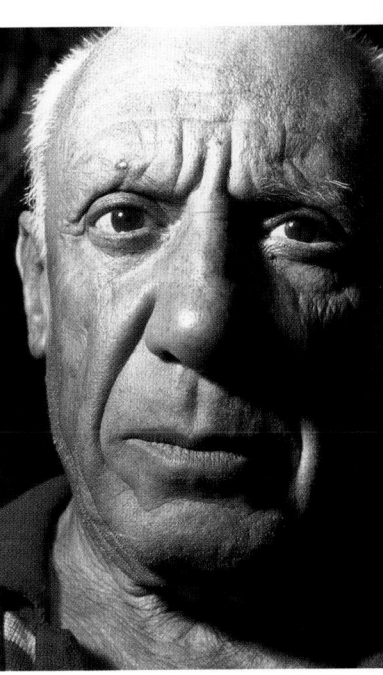

⬆ *Pablo Picasso*
The works of Spanish artist Picasso (1881–1973) are among the most expensive ever sold, with more £1-million paintings than any artist at auction.

Objets d'Art

top10 MOST EXPENSIVE WATERCOLOURS

WATERCOLOUR / ARTIST / SALE	PRICE (£)
1 La Moisson en Provence, Vincent van Gogh (Dutch; 1853–90), Sotheby's, London, 24 Jun 1997	8,000,000
2 Les Toits – 1882, Vincent van Gogh, Ader Picard & Tajan, Paris, 20 Mar 1990	2,900,107 (F.Fr 27,000,000)
3 Red Canoe, Winslow Homer (American; 1836–1910), Sotheby's, New York, 1 Dec 1999	2,750,000 ($4,400,000)
4 Die Sangerin L. Ais Fiordiligi, Paul Klee (Swiss; 1879–1940), Sotheby's, London, 28 Nov 1989	2,400,000 ($3,744,000)
5 Nature Morte au Melon Vert, Paul Cézanne (French;1839–1906), Sotheby's, London, 4 Apr 1989	2,300,000
6 The Stony Beach, Maurice Prendergast (American; 1859–1916), Christie's Rockefeller, New York, 23 May 2001	2,253,521 ($3,200,000)
7 John Biglin in Single Scull, Thomas Eakins (American; 1844–1916), Christie's, New York, 23 May 1990	1,893,490 ($3,200,000)
8 Heidelberg with a Rainbow, Joseph Mallord William Turner (British; 1775–1851), Sotheby's, London, 14 Jun 2001	1,850,000
9 Au Moulin Rouge, La Fille du Roi d'Egypte, Pablo Picasso (Spanish; 1881–1973), Sotheby's, London, 29 Nov 1994	1,650,000
10 Le Jardin des Lauvés, Vue sur Aix et la Cathedrale de Saint Sauveurt, Paul Cézanne, Phillips, New York, 7 May 2001	1,549,296 ($2,200,000)

top10 MOST EXPENSIVE MINIATURES

MINIATURE / ARTIST / SALE	PRICE (£)
1 Portrait of George Washington, John Ramage (Irish; c.1748–1802), Christie's, New York, 19 Jan 2001	825,408 ($1,216,000)
2 Two Orientals, Francisco José de Goya y Lucientes (Spanish; 1746–1828), Christie's, London, 3 Dec 1997	580,000
3 Maja and Celestina, Francisco José de Goya y Lucientes, Sotheby's, New York, 30 May 1991	294,118 ($500,000)
4 Portrait of George Villiers, Duke of Buckingham, Jean Petitot (French; 1607–91), Christie's, London, 30 Apr 1996	250,000
5 Man Clasping Hand from Cloud, possibly Lord, Thomas Howard, Nicholas Hilliard (British; 1547–1619), Christie's, London, 3 Mar 1993	160,000
6 Self-portrait, Frida Kahlo (Mexican; 1907–1954), Sotheby's, New York, 20 Nov 2000	141,844 ($200,000)
7 A Gentleman aged 52, Nicholas Hilliard, Christie's, London, May 2003	122,850
8 King George III when Prince of Wales Wearing Order of Garter, Jean-Etienne Liotard (Swiss; 1702–89), Christie's, London, 21 Oct 1997	115,000
9 Portrait of Henry Stuart, Earl of Ross and 1st Duke of Albany, attributed to Lievine Teerling-Bening (Flemish; 16th century), Bonhams, London, 20 Nov 1997	110,000
10 Portrait of Tsar Nicholas II in Uniform with Orders, Russian School (Russian; 20th century), Christie's, New York, 1 Dec 1995	91,503 ($140,000)

top10 MOST EXPENSIVE SCULPTURES

SCULPTURE / ARTIST / SALE	PRICE (£)
1 Danaïde, Constantin Brancusi (Romanian; 1876–1956), Christie's Rockefeller, New York, 7 May 2002	11,235,955 ($16,500,000)
2 Grande Femme Debout I, Alberto Giacometti (Swiss; 1901–66), Christie's Rockefeller, New York, 8 Nov 2000	9,067,068 ($13,000,000)
3 Grande Tête de Diego, Alberto Giacometti, Sotheby's, New York, 8 May 2002	8,516,147 ($12,500,000)
4 La Serpentine Femme à la Stele – l'Araignée, Henri Matisse (French; 1869–1954), Sotheby's, New York, 10 May 2000	8,328,489 ($12,750,000)
5 La Forêt, Alberto Giacometti, Christie's Rockefeller, New York, 7 May 2002	8,171,604 ($12,000,000)
6 Figure Decorative, Henri Matisse, Sotheby's, New York, 10 May 2001	8,095,741 ($11,500,000)
7 Petite Danseuse de Quatorze Ans, Edgar Degas (French; 1834–1917), Sotheby's, London, 27 Jun 2000	7,000,000
8 Petite Danseuse de Quatorze Ans, Edgar Degas, Sotheby's, New York, 11 Nov 1999	6,931,608 ($11,250,000)
9 Nu Couche I, Aurore, Henri Matisse, Phillips, New York, 7 May 2001	6,604,101 ($9,500,000)
10 Petite Danseuse de Quatorze Ans, Edgar Degas, Sotheby's, New York, 12 Nov 1996	6,542,283 ($10,800,000)

❶ Million-dollar President
George Washington sat for this miniature on 3 October 1789 as a gift for his wife. It became the first ever to be sold for over $1 million.

Record-Breaking Photographic Record

In 1906 American photographer Edward S. (Sheriff) Curtis (1862–1952) was commissioned by millionaire J.P. Morgan to produce a collection of photographs known as *The North American Indian*. The 20 volumes and 1,500 photographs that resulted present the most comprehensive visual record of native Americans in the early 20th century. The work occupied Curtis until 1930, and has become the most prized sets of photographs among collectors. In the past decade, several have changed hands for over £300,000, and in 2005 one was sold for a record $1.4 million.

◉ *Water level*
Maurice Prendergast's The Stony Beach *(1897) set a new record as the most expensive watercolour to be sold in the 21st century.*

top10 MOST EXPENSIVE **PHOTOGRAPHS**

PHOTOGRAPH* / PHOTOGRAPHER / SALE	PRICE (£)
1 The Pond – Moonlight (1904), Edward Steichen (American; 1879–1973), Sotheby's, New York, 14 Feb 2006	1,681,097 ($2,928,000)
2 Georgia O'Keeffe (Hands) (1919), Alfred Stieglitz (American; 1864–1946), Sotheby's, New York, 14 Feb 2006	845,142 ($1,472,000)
3 Georgia O'Keeffe (Nude) (1919), Alfred Stieglitz, Sotheby's, New York, 14 Feb 2006	780,837 ($1,360,000)
4 Untitled (Cowboy), Richard Prince (American, b.1949), Christie's, New York, 8 Nov 2005	715,268 ($1,248,000)
5 Athènes, Temple de Jupiter Olympien (1842), Joseph Philibert Girault de Prangey (French; 1804–92), Christie's, London, 20 May 2003	500,000
6 White Angel Breadline (1933), Dorothea Lange (American; 1895–1965), Sotheby's, New York, 11 Oct 2005	468,444 ($822,400)
7 The Breast (1921), Edward Weston (American; 1886–1958), Sotheby's, New York, 10 Oct 2005	467,060 ($822,400)
8 Grande vague – sète (c.1857), Gustave le Gray (French; 1820–82), Sotheby's, London, 27 Oct 1999	460,000
9 Untitled V (1997), Andreas Gursky (German; b.1955), Christie's, London, 6 Feb 2002	390,000
10 Mullein, Maine (1927), Paul Strand (American; 1890–1976), Phillips, New York, 15 Apr 2002	380,412 ($550,000)

* Single prints only

top10 PRICES FOR **FILM POSTERS** AT AUCTION

POSTER* / AUCTION	PRICE (£)
1 The Mummy (1932) Sotheby's, New York, 1 Mar 1997	278,477 ($453,500)
2 Metropolis (1927) Sotheby's, New York, 28 Oct 2000	246,067 ($357,750)
3 King Kong (1933) Sotheby's, New York, 16 Apr 1999	151,958 ($244,500)
4 Frankenstein (1931) Odyssey Auctions, Los Angeles, 11 Oct 1993	128,931 ($198,000)
5 Babe Comes Home (1927) Heritage online auction, 20 Nov 2003	81,286 ($138,000)
6 Men in Black (1934) Sotheby's, New York, 4 Apr 1998	66,142 ($109,750)
7 = Play Ball with Babe Ruth (1929) Sotheby's, New York, 16 Apr 1999	59,664 ($96,000)
= Three Little Pigskins (1934) Sotheby's, New York, 16 Apr 1999	59,664 ($96,000)
9 Casablanca (1942) Christie's, London, 27 Mar 2000	54,000
10 The Outlaw (1943) Christie's, London, 4 Mar 2003	52,875

* Highest priced example of each – other versions of some have also achieved high prices

In November 2005, the Reel Poster Gallery, London, sold a 1927 *Metropolis* poster privately (not at auction, and hence not included in this Top 10) for £397,762 ($690,000), a record for any poster.

Treasured Possessions

top10 MOST EXPENSIVE **BOOKS AND MANUSCRIPTS**

BOOK / MANUSCRIPT / SALE*	PRICE (£)#
1 The Codex Hammer (formerly Codex Leicester) (1506–10), Christie's, New York, USA, 11 Nov 1994	19,263,602 ($30,802,500)

This is one of Leonardo da Vinci's notebooks, which includes many scientific drawings and diagrams. It was purchased by Bill Gates, the billionaire founder of Microsoft.

2 The Rothschild Prayerbook (c.1503) Christie's, London, UK, 8 Jul 1999	8,581,500

This holds the world-record price for an illuminated manuscript.

3 The Gospels of Henry the Lion (c.1173–75) Sotheby's, London, UK, 6 Dec 1983	7,400,000

At the time of its sale, it became the most expensive manuscript, book or work of art other than a painting ever sold.

4 John James Audubon's The Birds of America (1827–38), Christie's, New York, USA, 10 Mar 2000	6,042,768 ($8,802,500)

The record for any printed book. A facsimile reprint of Audubon's *The Birds of America* published in 1985 by Abbeville Press, New York, was once listed at $30,000 (£15,000), making it the most expensive book ever published.

5 The Canterbury Tales, Geoffrey Chaucer (c.1476–77), Christie's, London, UK, 8 Jul 1998	4,621,500

Printed by William Caxton, and purchased by Sir Paul Getty. The record for a work of English literature. In 1776, the same volume had changed hands for just £6.

6 Comedies, Histories, and Tragedies, The First Folio of William Shakespeare (1623) Christie's, New York, USA, 8 Oct 2001	4,171,854 ($6,166,000)

This sale marks the world auction record for a 17th-century book.

7 The Gutenberg Bible (1455) Christie's, New York, USA, 22 Oct 1987	3,264,688 ($5,390,000)

One of the first books ever printed, by Johann Gutenberg and Johann Fust.

8 The Northumberland Bestiary (c.1250–60) Sotheby's, London, UK, 29 Nov 1990	2,700,000

9 The Cornaro Missal (c.1503) Christie's, London, UK, 8 Jul 1999	2,600,000

This manuscript, formerly owned by the Barons Nathaniel and Albert Von Rothschild, achieved a world-record price for an Italian manuscript.

10 The Burdett Psalter and Hours (c.1282–86) Sotheby's, London, UK, 23 Jun 1998	2,500,000

* Excludes collections
# Includes buyer's premium

top10 MOST EXPENSIVE **TOYS EVER SOLD** AT AUCTION

TOY / SALE	PRICE (£)
1 Kämmer and Reinhardt doll, Sotheby's, London, 8 Feb 1994	188,500
2 Titania's Palace, Christie's, London, 10 Jan 1978	135,000

A doll's house with 2,000 items of furniture.

3 The Charles, Christie's, New York, 14 Dec 1991	127,483 ($231,000)

A fire hose-reel made by American manufacturer George Brown & Co (c.1875).

4 Louis Vuitton Steiff teddy bear (2000), Christie's, Monaco, 14 Oct 2000	125,831
5 'Teddy Girl', a 1904 Steiff teddy bear, Christie's, London, 5 Dec 1994	110,000
6 Kämmer and Reinhardt bisque character doll, German (c.1909), Sotheby's, London, 17 Oct 1996	108,200

Previously sold at Sotheby's, London, 16 Feb 1989, for £90,200 (see No.8 entry below).

7 Black mohair Steiff teddy bear (c.1912), Christie's, London, 4 Dec 2000	91,750

One of a number of black Steiff bears brought out in the UK after the sinking of the *Titanic* that have since become known as 'Mourning' teddies.

8 Kämmer and Reinhardt bisque character doll, German (c.1909), Sotheby's, London, 16 Feb 1989	90,200
9 Hornby 00-gauge train set, Christies, London, 27 Nov 1992	80,178

The largest train set ever sold at auction.

10 William and Mary wooden doll, English, (c.1690), Sotheby's, London, 24 Mar 1987	67,000

⊙ Bear market
This rare Steiff teddy bear's high price results from its association with the Titanic, *the 1912 sinking of which it commemorates.*

A price above rubies
The iconic ruby slippers worn by Judy Garland in The Wizard of Oz *– one of seven pairs – made a record price at auction.*

top10 ITEMS OF **FILM MEMORABILIA** SOLD AT AUCTION*

ITEM / SALE	PRICE (£)
1 David O. Selznick's Oscar for 'Gone with the Wind' **(1939)**, Sotheby's, New York, 12 Jun 1999 ($1,542,500) Bought by Michael Jackson.	954,104
2 Marilyn Monroe's 'Happy Birthday Mr President' dress **(1962)**, Christie's, New York, 27 Oct 1999 ($1,267,000)	767,042
3 Judy Garland's ruby slippers from 'The Wizard of Oz' **(1939)**, Christie's, New York, 26 May 2000 ($666,000)	453,815
4 Bette Davis's Oscar for 'Jezebel' **(1938)**, Christie's, New York, 19 Jul 2001 ($578,000) Bought by Steven Spielberg.	407,407
5 Vivien Leigh's Oscar for 'Gone with the Wind', Sotheby's, New York, 15 Dec 1993 ($562,500)	378,737
6 Clark Gable's Oscar for 'It Happened One Night' **(1934)**, Christie's, Los Angeles, 15 Dec 1996 ($607,500)	366,770
7 Statue of the falcon from 'The Maltese Falcon' **(1941)**, Christie's, New York, 6 Dec 1994 ($398,500)	255,580
8 Judy Garland's blue-and-white gingham dress from 'The Wizard of Oz', Christie's, London, 9 Dec 1999	199,500
9 James Bond's Aston Martin DB5 from 'Goldfinger' **(1964)**, Sotheby's, New York, 28 Jun 1986 ($275,000)	179,915
10 Marlon Brando's script for 'The Godfather', Christie's, New York, 30 Jun 2005 ($312,800)	173,373

* Excluding posters and animation cels

top10 MOST EXPENSIVE **MUSICAL INSTRUMENTS**

INSTRUMENT* / DETAILS	SALE	PRICE (£)
1 John Lennon's Steinway Model Z upright piano	Fleetwood-Owen online auction, London and New York, Hard Rock Café, 17 Oct 2000	1,450,000
2 'Kreutzer' violin by Antonio Stradivari (1727)	Christie's, London, 1 Apr 1998	947,500
3 'Cholmondeley' violincello by Antonio Stradivari	Sotheby's, London, 22 Jun 1998	682,000
4 Jerry Garcia's 'Tiger' guitar	Guernsey's at Studio 54, New York, 9 May 2002	657,850 ($957,500)
5 Eric Clapton's 1964 Gibson acoustic ES-335	Christie's, New York, 25 Jun 2004	465,659 ($847,500)
6 Single-manual harpsichord by Joseph Joannes Couchet, Antwerp (1679)	Sotheby's, London, 21 Nov 2001	267,500
7 Steinway grand piano, decorated by Lawrence Alma-Tadema and Edward Poynter for Henry Marquand (1884–87)	Sotheby Parke Bernet, New York, 26 Mar 1980	163,000 ($390,000)
8 Double bass by Domenico Montagnana	Sotheby's, London, 16 Mar 1999	155,500
9 Viola by Giovanni Paolo Maggini	Christie's, London, 20 Nov 1984	129,000
10 Verne Powell's platinum flute	Christie's, New York, 18 Oct 1986	126,200 ($187,000)

* Most expensive example only for each type of instrument

MUSIC

Singles

↥ **All-time hit** *Elton John's tribute to Princess Diana is the bestselling single ever.*

top10 SINGLES OF **ALL TIME**

TITLE / ARTIST/GROUP	YEAR	SALES EXCEED
1 Candle in the Wind (1997)/Something about the Way You Look Tonight, Elton John	1997	37,000,000
2 White Christmas, Bing Crosby	1942	30,000,000
3 Rock Around the Clock, Bill Haley & His Comets	1954	17,000,000
4 I Want to Hold Your Hand, The Beatles	1963	12,000,000
5 = It's Now or Never, Elvis Presley	1960	10,000,000
= Hey Jude, The Beatles	1968	10,000,000
= I Will Always Love You, Whitney Houston	1992	10,000,000
8 = Diana, Paul Anka	1957	9,000,000
= Hound Dog/Don't Be Cruel, Elvis Presley	1956	9,000,000
10 = (Everything I Do) I Do it for You, Bryan Adams	1991	8,000,000
= I'm a Believer, The Monkees	1966	8,000,000

Global sales are notoriously difficult to calculate, since for many decades, little statistical research on record sales was done in a large part of the world. 'Worldwide' is thus usually taken to mean the known minimum 'western world' sales. It took 55 years for a record to overtake Bing Crosby's 1942 *White Christmas*, although the song, as also recorded by others and sold as sheet music, has achieved such enormous total sales that it would still appear in first position in any list of bestselling songs.

top10 UK **SINGLES** OF 2005

TITLE / ARTIST/GROUP

1 (Is This The Way To) Amarillo, Tony Christie featuring Peter Kay

2 That's My Goal, Shayne Ward

3 Crazy Frog, Axel F

4 You're Beautiful, James Blunt

5 Don't Cha, Pussycat Dolls featuring Busta Rhymes

6 All About You/You've Got A Friend, McFly

7 Lonely, Akon

8 Hung Up, Madonna

9 You Raise Me Up, Westlife

10 Push The Button, Sugababes

Source: The Official UK Charts Company

Total singles sales for 2005 were down 19.91 per cent, with Tony Christie's *Amarillo* the only one to be certified gold.

top10 UK **DOWNLOADS** OF 2005

TITLE / ARTIST/GROUP

1 You're Beautiful, James Blunt

2 Hung Up, Madonna

3 Bad Day, Daniel Powter

4 Push The Button, Sugababes

5 Feel Good Inc., Gorillaz

6 Don't Cha, Pussycat Dolls featuring Busta Rhymes

7 That's My Goal, Shayne Ward

8 (Is This The Way To) Amarillo, Tony Christie featuring Peter Kay

9 Gold Digger, Kanye West featuring Jamie Foxx

10 I Like The Way, Bodyrockers

Source: The Official UK Charts Company

In contrast to the declining fortunes of singles, the age of the iPOD has created an entirely new market, with legal downloads increasing by 3,573 per cent to over 26 million.

top10 SINGLES OF **ALL TIME** IN THE UK

TITLE / ARTIST/GROUP / YEAR OF ENTRY	EST. UK SALES
1 Candle In The Wind (1997)/Something About the Way You Look Tonight, Elton John, 1997	4,868,000
2 Do They Know It's Christmas?, Band Aid, 1984	3,550,000
3 Bohemian Rhapsody, Queen, 1975/1991	2,130,000
4 Mull of Kintyre, Wings, 1977	2,050,000
5 Rivers of Babylon/Brown Girl in the Ring, Boney M, 1978	1,995,000
6 You're the One that I Want, John Travolta and Olivia Newton-John, 1978	1,975,000
7 Relax, Frankie Goes to Hollywood, 1984	1,910,000
8 She Loves You, The Beatles, 1963	1,890,000
9 Unchained Melody, Robson Green and Jerome Flynn, 1995	1,844,000
10 Mary's Boy Child/Oh My Lord, Boney M, 1978	1,790,000

Source: BPI/The Official UK Charts Company

Seventy-eight singles have sold over 1 million copies apiece in the UK during the last 50 years, and these are the cream of that crop. The Band Aid single had a number of special circumstances surrounding it, and it took the remarkable response to the death of Diana, Princess of Wales, to generate sales that were capable of overtaking it. Two years – 1978, with its two giant hits from Boney M, and 1984 – were the all-time strongest for million-selling singles, and this chart fittingly has representatives from each.

top10 SINGLES THAT STAYED **LONGEST IN THE UK CHARTS**

	TITLE / ARTIST/GROUP	FIRST CHART ENTRY	WEEKS IN CHARTS
1	My Way, Frank Sinatra	1969	124
2	Amazing Grace, Judy Collins	1970	66
3	Relax, Frankie Goes to Hollywood	1983	59
4 =	Rock Around The Clock, Bill Haley & His Comets	1955	57
=	Release Me, Engelbert Humperdinck	1967	57
6	Stranger on the Shore, Mr Acker Bilk	1961	55
7	Blue Monday, New Order	1983	49
8	I Love You Because, Jim Reeves	1964	47
9 =	Let's Twist Again, Chubby Checker	1961	44
=	All Right Now, Free	1970	44

Source: Music Information Database

◗ The King still rules
Fifty years after his first UK chart entry and 30 years since his death, Elvis Presley maintains his commanding lead with most weeks and most singles at No.1.

top10 ARTISTS WITH THE **MOST WEEKS AT NO. 1** IN THE UK

ARTIST/GROUP / WEEKS AT NO. 1	
1	Elvis Presley 80
2	The Beatles 69
3	Cliff Richard 44
4	Frankie Laine 32
5	Abba 31
6 =	Madonna 23
=	Wet Wet Wet 23
8 =	Spice Girls 21
=	Take That 21
10 =	Queen 20
=	Slade 20

Source: Music Information Database

top10 ARTISTS WITH THE **MOST NO. 1 SINGLES** IN THE UK

ARTIST/GROUP / NO. 1 SINGLES	
1	Elvis Presley 21
2	The Beatles 17
3	Cliff Richard 14
4	Westlife 13
5	Madonna 11
6 =	Abba 9
=	Spice Girls 9
8 =	Oasis 8
=	Rolling Stones 8
=	Take That 8

Source: Music Information Database

Albums

top10 SLOWEST UK ALBUM CHART RISES TO NO.1

	ARTIST/GROUP / TITLE	WEEKS TO REACH NO.1
1	**Tyrannosaurus Rex**, My People Were Fair and Had Sky in Their Hair, But Now They're Content to Wear Stars on Their Brows	199
2	**Abba**, Abba Gold	117
3	**Elvis Presley**, 40 Greatest Hits	114
4	**Various Artists**, Fame (Original Soundtrack)	98
5	**Shania Twain**, Come on Over	88
6	**Cranberries**, Everybody Else is Doing It, So Why Can't We?	67
7	**David Gray**, White Ladder	66
8	**Mike Oldfield**, Tubular Bells	65
9	**Ace of Base**, Happy Nation	54
10	**Fleetwood Mac**, Rumours	49

Source: Music Information Database

In addition to heading this list, the Tyrannosaurus Rex album also holds the distinction of being the album with the longest title ever to chart. It originally charted in July 1968, but had to wait until the heyday of T. Rex (the name the group were by then using) to re-chart in May 1972 as one-half of a double album repackage with *Prophets, Seers and Sages: The Angels of the Ages*, when it hit UK No.1. The resurrection of the 1975 Elvis Presley *40 Greatest Hits* collection was undoubtedly spurred on by his death in 1977.

top10 ALBUMS THAT STAYED LONGEST IN THE UK CHART

	TITLE / ARTIST/GROUP	YEAR OF ENTRY	TOTAL WEEKS
1	**Rumours**, Fleetwood Mac	1977	477
2	**Bat Out of Hell**, Meat Loaf	1978	473
3	**Greatest Hits**, Queen	1981	439
4 =	**The Sound of Music**, Soundtrack	1965	363
=	**Dark Side of The Moon**, Pink Floyd	1973	363
6	**Legend**, Bob Marley and the Wailers	1984	339
7	**Bridge Over Troubled Water**, Simon and Garfunkel	1970	307
8	**South Pacific**, Soundtrack	1958	288
9	**Greatest Hits**, Simon and Garfunkel	1972	283
10	**Tubular Bells**, Mike Oldfield	1973	276

Source: Music Information Database

The 10 longest-staying records virtually took up residence in the album charts (the Top 50, 75 or 100, depending on the years during which the charts were compiled), remaining there for periods ranging from over five years for *Tubular Bells* to the astonishing nine-year occupation of Meat Loaf's *Bat Out of Hell*. Uk long-stayer Fleetwood Mac's *Rumours* total included two chart re-entries in 1988 and 1997. In the USA, the album stayed at the top of the charts for 31 weeks, second only to the 37 weeks of Michael Jackson's *Thriller*, and sold 19 million copies.

top10 ARTISTS WITH THE MOST CONSECUTIVE UK TOP 10 ALBUMS

	ARTIST/GROUP	PERIOD	ALBUMS
1	Elvis Presley	Nov 1958–Jul 1964	17
2	Queen	Nov 1974–Jun 1989	14
3 =	Rolling Stones	Apr 1964–May 1971	13
=	David Bowie	May 1973–Jan 1981	13
=	Madonna	Feb 1984–Oct 2000	13
6 =	Bob Dylan	May 1965–Nov 1970	12
=	Bob Dylan	Feb 1974–Nov 1983	12
=	Depèche Mode	Nov 1981–Oct 1998	12
9 =	Cliff Richard	Apr 1959–Jul 1964	11
=	Led Zeppelin	Apr 1969–Oct 1990	11
=	Elton John	Jun 1972–Nov 1978	11

Source: Music Information Database

top10 ALBUMS WITH THE MOST CONSECUTIVE WEEKS AT NO.1 IN THE UK

	TITLE / ARTIST/GROUP / YEAR OF ENTRY	CONSECUTIVE WEEKS AT NO.1
1	**South Pacific**, Soundtrack, 1958	70
2	**Please Please Me**, The Beatles, 1963	30
3	**Sgt. Pepper's Lonely Hearts Club Band**, The Beatles, 1967	23
4 =	**With The Beatles**, The Beatles, 1963	21
=	**A Hard Day's Night**, The Beatles, 1964	21
6	**South Pacific**, Soundtrack, 1960	19
7 =	**The Sound of Music**, Soundtrack, 1966	18
=	**Saturday Night Fever**, Soundtrack, 1978	18
9	**Blue Hawaii**, Elvis Presley, 1962	17
10	**Summer Holiday**, Cliff Richard and the Shadows, 1963	14

Source: Music Information Database

↑ Twain makes her mark

Canadian singer Shania Twain's Come On Over *album has sold over 39 million copies worldwide, making it the bestselling of all time by a solo female artist.*

top10 ALBUMS OF **ALL TIME**

TITLE / ARTIST/GROUP	YEAR OF ENTRY
1 Thriller, Michael Jackson	1982
2 Dark Side of the Moon, Pink Floyd	1973
3 Their Greatest Hits 1971–1975, The Eagles	1976
4 The Bodyguard, Soundtrack	1992
5 Rumours, Fleetwood Mac	1977
6 Sgt. Pepper's Lonely Hearts Club Band, The Beatles	1967
7 Led Zeppelin IV, Led Zeppelin	1971
8 Greatest Hits, Elton John	1974
9 Come On Over, Shania Twain	1997
10 Jagged Little Pill, Alanis Morissette	1995

Total worldwide sales of albums have traditionally been notoriously hard to gauge, but even with the huge expansion of the album market during the 1980s, and multiple million sales of many major releases, this Top 10 is still élite territory.

top10 ALBUMS THAT STAYED **LONGEST AT NO.1** IN THE UK

TITLE / ARTIST/GROUP	WEEKS AT NO.1
1 South Pacific, Soundtrack	115
2 The Sound of Music, Soundtrack	70
3 Bridge Over Troubled Water, Simon and Garfunkel	41
4 Please Please Me, The Beatles	*30
5 Sgt. Pepper's Lonely Hearts Club Band, The Beatles	27
6 G.I. Blues, Elvis Presley/Soundtrack	22
7 = A Hard Day's Night, The Beatles/Soundtrack	*21
= With The Beatles, The Beatles	*21
9 = Blue Hawaii, Elvis Presley/Soundtrack	18
= Saturday Night Fever, Soundtrack	*18

* Continuous run

Source: Music Information Database

Male Solo Artists

top10 MALE SOLO ALBUMS IN THE UK, 2005

	TITLE	ARTIST
1	Back to Bedlam	James Blunt
2	Intensive Care	Robbie Williams
3	Curtain Call – The Hits	Eminem
4	Life in Slow Motion	David Gray
5	The Definitive Collection	Tony Christie
6	The Massacre	50 Cent
7	In Between Dreams	Jack Johnson
8	Trouble	Akon
9	Keep On	Will Young
10	It's Time	Michael Bublé

Source: The Official UK Charts Company

➔ Curtain call?
Eminem's 'greatest hits' compilation album Curtain Call was not released until December 2005, but its debut at UK No.1 ensured it a prominent place among the year's Top 10 releases. Its title prompted rumours that it was to be his last release.

top10 MALE SOLO SINGERS WITH THE MOST NO.1 SINGLES IN THE UK

	ARTIST/GROUP	NO.1 SINGLES
1	Elvis Presley	22
2	Cliff Richard	14
3	Michael Jackson	7
	= George Michael	7
5	= Eminem	6
	= Elton John	6
	= Rod Stewart	6
	= Robbie Williams	6
9	= Frank Ifield	4
	= Frankie Laine	4
	= Guy Mitchell	4
	= Will Young	4

Source: Music Information Database

top10 YOUNGEST MALE SOLO SINGERS TO HAVE A NO.1 SINGLE IN THE UK

	ARTIST / TITLE	YEAR	AGE* YRS	MTHS	DAYS
1	Little Jimmy Osmond, Long Haired Lover from Liverpool	1972	9	8	7
2	Donny Osmond, Puppy Love	1972	14	6	30
3	Paul Anka, Diana	1957	16	1	1
4	Gareth Gates", Unchained Melody	2002	17	8	18
5	Gareth Gates, Anyone of Us (Stupid Mistake)	2002	18	0	8
6	Glenn Medeiros, Nothing's Gonna Change My Love	1988	18	0	15
7	Craig Douglas, Only Sixteen	1959	18	0	27
8	Gareth Gates, Suspicious Minds	2002	18	2	23
9	Cliff Richard, Living Doll	1959	18	9	18
10	Craig David, Fill Me In	2000	18	11	0

* During first week of debut No.1 UK single
" Youngest British solo No.1

Source: Music Information Database

top10 ALBUMS BY MALE SOLO SINGERS IN THE UK

TITLE / SINGER / YEAR

1 Bad, Michael Jackson, 1987
2 Thriller, Michael Jackson, 1982
3 I've Been Expecting You, Robbie Williams, 1998
4 The Very Best of Elton John, Elton John, 1990
5 White Ladder, David Gray, 2000
6 Life Thru a Lens, Robbie Williams, 1997
7 But Seriously..., Phil Collins, 1989
8 Sing When You're Winning, Robbie Williams, 2000
9 Bat Out of Hell, Meat Loaf, 1978
10 Tubular Bells, Mike Oldfield, 1973

Source: Music Information Database

The certified sales of the Top 10 albums range from the 13 x platinum of Michael Jackson's *Bad* to the 7 x platinum of Mike Oldfield's *Tubular Bells*, equivalent to 3.9 million and 2.1 million, respectively. Sales at this sort of level achieved by Jackson's *Bad* and *Thriller* (11 x platinum, 3.3 million sales) mean that approximately one in every six British households, or one in every 15 inhabitants, owns a copy of one or both of these mega-sellers.

top10 SINGLES BY MALE SOLO SINGERS IN THE UK

TITLE / SINGER/GROUP / YEAR

1 Candle in the Wind (1997)/Something About the Way You Look Tonight, Elton John, 1997
2 Anything is Possible/Evergreen, Will Young, 2002
3 I Just Called to Say I Love You, Stevie Wonder, 1984
4 (Everything I Do) I Do It For You, Bryan Adams, 1991
5 Tears, Ken Dodd, 1965
6 Imagine, John Lennon, 1975
7 Careless Whisper, George Michael, 1984
8 Release Me, Engelbert Humperdinck, 1967
9 Unchained Melody, Gareth Gates, 2002
10 Diana, Paul Anka, 1957

Source: The Official UK Charts Company

This list represents a time shaft through the history of British popular music, with singles from each of the six decades reflecting the sometimes unpredictable taste of the British public for, predominantly, romantic ballads.

top10 TOURS IN THE US BY MALE SOLO ARTISTS, 2005*

ARTIST / TOTAL ($)

Neil Diamond
$71,339,710

Kenny Chesney
$63,029,422

Paul McCartney
$59,684,076

Rod Stewart
$48,943,773

Elton John
$45,524,280

Jimmy Buffett
$40,956,723

Toby Keith
$32,434,946

Bruce Springsteen
$31,752,514

Sting
$23,832,116

Eminem/50 Cent
$21,248,713

* November 17, 2004 to November 15, 2005

Source: 'Billboard' magazine

115

Female Solo Artists

top10 YOUNGEST FEMALE SOLO SINGERS TO HAVE A NO.1 SINGLE IN THE UK

	SINGER / TITLE	YEAR	YRS	AGE MTHS	DAYS
1	Helen Shapiro, You Don't Know	1961	14	10	13
2	Billie, Because We Want To	1998	15	9	20
3	Billie, Girlfriend	1998	16	0	25
4	Tiffany, I Think We're Alone Now	1988	16	3	28
5	Nicole, A Little Peace	1982	17	0	0
6	Britney Spears, ...Baby One More Time	1999	17	2	25
7	Sandie Shaw, (There's) Always Something There to Remind Me	1964	17	7	26
8	LeAnn Rimes, Can't Fight the Moonlight	2000	18	2	29
9	Mary Hopkin, Those Were the Days	1968	18	4	22
10	Sonia, You'll Never Stop Me Loving You	1989	18	5	9

Source: Music Information Database

The ages are those of each artist on the publication date of the chart in which she achieved her first No.1 single. All were teenagers when they had their first chart-toppers, as were Christina Aguilera and Connie Francis, who just fail to make the list.

top10 OLDEST FEMALE SOLO SINGERS TO HAVE A NO.1 SINGLE IN THE UK

	SINGER / TITLE	YEAR	YRS	AGE MTHS	DAYS
1	Cher, Believe	1998	52	5	12
2	Madonna, Hung Up	2005	47	3	4
3	Barbra Streisand, Woman in Love	1980	38	6	1
4	Vera Lynn, My Son, My Son	1954	37	7	25
5	Kylie Minogue, Slow	2003	35	5	18
6	Jennifer Lopez, Get Right	2005	34	7	3
7	Nicole Kidman, Something Stupid	2001	34	6	2
8	Kylie Minogue, Can't Get You Out of My Head	2001	33	4	1
9	Tammy Wynette, Stand By Your Man	1975	33	0	12
10	Kitty Kallen, Little Things Mean a Lot	1954	32	3	16

Source: Music Information Database

The ages shown are those of each artist on the publication date of the chart in which her last No.1 single reached the top. Coincidentally, since the other entries are of more recent vintage, two entries date from the same year – 1954 – when a decade after acquiring her status as the 'Forces' Sweetheart', Vera Lynn achieved her one and only No.1 record and Kitty Kallen her unique chart hit in the UK, where it hit the No.1 slot for a single week.

top10 SINGLES BY FEMALE SOLO SINGERS IN THE UK

	TITLE / SINGER	YEAR
1	Believe, Cher	1998
2	...Baby One More Time, Britney Spears	1999
3	I Will Always Love You, Whitney Houston	1992
4	My Heart Will Go On, Celine Dion	1998
5	The Power of Love, Jennifer Rush	1985
6	Think Twice, Celine Dion	1994
7	Saturday Night, Whigfield	1994
8	Can't Get You Out of My Head, Kylie Minogue	2001
9	Don't Cry For Me Argentina, Julie Covington	1976
10	Torn, Natalie Imbruglia	1997

Source: Music Information Database

Perhaps the most significant aspect of this list is how comparatively recent most of its entries are. Only one of these singles was released before 1980. Statistically, a female artist has stood a better chance of major chart success since the 1980s than in any of pop music's earlier eras.

top10 ALBUMS BY FEMALE SOLO SINGERS IN THE UK

	TITLE / SINGER	YEAR
1	The Immaculate Collection, Madonna	1990
2	Jagged Little Pill, Alanis Morissette	1995
3	Come On Over, Shania Twain	1997
4	No Angel, Dido	2000
5	Tracy Chapman, Tracy Chapman	1998
6	Simply the Best, Tina Turner	1991
7	Come Away with Me, Norah Jones	2002
8	Falling Into You, Celine Dion	1996
9	True Blue, Madonna	1986
10	Life For Rent, Dido	2003

Source: Music Information Database

the10 FIRST FEMALE SINGERS TO HAVE A NO.1 HIT IN THE UK

	ARTIST	TITLE	DATE AT NO.1
1	Jo Stafford	You Belong to Me	16 Jan 1953
2	Kay Starr	Comes A-Long A-Love	23 Jan 1953
3	Lita Roza	(How Much Is That) Doggie in the Window?	17 Apr 1953
4	Doris Day	Secret Love	16 Apr 1954
5	Kitty Kallen	Little Things Mean a Lot	10 Sep 1954
6	Vera Lynn	My Son, My Son	5 Nov 1954
7	Rosemary Clooney	This Ole House	26 Nov 1954
8	Ruby Murray	Softly Softly	18 Feb 1955
9	Alma Cogan	Dreamboat	15 Jul 1955
10	Anne Shelton	Lay Down Your Arms	21 Sep 1956

Source: Music Information Database

The UK singles chart was launched in November 1952. US singer Jo Stafford's *You Belong to Me* replaced the inaugural chart-topper (Al Martino's *Here In My Heart*), with Kay Starr's single becoming the UK's third chart-topper a week later. With a cover version of a US No.1 by Patti Page, Lita Roza became the first UK female artist to reach the summit, six months into the life of the chart.

⬆ Red hot
Despite reaching only No.7 on the UK album charts, Mariah Carey's The Emancipation of Mimi *sold solidly, in 2006 receiving the Grammy award for 'Best Contemporary R&B Album'.*

top10 ALBUMS BY FEMALE SOLO SINGERS IN THE UK, 2005

	TITLE	ARTIST
1	Eye to the Telescope	KT Tunstall
2	Breakaway	Kelly Clarkson
3	Piece By Piece	Katie Melua
4	Confessions on a Dance Floor	Madonna
5	Love. Angel. Music. Baby.	Gwen Stefani
6	The Emancipation of Mimi	Mariah Carey
7	Greatest Hits	Mariah Carey
8	Guilty Too	Barbra Streisand
9	Living a Dream	Katherine Jenkins
10	Mind Body & Soul	Joss Stone

Source: The Official UK Charts Company

Groups & Duos

top10 ALBUMS BY GROUPS OR DUOS IN THE UK, 2005

	TITLE	GROUP/DUO
1	X&Y	Coldplay
2	Employment	Kaiser Chiefs
3	Demon Days	Gorillaz
4	Face to Face	Westlife
5	Forever Faithless – The Greatest Hits	Faithless
6	Hot Fuss	Killers
7	Don't Believe The Truth	Oasis
8	Ancora	Il Divo
9	American Idiot	Green Day
10	Scissor Sisters	Scissor Sisters

Source: The Official UK Charts Company

top10 DUOS IN THE UK

	DUO	TOTAL CHART HITS
1	Pet Shop Boys	37
2	Erasure	31
3	= Everly Brothers	30
	= T. Rex	30
5	Eurythmics	29
6	Roxette	25
7	Everything But the Girl	23
8	Carpenters	21
9	= Basement Jaxx	17
	= Daryl Hall & John Oates	17
	= Tears For Fears	17

Source: Music Information Database

Pet Shop Boys started their chart career hesitantly: *West End Girls* was released in 1984 without charting, and it was not until a re-recorded version appeared over a year later that they began their glittering career, with four No.1s.

top10 GROUPS AND DUOS WITH THE MOST NO.1 SINGLES IN THE UK

	GROUP/DUO	NO.1 SINGLES
1	The Beatles	17
2	Westlife*	13
3	= Abba	9
	= The Spice Girls	9
5	= Oasis	8
	= Rolling Stones	8
	= Take That	8
8	U2	7
9	= Blondie	6
	= Boyzone	6
	= Slade	6

* Including one with Mariah Carey

Source: Music Information Database

top10 SINGLES BY GROUPS IN THE UK

	TITLE / GROUP	YEAR
1	Bohemian Rhapsody, Queen	1975
2	Mull of Kintyre/Girls' School, Wings	1977
3	Rivers of Babylon/Brown Girl in the Ring, Boney M	1978
4	Relax, Frankie Goes To Hollywood	1984
5	She Loves You, The Beatles	1963
6	Mary's Boy Child/Oh My Lord, Boney M	1978
7	Love is All Around, Wet Wet Wet	1994
8	I Want to Hold Your Hand, The Beatles	1963
9	Barbie Girl, Aqua	1997
10	Can't Buy Me Love, The Beatles	1964

Source: The Official UK Charts Company

Not only was Queen's *Bohemian Rhapsody* the biggest-selling single by a group in the UK, but more than one poll has ranked it at the top 10 of a list of '100 Greatest Singles' of all time. Its total sales in the UK alone are over 2.13 million.

top10 SINGLES BY DUOS IN THE UK

	TITLE / DUO	YEAR
1	You're The One That I Want, John Travolta and Olivia Newton-John	1978
2	Unchained Melody/(There'll Be Bluebirds Over the) White Cliffs of Dover, Robson and Jerome	1995
3	Summer Nights, John Travolta and Olivia Newton-John	1978
4	Last Christmas/Everything She Wants, Wham!	1984
5	Tainted Love, Soft Cell	1981
6	I Believe/Up On the Roof, Robson and Jerome	1995
7	Especially For You, Kylie Minogue and Jason Donovan	1988
8	Unchained Melody, Righteous Brothers	1990
9	Sweet Like Chocolate, Shanks and Bigfoot	1999
10	Truly Madly Deeply, Savage Garden	1998

Source: Music Information Database

Released in the UK on 1 May 1978, *You're The One That I Want* from *Grease*, the top film of the year, stayed at No.1 for eight weeks and in the charts for 26 weeks, achieving platinum status by 1 July. It was followed by *Summer Nights*, released 1 September, which stayed at No.1 for seven weeks and was certified platinum on 1 October, and two reaching No.2.

top10 **ALBUMS BY GROUPS** IN THE UK

TITLE / GROUP	YEAR
1 Sgt. Pepper's Lonely Hearts Club Band, The Beatles	1967
2 (What's the Story), Morning Glory, Oasis	1995
3 Brothers in Arms, Dire Straits	1985
4 Abba Gold Greatest Hits, Abba	1990
5 Stars, Simply Red	1991
6 Greatest Hits (Volume One), Queen	1981
7 Spice, The Spice Girls	1996
8 Rumours, Fleetwood Mac	1977
9 Talk On Corners, Corrs	1997
10 The Man Who, Travis	1999

Source: BPI

The Beatles' *Sgt. Pepper*, the seminal album from the 1967 'Summer of Love', sold 250,000 copies in the UK in its first week and 500,000 within the month, staying at No. 1 for 27 weeks.

⬆ *Tour de force*
Bono of U2, whose Vertigo tour topped $260 million in 2005.

top10 **TOURS** IN THE US, 2005*

ARTIST	TOTAL ($)
1 U2	260,119,588
2 Rolling Stones	140,845,375
3 The Eagles	116,907,647
4 Dave Matthews Band	45,015,384
5 Green Day	36,537,583
6 Motley Crue	33,785,715
7 Rascal Flatts	26,349,676
8 Coldplay	23,573,443
9 Trans-Siberian Orchestra	22,559,636
10 Tom Petty and the Heartbreakers	22,085,839

* 17 November 2004 to 15 November 2005

Source: 'Billboard' magazine

Gold & Platinum Discs

the first 10 GOLD ALBUMS IN THE UK

	ALBUM	ARTIST
1	Tubular Bells	Mike Oldfield
2	Goodbye Yellow Brick Road	Elton John
3	Bread Winners	Jack Jones
4	I'm a Writer Not a Fighter	Gilbert O'Sullivan
5	Goats Head Soup	The Rolling Stones
6	Sing It Again Rod	Rod Stewart
7	Pin Ups	David Bowie
8	We Can Make It	Peters & Lee
9	For Your Pleasure	Roxy Music
10	Sladest	Slade

Source: BPI

The BPI began awarding certifications in 1973, with Mike Oldfield's *Tubular Bells* being the sole recipient of a gold award on New Year's Day. The remaining nine records on this list were certified in October and November of that year.

↑ *Golden boys*
The Rolling Stones, still touring after 44 years, have earned 21 gold albums.

top 10 GROUPS WITH THE MOST GOLD ALBUMS IN THE UK

	GROUP	GOLD ALBUM AWARDS
1	Queen	25
2	The Rolling Stones	21
3	Status Quo	19
4	= The Beatles	16
	= Genesis	16
6	= Abba	15
	= UB40	15
8	= Iron Maiden	14
	= Roxy Music	14
10	U2	13

Source: BPI

Having careers that began in the 1960s, several of the groups listed would have qualified for even more gold discs if they had been awarded prior to their introduction by the BPI (British Phonographic Industry) on 1 April 1973. Gold awards are presented for sales of 100,000 albums, cassettes or CDs – but 200,000 for budget-priced products.

top 10 MALE ARTISTS WITH THE MOST PLATINUM ALBUMS IN THE UK

	ARTIST	PLATINUM ALBUM AWARDS
1	Robbie Williams	49
2	Michael Jackson	42
3	Phil Collins	34
4	Elton John	28
5	George Michael	25
6	Rod Stewart	19
7	Meat Loaf	17
8	= Chris Rea	15
	= Cliff Richard	15
10	Eminem	14

Source: BPI

Platinum albums in the UK are those that have achieved sales of 300,000. In the UK multi-platinum albums are those that have sold multiples of 300,000, so a quadruple platinum album denotes sales of 1.2 million units and so on. A UK platinum certification represents about one sale per 200 inhabitants, in contrast to the USA's ratio of one sale per 300 people.

top 10 MALE ARTISTS WITH THE MOST GOLD ALBUMS IN THE UK

	ARTIST	GOLD ALBUM AWARDS
1	Rod Stewart	27
2	Cliff Richard*	25
3	Elton John	24
4	Paul McCartney#	21
5	= David Bowie	18
	= Neil Diamond	18
7	= James Last†	17
	= Elvis Presley	17
9	Mike Oldfield	16
10	Prince☆	15

* Including two with the Shadows
# Including eight with Wings
† Including two with Richard Clayderman
☆ Including one with the New Power Generation

Source: BPI

Gold discs have been awarded in the UK by the BPI (British Phonographic Industry) since 1 April 1973. They are presented for sales of 400,000 singles or 100,000 albums, cassettes or CDs – but 200,000 for budget-priced products.

top10 FEMALE ARTISTS WITH THE MOST GOLD ALBUMS IN THE UK

	ARTIST	GOLD ALBUM AWARDS
1	Diana Ross*	18
2	Barbra Streisand#	17
3	Madonna	15
4	Mariah Carey	12
5	Celine Dion†	11
6	Donna Summer	10
7	= Cher	9
	= Tina Turner	9
9	= Kate Bush	8
	= Kylie Minogue	8

* Including one with Marvin Gaye and one with Michael Jackson
# Including one with Kris Kristofferson and one with Celine Dion
† Including one with Barbra Streisand

Source: BPI

With a gold award for her *Love and Life* album in 2001, Diana Ross has received gold discs for releases across four decades.

→ Platinum blonde
Madonna's 22-year UK album career has seen her with all 17 albums entering the Top 10 and 9 reaching No.1. Most have achieved sustained sales – hence her more than twice as many platinum albums as her closest rival Celine Dion. With overall album sales in decline, Madonna's place in this list seems unassailable.

top10 FEMALE ARTISTS WITH THE MOST PLATINUM ALBUMS IN THE UK

	ARTIST	PLATINUM ALBUM AWARDS
1	Madonna	49
2	Celine Dion	24
3	Tina Turner	22
4	Kylie Minogue	20
5	Whitney Houston*	18
6	Dido	16
7	Shania Twain	15
8	Enya	13
9	= Cher	11
	= Alanis Morissette	11

* Not including the album, *The Bodyguard*

Source: BPI

top10 GROUPS WITH THE MOST PLATINUM ALBUMS IN THE UK

	GROUP	PLATINUM ALBUM AWARDS
1	Simply Red	44
2	U2	37
3	Queen	36
4	Oasis	34
5	Dire Straits	27
6	Fleetwood Mac	26
7	Westlife	24
8	Abba	22
9	R.E.M.	20
10	Coldplay	19

Source: BPI

the10 LATEST WINNERS OF THE BRIT AWARD FOR **BEST BRITISH GROUP**

YEAR	GROUP
2006	Kaiser Chiefs
2005	Franz Ferdinand
2004	The Darkness
2003	Coldplay
2002	Travis
2001	Coldplay
2000	Travis
1999	Manic Street Preachers
1998	The Verve
1997	Manic Street Preachers

A precursor of the BRITs in 1977 presented this award to the Beatles – even though the group had split in 1970. It became an annual event in 1982 when first winner in this category was Police. Double winners include Dire Straits, Travis and Coldplay.

the10 LATEST WINNERS OF THE BRIT AWARD FOR **BEST SINGLE BY A BRITISH ARTIST**

YEAR	TITLE	ARTIST / GROUP
2006	Speed of Sound	Coldplay
2005	Your Game	Will Young
2004	White Flag	Dido
2003	Just a Little	Liberty X
2002	Don't Stop Movin'	S Club 7
2001	Rock DJ	Robbie Williams
2000	She's the One	Robbie Williams
1999	Angels	Robbie Williams
1998	Never Ever	All Saints
1997	Wannabe	The Spice Girls

At the 1977 awards, this category was shared by two singles that have since become regarded as British classics: Queen's *Bohemian Rhapsody* and Procol Harum's *A White Shade of Pale*.

the10 LATEST WINNERS OF THE BRIT AWARD FOR **BEST BRITISH MALE SOLO ARTIST**

YEAR	ARTIST
2006	James Blunt
2005	The Streets
2004	Daniel Bedingfield
2003	Robbie Williams
2002	Robbie Williams
2001	Robbie Williams
2000	Tom Jones
1999	Robbie Williams
1998	Finlay Quaye
1997	George Michael

Cliff Richard was the first winner in this category in 1977, and again in 1982. Robbie Williams's three consecutive wins and total of four are unique. Phil Collins has also won this award three times.

the10 LATEST WINNERS OF THE BRIT AWARD FOR **OUTSTANDING CONTRIBUTION TO MUSIC***

YEAR	ARTIST
2006	Paul Weller
2005	Bob Geldof
2004	Duran Duran
2003	Tom Jones
2002	Sting
2001	U2
2000	Spice Girls
1999	Eurythmics
1998	Fleetwood Mac
1997	Bee Gees

* Formerly 'Outstanding Contribution to the British Record Industry'

The first award in 1977 was shared between L.G. Wood of record company EMI and the Beatles. John Lennon in 1982 and Freddie Mercury in 1992 both received the award posthumously.

the10 LATEST WINNERS OF THE BRIT AWARD FOR **BEST BRITISH FEMALE SOLO ARTIST**

YEAR	ARTIST
2006	KT Tunstall
2005	Joss Stone
2004	Dido
2003	Ms Dynamite
2002	Dido
2001	Sonique
2000	Beth Orton
1999	Des'ree
1998	Shola Ama
1997	Gabrielle

Between 1984 and 1996, Annie Lennox won this award on a record six occasions. No other singer has come close, with only Alison Moyet, Lisa Stansfield and Dido achieving double wins.

the10 LATEST WINNERS OF THE BRIT AWARD FOR **BEST BRITISH BREAKTHROUGH ARTIST***

YEAR	ARTIST
2006	Arctic Monkeys
2005	Keane
2004	Busted
2003	Will Young
2002	Blue
2001	A1
2000	S Club 7
1999	Belle and Sebastian
1998	Stereophonics
1997	Kula Shaker

* 'Best British Newcomer' until 2002

This category has proved both prophetic in identifying solo singers and groups at the beginning of their careers, who have gone on to achieve critical and commercial success, and some whose subsequent performance has been unremarkable.

the10 LATEST WINNERS OF THE BRIT AWARD FOR **BEST BRITISH ALBUM***

YEAR	ALBUM	ARTIST
2006	X&Y	Coldplay
2005	Hopes and Fears	Keane
2004	Permission to Land	The Darkness
2003	A Rush of Blood to the Head	Coldplay
2002	No Angel	Dido
2001	Parachutes	Coldplay
2000	The Man Who	Travis
1999	This is My Truth, Tell Me Yours	Manic Street Preachers
1998	Urban Hymns	The Verve
1997	Everything Must Go	Manic Street Preachers

* Previously 'Best Album'

➔ *Coldplay's code play*
The cover of 2006 winners Chris Martin and Coldplay's third album X&Y depicts its title converted into an alphanumeric coding.

Classical Music

top10 CLASSICAL WORKS*

COMPOSER / TITLE

1 Sergei Rachmaninov, Piano Concerto No. 2 in C minor
2 Ralph Vaughan Williams, The Lark Ascending
3 Wolfgang Amadeus Mozart, Clarinet Concerto in A
4 Ludwig van Beethoven,
  Piano Concerto No. 5 in E flat major (The Emperor)
5 Max Bruch, Violin Concerto No. 1 in G minor
6 Ludwig van Beethoven, Symphony No. 6 Pastoral
7 Edward Elgar, Cello Concerto in E minor
8 Edward Elgar, Enigma Variations
9 Karl Jenkins, The Armed Man (A Mass for Peace)
10 Edvard Grieg, Piano Concerto in A minor

* Based on Classic FM Hall of Fame 2005

⏻ *Grand opera*
*The restored Roman amphitheatre of Verona, Italy, is the world's largest venue
that regularly stages opera, especially during the city's annual festival.*

top10 WORKS BY BRITISH COMPOSERS*

COMPOSER / TITLE

1 Ralph Vaughan Williams, The Lark Ascending
2 Edward Elgar, Cello Concerto in E minor
3 Edward Elgar, Enigma Variations
4 Karl Jenkins, The Armed Man (A Mass for Peace)
5 Ralph Vaughan Williams,
  Fantasia on a Theme by Thomas Tallis
6 Gustav Holst, The Planets
7 George Friedrich Handel, Messiah
8 George Friedrich Handel, Zadok the Priest
9 George Friedrich Handel, Solomon
10 Peter Maxwell Davies, Farewell to Stromness

* Based on Classic FM Hall of Fame 2005

top10 LARGEST **OPERA THEATRES**

	THEATRE	LOCATION	CAPACITY*
1	Arena di Verona#	Verona, Italy	15,000
2	Metropolitan Opera House	New York, USA	3,800
3	NHK Hall	Tokyo, Japan	3,677
4	Civic Opera House	Chicago, USA	3,563
5	Music Hall	Cincinnati, USA	3,516
6	Music Hall	Dallas, USA	3,420
7	War Memorial Opera House	San Francisco, USA	3,176
8	The Hummingbird Centre	Toronto, Canada	3,167
9	Dorothy Chandler Pavilion	Los Angeles, USA	3,098
10	Civic Theatre	San Diego, USA	2,992
	Royal Opera House	*London, UK*	*2,267*

* Seating capacity only, excluding standing
# Open-air venue

Although there are many more venues in the world where opera is also performed, such as the 13,000-seat Municipal Opera Theatre ('Muny') open-air auditorium, St Louis, USA, this list is limited to those where the principal performances are opera.

top10 MOST PROLIFIC **CLASSICAL COMPOSERS**

	COMPOSER / NATIONALITY / DATES	HOURS OF MUSIC
1	Joseph Haydn (Austrian; 1732–1809)	340
2	George Handel (German-English; 1685–1759)	303
3	Wolfgang Amadeus Mozart (Austrian; 1756–91)	202
4	Johann Sebastian Bach (German; 1685–1750)	175
5	Franz Schubert (German; 1797–1828)	134
6	Ludwig van Beethoven (German; 1770–1827)	120
7	Henry Purcell (English; 1659–95)	116
8	Giuseppe Verdi (Italian; 1813–1901)	87
9	Anton Dvorák (Czech; 1841–1904)	79
10	= Franz Liszt (Hungarian; 1811–86)	76
	= Peter Tchaikovsky (Russian; 1840–93)	76

This list is based on a survey conducted by *Classical Music* magazine, which ranked classical composers by the total number of hours of music each composed. If the length of the composer's working life is brought into the calculation, Schubert wins: his 134 hours were composed in a career of 18 years, giving an average of 7 hours 27 minutes per annum. The same method would place Tchaikovsky ahead of Liszt: although both composed 76 hours of music, Tchaikovsky worked for 30 years and Liszt for 51, giving them annual averages of 2 hours 32 minutes and 1 hour 29 minutes, respectively.

top10 **CLASSICAL ALBUMS** IN THE UK

	TITLE	PERFORMER / ORCHESTRA	YEAR
1	The Three Tenors In Concert	José Carreras, Placido Domingo, Luciano Pavarotti	1990
2	Il Divo	Il Divo	2004
3	The Essential Pavarotti	Luciano Pavarotti	1990
4	Ancora	Il Divo	2005
5	Vivaldi: The Four Seasons	Nigel Kennedy/English Chamber Orchestra	1989
6	The Three Tenors – In Concert 1994	José Carreras, Placido Domingo, Luciano Pavarotti, Zubin Mehta	1994
7	The Voice	Russell Watson	2000
8	Voice of an Angel	Charlotte Church	1998
9	Pure	Hayley Westenra	2003
10	Encore	Russell Watson	2002

Source: Music Information Database

top10 OPERAS **MOST FREQUENTLY PERFORMED** AT THE ROYAL OPERA HOUSE, COVENT GARDEN, 1833–2005

	OPERA	COMPOSER	FIRST PERFORMANCE	TOTAL*
1	La Bohème	Giacomo Puccini	2 Oct 1897	545
2	Carmen	Georges Bizet	27 May 1882	495
3	Aïda	Giuseppi Verdi	22 Jun 1876	481
4	Rigoletto	Giuseppi Verdi	14 May 1853	465
5	Faust	Charles Gounod	18 Jul 1863	442
6	Tosca	Giacomo Puccini	12 Jul 1900	415
7	Don Giovanni	Wolfgang Amadeus Mozart	17 Apr 1834	414
8	La Traviata	Giuseppi Verdi	25 May 1858	391
9	Madama Butterfly	Giacomo Puccini	10 Jul 1905	366
10	Norma	Vincenzo Bellini	12 Jul 1833	355

* To 1 Jan 2005

Most of the works listed were first performed at Covent Garden within a few years of their world premieres (in the case of *Tosca*, in the same year). Although some were considered controversial at the time, all of them are now regarded as important components of the classic opera repertoire.

Musicals

⬆ *... and all that jazz*
Chicago's earnings of $300 million worldwide make it the highest-earning musical film of the 21st century.

top10 MUSICAL **FILMS OF THE 1960S**

FILM	YEAR
1 The Sound of Music	1965
2 Mary Poppins	1964
3 My Fair Lady	1964
4 Funny Girl	1968
5 Let's Make Love	1960
6 West Side Story	1961
7 Oliver!	1968
8 Thoroughly Modern Millie	1967
9 Hello Dolly!	1969
10 Paint Your Wagon	1969

Improvements in colour and sound technology prompted a wave of popular musicals in the 1960s. With the exception of *Mary Poppins*, the entire Top 10 were successful stage productions.

top10 FAVOURITE **MUSICALS IN THE UK**

FILM
1 Les Misérables
2 The Phantom of the Opera
3 Seven Brides for Seven Brothers
4 The King and I
5 Sunset Boulevard
6 Evita
7 Chess
8 The Rocky Horror Show
9 Follies
10 Hair

Source: BBC Radio 2

A six-month survey of 50 candidate shows conducted by BBC Radio 2 in 2005 received 400,000 votes: *Les Misérables* achieved some 40 per cent of the total.

top10 **MUSICAL** FILMS

FILM	YEAR
1 Grease	1978
2 Chicago	2002
3 Saturday Night Fever	1977
4 8 Mile	2002
5 Moulin Rouge!	2001
6 The Sound of Music	1965
7 The Phantom of the Opera	2004
8 Evita	1996
9 The Rocky Horror Picture Show	1975
10 Staying Alive	1983

Traditional musicals (films in which the cast actually sing) and films in which a musical soundtrack is a major component of the film are included here. With a few notable exceptions, in recent years animated films with an important musical content appear to have taken over from these, with *Beauty and the Beast*, *Aladdin*, *The Lion King*, *Pocahontas*, *The Prince of Egypt*, *Tarzan* and *Monsters, Inc.* also winning Best Original Song Oscars.

top10 **LONGEST-RUNNING** MUSICALS **ON BROADWAY**

	SHOW	RUN	PERFORMANCES
1	The Phantom of the Opera	26 Jan 1988–	7,579*
2	Cats	23 Sep 1982–10 Sep 2000	7,485
3	Les Misérables	12 Mar 1987–18 May 2003	6,680
4	A Chorus Line	25 Jul 1975–28 Apr 1990	6,137
5	Beauty and the Beast	9 Mar 1994–	4,909*
6	Miss Saigon	11 Apr 1991–28 Jan 2001	4,092
7	Rent	29 Apr 1996–	4,141*
8	Chicago	14 Nov 1996–	3,894*
9	The Lion King	13 Nov 1997–	3,526*
10	42nd Street	18 Aug 1980–8 Jan 1989	3,486*

* Still running; total as at 31 March 2006

All the longest-running musicals date from the past 40 years. Prior to these record-breakers, the longest runner of the 1940s was *Oklahoma!*, which debuted in 1943 and ran for 2,212 performances up to 1948, and from the 1950s *My Fair Lady*, which opened in 1956 and closed in 1962 after 2,717 performances. With 3,388 performances, *Grease* – which opened in 1972 and closed in 1980 – just fails to enter the Top 10.

top10 **LONGEST-RUNNING** MUSICALS **IN THE UK**

	SHOW / RUN	PERFORMANCES*
1	Cats (1981–2002)	8,949
2	Les Misérables (1985–)	8,434#
3	The Phantom of the Opera (1986–)	8,099#
4	Starlight Express (1984–2002)	7,406
5	Miss Saigon (1989–99)	4,263
6	Jesus Christ, Superstar (1972–80)	3,357
7	Evita (1978–86)	2,900
8	Oliver! (1960–66)	2,618
9	The Sound of Music (1961–67)	2,386
10	Salad Days (1954–60)	2,283

* Continuous runs only
# Still running; total as at 31 March 2006

Despite closing at the Palace Theatre on 27 March 2004 and reopening at the Queen's Theatre on 3 April 2004, *Les Misérables* has been included as a continuous run, since it was the same production with the same cast.

the10 **LATEST WINNERS** OF THE LAURENCE OLIVIER AWARD FOR BEST NEW MUSICAL

YEAR	MUSICAL
2006	Billy Elliot
2005	The Producers
2004	Jerry Springer – The Opera
2003	Our House
2001*	Merrily We Roll Along
2000	Honk! The Ugly Duckling
1999	Kat and the Kings
1998	Beauty and the Beast
1997	Martin Guerre
1996	Jolson

* No award in 2002

➲ Top Cats
On 11 May 2001, Cats ended its London run on its 21st birthday, establishing an as-yet unbroken record as the UK's longest-running musical.

STAGE & SCREEN

Theatre

top10 **LONGEST-RUNNING NON-MUSICALS** IN THE UK

SHOW	PERFORMANCES
1 The Mousetrap (1952–)	22,227*
2 The Woman in Black (1989–)	6,866*
3 No Sex, Please – We're British (1971–81; 1982–86; 1986–87)	6,761
4 The Complete Works of William Shakespeare (abridged) (1996–2005)	4,266
5 Oh! Calcutta! (1970–74; 1974–80)	3,918
6 Run for Your Wife (1983–91)	2,638
7 There's a Girl in My Soup (1966–69; 1969–72)	2,547
8 Pyjama Tops (1969–75)	2,498
9 Sleuth (1970; 1972; 1973–75)	2,359
10 Worm's Eye View (1945–51)	2,245

* Still running; total as at 31 March 2006

Oh! Calcutta! is included here as it is regarded as a revue with music, rather than a musical.

the **LONGEST-RUNNING SHOWS** OF ALL TIME

SHOW / LOCATION / RUN	PERFORMANCES
1 The Golden Horseshoe Revue (Disneyland, California, 16 Jul 1955–12 Oct 86)	47,250
2 The Mousetrap (London, 25 Nov 1952–)	22,227*
3 The Fantasticks (New York, 3 May 1960–13 Jan 2002)	17,162
4 La Cantatrice Chauve (The Bald Soprano) (Paris, 16 Feb 1957–)	15,588*
5 Shear Madness (Boston, 31 Jan 1980–)	10,959*
6 The Drunkard (Los Angeles, 6 Jul 1933–17 Oct 1959)	9,477
7 The Mousetrap (Toronto, 19 Aug 1977–18 Jan 2004)	9,000
8 Cats (London, 11 May 1981–11 May 2002)	8,949
9 Les Misérables (London, 8 Oct 1985–)	8,434*
10 The Phantom of the Opera (London, 1986–)	8,099*

* Still running; total as at 31 March 2006

🕐 *Prince among actors*
American actor John Barrymore (1882–1942), the grandfather of film actress Drew Barrymore, was famed for his mastery of the demanding role of Hamlet, which he performed over 100 times in 1922–25.

top10 LONGEST SHAKESPEAREAN ROLES

	ROLE	PLAY	LINES
1	Hamlet	Hamlet	1,422
2	Falstaff	Henry IV, Parts I and II	1,178
3	Richard III	Richard III	1,124
4	Iago	Othello	1,097
5	Henry V	Henry V	1,025
6	Othello	Othello	860
7	Vincentio	Measure for Measure	820
8	Coriolanus	Coriolanus	809
9	Timon	Timon of Athens	795
10	Antony	Antony and Cleopatra	766

Hamlet's role comprises 11,610 words, but if multiple plays are considered, he is beaten by Falstaff who appears in *Henry IV*, Parts I and II, and in *The Merry Wives of Windsor*, his total of 1,614 lines making him the most talkative of all Shakespeare's characters. However, if more than one play (or parts of a play) are taken into account, others would increase their tallies, among them Richard III, who appears (as Richard, Duke of Gloucester) in *Henry VI*, Part III, and Henry V who appears (as Prince Hal) in *Henry IV*, where he speaks 117 lines, making his total 1,142. Rosalind's 668-line role in *As You Like It* is the longest female part in Shakespeare's works.

the10 LATEST WINNERS OF THE LAURENCE OLIVIER AWARD FOR BEST NEW PLAY*

YEAR#	PLAY	PLAYWRIGHT
2006	On the Shore of the Wide World	Simon Stephens
2005	The History Boys	Alan Bennett
2004	The Pillowman	Martin McDonagh
2003	Vincent in Brixton	Nicholas Wright
2002	Jitney	August Wilson
2001	Blue/Orange	Marie Jones
2000	Goodnight Children Everywhere	Richard Nelson
1999	The Weir	Conor McPherson
1998	Closer	Patrick Marber
1997	Stanley	Pam Gems

* 'BBC Award for Best Play' until 1996; 'Best New Play' thereafter
# Awards are for plays staged during the previous year

Presented by The Society of London Theatres (founded 1908), the award itself depicts Laurence (later Lord) Olivier (1907–89), after whom it is named in his celebrated role as Henry V at the Old Vic in 1937. Several earlier winners went on to become successful films, among them *Whose Life is it Anyway?* (play 1978, film 1981), *Glengarry Glen Ross* (1983/92) and *Les Liaisons Dangereuses* (1986/88 – as *Dangerous Liaisons*).

top10 MOST PRODUCED PLAYS BY SHAKESPEARE, 1878–2005

	PLAY	PRODUCTIONS
1	As You Like It	79
2 =	Twelfth Night	77
3 =	Hamlet	76
=	The Taming of the Shrew	76
5	A Midsummer Night's Dream	72
6	Much Ado About Nothing	71
7	The Merchant of Venice	70
8	Macbeth	66
9	The Merry Wives of Windsor	61
10	Romeo and Juliet	59

Source: Shakespeare Centre

This list is based on an analysis of Shakespearean productions rather than individual performances – 31 December 1878 to 31 December 2005 – at Stratford upon Avon and by the Royal Shakespeare Company in London and on tour.

top10 OLDEST LONDON THEATRES

	THEATRE	OPENING SHOW	OPENED
1	Theatre Royal, Drury Lane	The Humorous Lieutenant	7 May 1663
2	Sadler's Wells, Rosebery Avenue	Musical performances	3 Jun 1683
3	The Haymarket (Theatre Royal), Haymarket	La Fille à la Mode	29 Dec 1720
4	Royal Opera House, Covent Garden	The Way of the World	7 Dec 1732
5	The Adelphi (originally Sans Pareil), Strand	The Rout/Tempest Terrific/Vision in the Holyland	17 Nov 1806
6	The Old Vic (originally Royal Coburg), Waterloo Road	Trial by Battle/Alzora and Nerine/Midnight Revelry	11 May 1818
7	The Vaudeville, Strand	For Love or Money	16 Apr 1870
8	The Criterion, Piccadilly Circus	An American Lady	21 Mar 1874
9	The Savoy, Strand	Patience	10 Oct 1881
10	The Comedy, Panton Street	La Mascotte	15 Oct 1881

These are London's 10 oldest theatres still operating on their original sites – although most of them have been rebuilt, some several times. The Lyceum, built in 1771 as 'a place of entertainment', was not originally licensed as a theatre and, in its early years, was used for such events as circuses and exhibitions, with only occasional theatrical performances. The Savoy was gutted by fire in 1990, but was completely rebuilt and reopened in 1993.

Movie Mosts

Except where otherwise stated, film lists are ranked on cumulative world box office income. In keeping with the industry standard, in order to compare on a like-for-like basis, these are gross totals and disregard production and marketing costs (which are unreliable and often either exaggerated or understated), earnings from subsequent DVD releases and TV broadcasts. Inflation is also not taken into account. Unless they are meaningful (as with those comparing film opening weekends), the precise amounts are omitted.

top10 LONGEST FILMS EVER SCREENED

	TITLE	DIRECTOR/COUNTRY/YEAR	DURATION HR	MIN
1	The Cure for Insomnia	John Henry Timmis IV, USA, 1987	87	0
2	The Longest and Most Meaningless Movie in the World	Vincent Patouillard, UK, 1970	48	0
3	The Burning of the Red Lotus Temple	Star Film Company, China, 1928–31	27	0
4	Die Zweite Heimat	Edgar Reitz, West Germany, 1992	25	32
5	**** (aka Four Stars)	Andy Warhol, USA, 1967	25	0
6	Heimat - Eine deutsche Chronik	Edgar Reitz, West Germany, 1984	15	40
7	Berlin Alexanderplatz	Rainer Werner Fassbinder, West Germany/Italy, 1980	15	21
8	Resan (The Journey)	Peter Watkins, Sweden, 1987	14	33
9	Comment Yukong déplaca les montagnes (How Yukong moved the mountains)	Joris Ivens and Marceline Lorigan, France, 1976	12	43
10	Out 1: Noli me Tangere	Jacques Rivette and Suzanne Schiffman, France, 1971	12	9

Although the list includes such 'stunt' films as Andy Warhol's ****, all those listed have been screened commercially. *The Cure for Insomnia*, which depicts L .D. Groban reciting a 4,080-page poem, was shown in a cinema just once, in Chicago from 31 January to 3 February 1987. *The Longest and Most Meaningless Movie in the World* was later cut to a more manageable 1 hour 30 minutes, but remained just as meaningless.

⊙ A cast of thousands
The funeral sequence in Gandhi *was filmed on the anniversary of the event. The final screen time lasted just 2 minutes 5 seconds, but featured the greatest-ever crowd of extras.*

top10 FILMS WITH THE MOST EXTRAS

	FILM/COUNTRY/YEAR	EXTRAS
1	Gandhi*, UK, 1982	294,560
2	Kolberg, Germany, 1945	187,000
3	Monster Wangmagwi, South Korea, 1967	157,000
4	War and Peace, USSR, 1968	120,000
5	Ilya Muromets (The Sword and the Dragon)#, USSR, 1956	106,000
6	Dun-Huang (aka Ton ko), Japan, 1988	100,000
7	Razboiul independentei (The War of Independence), Romania, 1912	80,000
8	Around the World in 80 Days*, US, 1956	68,894
9 =	Intolerance, US, 1916	60,000
=	Dny Zrady (Days of Betrayal), Czechoslovakia, 1973	60,000

* Won 'Best Picture' Oscar
# Won 'Best Foreign Language' Oscar

Unlike the enormous numbers of extras in these films, the vast crowd scenes in recent productions, such as *The Lord of the Rings* trilogy, were computer generated.

top10 **FILM-PRODUCING** COUNTRIES

	COUNTRY	FEATURE FILMS PRODUCED (2004)
1	India	946
2	USA	611
3	Japan	310
4	China	212
5	France	203
6	Italy	134
7	Spain	133
8	UK	132
9	Germany	121
10	Russia	120

Source: Screen Digest

Based on the number of full-length feature films produced, Hollywood's 'golden age' was the 1920s and 1930s, with a peak of 854 films made in 1921, and its nadir 1978 with just 354. Even the output of India's mighty film industry has dwindled since 2002, when some 1,200 films were made.

➔ Monster budget
The estimated production budget of King Kong set a new record – and was more than 300 times greater than the $670,000 of the 1933 original – but it is set to be eclipsed by ever-more costly films.

top10 COUNTRIES WITH THE **MOST** CINEMA SCREENS

	COUNTRY	NUMBER OF CINEMA SCREENS (2004)
1	China	42,400
2	USA	36,594
3	India	11,000
4	France	5,295
5	Germany	4,870
6	Spain	4,388
7	Italy	3,566
8	UK	3,474
9	Mexico	3,197
10	Canada	2,974

Source: Film Distributors' Association

top10 FILM **BUDGETS**

	FILM	YEAR	BUDGET ($)
1	=Spider-Man 3	2007*	250,000,000
	=Superman Returns	2006	250,000,000
3	King Kong	2005	207,000,000
4	=Battle Angel	2007*	200,000,000
	=Spider-Man 2	2004	200,000,000
	=Titanic	1997	200,000,000
7	=Waterworld	1995	175,000,000
	=Wild, Wild West	1999	175,000,000
9	=The Polar Express	2004	170,000,000
	=Terminator 3: Rise of the Machines	2003	170,000,000
	=Van Helsing	2005	170,000,000

* Scheduled release

Film Hits

top10 FILMS OF **ALL TIME**

	FILM	YEAR	USA	GROSS INCOME ($) OVERSEAS	WORLD TOTAL
1	Titanic*	1997	600,788,188	1,244,246,000	1,845,034,188
2	The Lord of the Rings: The Return of the King*	2003	377,027,325	752,191,927	1,129,219,252
3	Harry Potter and the Sorcerer's Stone	2001	317,575,550	668,242,109	985,817,659
4	The Lord of the Rings: The Two Towers	2002	341,786,758	584,500,642	926,287,400
5	Star Wars: Episode I – The Phantom Menace	1999	431,088,297	493,229,257	924,317,554
6	Shrek 2#	2004	441,226,247	479,439,411	920,665,658
7	Jurassic Park	1993	357,067,947	562,636,053	919,700,000
8	Harry Potter and the Goblet of Fire	2005	288,801,149	601,400,000	890,201,149
9	Harry Potter and the Chamber of Secrets	2002	261,988,482	614,700,000	876,688,482
10	The Lord of the Rings: The Fellowship of the Ring	2001	314,776,170	556,592,194	871,368,364

* Won Best Picture Oscar
# Animated

Prior to the release of *Star Wars* in 1977, no film had ever made over $500 million globally. Since then, some 43 films have done so. *Titanic* remains the only film to have made over this amount in the USA alone, and just 11 films have exceeded this total outside the USA. To date, those in the Top 10, together with *Finding Nemo* (2003), *Star Wars: Episode III – Revenge of the Sith* (2005), *Spider-Man* (2002) and *Independence Day* (1996), are the only films to have earned over $800 million worldwide.

top10 **MOST PROFITABLE** FILMS OF ALL TIME*

	FILM	YEAR	BUDGET ($)	WORLD GROSS ($)	PROFIT RATIO
1	The Blair Witch Project	1999	35,000	248,662,839	7,104.65
2	American Graffiti	1973	750,000	115,000,000	153.33
3	Snow White and the Seven Dwarfs#	1937	1,488,000	187,670,866	126.12
4	The Rocky Horror Picture Show	1975	1,200,000	139,876,417	116.56
5	Rocky†	1976	1,100,000	117,235,147	106.58
6	Gone With the Wind†	1939	3,900,000	400,176,459	102.61
7	E.T. The Extra-Terrestrial	1982	10,500,000	792,910,554	75.52
8	My Big Fat Greek Wedding	2002	5,000,000	368,744,044	73.75
9	The Full Monty	1997	3,500,000	257,850,122	73.67
10	Star Wars☆	1977	11,000,000	775,398,007	70.49

* Minimum entry $100 million world gross
# Animated
† Won Best Picture Oscar
☆ Later retitled 'Star Wars: Episode IV – A New Hope'

top10 FILMS **WORLDWIDE**, 2005

	FILM	WORLDWIDE GROSS ($)*
1	Harry Potter and the Goblet of Fire	888,733,970
2	Star Wars: Episode III – Revenge of the Sith	848,480,152
3	The Chronicles of Narnia: The Lion, the Witch and the Wardrobe	663,891,914
4	War of the Worlds	591,413,297
5	King Kong	543,007,743
6	Madagascar#	527,890,631
7	Mr. and Mrs. Smith	477,671,954
8	Charlie and the Chocolate Factory	473,425,317
9	Batman Begins	371,853,783
10	Hitch	368,100,420

* Including income from ongoing US and overseas releases through 2006
# Animated

top10 **BLACK & WHITE** FEATURE FILMS

	FILM	YEAR
1	Young Frankenstein	1974
2	Manhattan	1979
3	Good Night, and Good Luck.	2005
4	Psycho	1960
5	Mom and Dad	1944
6	Paper Moon	1973
7	From Here to Eternity	1953
8	Some Like It Hot	1959
9	The Best Years of Our Lives*	1946
10	Lenny	1974

* Won Best Picture Oscar

These are exclusively monochrome films, rather than combination black and white and colour films (monochrome films with colour sequences, or vice versa), a category that would be led by *Schindler's List* (1993). The Top 10 includes some recent examples where the director opted for black and white rather than colour for aesthetic reasons, often to create the atmosphere of an earlier period.

⬆ Star turn
Star Wars: Episode III – Revenge of the Sith, *the world's top-earning film in 2005, completed the 28-year, six-episode* Star Wars *saga.*

top10 FILMS IN THE UK BY **ATTENDANCE**

	FILM	YEAR	ESTIMATED ATTENDANCE
1	Gone With The Wind*	1940	35,000,000
2	The Sound of Music*	1965	30,000,000
3	Snow White and the Seven Dwarfs	1938	28,000,000
4	Star Wars	1977	20,760,000
5	Spring in Park Lane	1948	20,500,000
6	The Best Years of Our Lives*	1947	20,400,000
7	The Jungle Book#	1968	19,800,000
8	Titanic*	1998	18,910,000
9	The Wicked Lady	1946	18,400,000
10	The Seventh Veil	1945	17,900,000

* Won Best Picture Oscar
# Animated

Source: British Film Institute

top10 FILMS IN THE **UK**, 2005

	FILM	UK GROSS (£)
1	Harry Potter and the Goblet of Fire	48,589,753
2	The Chronicles of Narnia: The Lion, the Witch and the Wardrobe	43,641,024
3	Star Wars: Episode III – Revenge of the Sith	39,433,983
4	Charlie and the Chocolate Factory	37,462,140
5	Wallace & Gromit: The Curse of the Were-Rabbit*	32,007,310
6	War of the Worlds	30,648,315
7	King Kong	30,038,677
8	Meet the Fockers	28,925,095
9	Madagascar*	22,654,878
10	Hitch	17,393,484

* Animated

This list is based on the actual number of people purchasing tickets at the UK box office. Because it takes account of the relatively greater numbers of tickets sold to children and other discounted sales (such as matinées for certain popular films), it differs both from lists that present total box-office receipts which, as ticket prices increase, tend to feature more recent films, and those that are adjusted for inflation. However, it is interesting to observe that if inflation were factored in, *Gone With the Wind* would also top the all-time list, outearning even mega-blockbuster *Titanic*.

Another Opening

top10 **JANUARY** OPENING WEEKENDS IN THE UK

FILM / YEAR	£
1 Meet the Fockers (2005)	7,917,661
2 Titanic (1998)	4,805,270
3 8 Mile (2003)	4,440,334
4 Catch Me If You Can (2003)	3,720,957
5 Scary Movie 3 (2004)	3,490,585
6 Vanilla Sky (2002)	2,978,264
7 Sleepy Hollow (2000)	2,848,933
8 Cast Away (2001)	2,807,312
9 The Last Samurai (2004)	2,723,081
10 Star Trek: Insurrection (1999)	2,706,800

top10 **FEBRUARY** OPENING WEEKENDS IN THE UK

FILM / YEAR	£
1 Monsters, Inc. (2002)	9,200,257
2 Toy Story 2 (2000)	7,971,539
3 Hannibal (2001)	6,402,540
4 Ocean's Eleven (2002)	5,095,062
5 A Bug's Life (1999)	4,204,678
6 Ocean's Twelve (2005)	3,394,100
7 What Women Want (2001)	3,375,075
8 School of Rock (2004)	2,742,356
9 Two Weeks Notice (2003)	2,636,050
10 Mrs Doubtfire (1994)	2,633,285

top10 **MARCH** OPENING WEEKENDS IN THE UK

FILM / YEAR	£
1 Starsky & Hutch (2004)	4,809,897
2 Hitch (2005)	4,309,540
3 Star Wars – Episode IV: A New Hope* (1997)	3,771,206
4 Toy Story (1996)	3,387,160
5 Ali G Indahouse (2002)	3,231,673
6 Ice Age (2002)	3,029,738
7 The Passion of the Christ (2004)	2,784,344
8 Robots (2005)	2,622,253
9 Blade II (2002)	2,450,226
10 Maid in Manhattan (2003)	2,424,584

* Re-release (Special Edition)

top10 **APRIL** OPENING WEEKENDS IN THE UK

FILM / YEAR	£
1 Bridget Jones's Diary (2001)	5,720,292
2 About a Boy (2002)	3,747,966
3 Scooby-Doo 2: Monsters Unleashed (2004)	3,549,487
4 Johnny English (2003)	3,435,342
5 Hitchhiker's Guide to the Galaxy (2005)	3,298,262
6 Pokémon: The First Movie (1996)	2,883,721
7 Kill Bill: Vol. 2 (2004)	2,768,832
8 Scream 3 (2000)	2,449,937
9 Kevin & Perry Go Large (2000)	2,404,517
10 The Ring Two (2005)	2,062,792

top10 **MAY** OPENING WEEKENDS IN THE UK

FILM / YEAR	£
1 Harry Potter and the Prisoner of Azkaban (2004)	23,882,688
2 Star Wars: Episode III: Revenge of the Sith (2005)	14,361,469
3 The Matrix Reloaded (2003)	12,165,276
4 Star Wars: Episode II: Attack of the Clones (2002)	11,386,209
5 The Day After Tomorrow (2004)	7,321,633
6 X2: X-Men United (2003)	7,037,861
7 Troy (2004)	6,151,581
8 The Mummy Returns (2001)	5,929,146
9 Van Helsing (2004)	5,429,632
10 Notting Hill (1999)	4,323,678

top10 **JUNE** OPENING WEEKENDS IN THE UK

FILM / YEAR	£
1 Spider-Man (2002)	9,426,969
2 Bruce Almighty (2003)	7,242,166
3 Batman & Robin (1997)	4,940,566
4 Shrek (2001)	4,686,210
5 Batman Begins (2005)	4,427,802
6 Mr & Mrs Smith (2005)	3,943,422
7 Chicken Run (2000)	3,848,755
8 The Mummy (1999)	3,771,429
9 The Matrix (1999)	3,384,948
10 Pearl Harbor (2001)	3,075,147

➲ Battle Royal
The Chronicles of Narnia: The Lion, The Witch and The Wardrobe *achieved a creditable fourth place in its December box office fight against the* Lord of the Rings *trilogy.*

top10 JULY OPENING WEEKENDS IN THE UK

FILM / YEAR	£
1 Shrek 2 (2004)	16,220,752
2 Star Wars: Episode I – The Phantom Menace (1999)	9,512,295
3 Spider-Man 2 (2004)	8,766,902
4 War of the Worlds (2005)	8,644,787
5 Charlie and the Chocolate Factory (2005)	7,972,168
6 Austin Powers: The Spy Who Shagged Me (1999)	6,005,087
7 The Lost World: Jurassic Park (1997)	5,666,917
8 Austin Powers in Goldmember (2002)	5,585,978
9 Madagascar (2005)	5,431,639
10 Scooby-Doo (2002)	5,129,109

top10 AUGUST OPENING WEEKENDS IN THE UK

FILM / YEAR	£
1 Men in Black (1997)	7,066,748
2 Independence Day (1996)	7,005,905
3 Men in Black II (2002)	6,191,428
4 Terminator 3: The Rise of the Machines (2003)	6,080,369
5 Planet of the Apes (2001)	5,445,983
6 X-Men (2000)	4,749,241
7 I, Robot (2004)	4,745,541
8 American Wedding (2003)	4,151,788
9 Pirates of the Caribbean (2003)	3,765,450
10 Cats & Dogs (2001)	3,707,358

top10 SEPTEMBER OPENING WEEKENDS IN THE UK

FILM / YEAR	£
1 Signs (2002)	3,767,713
2 Snatch (2000)	3,180,602
3 Scary Movie (2000)	2,887,451
4 Saving Private Ryan (1998)	2,704,522
5 Pride & Prejudice (2005)	2,529,947
6 Moulin Rouge! (2001)	2,403,378
7 Apollo 13 (1995)	2,358,966
8 The Italian Job (2003)	2,294,027
9 Artificial Intelligence: A.I. (2001)	2,285,786
10 There's Something About Mary (1998)	2,076,411

top10 OCTOBER OPENING WEEKENDS IN THE UK

FILM / YEAR	£
1 Wallace & Gromit: The Curse of the Were-Rabbit (2005)	9,374,932
2 Finding Nemo (2003)	7,590,845
3 Shark Tale (2004)	7,545,074
4 The Blair Witch Project (1999)	5,875,318
5 American Pie 2 (2001)	5,508,709
6 xXx (2002)	3,435,891
7 Bad Boys II (2003)	3,175,258
8 Kill Bill: Vol. 1 (2003)	2,955,190
9 Nanny McPhee (2005)	2,603,834
10 The Nutty Professor (1996)	2,278,236

top10 NOVEMBER OPENING WEEKENDS IN THE UK

FILM / YEAR	£
1 Harry Potter and the Chamber of Secrets (2002)	18,871,829
2 Harry Potter and the Philosopher's Stone (2001)	16,335,627
3 Harry Potter and the Goblet of Fire (2005)	14,933,901
4 Bridget Jones: The Edge of Reason (2004)	10,435,193
5 The Incredibles (2004)	9,874,782
6 Die Another Day (2002)	9,122,344
7 The Matrix Revolutions (2003)	8,712,350
8 Love Actually 2003	6,657,479
9 The World is Not Enough (1999)	6,273,584
10 The Sixth Sense (1999)	5,229,978

top10 DECEMBER OPENING WEEKENDS IN THE UK

FILM / YEAR	£
1 The Lord of the Rings: The Return of the King (2003)	15,021,761
2 The Lord of the Rings: The Two Towers (2002)	13,063,560
3 The Lord of the Rings: The Fellowship of the Ring (2001)	11,058,045
4 The Chronicles of Narnia: The Lion, the Witch and the Wardrobe (2005)	8,884,111
5 King Kong (2005)	6,944,740
6 Tomorrow Never Dies (1997)	3,656,746
7 How the Grinch Stole Christmas (2000)	3,063,799
8 Blade: Trinity (2004)	2,633,626
9 101 Dalmatians (1996)	2,360,762
10 Star Trek VIII: First Contact (1996)	2,352,700

AMAZING FACT

Opening Weekends

Much of the promotional budget of a film is dedicated to the opening weekend, when it may earn between a quarter and a third of its total box office revenue. However, reviews and word-of-mouth criticism, competition from other films and even bad weather may cause a decline in its subsequent audience. *Alien vs. Predator* (2004), for example, earned almost half its total US income during the first weekend, the rest in a lacklustre 15 weeks. Conversely, *Titanic* (1997) made less than five per cent of its record total during the first weekend.

Film Genres

top10 MAFIA FILMS

	FILM	YEAR
1	The Firm	1993
2	The Godfather*	1972
3	The Untouchables	1987
4	Road to Perdition	2002
5	Analyze This	1999
6	The Specialist	1994
7	The Godfather, Part III	1990
8	L.A. Confidential	1997
9	Donnie Brasco	1997
10	The Client	1994

* Won Best Picture Oscar

Although *The Godfather* trilogy – with *The Godfather, Part II* (1974) falling just outside the Top 10 – represents the apogee of the Mafia movie, its history dates back to the silent era. In recent years, comedies in which organized crime and Mafia stereotypes are satirized have been especially popular, as exemplified by several entries in this Top 10 – which have all earned over $100 million worldwide.

top10 PIRATE FILMS

	FILM	YEAR
1	Pirates of the Caribbean: The Curse of the Black Pearl	2003
2	Hook	1991
3	Peter Pan	2003
4	Peter Pan: Return to Never Land*	2002
5	Treasure Planet*	2002
6	Peter Pan*	1953
7	The Goonies	1985
8	Muppet Treasure Island	1996
9	Swiss Family Robinson	1960
10	The Island	1980

* Animated

After notable pirate film flops, such as *Pirates* (1986) and *Cutthroat Island* (1995), it seemed that the genre was finished, but then along came *Pirates of the Caribbean: The Curse of the Black Pearl*, which has earned so much worldwide that it is ranked as the 22nd highest-earning film of all time.

top10 COWBOY AND WESTERN FILMS

	FILM	YEAR
1	Dances with Wolves*	1990
2	The Mask of Zorro	1998
3	Wild Wild West	1999
4	Maverick	1994
5	City Slickers	1991
6	Brokeback Mountain	2005
7	Legends of the Fall	1994
8	Unforgiven*	1992
9	The Legend of Zorro	2005
10	Blazing Saddles	1974

* Won Best Picture Oscar

Westerns have a history that dates back to the birth of cinema: *The Great Train Robbery* (1903), which is credited as the first narrative film ever made, was also the first-ever Western. The animated *Spirit: Stallion of the Cimarron* (2002) falls just outside the Top 10, each of which has earned upwards of $100 million.

top10 SUPERHERO FILMS

	FILM	YEAR
1	Spider-Man	2002
2	Spider-Man 2	2004
3	The Incredibles*	2004
4	Batman	1989
5	X2: X-Men United	2003
6	Batman Begins	2005
7	The Mask	1994
8	Batman Forever	1995
9	Fantastic Four	2005
10	Superman	1978

* Animated

Superman makes a single showing in this Top 10, since it is in the unusual situation where the first film made a large amount (over $300 million) at the world box office, whereas each of its three sequels made progressively less.

top10 HORROR FILMS

	FILM	YEAR
1	Jurassic Park	1993
2	The Sixth Sense	1999
3	The Lost World: Jurassic Park	1997
4	Jaws	1975
5	The Mummy Returns	2001
6	The Mummy	1999
7	Signs	2002
8	Godzilla	1998
9	Jurassic Park III	2001
10	Hannibal	2001

This list encompasses supernatural and science-fiction horror films featuring monster creatures, such as dinosaurs and oversized sharks, as well as serial killers. It has long been a successful genre: each of the films listed has earned $350 million or more at the world box office.

top10 COMEDY FILMS

	FILM	YEAR
1	Forrest Gump*	1994
2	Pirates of the Caribbean: The Curse of the Black Pearl	2003
3	Men in Black	1997
4	Home Alone	1990
5	Meet the Fockers	2004
6	Ghost	1990
7	Bruce Almighty	2003
8	Mr. & Mrs. Smith	2005
9	Charlie and the Chocolate Factory	2005
10	Pretty Woman	1990

* Won Best Picture Oscar

Since the earliest days of Hollywood, comedy – including romantic comedies and other sub-genres – has consistently performed well at the box office: all those in the Top 10 have earned over $450 million worldwide, while each of the first six has earned in excess of half a billion dollars globally.

top10 JAMES BOND FILMS

FILM / BOND ACTOR / YEAR

1 Die Another Day
Pierce Brosnan 2002

2 The World is Not Enough
Pierce Brosnan 1999

3 GoldenEye
Pierce Brosnan 1995

4 Tomorrow Never Dies
Pierce Brosnan 1997

5 Moonraker
Roger Moore 1979

6 For Your Eyes Only
Roger Moore 1981

7 The Living Daylights
Timothy Dalton 1987

8 The Spy Who Loved Me
Roger Moore 1977

9 Octopussy
Roger Moore 1983

10 Licence to Kill
Timothy Dalton 1990

Ian Fleming wrote 12 James Bond novels, only two of which, *Moonraker* (1955) and *The Spy Who Loved Me* (1962), figure in this Top 10. After his death in 1964, *For Your Eyes Only*, *Octopussy*, *The Living Daylights* and *GoldenEye* were developed by other writers from his short stories, while subsequent releases were written without reference to Fleming's writings.

➔ High-yield Bond
Pierce Brosnan's four Bond films have made over $1.5 billion worldwide.

Animated Films

⬆ **Wild things**
Melman, Marty, Alex and Gloria, stars of 2005 cartoon smash Madagascar.

top10 **ANIMATED** FILMS

	FILM	YEAR	WORLDWIDE TOTAL GROSS ($)
1	Shrek 2*	2004	920,665,658
2	Finding Nemo#	2003	864,625,978
3	The Lion King#	1994	783,841,776
4	The Incredibles#	2004	631,436,092
5	Monsters, Inc.#	2001	529,061,238
6	Madagascar*	2005	527,890,631
7	Aladdin*	1992	504,050,219
8	Toy Story 2#	1999	485,015,179
9	Shrek*	2001	484,409,218
10	Tarzan#	1999	449,391,819

* DreamWorks
\# Disney

top10 **ANIMATED** FILMS **IN THE UK**

	FILM	YEAR	UK TOTAL GROSS (£)
1	Shrek 2*	2004	48,243,628
2	Toy Story 2#	2000	44,306,070
3	Monsters, Inc.#	2002	37,907,451
4	Finding Nemo#	2003	37,364,251
5	The Incredibles#	2004	32,277,041
6	Wallace & Gromit: The Curse of the Were-Rabbit*	2005	32,007,310
7	Chicken Run*	2000	29,514,237
8	A Bug's Life#	1999	29,449,272
9	Ice Age: The Meltdown	2006	26,248,217
10	Shrek*	2001	29,004,582

* DreamWorks
\# Disney

top10 ANIMATED **FILM BUDGETS**

	FILM	YEAR	BUDGET ($)
1	The Polar Express	2004	170,000,000
2	Tarzan	1999	145,000,000
3	Treasure Planet	2002	140,000,000
4	Final Fantasy: The Spirits Within	2001	137,000,000
5	Dinosaur	2000	128,000,000
6	Monsters, Inc.	2001	115,000,000
7	Home on the Range	2004	110,000,000
8	The Emperor's New Groove	2000	100,000,000
9	The Road to El Dorado	2000	95,000,000
10	Finding Nemo	2003	94,000,000

Snow White and the Seven Dwarfs (1937) established a record budget of $1.49 million. The $2.6-million budget for *Pinocchio* (1940) and $2.28 million for the original *Fantasia* (1940) were the two biggest of the 1940s, while *Sleeping Beauty* (1959) at $6 million was the highest of the 1950s. Since the 1990s, budgets of $50 million or more have become commonplace: *The Lion King* (1994) cost $79.3 million, while *Tarzan* has become the first to break through $100 million.

top10 ANIMATED FILMS BASED ON **TV SERIES**

	FILM	TV SERIES*	FILM YEAR
1	Pokémon: The First Movie	1997	1999
2	The Rugrats Movie	1991	1998
3	The SpongeBob SquarePants Movie	1999	2004
4	Pokémon: The Movie 2000	1997	2000
5	Rugrats in Paris: The Movie – Rugrats II	1991	2000
6	South Park: Bigger, Longer & Uncut	1997	1999
7	Beavis and Butt-head Do America	1993	1996
8	Pokémon 3: The Movie	1997	2001
9	The Wild Thornberrys Movie	1998	2002
10	Rugrats Go Wild	1991	2003

* Launched on TV in USA

Such is the fan following of many TV animated series that when they reach the big screen they attract huge audiences: the first five films in this list each earned in excess of $100 million, and the others have all made over $50 million each.

top10 ANIMATED **OPENING WEEKENDS** IN THE UK

	FILM	YEAR	OPENING WEEKEND GROSS (£)
1	Shrek 2	2004	16,220,752
2	The Incredibles	2004	9,874,782
3	Ice Age: The Meltdown	2006	9,775,974
4	Wallis & Gromit: The Curse of the Were-Rabbit	2005	9,374,932
5	Monsters, Inc.	2002	9,200,257
6	Toy Story 2	2000	7,971,539
7	Finding Nemo	2003	7,590,845
8	Shark Tale	2004	7,545,074
9	Madagascar	2005	5,431,639
10	Shrek	2001	4,686,210

➔ Baby boom
Tommy Pickles, voiced, like many other animated characters, by Elizabeth Daily, appeared in the popular Rugrats *films.*

Film Actors

top10 HIGHEST-EARNING FILM ACTORS

ACTOR	2005 INCOME ($)
1 Mel Gibson	185,000,000
2 Johnny Depp	37,000,000
3 Will Smith	35,000,000
4 Tobey Maguire	32,000,000
5 Tom Cruise	31,000,000
6 Denzel Washington	30,000,000
7 Adam Sandler	28,000,000
8 Matt Damon	27,000,000
9 Brad Pitt	25,000,000
10 Frankie Muniz	8,000,000

Source: Forbes magazine

top10 MEL GIBSON FILMS

FILM	YEAR
1 Signs	2002
2 What Women Want	2000
3 Lethal Weapon 3	1992
4 Ransom	1996
5 Lethal Weapon 4	1998
6 Lethal Weapon 2	1989
7 The Patriot	2000
8 Braveheart*	1995
9 Maverick	1994
10 Payback	1999

* Won Best Picture Oscar

top10 SAMUEL L. JACKSON FILMS

FILM	YEAR
1 Star Wars: Episode I – The Phantom Menace	1999
2 Jurassic Park	1993
3 Star Wars: Episode III – Revenge of the Sith	2005
4 Star Wars: Episode II - Attack of the Clones	2002
5 Die Hard: With a Vengeance	1995
6 Coming to America	1988
7 xXx	2002
8 Unbreakable	2000
9 Pulp Fiction	1994
10 S.W.A.T.	2003

top10 TOM CRUISE FILMS

FILM	YEAR
1 War of the Worlds	2005
2 Mission: Impossible II	2000
3 The Last Samurai	2003
4 Mission: Impossible	1996
5 Rain Man	1988
6 Minority Report	2002
7 Top Gun	1986
8 Jerry Maguire	1996
9 The Firm	1993
10 A Few Good Men	1992

top10 AL PACINO FILMS

FILM	YEAR
1 The Godfather*	1972
2 Heat	1995
3 Dick Tracy	1990
4 The Devil's Advocate	1997
5 The Godfather: Part III	1990
6 Scent of a Woman#	1992
7 Donnie Brasco	1997
8 Insomnia	2002
9 Sea of Love	1989
10 The Godfather: Part II	1974

* Won Best Picture Oscar
# Won Best Actor Oscar

top10 ROBERT DE NIRO FILMS

FILM	YEAR
1 Meet the Fockers	2004
2 Meet the Parents	2000
3 Heat	1995
4 The Untouchables	1987
5 Cape Fear	1991
6 Analyze This	1999
7 Sleepers	1996
8 Backdraft	1991
9 Hide and Seek	2005
10 Casino	1995

Here's Johnny!
Johnny Depp as Willy Wonka in Charlie and the Chocolate Factory, *his second chocolate-based film, and his fifth film since* Edward Scissorhands *under the direction of Tim Burton.*

top10 **JOHNNY DEPP** FILMS

FILM	YEAR
1 Pirates of the Caribbean: The Curse of the Black Pearl	2003
2 Charlie and the Chocolate Factory	2004
3 Sleepy Hollow	1999
4 Platoon	1986
5 Chocolat	2000
6 Donnie Brasco	1997
7 Finding Neverland	2004
8 Desperado II: Once Upon a Time in Mexico	2003
9 Secret Window	2004
10 Edward Scissorhands	1990

Seven of Johnny Depp's Top 10 films have earned over $100 million, his run of successes led – by a considerable margin – by *Pirates of the Caribbean*.

top10 **GEORGE CLOONEY** FILMS

FILM	YEAR
1 Ocean's Eleven	2001
2 Ocean's Twelve	2004
3 The Perfect Storm	2000
4 Batman & Robin	1997
5 Spy Kids	2001
6 Intolerable Cruelty	2003
7 The Peacemaker	1997
8 Three Kings	1999
9 One Fine Day	1996
10 The Thin Red Line	1998

Already well-known as Dr Doug Ross in TV series *ER* – as well as some best-forgotten early film parts, such as *Return of the Killer Tomatoes!* (1988) – George Clooney has appeared in a run of successful films during the past 10 years. He also provided voices for the animated *South Park: Bigger, Longer & Uncut* (1999).

top10 **BRAD PITT** FILMS

FILM	YEAR
1 Troy	2004
2 Mr. & Mrs. Smith	2005
3 Ocean's Eleven	2001
4 Ocean's Twelve	2004
5 Se7en	1995
6 Interview with the Vampire: The Vampire Chronicles	1994
7 Twelve Monkeys	1995
8 Sleepers	1996
9 Legends of the Fall	1994
10 The Mexican	2001

Although *Troy* earned almost $500 million worldwide, Brad Pitt's action comedies have been among his most successful films. Including the four films in his Top 10, he has appeared in 10 films or TV series with a number in the title.

Film Actresses

top10 HIGHEST-EARNING FILM ACTRESSES

	ACTRESS	2005 INCOME ($)
1	Bette Midler	31,000,000
2	Drew Barrymore	22,000,000
3	Jennifer Aniston	18,500,000
4	Jennifer Lopez	17,000,000
5	Nicole Kidman	14,500,000
6	Jennifer Garner	14,000,000
7	Cameron Diaz	13,000,000
8	Naomi Watts	11,500,000
9	Lindsay Lohan	11,000,000
10	Sandra Bullock	10,500,000

Source: Forbes magazine

top10 CAMERON DIAZ FILMS

	FILM	YEAR
1	There's Something About Mary	1998
2	The Mask	1994
3	My Best Friend's Wedding	1997
4	Charlie's Angels	2000
5	Charlie's Angels: Full Throttle	2003
6	Vanilla Sky	2001
7	Gangs of New York	2002
8	Any Given Sunday	1999
9	In Her Shoes	2005
10	The Sweetest Thing	2002

Cameron Diaz's Top 10 films include some of the highest earning of recent years. She also provided the voice of Princess Fiona in *Shrek* (2001) and *Shrek 2* (2004) – which have outearned all of them.

← Pay acceleration
Cameron Diaz earned $20 million for her role in Charlie's Angels: Full Throttle *(2003) – 10 times the amount she received for* There's Something About Mary *(1998).*

top10 NICOLE KIDMAN FILMS

	FILM	YEAR
1	Batman Forever	1995
2	The Others	2001
3	Moulin Rouge!	2001
4	Cold Mountain	2003
5	Days of Thunder	1990
6	The Interpreter	2005
7	Eyes Wide Shut	1999
8	Far and Away	1992
9	Bewitched	2005
10	The Peacemaker	1997

top10 SANDRA BULLOCK FILMS

	FILM	YEAR
1	Speed	1994
2	Miss Congeniality	2000
3	Two Weeks Notice	2002
4	While You Were Sleeping	1995
5	Speed 2: Cruise Control	1997
6	A Time to Kill	1996
7	The Net	1995
8	Miss Congeniality 2: Armed and Fabulous	2005
9	Forces of Nature	1999
10	Crash	2005

top10 JUDI DENCH FILMS

	FILM	YEAR
1	Die Another Day	2002
2	The World is Not Enough	1999
3	GoldenEye	1995
4	Tomorrow Never Dies	1997
5	Shakespeare in Love	1998
6	Chocolat	2000
7	The Chronicles of Riddick	2004
8	Pride and Prejudice	2005
9	The Shipping News	2001
10	Tea with Mussolini	1999

top10 **CATHERINE ZETA-JONES** FILMS

	FILM	YEAR
1	Ocean's Twelve	2004
2	Chicago*	2002
3	The Mask of Zorro	1998
4	Entrapment	1999
5	Traffic	2000
6	The Terminal	2004
7	The Haunting	1999
8	America's Sweethearts	2001
9	The Legend of Zorro	2005
10	Intolerable Cruelty	2003

* Won Best Picture Oscar

In little over 12 years, Catherine Zeta-Jones has graduated from British TV series *The Darling Buds of May* (1991–93), in which she appeared as Mariette Larkin, to starring roles in major Hollywood blockbusters, all of which have grossed over $100 million worldwide.

● *Strong poison*
Uma Thurman received $5 million for her Batman and Robin *role as Poison Ivy – and $12 million for each of the* Kill Bill *films.*

top10 **UMA THURMAN** FILMS

	FILM	YEAR
1	Batman & Robin	1997
2	Pulp Fiction	1994
3	Kill Bill: Vol. 1	2003
4	Kill Bill: Vol. 2	2004
5	Paycheck	2003
6	Be Cool	2005
7	The Truth About Cats & Dogs	1996
8	The Avengers	1998
9	Final Analysis	1992
10	Dangerous Liaisons	1988

top10 **CATE BLANCHETT** FILMS

	FILM	YEAR
1	The Lord of the Rings: The Return of the King	2003
2	The Lord of the Rings: The Two Towers	2002
3	The Lord of the Rings: The Fellowship of the Ring	2001
4	The Aviator	2004
5	The Talented Mr Ripley	1999
6	Bandits	2001
7	Elizabeth	1998
8	The Gift	2000
9	The Missing	2003
10	The Life Aquatic With Steve Zissou	2004

top10 **SCARLETT JOHANSSON** FILMS

	FILM	YEAR
1	The Horse Whisperer	1998
2	The Island	2005
3	Lost in Translation	2003
4	Home Alone 3	1997
5	Match Point	2005
6	Just Cause	1995
7	In Good Company	2004
8	Eight Legged Freaks	2002
9	Girl with a Pearl Earring	2003
10	The Man Who Wasn't There	2001

Film Directors

⬆ **Glowing report** Minority Report, *Spielberg's first blockbuster of the 21st century, earned over $350 million worldwide.*

top10 **HIGHEST-EARNING** DIRECTORS

	DIRECTOR	FILMS	HIGHEST-EARNING FILM	TOTAL US GROSS OF ALL FILMS ($)
1	Steven Spielberg	24	E.T.: the Extra-Terrestrial	3,505,000,223
2	Robert Zemeckis	13	Forrest Gump	1,715,281,884
3	George Lucas	6	Star Wars: Episode IV – A New Hope	1,700,470,625
4	Chris Columbus	12	Harry Potter and the Sorcerer's Stone	1,567,938,485
5	Ron Howard	16	Dr Seuss's How the Grinch Stole Christmas	1,388,746,933
6	Peter Jackson	8	The Lord of the Rings: The Return of the King	1,270,962,886
7	Tim Burton	13	Batman	1,247,173,343
8	Richard Donner	17	Lethal Weapon 2	1,217,512,205
9	James Cameron	8	Titanic	1,150,831,308
10	Andrew Adamson	3	Shrek 2	998,070,204

While the cumulative total US box office income of all the films of these directors provides a comparative view of the overall earning power of the group, the most impressive representative is George Lucas, with relatively few but extremely high-grossing releases, an unrivalled per-picture average of over $283 million.

top10 FILMS DIRECTED BY **STEVEN SPIELBERG**

	FILM	YEAR
1	Jurassic Park	1993
2	E.T.: the Extra-Terrestrial	1982
3	The Lost World: Jurassic Park	1997
4	War of the Worlds	2005
5	Indiana Jones and the Last Crusade	1989
6	Saving Private Ryan	1998
7	Jaws	1975
8	Raiders of the Lost Ark	1981
9	Minority Report	2002
10	Catch Me if You Can	2002

Steven Spielberg has directed some of the most successful films of all time: the top six in this list appear among the 50 highest-earning films of all time worldwide, while the cumulative world box-office gross of his Top 10 alone amounts to an unrivalled $5.5 billion.

top10 DIRECTORS, 2005

	DIRECTOR	FILM(S) OF YEAR	WORLD TOTAL (US$)
1	Mike Newell	Harry Potter and the Goblet of Fire	891,338,639
2	George Lucas	Star Wars: Episode III – Revenge of the Sith	848,797,674
3	Andrew Adamson	The Chronicles of Narnia: The Lion, the Witch and the Wardrobe	677,522,946
4	Steven Spielberg	War of the Worlds	591,416,316
5	Tim Burton	Charlie and the Chocolate Factory/Corpse Bride*	590,520,433
6	Peter Jackson	King Kong	544,456,306
7	Eric Darnell	Madagascar*	527,890,631
8	Jay Roach	Meet the Fockers#	515,291,929
9	Doug Liman	Mr. & Mrs. Smith	477,671,954
10	Christopher Nolan	Batman Begins	371,853,783

* Animated
# Late 2004 release

top10 FILMS DIRECTED BY WOMEN

	FILM	DIRECTOR	YEAR
1	Shrek*	Victoria Jenson#	2001
2	What Women Want	Nancy Meyers	2000
3	Deep Impact	Mimi Leder	1998
4	Look Who's Talking	Amy Heckerling	1989
5	Doctor Dolittle	Betty Thomas	1998
6	Bridget Jones's Diary	Sharon Maguire	2001
7	Something's Gotta Give	Nancy Meyers	2003
8	You've Got M@il	Nora Ephron	1998
9	Sleepless in Seattle	Nora Ephron	1993
10	The Prince of Egypt*	Brenda Chapman†	1998

* Animated
# Co-director with Andrew Adamson
† Co-director with Steve Hickner and Simon Wells

top10 FILMS DIRECTED BY RIDLEY SCOTT

	FILM	YEAR
1	Gladiator	2000
2	Hannibal	2001
3	Kingdom of Heaven	2005
4	Black Hawk Down	2001
5	Black Rain	1989
6	Alien	1979
7	G.I. Jane	1997
8	Matchstick Men	2003
9	Thelma & Louise	1991
10	Blade Runner	1982

British director Sir Ridley Scott (b. 1937) began his career in television and as a maker of such celebrated TV commercials as the Hovis bread advertisement (1974), but has been directing films since the late 1970s with *The Duellists* (1977) and especially *Alien* launching a run of box office hits – although *1492: Conquest of Paradise*, with an estimated budget of $47 million and a US gross of just over $7 million, may be regarded as a notable 'flop'. He is credited with relaunching the epic 'sword and sandal' genre with the enormously successful *Gladiator* ($458 million worldwide) and *Kingdom of Heaven*. He was knighted in 2003.

top10 FILMS DIRECTED BY CHRIS COLUMBUS

	FILM	YEAR
1	Harry Potter and the Sorcerer's Stone	2001
2	Harry Potter and the Chamber of Secrets	2002
3	Home Alone	1990
4	Mrs. Doubtfire	1993
5	Home Alone 2: Lost in New York	1992
6	Stepmom	1998
7	Nine Months	1995
8	Bicentennial Man	1999
9	Adventures in Babysitting	1987
10	Only the Lonely	1991

➜ *Heaven-sent*
Ridley Scott on the set of Kingdom of Heaven. *His Top 10 films have earned almost $1.7 billion worldwide.*

top10 FILMS DIRECTED BY TIM BURTON

	FILM	YEAR
1	Charlie and the Chocolate Factory	2005
2	Batman	1989
3	Planet of the Apes	2001
4	Batman Returns	1992
5	Sleepy Hollow	1999
6	Big Fish	2003
7	Tim Burton's Corpse Bride*	2005
8	Mars Attacks!	1996
9	Edward Scissorhands	1990
10	Beetlejuice	1988

* Animated; co-directed with Mike Johnson

Film Studios

The Studios

A small group of studios once controlled the entire film industry, owning production facilities and acting as producers, distributors and, before the 1950s, through their ownership of cinema chains, exhibitors. The definition of a 'studio' is no longer clear-cut: some of the original studios no longer exist, while as a result of mergers and takeovers, most of the leading names are now components of large global media conglomerates operating alongside some newer independent studios, such as Artisan and Dimension, the specialist studio within Miramax. Studios are primarily financial and distribution organizations with the actual production undertaken by independent production companies – often more than one may be involved in a co-production. The films listed here represent the Top 10 productions distributed by each of the major studios within the USA, but based on total global revenue – although in many instances different companies may have acted as distributors outside the USA.

⊙ **Set for success**
Peter Jackson directs Naomi Watts in King Kong. Worldwide it is Universal Studios' biggest hit of the century so far.

top10 SONY (+ COLUMBIA/TRISTAR) FILMS

	FILM	YEAR
1	Spider-Man	2002
2	Spider-Man 2	2004
3	Men in Black	1997
4	Terminator 2: Judgment Day	1991
5	Men in Black II	2002
6	Terminator 3: Rise of the Machines	2003
7	Hitch	2005
8	Air Force One	1997
9	As Good as It Gets	1997
10	Close Encounters of the Third Kind	1977/80

top10 UNIVERSAL FILMS

	FILM	YEAR
1	E.T. the Extra-Terrestrial	1982
2	Jurassic Park	1993
3	The Lost World: Jurassic Park	1997
4	King Kong	2005
5	Meet the Fockers	2004
6	Bruce Almighty	2003
7	Jaws	1975
8	The Mummy Returns	2001
9	The Mummy	1999
10	Back to the Future	1985

top10 STUDIOS, 2005

	STUDIO	FILMS RELEASED	TOTAL US GROSS, 2005 ($)
1	Warner Bros	25	1,377,106,137
2	Fox	21	1,353,871,333
3	Universal	24	1,010,193,093
4	Buena Vista	23	921,523,769
5	Sony	26	917,764,099
6	Paramount	17	832,177,664
7	Dreamworks SKG	10	501,837,191
8	New Line	13	420,532,445
9	Lions Gate	20	283,992,663
10	Dimension	7	185,149,258

top10 PARAMOUNT FILMS

	FILM	YEAR
1	Titanic*	1997
2	Forrest Gump*	1994
3	War of the Worlds	2005
4	Mission: Impossible II	2000
5	Ghost	1990
6	Indiana Jones and the Last Crusade	1989
7	Saving Private Ryan	1998
8	Mission: Impossible	1996
9	Grease	1978
10	Raiders of the Lost Ark	1981

* Won Best Picture Oscar

top10 NEW LINE FILMS

	FILM	YEAR
1	The Lord of the Rings: The Return of the King*	2003
2	Lord of the Rings: The Two Towers	2002
3	Lord of the Rings: The Fellowship of the Ring	2001
4	The Mask	1994
5	Rush Hour 2	2001
6	Se7en	1995
7	Austin Powers: The Spy who Shagged Me	1999
8	Austin Powers in Goldmember	2002
9	Wedding Crashers	2005
10	Rush Hour	1998

* Won Best Picture Oscar

top10 **20TH CENTURY** FOX FILMS

	FILM	YEAR
1	Star Wars: Episode I – The Phantom Menace	1999
2	Star Wars: Episode III – Revenge of the Sith	2005
3	Independence Day	1996
4	Star Wars: Episode IV – A New Hope	1977
5	Star Wars: Episode II – Attack of the Clones	2002
6	Star Wars: Episode VI – Return of the Jedi	1983
7	The Day After Tomorrow	2004
8	Star Wars: Episode V – The Empire Strikes Back	1980
9	Home Alone	1990
10	Mr. & Mrs. Smith	2005

William Fox founded a film production company in 1912. It was merged with 20th Century Pictures in 1935 and achieved some of its greatest successes, especially a series of musicals starring Betty Grable, in the 1940s. Despite the box-office success of *The Sound of Music* (1965) the studio suffered a number of setbacks, including the failure of the colossally expensive *Cleopatra* (1963). Its return to prosperity began in the 1970s with *The French Connection* (1971) and was consolidated by the outstanding achievement of *Star Wars* (1977) and its successors.

top10 **WARNER BROS** FILMS

	FILM	YEAR
1	Harry Potter and the Sorcerer's Stone	2001
2	Harry Potter and the Goblet of Fire	2005
3	Harry Potter and the Chamber of Secrets	2002
4	Harry Potter and the Prisoner of Azkaban	2004
5	The Matrix Reloaded	2003
6	Troy	2004
7	Twister	1996
8	Charlie and the Chocolate Factory	2005
9	The Matrix	1999
10	Ocean's Eleven	2001

The coming of sound launched Warner Bros into its important place in cinema history, with *The Jazz Singer* (1927). In the 1960s its feature films took a lesser role as the company focused on TV production, although a handful, among them *Bonnie and Clyde* (1967), were notable box-office draws. In the 1970s Warner Bros embarked on an era of notable success that began with *The Exorcist* (1973). *Batman* (1989) became one of the then highest-earning films ever – though now far eclipsed by the enormous global success of the *Harry Potter* series.

⊕ *Fire power*
Daniel Radcliffe as the eponymous hero of Harry Potter and the Goblet of Fire, *the latest blockbuster in this highly successful series.*

Oscar-winning Films

top10 FILMS TO WIN THE **MOST OSCARS***

FILM	YEAR	NOMINATIONS	AWARDS
1 = Ben-Hur	1959	12	11
= Titanic	1997	14	11
= The Lord of the Rings: The Return of the King	2003	11	11
4 West Side Story	1961	11	10
5 = Gigi	1958	9	9
= The Last Emperor	1987	9	9
= The English Patient	1996	12	9
8 = Gone With the Wind	1939	13	8#
= From Here to Eternity	1953	13	8
= On the Waterfront	1954	12	8
= My Fair Lady	1964	12	8
= Cabaret†	1972	10	8
= Gandhi	1982	11	8
= Amadeus	1984	11	8

* Oscar® is a Registered Trade Mark
# Plus two special awards
† Did not win Best Picture Oscar

Ten other films have won seven Oscars each: *Going My Way* (1944), *The Best Years of Our Lives* (1946), *The Bridge on the River Kwai* (1957), *Lawrence of Arabia* (1962), *Patton* (1970), *The Sting* (1973), *Out of Africa* (1985), *Dances With Wolves* (1991), *Schindler's List* (1993) and *Shakespeare in Love* (1998). A further nine films have each won six Oscars, most recently *Chicago* (2002), including the award for Best Picture.

top10 FILMS TO WIN THE **MOST OSCARS** WITHOUT WINNING BEST PICTURE

FILM	YEAR	WINS
1 Cabaret	1972	8
2 = A Place in the Sun	1951	6
= Star Wars	1977	6
4 = Wilson	1944	5
= The Bad and the Beautiful	1952	5
= The King and I	1956	5
= Mary Poppins	1964	5
= Doctor Zhivago	1965	5
= Who's Afraid of Virginia Woolf?	1966	5
= Saving Private Ryan	1998	5
= The Aviator	2004	5

top10 FILMS **NOMINATED** FOR THE MOST OSCARS

FILM	YEAR	AWARDS	NOMINATIONS
1 = All About Eve	1950	6	14
= Titanic	1997	11	14
3 = Gone With the Wind	1939	8*	13
= From Here to Eternity	1953	8	13
= Mary Poppins#	1964	5	13
= Who's Afraid of Virginia Woolf?#	1966	5	13
= Forrest Gump	1994	6	13
= Shakespeare in Love	1998	7	13
= The Lord of the Rings: The Fellowship of the Ring#	2001	4	13
= Chicago	2002	6	13

* Plus two special awards
# Did not win Best Picture Oscar

Thirteen is not an unlucky number where Oscar nominations are concerned, no fewer than eight films having received that total. They and the two with 14 are those that received the greatest share of votes from Academy members (over 5,800, including previous nominees and winners), using a system that creates a shortlist of five nominees in each of 24 categories.

the10 FILMS WITH THE **MOST NOMINATIONS** WITHOUT A SINGLE WIN

FILM	YEAR	NOMINATIONS
1 = The Turning Point	1977	11
= The Color Purple	1985	11
3 Gangs of New York	2002	10
4 = The Little Foxes	1941	9
= Peyton Place	1957	9
6 = Quo Vadis	1951	8
= The Nun's Story	1959	8
= The Sand Pebbles	1966	8
= The Elephant Man	1980	8
= Ragtime	1981	8
= The Remains of the Day	1993	8

Gangs of New York is the latest of a number of films that have received an impressive tally of nominations, but no wins in any category. *The Broadway Melody* (1928–29), *Grand Hotel* (1931–32) and *Mutiny on the Bounty* (1935) are the only films to win Best Picture but to receive no other awards in any category.

↑ Crash drama
Thandie Newton and Matt Dillon in Crash, winner of three Oscars including Best Picture.

top10 **HIGHEST-EARNING** BEST PICTURE OSCAR WINNERS

	FILM	YEAR*	WORLD BOX OFFICE ($)
1	Titanic	1997	1,845,000,000
2	The Lord of the Rings: The Return of the King	2003	1,118,900,000
3	Forrest Gump	1994	677,400,000
4	Gladiator	2000	457,600,000
5	Dances With Wolves	1990	424,200,000
6	Rain Man	1988	416,000,000
7	Gone With the Wind	1939	400,200,000
8	American Beauty	1999	356,300,000
9	Schindler's List	1993	321,300,000
10	A Beautiful Mind	2001	313,500,000

* Of release; Academy Awards are made the following year

the10 LATEST **BEST PICTURE** OSCAR WINNERS

YEAR	FILM	DIRECTOR
2005	Crash	Paul Haggis*
2004	Million Dollar Baby	Clint Eastwood
2003	The Lord of the Rings: The Return of the King	Peter Jackson
2002	Chicago	Rob Marshall*
2001	A Beautiful Mind	Ron Howard
2000	Gladiator	Ridley Scott*
1999	American Beauty	Sam Mendes
1998	Shakespeare in Love	John Madden*
1997	Titanic	James Cameron
1996	The English Patient	Anthony Minghella

* Did not also win 'Best Director' Oscar

Oscar-winning Actors

the10 LATEST **BEST ACTOR** OSCAR WINNERS

YEAR	ACTOR / FILM
2005	Philip Seymour Hoffman / Capote
2004	Jamie Foxx / Ray
2003	Sean Penn / Mystic River
2002	Adrien Brody / The Pianist
2001	Denzel Washington / Training Day
2000	Russell Crowe / Gladiator*
1999	Kevin Spacey / American Beauty*
1998	Roberto Benigni / Life is Beautiful
1997	Jack Nicholson / As Good As It Gets
1996	Geoffrey Rush / Shine

* Won Best Picture Oscar

top10 ACTORS WITH THE MOST NOMINATIONS **WITHOUT A WIN***

	ACTOR	NOMINATIONS
1	=Richard Burton	7
	=Peter O'Toole	7
2	=Albert Finney	5
	=Arthur Kennedy	5
4	=Warren Beatty	4
	=Charles Boyer	4
	=Jeff Bridges	4
	=Montgomery Clift	4
	=Ed Harris	4
	=Claude Rains	4
	=Mickey Rooney	4

* In any acting categories

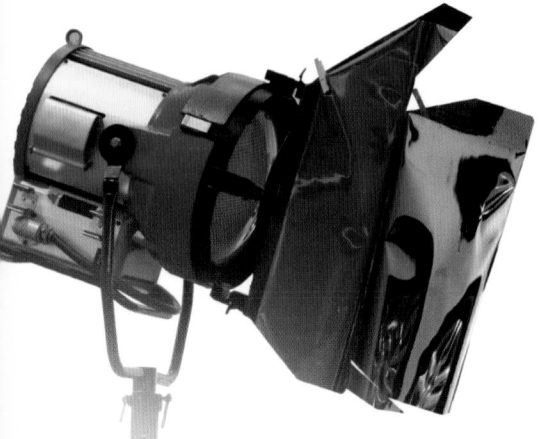

top10 **YOUNGEST** OSCAR-WINNING ACTORS

	ACTOR	AWARD / FILM	YEAR	AGE* YRS	MTHS	DAYS
1	Vincent Winter	Special Award: Outstanding Performance (The Little Kidnappers)	1954	7	3	1
2	Jon Whiteley	Special Award: Outstanding Juvenile Performance (The Little Kidnappers)	1954	10	1	11
3	Ivan Jandl	Special Award: Outstanding Juvenile Performance of 1948 (The Search)	1948	12	2	0
4	Claude Jarman Jr	Special Award: Outstanding Child Actor of 1946 (The Yearling)	1946	12	5	14
5	Bobby Driscoll	Special Award: Outstanding Juvenile Actor of 1949 (The Window)	1949	13	0	20
6	Mickey Rooney	Special Award for juvenile players setting a high standard of ability and achievement#	1938	18	5	0
7	Timothy Hutton	Best Supporting Actor (Ordinary People)	1980	20	7	15
8	George Chakiris	Best Supporting Actor (West Side Story)	1961	26	7	1
9	Cuba Gooding Jr	Best Supporting Actor (Jerry Maguire)	1996	29	3	22
10	Adrien Brody	Best Actor (The Pianist)	2002	29	11	9

* As at date of award ceremony
# Shared with fellow teen star Deanna Durbin

Jackie Cooper was nine at the time of his nomination as Best Actor for his part in *Skippy* (1930–31 Academy Awards), while eight-year-old Justin Henry is the youngest-ever Oscar nominee for Best Supporting Actor, for his role in *Kramer vs Kramer* (1979).

top10 **OLDEST** OSCAR-WINNING ACTORS

	ACTOR	FILM	YEAR	YRS	AGE* MTHS	DAYS
1	George Burns	The Sunshine Boys	1975	80	2	9
2	Melvyn Douglas	Being There	1979	79	0	9
3	John Gielgud	Arthur	1981	77	11	15
4	Don Ameche	Cocoon	1985	77	9	24
5	Henry Fonda	On Golden Pond	1981	76	10	13
6	Edmund Gwenn	Miracle on 34th Street	1947	72	5	24
7	Jack Palance	City Slickers	1991	72	0	1
8	John Houseman	The Paperchase	1973	71	6	0
9	Morgan Freeman	Million Dollar Baby#	2004	67	8	27
10	Charles Coburn	The More the Merrier	1943	66	8	13

* As at date of award ceremony
# Won Best Picture Oscar

All of the Academy Awards listed above are for Best Supporting Actor, apart from Henry Fonda's Best Actor award for *On Golden Pond*. The oldest person to win the Best Actor award prior to Fonda was John Wayne, who was 62 when he received his 1969 award for *True Grit*. Richard Farnsworth was 80 when nominated for *The Straight Story* (1999).

⬅ **Mr Cool**
Paul Newman in Cool Hand Luke (1967). As well as his nine acting nominations, he received one as a director and has won both an Honorary Oscar and the prestigious Jean Hersholt Humanitarian Award.

top10 ACTORS WITH THE MOST NOMINATIONS *

	ACTOR	WINS		NOMS.
		SUPPORTING	BEST	
1	Jack Nicholson	1	2	12
2	Laurence Olivier	0	1	10
3	=Paul Newman	0	1	9
	=Spencer Tracy	0	2	9
5	=Marlon Brando	0	2	8
	=Jack Lemmon	1	1	8
	=Al Pacino	0	1	8
8	=Richard Burton	0	0	7
	=Dustin Hoffman	0	2	7
	=Peter O'Toole	0	0	7

* In all acting categories

Oscar-winning Actresses

top10 ACTRESSES WITH THE **MOST OSCAR NOMINATIONS**＊

	ACTOR	WINS SUPPORTING	WINS BEST	NOMS.
1	Meryl Streep	1	1	13
2	Katharine Hepburn	0	4	12
3	Bette Davis	0	2	10
4	Geraldine Page	0	1	8
5 =	Ingrid Bergman	1	2	7
=	Jane Fonda	0	2	7
=	Greer Garson	0	1	7
8 =	Ellen Burstyn	0	1	6
=	Deborah Kerr	0	0	6
=	Jessica Lange	1	1	6
=	Vanessa Redgrave	1	0	6
=	Thelma Ritter	0	0	6
=	Norma Shearer	0	0	6
=	Maggie Smith	1	1	6
=	Sissy Spacek	0	1	6

＊ In all acting categories

top10 **YOUNGEST** OSCAR-WINNING ACTRESSES

	ACTRESS	AWARD/FILM (WHERE SPECIFIED)	YEAR	AGE* YRS	MTHS	DAYS
1	Shirley Temple	Special Award – Outstanding Contribution during 1934	1934	6	10	4
2	Margaret O'Brien	Special Award – Outstanding Child Actress of 1944 (Meet Me in St Louis)	1944	8	2	0
3	Tatum O'Neal	Best Supporting Actress (Paper Moon)	1973	10	4	28
4	Anna Paquin	Best Supporting Actress (The Piano)	1993	11	7	25
5	Hayley Mills	Special Award: Outstanding Juvenile Performance of 1960 (Pollyanna)	1960	13	11	30
6	Peggy Ann Garner	Special Award: Outstanding Child Performer of 1945 (A Tree Grows in Brooklyn)	1945	14	4	18
7	Patty Duke	Best Supporting Actress (The Miracle Worker)	1962	16	3	25
8	Deanna Durbin	Special Award for juvenile players setting a high standard of ability and achievement#	1938	17	2	19
9	Judy Garland	Special Award (Wizard of Oz)	1939	17	8	19
10	Marlee Matlin	Best Actress (Children of a Lesser God)	1986	21	7	6

* Age at time of award ceremony
# Shared with fellow teen star Mickey Rooney

British actress Hayley Mills, the 12th and last winner of the Special Award miniature Oscar, won her award precisely one day before her 14th birthday. Subsequent winners have had to compete on the same basis as adult actors and actresses for the major acting awards. Tatum O'Neal is thus the youngest winner of – as well as the youngest-ever nominee for – an 'adult' Oscar. The youngest Best Actress nominee is Keisha Castle-Hughes (Australia), who was 13 in 2004 when she was nominated for her role in *Whale Rider*.

AMAZING FACT

Why Oscar?

The Academy Awards or 'Oscars' have been presented since 1929. The actual award is a gold-plated statuette made of antimony, copper and tin, standing 34.3 cm (13.5 in) high and weighing 3.85 kg (8 lb 8 oz). According to legend, Academy librarian Margaret Herrick named it when she commented, 'It looks just like my Uncle Oscar!' The name stuck as a universally recognized symbol of excellence in film-making.

the10 LATEST ACTRESSES TO WIN **TWO BEST ACTRESS OSCARS**

	ACTRESS	FIRST WIN	YEAR	SECOND WIN	YEAR
1	Hilary Swank	Boys Don't Cry	1999	Million Dollar Baby*	2004
2	Jodie Foster	The Accused	1988	The Silence of the Lambs*	1991
3	Sally Field	Norma Rae	1979	Places in the Heart	1984
4	Jane Fonda	Klute	1971	Coming Home	1978
5	Glenda Jackson	Women in Love	1970	A Touch of Class	1973
6	Katharine Hepburn	The Lion in Winter	1968	On Golden Pond	1981
7	Katharine Hepburn	Morning Glory	1932/33	Guess Who's Coming to Dinner?	1967
8	Elizabeth Taylor	Butterfield 8	1960	Who's Afraid of Virginia Woolf	1966
9	Ingrid Bergman	Gaslight	1944	Anastasia	1956
10	Vivien Leigh	Gone With the Wind*	1939	A Streetcar Named Desire	1951

* Won Best Picture Oscar

Katharine Hepburn is the only actress to win a third and a fourth Best Actress Oscar. Other double winners were Olivia de Havilland for *To Each His Own* (1946) and *The Heiress* (1949) and Louise Rainer for *The Great Ziegfeld* (1936) and *The Good Earth* (1937). The only actors with doubles are Marlon Brando, Gary Cooper, Tom Hanks, Dustin Hoffman, Fredric March, Jack Nicholson and Spencer Tracy.

the10 LATEST ACTRESSES TO RECEIVE THREE OR MORE **CONSECUTIVE OSCAR NOMINATIONS**

	ACTRESS	NOMINATIONS*	YEARS
1	Reneé Zellweger	3	2001–03
2	Glenn Close	3	1982–84
3	Meryl Streep	3	1981–83
4	Jane Fonda	3	1977–79
5	Elizabeth Taylor	4	1957–60
6	Deborah Kerr	3	1956–58
7	Thelma Ritter	4	1950–53
8	Jennifer Jones	4	1943–46
9	Ingrid Bergman	3	1943–45
10	Greer Garson	5	1941–45

* In Best Actress or Best Supporting Actress categories

top10 **OLDEST** OSCAR-WINNING ACTRESSES

	ACTRESS	FILM	YEAR	YRS	AGE* MTHS	DAYS
1	Jessica Tandy	Driving Miss Daisy#	1989	80	9	21
2	Peggy Ashcroft	A Passage to India	1984	77	3	3
3	Katharine Hepburn	On Golden Pond	1981	74	4	11
4	Ruth Gordon	Rosemary's Baby	1968	72	5	15
5	Margaret Rutherford	The VIPs	1963	71	11	2
6	Helen Hayes	Airport	1970	70	5	25
7	Ethel Barrymore	None But the Lonely Heart	1944	65	7	0
8	Josephine Hull	Harvey	1950	65	1	26
9	Judi Dench	Shakespeare in Love#	1998	64	3	12
10	Beatrice Straight	Network	1976	62	7	26

* Age at time of award ceremony
# Won Best Picture Oscar

All of the Academy Awards listed here are for Best Supporting Actress, apart from Katharine Hepburn, whose win was in the Best Actress category (as were all 12 of the nominations she received from 1933 to 1981).

Jessica Tandy is the oldest nominee and oldest winner of a Best Actor/Actress Academy Award ever. Among the female seniors who received nominations but did not win are May Robson, 75 when she was nominated as Best Actress in *Lady for a Day* (1933), and Gloria Stuart (87) for Best Supporting Actress in *Titanic* (1997).

the10 LATEST **BEST ACTRESS** OSCAR WINNERS

YEAR	ACTRESS	FILM
2005	Reese Witherspoon	Walk the Line
2004	Hilary Swank	Million Dollar Baby*
2003	Charlize Theron	Monster
2002	Nicole Kidman	The Hours
2001	Halle Berry	Monster's Ball
2000	Julia Roberts	Erin Brockovich
1999	Hilary Swank	Boys Don't Cry
1998	Gwyneth Paltrow	Shakespeare in Love*
1997	Helen Hunt	As Good As It Gets
1996	Frances McDormand	Fargo

* Won Best Picture Oscar

↻ *Something to smile about*
Following her Best Actress Oscar win for Walk the Line, *Reese Witherspoon is reported to be receiving $29 million for her role in* Our Family Trouble *(2007), beating Julia Roberts's $24 million for* Mona Lisa Smile *(2003) and making her Hollywood's highest-paid female star.*

DVD & Video

top10 BESTSELLING **DVDS IN THE UK***

TITLE

1 The Lord of the Rings: The Fellowship of the Ring
2 The Lord of the Rings: The Two Towers
3 The Lord of the Rings: The Return of the King
4 Pirates of the Caribbean: The Curse of the Black Pearl
5 Shrek 2
6 Harry Potter and the Prisoner of Azkaban
7 Finding Nemo
8 The Matrix
9 Harry Potter and the Chamber of Secrets
10 Love Actually

* To 1 Jan 2006

Source: British Video Association/The Official UK Charts Company

The 1999 release of *The Matrix* marks it out as the earliest DVD in this all-time list. Later releases have benefited from the annual increase in DVD market penetration: it is estimated that while some 25 per cent of UK homes owned a DVD player in 2002, this figure grew to 45 per cent in 2003, 62 percent in 2004 and 75 per cent in 2005.

top10 BESTSELLING **VIDEOS** IN THE UK***

TITLE

1 The Lord of the Rings: The Fellowship of the Ring
2 Titanic
3 The Lord of the Rings: The Two Towers
4 Shrek
5 The Lion King
6 The Jungle Book
7 The Matrix
8 Dirty Dancing
9 Gladiator
10 Snow White and the Seven Dwarfs

* To 1 Jan 2006; includes VHS and DVD formats

Source: British Video Association/The Official UK Charts Company

Already 55 years old when it appeared on video in 1992, animated Disney classic *Snow White and the Seven Dwarfs* immediately topped the all-time list. Its status was soon eclipsed by the 1993 release of the 1967 film *The Jungle Book*, the 4.5-million-copy sale of which sustained its rank until *Titanic* in 1998. With more recent releases, DVD has overtaken VHS as the format of choice.

top10 **BESTSELLING MUSIC DVDS** IN THE UK, 2005

TITLE / ARTIST/GROUP

1 Now That's What I Call a Music Quiz
2 Live 8 – July 2nd 2005
3 The Number Ones Tour, Westlife
4 Family Jewels, AC/DC
5 The Rock 'n' Roll Show, Daniel O'Donnell
6 Elvis by the Presleys
7 Live at Wembley Stadium, Queen
8 Vertigo 2005 – Live from Chicago, U2
9 Some Kind of Monster, Metallica
10 Return of the Champions, Queen & Paul Rodgers

Source: British Video Association/The Official UK Charts Company

A diverse range of music DVDs captured the British public's imagination this year. Offerings included the Live 8 and U2 concerts, a documentary about Elvis Presley, combining interviews with members of his family and performance footage, stage shows by Irish boy band Westlife, singer Daniel O'Donnell and the original and current Queen line-up, and studio sessions from heavy metal masters Metallica and AC/DC's TV appearances.

top10 **FILM-INSPIRED** COMPUTER GAMES IN THE UK, 2005

TITLE	UK PUBLISHER
1 Star Wars: Episode III – Revenge of the Sith	LucasArts
2 Star Wars: Battlefront II	LucasArts
3 King Kong: Official Game of the Movie	Ubisoft
4 Harry Potter and the Goblet of Fire	Electronic Arts
5 Lego Star Wars	TT Games/Eidos
6 The Incredibles	THQ
7 Madagascar	Activision
8 Spider-Man 2	Activision
9 Narnia: The Lion, the Witch and the Wardrobe	Disney/Buena Vista Games
10 The SpongeBob SquarePants Movie	THQ

Source: ©ELSPA

Although computer games, derived from sources ranging from sport to TV quiz shows, remain ever popular, those based on blockbuster movies are among the bestselling, with the symbiotic publicity for simultaneously released films and games increasingly evident. Such is the intimacy of this link that the process has also worked in reverse, with games such as *Super Mario Bros.* and *Tomb Raider* subsequently inspiring successful films.

top10 BESTSELLING **DVDS IN THE UK, 2005**

TITLE

1 The Incredibles
2 Bridget Jones: The Edge of Reason
3 Madagascar
4 Star Wars: Episode III – Revenge of the Sith
5 War of the Worlds
6 Charlie and the Chocolate Factory
7 Shark Tale
8 Meet the Fockers
9 The Bourne Supremacy
10 Dodgeball: A True Underdog Story

Source: British Video Association/The Official UK Charts Company

An estimated 211 million DVDs were sold in 2005, while VHS sales fell to 10.4 million. Several major retailers announced that they will phase VHS out altogether.

⬆ Incredible success
The DVD of The Incredibles *sold over two million copies in the UK alone, adding to its $631 million worldwide box-office takings.*

top10 **MOST-RENTED DVDS AND VIDEOS** IN THE UK, 2005

FILM

1 Collateral
2 Meet the Fockers
3 Man on Fire
4 The Bourne Supremacy
5 National Treasure
6 Dodgeball: A True Underdog Story
7 Hitch
8 The Terminal
9 Layer Cake
10 Bridget Jones: The Edge of Reason

Source: British Video Association/MRIB

top10 **MOST-RENTED VIDEOS** IN THE UK*

TITLE

1 Four Weddings and a Funeral
2 Dirty Dancing
3 Basic Instinct*
4 Crocodile Dundee
5 Gladiator
6 Sister Act
7 Forrest Gump
8 The Sixth Sense
9 Home Alone
10 Ghost

* To 1 Jan 2006; includes VHS and DVD formats

Source: British Video Association/MRIB

top10 **VIDEO PIRACY** COUNTRIES

	COUNTRY	EST. LOSSES, 2005* ($)
1	Mexico	483,000,000
2	Russia	266,000,000
3	China	244,000,000
4	Italy	161,000,000
5	Thailand	149,000,000
6	Brazil	120,000,000
7	Canada	118,000,000
8 =	Hungary	102,000,000
=	Poland	102,000,000
10	Taiwan	98,000,000

* Or latest year for which data available, including illicit broadcasts

Source: International Intellectual Property Alliance (IIPA)

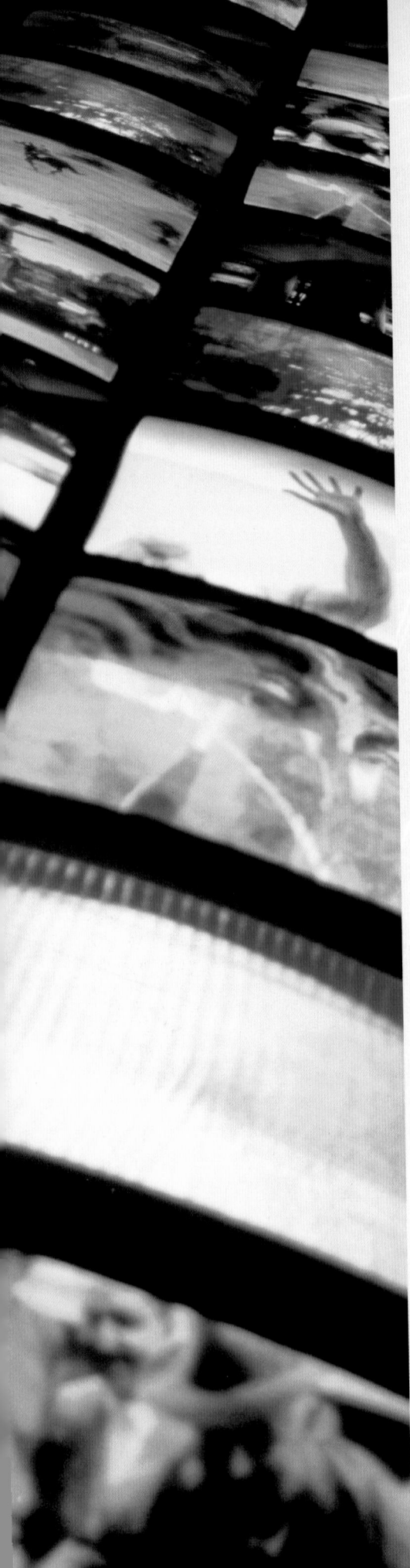

TV & Radio

top10 TV COUNTRIES

	COUNTRY	TV HOUSEHOLDS*
1	China	186,679,720
2	USA	112,884,190
3	India	83,512,900
4	Japan	48,842,920
5	Brazil	48,390,910
6	Russia	40,822,010
7	Germany	38,715,850
8	Indonesia	34,334,330
9	UK	25,269,160
10	France	24,369,170
	World total	*1,176,019,000*

* Households with colour TVs, 2007 forecast

Source: Euromonitor

Both local and national television in China is state controlled. CCTV (China Central Television), the principal broadcaster, offers 16 channels with a wide range of programmes.

top10 RADIO STATIONS IN THE UK

	STATION	% 2004–2005*
1	BBC Radio 2	27.2
2	BBC Radio 1	20.4
3	BBC Radio 4	19.3
4	BBC Radio 5 Live	12.7
5	Classic FM	12.6
6	Virgin (AM/FM)	5.1
7	talkSPORT	4.6
8	BBC Radio 3	4.2
9	BBC World Service	2.6
10	BBC Asian Network	1.0

* Of viewers listening for at least 15 minutes per week

Source: 'BBC Annual Report and Accounts 2004–2005'

The successor to the Light Programme, Radio 2, now Britain's most popular radio station, first broadcast on 30 September 1967 – its debut single was Julie Andrews' 'The Sound of Music'.

the10 LATEST WINNERS OF THE BAFTA BEST ACTRESS AWARD

YEAR	ACTRESS / PROGRAMME
2005	Anamaria Marinca, Sex Traffic
2004	Julie Walters, The Canterbury Tales: The Wife of Bath's Tale
2003	Julie Walters, Murder
2002	Julie Walters, My Beautiful Son (ITV1)
2001	Judi Dench, Last of the Blonde Bombshells
2000	Thora Hird, Lost for Words
1999	Thora Hird, Talking Heads: Waiting for the Telegram
1998	Daniela Nardini, This Life
1997	Gina McKee, Our Friends in the North
1996	Jennifer Ehle, Pride and Prejudice

In 1959 the British Film Academy (1948) and the Guild of Television Producers and Directors (1954) amalgamated to form the Society of Film and Television Arts. In 1975 it changed its name to BAFTA (the British Academy of Film and Television Arts).

the10 LATEST WINNERS OF THE BAFTA BEST ACTOR AWARD

YEAR	ACTOR / PROGRAMME
2005	Rhys Ifans, Not Only But Always
2004	Bill Nighy, State of Play
2003	Albert Finney, The Gathering Storm
2002	Michael Gambon, Perfect Strangers
2001	Michael Gambon, Longitude
2000	Michel Gambon, Wives & Daughters
1999	Tom Courtenay, A Rather English Marriage
1998	Simon Russell-Beale, A Dance to the Music of Time
1997	Nigel Hawthorne, The Fragile Heart
1996	Robbie Coltrane, Cracker

Prior to 1998, BAFTA film and television awards were presented in the same ceremony as those for films. A separate event is now held, with awards in 20 categories.

top 10 TELEVISION AUDIENCES IN THE UK

	PROGRAMME	BROADCAST	AUDIENCE
1	1966 World Cup Final: England v West Germany	30 Jul 1966	32,300,000
2	Funeral of Diana, Princess of Wales	6 Sep 1997	32,100,000
3	The Royal Family documentary	21 Jun 1969	30,690,000
4	EastEnders Christmas episode (Den divorces Angie)	25 Dec 1986	30,150,000
5	Apollo 13 splashdown	17 Apr 1970	28,600,000
6	Cup Final Replay: Chelsea v Leeds United	28 Apr 1970	28,490,000
7	Wedding of Prince Charles and Lady Diana Spencer	29 Jul 1981	28,400,000
8	Wedding of Princess Anne and Capt Mark Phillips	14 Nov 1973	27,600,000
9	Coronation Street (Alan Bradley killed by a tram)	19 Mar 1989	26,930,000
10	Only Fools and Horses (Batman and Robin episode)	29 Dec 1996	24,350,000

Source: British Film Institute

top 10 LONGEST-RUNNING PROGRAMMES ON BBC RADIO

	PROGRAMME	FIRST BROADCAST
1	The Week's Good Cause	24 Jan 1926
2	The Shipping Forecast	26 Jan 1926
3	Choral Evensong	7 Oct 1926
4	Daily Service	2 Jan 1928*
5	The Week in Westminster	6 Nov 1929
6	Sunday Half Hour	14 Jul 1940
7	Desert Island Discs	29 Jan 1942
8	Saturday Night Theatre	3 Apr 1943
9	Composer of the Week#	2 Aug 1943
10	From Our Own Correspondent	4 Oct 1946

* Experimental broadcast; national transmission began December 1929
# Formerly 'This Week's Composer'

In addition to these 10 long-running programmes, a further six that started in the 1940s are still on the air: with *Woman's Hour*, first broadcast on 7 October 1946, and *Down Your Way* (29 December 1946) the oldest.

top 10 COUNTRIES WITH THE MOST TV STATIONS

	COUNTRY	TELEVISION STATIONS
1	Russia	7,306
2	China	3,240
3	USA	2,218
4	Serbia and Montenegro	771
5	Turkey	635
6	France	584
7	India	562
8	South Africa	556
9	Germany	373
10	Norway	360
	UK	*228*

Source: Central Intelligence Agency, 'The World Factbook 2006'

In addition to these, some countries have numerous 'repeater stations' that relay signals: Germany has 8,042, the UK 3,523, Norway 2,729 and Turkey 2,394.

top 10 RADIO-OWNING COUNTRIES

	COUNTRY	RADIOS PER 1,000 POPULATION, 2003*
1	Norway	3,324
2	Sweden	2,811
3	USA	2,109
4	Australia	1,999
5	Finland	1,624
6	UK	1,445
7	Denmark	1,400
8	Estonia	1,136
9	Canada	1,047
10	South Korea	1,034
	World average	*419*

* Or latest year for which data available

Source: World Bank, 'World Development Indicators 2005'

These figures stand in sharp contrast to those of developing countries such as Malawi, where the ratio is four radios per 1,000, or 250 people to every radio.

top 10 CABLE TELEVISION COUNTRIES

	COUNTRY	CABLE TV SUBSCRIBERS, 2004
1	China	96,380,000
2	USA	66,100,200
3	Japan	24,683,900
4	Germany	19,350,000
5	South Korea	14,200,000
6	Canada	7,608,300
7	Russia	6,396,400
8	Netherlands	6,390,000
9	Argentina	5,900,000
10	Taiwan	4,856,000
	World	*317,047,500*
	UK	*3,288,000*

Source: International Telecommunication Union, 'World Telecommunication/ICT Development Report 2006'

COMMERCIAL WORLD

Workers of the World

top10 COMPANIES WITH THE **MOST EMPLOYEES**

COMPANY / COUNTRY	INDUSTRY	EMPLOYEES
1 Wal-Mart Stores, USA	Retail	1,400,000
2 McDonald's, USA	Fast food restaurants	438,000
3 Siemens, Germany	Electronics	430,000
4 Carrefour, France	Food markets	419,040
5 PetroChina, China	Oil and gas	417,229
6 China Petroleum and Chemical, China	Oil and gas	400,513
7 DaimlerChrysler, Germany	Automotive	384,723
8 United Parcel Service, USA	Package delivery	355,000
9 Deutsche Post, Germany	Post and courier	348,781
10 Volkswagen Group, Germany	Automotive	334,873

Source: Forbes 2000

top10 COUNTRIES WITH THE HIGHEST PROPORTION OF **CHILD WORKERS**

COUNTRY	PERCENTAGE OF 5–14-YEAR-OLDS AT WORK, 1999–2004 MALE	FEMALE	TOTAL
1 = Niger	69	64	66
= Nigeria	69	64	66
3 Togo	62	59	60
4 = Burkina Faso	n/a	n/a	57
= Chad	60	55	57
= Ghana	57	57	57
= Sierra Leone	57	57	57
8 Central African Rep.	54	57	56
9 Guinea-Bissau	54	54	54
10 = Cameroon	52	50	51
= Costa Rica	71	29	51
World average	*18*	*17*	*18*

Source: UNICEF, 'The State of the World's Children 2006'

Despite the efforts of bodies such as the International Labour Organization's International Programme on the Elimination of Child Labour to combat the exploitation of children in often dangerous work, over half the children in these countries work. According to UNICEF's definitions, this may be a combination of economic activity (paid labour) and of domestic work (in the case of those aged 12 to 14) totalling at least 14 hours of economic activity or a combination of 42 hours of economic activity and domestic work per week.

top10 **OCCUPATIONS** IN THE UK 100 YEARS AGO

OCCUPATION	EMPLOYEES
1 Farmers and gardeners	2,262,454
2 Domestic service	2,199,517
3 Conveyance (road, rail, canal, etc)	1,497,629
4 Textile manufacturing	1,462,001
5 Clothing makers and dealers	1,395,795
6 Builders	1,335,820
7 Metal workers	1,175,715
8 Miners and quarry workers	943,880
9 Food trade	865,777
10 Professional (clergymen, teachers, lawyers, etc)	733,582

At the beginning of the 20th century, there were 18,261,146 in the UK labour force.

top10 **OCCUPATIONS** IN THE UK

JOB SECTOR	EMPLOYEES, 2004
1 Real estate renting and business activities	4,010,000
2 Manufacturing	3,192,000
3 Health and social work	2,843,000
4 Retail (except motor and repair of personal/household goods)	2,803,000
5 Education	2,245,000
6 Hotels and restaurants	1,788,000
7 Transport, storage and communication	1,544,000
8 Public administration and defence	1,454,000
9 Construction	1,232,000
10 Wholesale and commission trade (excluding motor)	1,097,000
Total (including sectors outside Top 10)	*25,548,000*

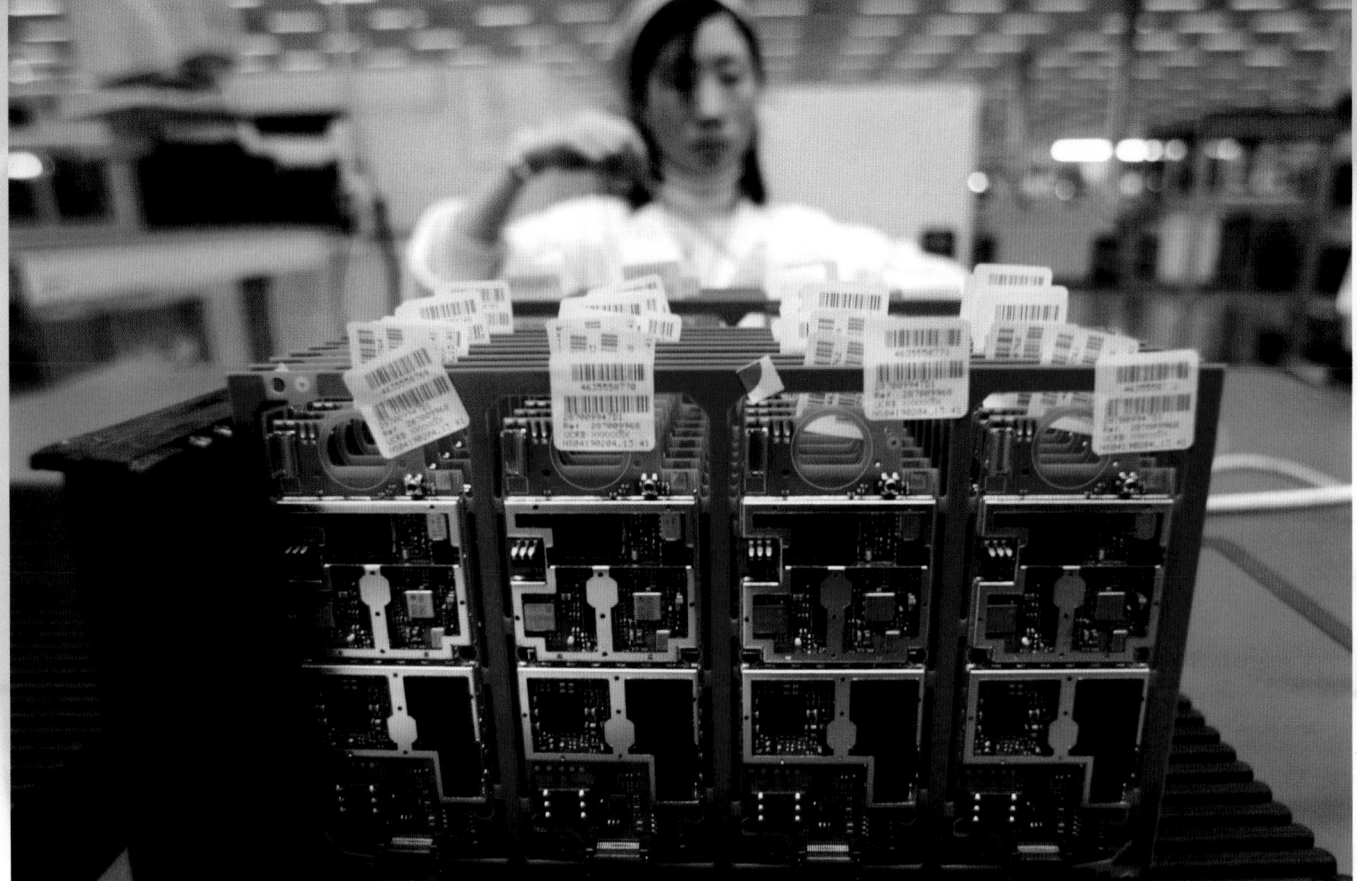

↑ *Flying start*
With China's vast labour force at its disposal, Ningbo Bird has become the country's largest manufacturer of mobile phones.

top10 COUNTRIES WITH THE MOST WORKERS

COUNTRY	WORKERS*
1 China	778,100,000
2 India	472,000,000
3 USA	147,401,000
4 Indonesia	105,700,000
5 Brazil	82,590,000
6 Russia	71,680,000
7 Japan	66,660,000
8 Bangladesh	64,020,000
9 Nigeria	54,360,000
10 Vietnam	45,740,000
UK	*29,600,000*

* 2004 or latest year available; based on people aged 15–64, currently employed; exclude unpaid groups

Source: Central Intelligence Agency/International Labour Organization

Labour statistics include employed and unemployed people aged 15 to 64, but exclude unpaid groups, such as students, housewives and retired people. In some countries, those involved in subsistence agriculture or informal work activities often go unrecorded.

top10 COUNTRIES WORKING THE LONGEST HOURS

COUNTRY	AVERAGE ANNUAL HOURS PER PERSON*
1 Korea	2,380
2 Czech Republic	1,986
3 Poland	1,983
4 Slovakia	1,958
5 Greece	1,925
6 Mexico	1,848
7 New Zealand	1,826
8 USA	1,824
9 Australia	1,816
10 Hungary	1,806
UK	*1,669*

* In employment, 2004 – total (employed and self-employed) or employed only, depending on source; OECD countries only

Source: Organization for Economic Cooperation and Development (OECD)

Historical assessments of hours worked suggest that in the mid-19th century, the average US employee worked up to 3,650 hours a year, equivalent to 10 hours a day.

the10 COUNTRIES WITH HIGHEST UNEMPLOYMENT

COUNTRY	EST. % LABOUR FORCE UNEMPLOYED, 2005*
1 Nauru	90
2 Liberia	85
3 =Turkmenistan	60
=Zimbabwe	60
5 =Djibouti	50
=East Timor	50
=Tajikistan	50
=Zambia	50
9 Senegal	48
10 Nepal	47
UK	*4.7*

* Or latest year; in those countries for which data available

Source: CIA, 'World Factbook, 2005'

The Global Economy

top10 COUNTRIES BY **GROSS NATIONAL INCOME**

COUNTRY / % OF WORLD TOTAL / GNI, 2004 ($)

1 USA 30.5 12,150,931,000,000

2 Japan 11.9 4,749,910,000,000

3 Germany 6.2 2,488,974,000,000

4 UK 5.1 2,016,393,000,000

5 France 4.7 1,858,731,000,000

6 China 4.2 1,676,846,000,000

7 Italy 3.8 1,503,562,000,000

8 Canada 2.3 905,629,000,000

9 Spain 2.2 875,817,000,000

10 Mexico 1.8 703,080,000,000

*World total 100.0
39,833,561,000,000*

Source: World Bank

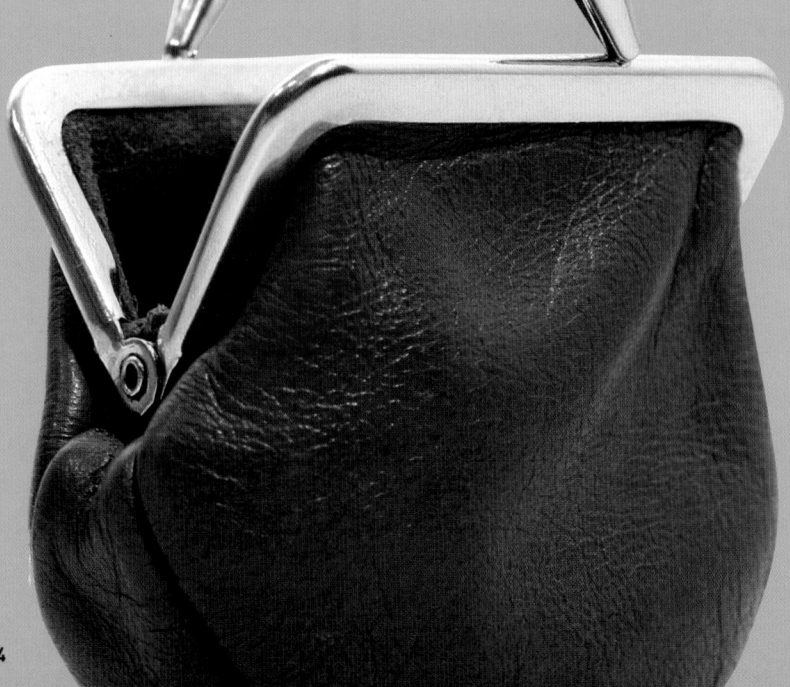

top10 SOURCES OF **UK GOVERNMENT INCOME**

	SOURCE	EST. INCOME, 2006–07 (£)
1	Income Tax	144,000,000,000
2	National Insurance contributions	89,600,000,000
3	Value Added Tax	76,500,000,000
4	Corporation Tax	49,000,000,000
5	Fuel duties	24,000,000,000
6	Council Tax	22,000,000,000
7	Business rates	21,400,000,000
8	Stamp duties	12,200,000,000
9	Tobacco duties	8,100,000,000
10	Alcohol duties	8,000,000,000

Source: HM Treasury

top10 AREAS OF **UK GOVERNMENT EXPENDITURE**

	DEPARTMENT	EST. EXPENDITURE, 2006–07 (£)
1	Social security benefits	138,300,000,000
2	Health	82,000,000,000
3	Education and Skills	53,400,000,000
4	Defence	32,600,000,000
5	Local Government	22,500,000,000
6	Scotland	22,200,000,000
7	Tax credits	15,600,000,000
8	Home Office	13,100,000,000
9	Wales	11,700,000,000
10	Works and Pensions	7,800,000,000

Source: HM Treasury

AMAZING FACT

Tax Return

Government income has escalated phenomenally in the past 100 years. In 1906, the UK's total income was £146 million or £3.40 per capita. In 2006, the Treasury's estimate was £516.4 billion – 3,537 times as much – or £8,530.88 per capita.

top10 RICHEST COUNTRIES

	COUNTRY	GDP* PER CAPITA, 2004 ($)
1	Luxembourg	69,737
2	Norway	54,600
3	Switzerland	49,300
4	Ireland	45,675
5	Denmark	44,808
6	Iceland	41,804
7	USA	39,935
8	Sweden	38,493
9	Qatar	37,610
10	Netherlands	37,326
	World average	*6,411*
	UK	*35,548*

* Gross Domestic Product

Source: International Monetary Fund

the10 POOREST COUNTRIES

	COUNTRY	GDP* PER CAPITA, 2004 ($)
1	Burundi	90
2	Dem. Rep. of the Congo	111
3	Ethiopia	113
4	Myanmar	127
5	Eritrea	139
6	Malawi	152
7	Guinea-Bissau	177
8	Sierra Leone	202
9	Rwanda	214
10	Afghanistan	228

Source: International Monetary Fund

the10 COUNTRIES MOST IN DEBT

	COUNTRY	EXTERNAL DEBT*, 2004–05 ($)
1	USA	8,837,000,000,000
2	UK	7,107,000,000,000
3	Germany	3,626,000,000,000
4	France	2,826,000,000,000
5	Italy	1,682,000,000,000
6	Netherlands	1,645,000,000,000
7	Japan	1,545,000,000,000
8	Spain	1,249,000,000,000
9	Ireland	1,049,000,000,000
10	Belgium	980,000,000,000

*External debt is total public and private debt owed to non-residents repayable in foreign currency, goods or services.

Source: World Bank

top10 MOST EXPENSIVE COUNTRIES IN WHICH TO BUY A BIG MAC

COUNTRY / COST OF A BIG MAC* ($)

A regular feature of the magazine since 1986, *The Economist*'s Big Mac index is based on the concept of 'Purchasing Power Parity', which assumes that an identical amount of goods and services should cost the same in all countries, comparing the value of countries' currencies against the standard US price of a Big Mac. The cheapest in the survey was China at $1.30, with Malaysia at $1.47.

1 Switzerland
$4.93

2 Denmark
$4.49

3 Sweden
$4.15

4 UK
$3.32

5 USA
$3.15

6 New Zealand
$3.08

7 Turkey
$3.07

8 Canada
$3.01

9 Chile
$2.98

10 Brazil
$2.74

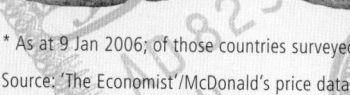
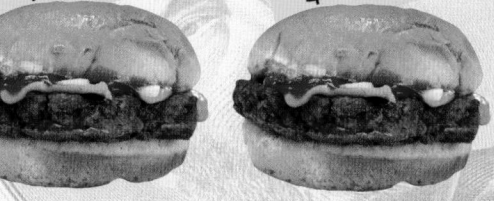

* As at 9 Jan 2006; of those countries surveyed

Source: 'The Economist'/McDonald's price data

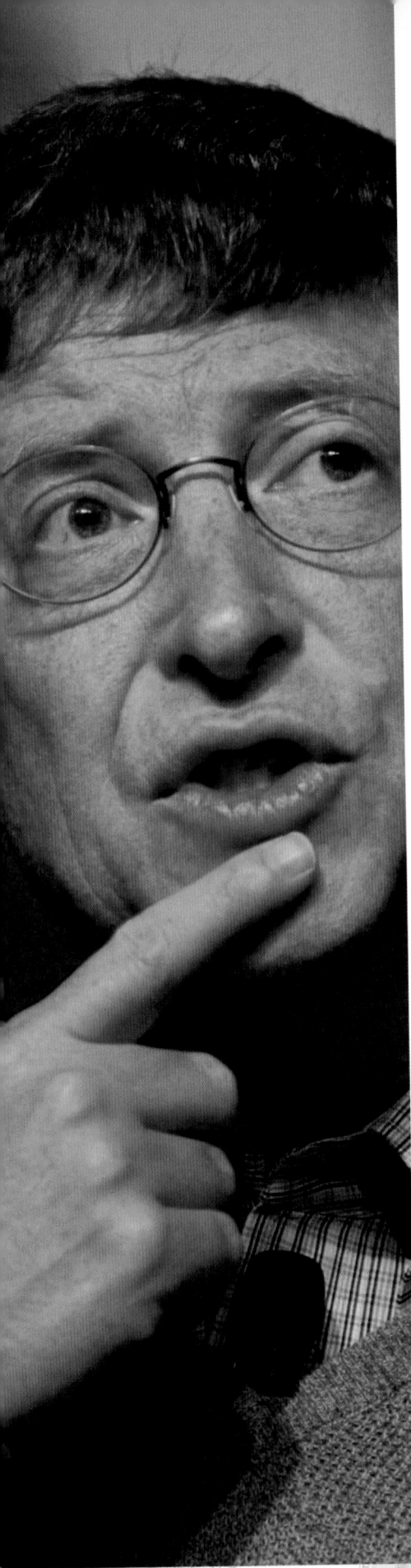

Personal Wealth

top10 **RICHEST** MEN*

NAME / COUNTRY (CITIZEN / RESIDENCE)	SOURCE	NET WORTH ($)
1 William H. Gates III, USA	Microsoft (software)	50,000,000,000
2 Warren Edward Buffett, USA	Berkshire Hathaway (investments)	42,000,000,000
3 Carlos Slim Helu, Mexico	Communications	30,000,000,000
4 Ingvar Kamprad, Sweden/ Switzerland	Ikea (home furnishings)	28,000,000,000
5 Lakshmi Mittal, India/UK	Mittal Steel	25,500,000,000
6 Paul Gardner Allen, USA	Microsoft (software)	22,000,000,000
7 Bernard Arnault, France	Louis Vuitton (luxury goods)	21,500,000,000
8 Prince Alwaleed Bin Talal Alsaud, Saudi Arabia	Investments	20,000,000,000
9 Li Ka-shing, China	Diverse investments	18,800,000,000
10 Roman Abramovich, Russia	Oil	18,200,000,000

* Excluding rulers and family fortunes

Source: Forbes magazine, The World's Richest People 2006

❸ World's wealthiest
Bill Gates has devoted a large share of his vast fortune to research, to rid the world of killer diseases.

top10 **RICHEST** WOMEN*

NAME / COUNTRY	SOURCE	NET WORTH ($)
1 Liliane Bettencourt, France	L'Oréal	16,000,000,000
2 Alice L. Walton, USA	Wal-Mart	15,700,000,000
3 Helen R. Walton, USA	Wal-Mart	15,600,000,000
4 Abigail Johnson, USA	Finance	12,500,000,000
5 = Anne Cox Chambers, USA	Media/entertainment	12,400,000,000
= Barbara Cox Anthony, USA	Media/entertainment	12,400,000,000
7 Jacqueline Mars, USA	Candy	10,000,000,000
8 Susanne Klatten, Germany	Pharmaceuticals	8,100,000,000
9 Johanna Quandt, Germany	BMW cars	6,100,000,000
10 Shari Arison, Israel	Carnival cruise line	5,200,000,000

* Excluding rulers and family fortunes

Source: Forbes magazine, The World's Richest People 2006

top10 HIGHEST-EARNING **CELEBRITIES**

CELEBRITY*	PROFESSION	EARNINGS# ($)
1 George Lucas	Film producer/director	290,000,000
2 Oprah Winfrey	Talk show host/producer	225,000,000
3 Mel Gibson	Film producer/director/actor	185,000,000
4 Tiger Woods	Golfer	87,000,000
5 Steven Spielberg	Film producer/director	80,000,000
6 Dan Brown	Author	76,500,000
7 Jerry Bruckheimer	Film and TV producer	66,000,000
8 Michael Schumacher	Racing driver	60,000,000
9 J.K. Rowling	Author	59,100,000
10 David Copperfield	Magician	57,000,000

* US, unless otherwise stated
# June 2004–June 2005

Source: Forbes magazine, 'The Celebrity 100', 2005

top10 HIGHEST-EARNING **DEAD CELEBRITIES**

CELEBRITY	PROFESSION	DEATH	EARNINGS, 2005 ($)
1 Elvis Presley	Rock star	16 Aug 1977	37,000,000
2 Charles Schultz	'Peanuts' cartoonist	12 Feb 2000	35,000,000
3 John Lennon	Rock star	8 Dec 1980	22,000,000
4 Andy Warhol	Artist	22 Feb 1987	16,000,000
5 Theodor 'Dr Seuss' Geisel	Author	24 Sep 1991	10,000,000
6 Marlon Brando	Actor	1 Jul 2004	9,000,000
7 = Marilyn Monroe	Actress	5 Aug 1962	8,000,000
= J.R.R. Tolkien	Author	2 Sep 1973	8,000,000
9 = Irving Berlin	Songwriter	22 Sep 1989	7,000,000
= Johnny Cash	Musician	12 Sep 2003	7,000,000
= George Harrison	Rock star	29 Nov 2001	7,000,000

Source: Forbes magazine, 'Top-Earning Dead Celebrities', 2005

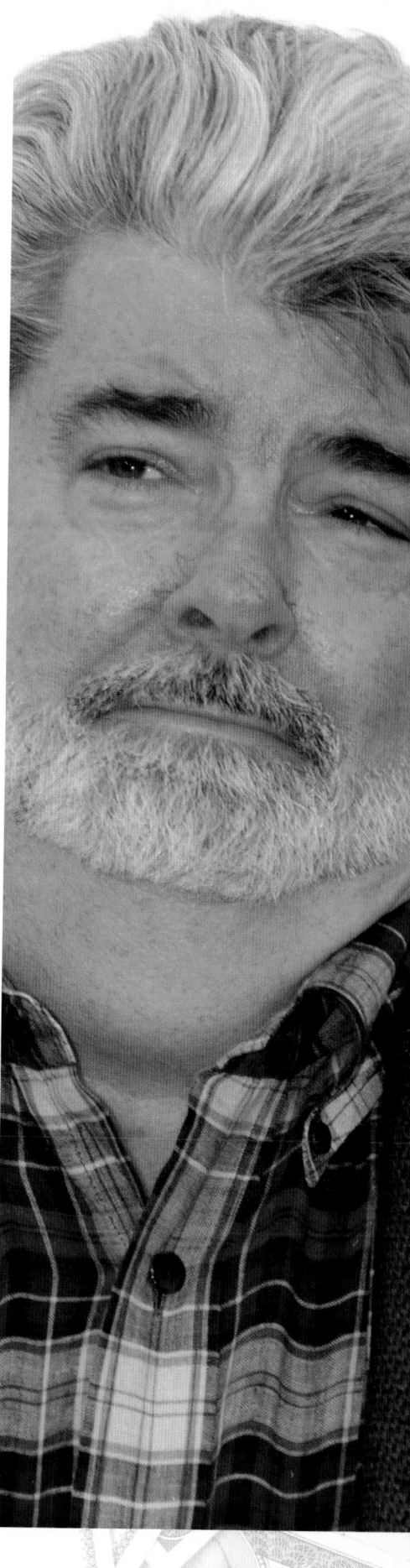

➲ By George!
George Lucas's success as the writer and producer of the Star Wars *series and other blockbusters places him first among the world's richest celebrities.*

Brand Image

top10 MOST-ADVERTISED PRODUCTS*

	CATEGORY	WORLD ADVERTISING SPENDING, 2004 ($)
1	Automotive	22,693,000,000
2	Personal care	17,163,000,000
3	Entertainment and media	10,459,000,000
4	Pharmaceuticals	8,197,000,000
5	Food	8,015,000,000
6	Soft drinks	3,331,000,000
7	Electronics	3,186,000,000
8	Restaurants	3,148,000,000
9	Cleaning products	2,982,000,000
10	Computers	2,973,000,000

* Based on total worldwide spend by Top 100 companies

Source: 'Advertising Age Global Marketing Report 2005'

World spending on advertising in all media in 2004 totalled $94 billion, with that for 2005 forecast to top $100 billion. Falling outside the Top 10, but with spending in excess of $2 billion each, are telecommunications, retailers, alcohol and financial services.

top10 GLOBAL RETAILERS

	COMPANY / COUNTRY	RETAIL SALES, 2004 ($)*
1	Wal-Mart, USA	285,222,000,000
2	Carrefour, France	89,568,000,000
3	Home Depot, USA	73,094,000,000
4	Metro, Germany	69,781,000,000
5	Tesco, UK	62,505,000,000
6	Kroger, USA	56,434,000,000
7	Costco, USA	47,146,000,000
8	Target, USA	45,682,000,000
9	Koninklijke, Netherlands	44,793,000,000
10	Aldi, Germany	42,906,000,000

* Financial year

Source: Deloitte/Stores '2006 Global Powers of Retailing'

In 2004 the total sales of the Top 250 global retailers was $2.84 trillion – almost one-third of the estimated world total of $9 trillion. Even those at the bottom of this extended list sold over $2.3 billion-worth of goods.

top10 MOST VALUABLE GLOBAL BRANDS

	BRAND NAME*	INDUSTRY	BRAND VALUE, 2005 ($)
1	Coca-Cola	Beverages	67,525,000,000
2	Microsoft	Technology	59,941,000,000
3	IBM	Technology	53,376,000,000
4	General Electric	Diversified	46,996,000,000
5	Intel	Technology	35,588,000,000
6	Nokia, Finland	Technology	26,452,000,000
7	Disney	Leisure	26,441,000,000
8	McDonald's	Food retail	26,014,000,000
9	Toyota, Japan	Automobiles	24,837,000,000
10	Marlboro	Tobacco	21,189,000,000

* All US-owned unless otherwise stated

Source: Interbrand/BusinessWeek

Brand consultants Interbrand use a method of estimating value that takes account of the profitability of individual brands within a business (rather than the companies that own them), as well as such factors as their potential for growth.

top10 OLDEST FAMILY BUSINESSES IN THE WORLD

	BUSINESS	LOCATION	FOUNDED
1	Kongo Gumi (construction)	Osaka, Japan	578
2	Hoshi Ryokan (hotel)	Komatsu, Japan	718
3	=Château de Goulaine (vineyard)	Haute Goulaine, France	1000
	=Fonderia Pontificia Marinelli (bell foundry)	Agnone, Italy	1000
5	Barone Ricasoli (wine and olive oil)	Siena, Italy	1141
6	Barovier & Tos (glassmaking)	Venice, Italy	1295
7	Pilgrim Haus (hotel)	Soest, Germany	1304
8	Richard de Bas (papermaking)	Ambert d'Auvergne, France	1326
9	Torrini Firenze (goldsmiths)	Florence, Italy	1369
10	Antinori (winemakers)	Florence, Italy	1385

Source: 'Family Business Magazine'

⬆ Great Wal-Mart of China
*The world's largest retailer Wal-Mart opened its first store in China in
1996. It now operates 47 units in 22 cities, employing over 25,000 people.*

top10 **GLOBAL** INDUSTRIAL COMPANIES

COMPANY / LOCATION	SECTOR	ANNUAL REVENUE ($)
1 Exxon Mobil, USA	Oil, gas	328,213,000,000
2 Wal-Mart Stores, Inc., USA	Retailing	312,427,000,000
3 Royal Dutch/Shell Group, Netherlands/UK	Oil, gas, chemicals	306,731,000,000
4 BP plc, UK	Oil, gas	249,465,000,000
5 General Motors Corp., USA	Motor vehicles	192,604,000,000
6 Chevron Corp., USA	Oil, gas	184,922,000,000
7 Ford Motor Co., USA	Motor vehicles	178,101,000,000
8 DaimlerChrysler AG, Germany	Motor vehicles	177,040,000,000
9 Toyota Motor, Japan	Motor vehicles	173,086,000,000
10 ConcoPhillips Company, USA	Oil, gas	162,405,000,000

Source: Forbes, 2,000 Largest Companies, 17 April 2006

top10 **GROCERY BRANDS** IN THE UK, 2004

BRAND	SALES, 2004 (£)
1 Coca-Cola	894,668,481
2 Walker's crisps	409,614,250
3 Warburton's bakery	381,032,729
4 Cadbury's Dairy Milk	319,892,000
5 Nescafé instant coffee	313,687,000
6 Müller yoghurt	312,108,921
7 Kingsmill bakery	301,738,999
8 Hovis bakery	301,074,736
9 Andrex toilet tissue	283,281,492
10 Robinsons soft drinks	266,112,898

Source: ACNielsen/Checkout, 'Top 100 Grocery Brands 2005'

Food Business

top10 GLOBAL **CONFECTIONERY** BRANDS

	BRAND	COMPANY	% OF GLOBAL MARKET
1	M&Ms	Mars Inc.	2.13
2	Snickers	Mars Inc.	2.10
3	Reese's	Hershey Foods Corp.	1.35
4	Milka	Kraft Foods Inc.	1.08
5	Orbit	William Wrigley Jr Co.	0.97
6 =	Extra	William Wrigley Jr Co.	0.94
=	Mars	Mars Inc.	0.94
8	Trident	Cadbury Schweppes plc	0.86
9	Lindt	Chocoladefabriken Lindt & Sprüngli AG	0.83
10	Artisanal	Artisanal	0.81

Source: Euromonitor, 'The World Market for Packaged Food, 2005'

top10 FAST FOOD **COMPANIES**

	COMPANY	GLOBAL SALES ($)
1	McDonald's Corp.	45,933,000,000
2	Yum! Brands Inc. (KFC, Taco Bell, Pizza Hut)	24,418,000,000
3	Burger King Corp.	11,100,000,000
4	Wendy's International Inc.	10,200,000,000
5	Doctor's Associates Inc. (Subway)	6,523,000,000
6	Darden Restaurants Inc.	4,655,000,000
7	Domino's Pizza Inc.	4,193,000,000
8	Brinker International Inc.	3,807,000,000
9	Applebee's International Inc.	3,593,000,000
10	Starbucks Corp.	3,450,000,000

Source: Euromonitor, 'The World Market for Consumer Foodservice, 2004'

top10 **RESTAURANT CHAINS** IN THE UK

	CHAIN	OUTLETS
1	Enterprise Inns	10,035
2	Punch Taverns	7,800
3	The Union Pub Company	1,617
4	McDonald's	1,250
5	Scottish & Newcastle	1,100
6	Greggs	1,004
7	Pizza Hut	793
8 =	Avebury Taverns	700
=	Burger King	700
10	KFC	609

Source: Euromonitor, 'Consumer Foodservice in the UK, 2005'

top10 FAST FOOD **COUNTRIES**

COUNTRY / GLOBAL SALES ($)

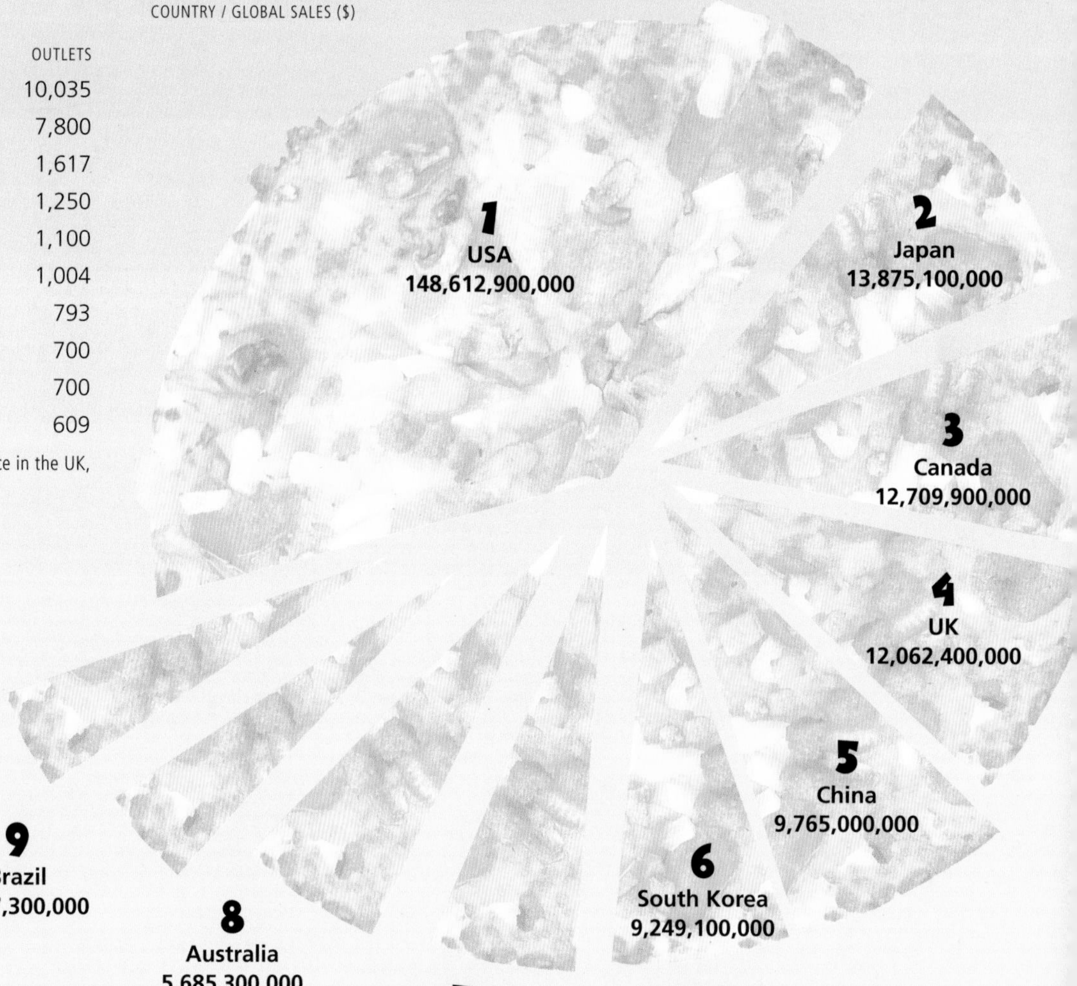

1 USA 148,612,900,000

2 Japan 13,875,100,000

3 Canada 12,709,900,000

4 UK 12,062,400,000

5 China 9,765,000,000

6 South Korea 9,249,100,000

7 Germany 7,376,900,000

8 Australia 5,685,300,000

9 Brazil 4,967,300,000

10 India 4,914,700,000

Source: Euromonitor, 'The World Market for Consumer Foodservice, 2004'

top10 **RESTAURANT TYPES** IN THE UK

	TYPE	OUTLETS	SALES (£)
1	Various*	16,222	2,769,100,000
2	Indian	6,646	1,886,600,000
3	Pizza	4,550	946,700,000
4	Chinese	3,284	707,900,000
5	Japanese	246	66,600,000
6	Thai	695	66,200,000
7	Mexican	190	33,700,000
8	Indonesian/Malaysian/Singaporean	145	16,400,000
9	Korean	54	8,400,000
10	Vietnamese	60	7,800,000

* Not identified by nationality

Source: Euromonitor, 'Consumer Foodservice in the UK, 2005'

➲ Exotic eating
Britain's first Indian restaurant, the Hindostanee Coffee House, opened in 1809, since when its cuisine, alongside that of China and many other countries, has been enthusiastically adopted across the UK.

top10 COUNTRIES THAT SPEND THE MOST **EATING OUT**

	COUNTRY	GLOBAL SALES ($)
1	USA	175,946,100,000
2	China	100,310,000,000
3	Japan	89,197,700,000
4	India	87,167,200,000
5	Italy	36,233,400,000
6	France	31,740,400,000
7	South Korea	15,297,100,000
8	Germany	14,514,100,000
9	Spain	14,013,300,000
10	Mexico	11,725,500,000
	UK	*10,685,800,000*

Source: Euromonitor, 'The World Market for Consumer Foodservice, 2004'

top10 COUNTRIES WITH **MOST CAFÉS AND BARS**

	COUNTRY	GLOBAL SALES ($)
1	Japan	55,222,900,000
2	Italy	24,094,200,000
3	USA	13,951,100,000
4	UK	12,398,500,000
5	South Korea	11,273,800,000
6	Spain	11,059,500,000
7	Brazil	7,436,100,000
8	Canada	3,618,200,000
9	Thailand	3,307,100,000
10	India	2,787,700,000

Source: Euromonitor, 'The World Market for Consumer Foodservice, 2004'

top10 **STREET FOOD** SALES COUNTRIES*

	COUNTRY	GLOBAL SALES ($)
1	USA	9,357,200,000
2	Thailand	4,699,000,000
3	Venezuela	3,541,200,000
4	India	3,295,000,000
5	UK	2,064,500,000
6	Brazil	1,411,200,000
7	Germany	1,313,700,000
8	France	855,600,000
9	Russia	824,600,000
10	Indonesia	817,900,000

* Sales from stalls and kiosks

Source: Euromonitor, 'The World Market for Consumer Foodservice, 2004'

Drinks Industry

top10 **WINE-PRODUCING** COUNTRIES

COUNTRY	ANNUAL PRODUCTION LITRES	PINTS
1 France	5,338,900,000	9,295,145,000
2 Italy	5,009,300,000	8,815,130,000
3 Spain	3,050,000,000	5,367,246,000
4 USA	1,920,000,000	3,378,725,000
5 Argentina	1,583,500,000	2,786,568,000
6 China	1,080,000,000	1,900,533,000
7 Australia	1,016,300,000	1,788,436,000
8 Germany	889,100,000	1,564,596,000
9 Portugal	778,900,000	1,370,671,000
10 South Africa	647,100,000	1,138,736,000
World total	26,473,000,000	46,585,941,000

Source: Commission for Distilled Spirits

The rise of New World and Southern Hemisphere wine-producing countries is the most notable recent development, ending the industry's centuries-old domination by European vineyards – since 1980, Australia's production has increased by over 200 per cent.

top10 **BEER-PRODUCING** COUNTRIES

COUNTRY	ANNUAL PRODUCTION LITRES	PINTS
1 China	23,580,000,000	41,494,975,000
2 USA	23,456,200,000	41,277,118,000
3 Germany	10,833,600,000	19,064,460,000
4 Brazil	8,600,000,000	15,133,875,000
5 Russia	7,200,000,000	12,670,221,000
6 Japan	6,930,400,000	12,195,792,000
7 Mexico	6,370,000,000	11,209,626,000
8 UK	5,667,200,000	9,972,872,000
9 Spain	2,786,000,000	4,902,671,000
10 Poland	2,610,000,000	4,592,955,000
World total	144,322,500,000	253,971,952,000

Source: Commission for Distilled Spirits

top10 **BREWERS**

BREWERY / COUNTRY	PRODUCTION, 2004 LITRES	PINTS
1 InBev (Belgium)	18,370,000,000	32,322,000,000
2 SABMiller (USA)	17,500,000,000	30,791,000,000
3 Anheuser-Busch (USA)	14,420,000,000	25,372,000,000
4 Heineken (Netherlands)	11,160,000,000	19,636,000,000
5 Carlsberg (Denmark)	6,700,000,000	11,788,000,000
6 Molson Coors (USA)	5,760,000,000	10,134,000,000
7 Scottish & Newcastle (UK)	5,150,000,000	9,061,000,000
8 Modelo (Mexico)	4,280,000,000	7,530,000,000
9 Tsingtao (China)	3,710,000,000	6,527,000,000
10 Kirin (Japan)	3,600,000,000	6,334,000,000

top10 CHAMPAGNE-IMPORTING COUNTRIES

COUNTRY	BOTTLES IMPORTED, 2003
1 UK	34,465,159
2 USA	18,957,031
3 Germany	12,053,665
4 Belgium	9,143,810
5 Italy	8,506,287
6 Switzerland	5,596,549
7 Japan	5,013,705
8 Netherlands	2,575,838
9 Spain	2,158,056
10 Australia	1,659,441

Source: Comité Interprofessionnel du Vin de Champagne (CIVC)

top10 CARBONATED SOFT DRINK CONSUMERS

COUNTRY	ANNUAL CONSUMPTION PER CAPITA LITRES	PINTS
1 USA	195.8	344.5
2 Mexico	126.0	222.0
3 Norway	122.0	215.0
4 Ireland	121.4	214.0
5 Canada	117.1	206.1
6 Belgium	109.3	192.3
7 Australia	103.2	182.0
8 Netherlands	99.8	175.6
9 Chile	99.7	175.4
10 Spain	98.3	173.0
World average	*28.5*	*50.1*
UK	*88.1*	*155.0*

Source: Euromonitor

In marked contrast to the countries in the Top 10, India (2 litres per capita) and Indonesia (3.2 litres) and many African nations are among the lowest consumers in a world market that in 2003 drank 179.4 billion litres – equivalent to almost 60,000 Olympic swimming pools full!

top10 BOTTLED WATER DRINKERS

COUNTRY	CONSUMPTION PER CAPITA, 2003 LITRES	PINTS
1 Italy	177.1	311.7
2 Spain	156.7	275.8
3 France	152.5	268.4
4 Mexico	152.1	267.7
5 Belgium	130.1	229.0
6 Germany	118.6	208.7
7 Switzerland	112.0	197.1
8 Austria	98.0	172.4
9 Portugal	96.8	170.3
10 Argentina	81.4	143.2
World average	*22.9*	*40.3*
UK	*28.7*	*50.5*

Source: Euromonitor

Worldwide consumption of bottled mineral water has more than doubled in the past decade, hitting a 2003 total of 144.5 billion litres (254.3 billion pints). Although its total consumption of 18.3 billion litres (32.2 billion pints) makes it the world's leading overall consumer, on a per capita basis the USA remains unusually absent from the Top 10.

top10 COFFEE-PRODUCING COUNTRIES

COUNTRY	PRODUCTION, 2005 (TONNES)
1 Brazil	2,179,270
2 Vietnam	990,000
3 Indonesia	762,006
4 Colombia	682,580
5 Mexico	310,861
6 India	275,400
7 Ethiopia	260,000
8 Guatemala	216,600
9 Honduras	190,640
10 Uganda	186,000
World total	*7,718,531*

Source: Food and Agriculture Organization of the United Nations

top10 TEA-PRODUCING COUNTRIES

COUNTRY	PRODUCTION, 2005 (TONNES)
1 China	900,500
2 India	852,800
3 Sri Lanka	308,090
4 Kenya	295,000
5 Turkey	202,000
6 Indonesia	171,410
7 Vietnam	110,000
8 Japan	100,000
9 Argentina	64,000
10 Bangladesh	55,627
World total	*3,200,877*

Source: Food and Agriculture Organization of the United Nations

Farming

top10 COUNTRIES WITH THE MOST FARMLAND

	COUNTRY	AGRICULTURAL LAND, 2003 (HECTARES)
1	China	554,851,000
2	Australia	439,500,000
3	USA	409,300,000
4	Brazil	263,600,000
5	Russia	216,277,000
6	Kazakhstan	207,784,000
7	India	180,804,000
8	Saudi Arabia	173,798,000
9	Sudan	134,600,000
10	Mongolia	130,500,000
	World total	*4,973,406,000*
	UK	*16,956,000*

Source: Food and Agriculture Organization of the United Nations

top10 WHEAT-PRODUCING COUNTRIES

	COUNTRY	PRODUCTION, 2005 (TONNES)
1	China	96,160,250
2	India	72,000,000
3	USA	57,105,552
4	Russia	45,500,000
5	France	36,922,000
6	Canada	25,546,900
7	Australia	24,067,000
8	Germany	23,578,000
9	Pakistan	21,591,400
10	Turkey	21,000,000
	World total	*626,466,585*
	UK	*14,950,000*

Source: Food and Agriculture Organization of the United Nations

top10 CATTLE COUNTRIES

	COUNTRY	CATTLE, 2005
1	Brazil	192,000,000
2	India	185,000,000
3	China	115,229,500
4	USA	95,848,000
5	Argentina	50,768,000
6	Ethiopia	38,500,000
7	Sudan	38,325,000
8	Mexico	31,476,600
9	Australia	26,900,000
10	Colombia	25,000,000
	World	*1,355,187,580*
	UK	*10,378,023*

Source: Food and Agriculture Organization of the United Nations

top10 COUNTRIES WHERE SHEEP MOST OUTNUMBER PEOPLE

	COUNTRY	SHEEP POPULATION, 2005	HUMAN POPULATION, 2005	SHEEP PER PERSON
1	New Zealand	40,009,000	4,035,461	9.91
2	Australia	106,000,000	20,090,437	5.27
3	Mongolia	11,686,400	2,791,272	4.18
4	Mauritania	8,850,000	3,086,859	2.86
5	Uruguay	9,712,000	3,415,920	2.84
6	Turkmenistan	13,000,000	4,952,081	2.62
7	Iceland	454,000	296,737	1.52
8	Namibia	2,900,000	2,030,692	1.42
9	Sudan	48,000,000	40,187,486	1.19
10	Ireland	4,556,700	4,015,676	1.13
	World average	*1,079,735,160*	*6,451,058,790*	*0.16*
	UK	*35,253,048*	*60,441,457*	*0.58*

Source: Food and Agriculture Organization of the United Nations/ US Census Bureau

You say 'tomato'...
The tomato – botanically a fruit – is celebrated in the annual Tomatina festival in Buñol, Valencia, Spain, during which some 30,000 people do battle with over 100,000 kg (240,000 lb) of tomatoes.

top10 **FRUIT** CROPS

	CROP	PRODUCTION, 2005 (TONNES)
1	Tomatoes	124,748,292
2	Watermelons	95,292,051
3	Bananas	72,464,562
4	Grapes	66,533,393
5	Apples	63,488,907
6	Oranges	59,858,474
7	Coconuts	55,037,524
8	Plantains	33,407,921
9	Cantaloupes and other melons	28,321,159
10	Mangoes	27,966,749

Source: Food and Agriculture Organization of the United Nations

top10 **VEGETABLE** CROPS

	CROP*	PRODUCTION, 2005 (TONNES)
1	Sugar cane	1,293,220,050
2	Potatoes	321,974,152
3	Sugar beets	241,985,317
4	Soybeans	209,531,558
5	Sweet potatoes	129,888,827
6	Cabbages	69,480,505
7	Onions (dry)	57,594,350
8	Cucumbers and gherkins	41,743,840
9	Yams	39,897,327
10	Aubergines	30,517,767

* Excluding cereals

Source: Food and Agriculture Organization of the United Nations

This includes only vegetables grown for human and annual consumption. Among non-food vegetable crops, cotton is the most important, with a total annual production of over 70 million tonnes, while rubber, tobacco, jute and other fibres are also economically significant.

top10 **RICE*-PRODUCING** COUNTRIES

	COUNTRY	PRODUCTION, 2005 (TONNES)
1	China	184,254,000
2	India	129,000,000
3	Indonesia	53,984,592
4	Bangladesh	40,054,000
5	Vietnam	36,341,000
6	Thailand	27,000,000
7	Myanmar	22,000,000
8	Philippines	14,800,000
9	Brazil	13,140,900
10	Japan	10,989,000
	World total	*614,654,895*

* Paddy rice only

Source: Food and Agriculture Organization of the United Nations

top10 COUNTRIES WITH THE **MOST AGRICULTURAL WORKERS**

	COUNTRY	% OF TOTAL WORKFORCE	AGRICULTURAL WORKERS, 2003
1	China	65	510,573,000
2	India	58	273,515,000
3	Indonesia	46	50,254,000
4	Bangladesh	53	39,466,000
5	Vietnam	66	28,582,000
6	Pakistan	46	26,173,000
7	Ethiopia	81	25,056,000
8	Myanmar	69	18,671,000
9	Nigeria	31	15,178,000
10	Turkey	44	14,779,000
	World	*43*	*1,340,460,000*
	UK	*1.7*	*501,000*

Source: Food and Agriculture Organization of the United Nations

Rich Resources

top10 COUNTRIES WITH THE MOST GOLD

COUNTRY	GOLD RESERVES* (TROY OUNCES)	(TONNES)
1 USA	261,497,718	8,133.5
2 Germany	110,206,169	3,427.8
3 France	90,681,049	2,820.5
4 Italy	78,827,086	2,451.8
5 Switzerland	41,477,618	1,290.1
6 Japan	24,601,715	765.2
7 Netherlands	22,341,521	694.9
8 China	19,290,420	600.0
9 Spain	14,715,375	457.7
10 Taiwan	13,609,391	423.3

* As at March 2006

Source: World Gold Council

Gold reserves are the government holdings of gold in each country – which are often far greater than the gold owned by private individuals. In the days of the 'Gold Standard', this provided a tangible measure of a country's wealth, guaranteeing the convertibility of its currency, and determined such factors as exchange rates. Though less significant today, gold reserves remain a component in calculating a country's international reserves, alongside its holdings of foreign exchange and SDRs (Special Drawing Rights).

AMAZING FACT

Gold Record

The world's total gold reserves are estimated at 30,836.8 tonnes, worth about $583 billion. However, these account for only one-fifth of all the gold ever mined, estimated at some 150,000 tonnes, the rest having been made into jewellery and coins, or used in dentistry and industrial processes. The total – worth $2.845 trillion at today's price – could be stretched into a wire that would circle the Earth 9 million times, but if made into a sphere would be only 25 metres (82 ft) in diameter.

top10 GOLD-PRODUCING COUNTRIES

COUNTRY	% OF WORLD TOTAL	2004 PRODUCTION (TONNES)
1 South Africa	13.9	342.7
2 USA	10.6	261.8
3 Australia	10.5	258.4
4 China	8.8	217.3
5 Russia	7.4	181.6
6 Peru	7.0	173.2
7 Canada	5.2	128.5
8 Indonesia	4.6	114.2
9 Uzbekistan	3.4	83.7
10 Ghana	2.3	57.6
World total	*100.0*	*2,464.4*

Source: Gold Fields Mineral Services Ltd, 'Gold Survey 2004'

Since hitting an all-time high of 619.5 tonnes in 1993, the output by South Africa, the world's dominant gold producer, has steadily declined, as has that of Australia, which peaked at 313.2 tonnes in 1997.

top10 SILVER PRODUCERS

	COUNTRY	PRODUCTION, 2004 (TONNES)
1	Peru	3,060
2	Mexico	2,700
3	China*	2,450
4	Australia	2,237
5	Chile	1,360
6	Canada	1,336
7	Russia*	1,277
8	= Poland	1,250
	= USA	1,250
10	Kazakhstan	733
	World total	*19,700*

* Estimated

Source: US Geological Survey, 'Minerals Yearbook'

top10 PLATINUM PRODUCERS

	COUNTRY	PRODUCTION, 2004 (KILOS)	(LBS)
1	South Africa	160,013	352,767
2	Russia*	36,000	79,366
3	Canada	7,000	15,432
4	Zimbabwe	4,438	9,784
5	USA	4,040	8,906
6	Colombia	1,400	3,086
7	Japan	780	1,719
8	Finland	500	1,102
9	Poland	20	44
10	Serbia & Montenegro	5	11
	World total	*214,000*	*471,788*

* Estimated

Source: US Geological Survey, 'Minerals Yearbook'

top10 URANIUM-PRODUCING COUNTRIES

	COUNTRY	PRODUCTION, 2004 (TONNES)
1	Canada	11,597
2	Australia	8,982
3	Kazakhstan	3,719
4	Niger	3,282
5	Russia*	3,200
6	Namibia	3,038
7	Uzbekistan	2,016
8	USA	846
9	Ukraine*	800
10	South Africa	755
	World total	*40,219*

* Estimated

Source: World Nuclear Association

In 2004 some 7,200 tonnes, or 18 per cent of the world's uranium output, came from a single Canadian mine, McArthur River, Canada.

top10 DIAMOND PRODUCERS (BY VOLUME)

COUNTRY
VALUE, 2004 ($) / VOLUME, 2004 (CARATS)

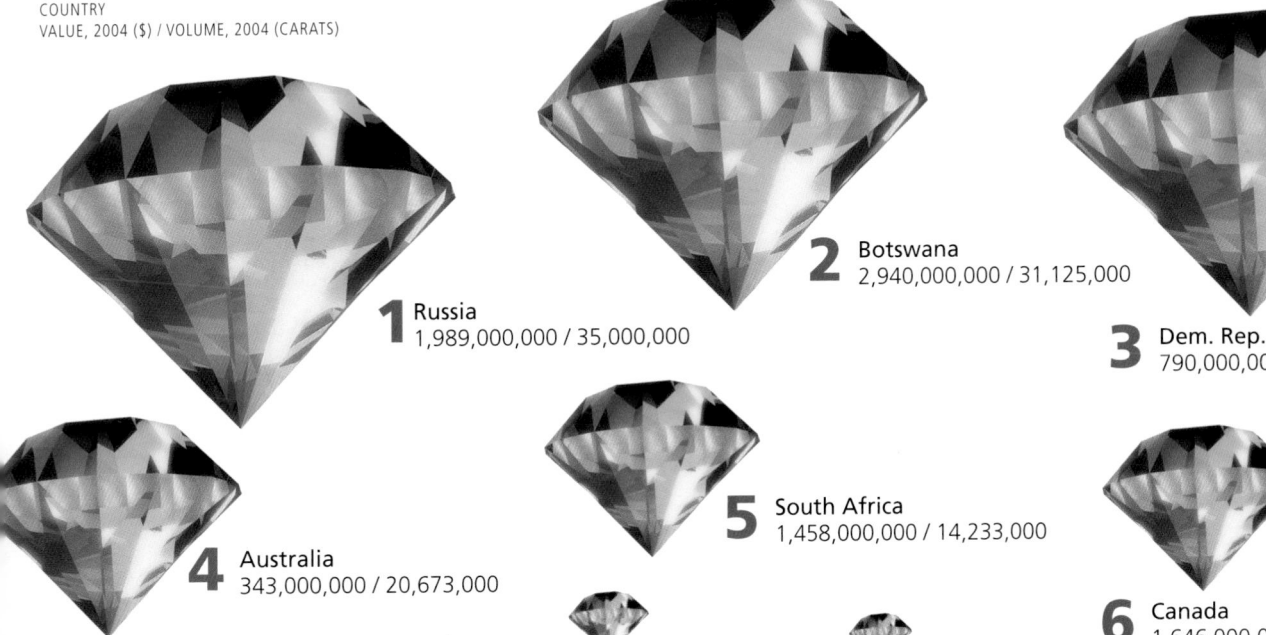

1 Russia
1,989,000,000 / 35,000,000

2 Botswana
2,940,000,000 / 31,125,000

3 Dem. Rep. of Congo
790,000,000 / 29,000,000

4 Australia
343,000,000 / 20,673,000

5 South Africa
1,458,000,000 / 14,233,000

6 Canada
1,646,000,000 / 12,618,000

7 Angola
1,300,000,000 / 7,500,000

8 Namibia
698,000,000 / 2,011,000

9 Ghana
26,000,000 / 900,000

10 Brazil
35,000,000 / 700,000

Source: Diamond Facts 2005

Oil Essentials

top10 COUNTRIES WITH THE **GREATEST** OIL-REFINING CAPACITY

	COUNTRY	BARRELS PER DAY, 2005*
1	USA	17,042,000
2	China	5,818,000
3	Russia	5,412,000
4	Japan	4,531,000
5	South Korea	2,598,000
6	India	2,513,000
7	Germany	2,314,000
8	Italy	2,294,000
9	Saudi Arabia	2,061,000
10	France	1,977,000
	UK	*1,813,000*

* One barrel = 159 litres

Source: BP Statistical Review of World Energy 2005

In 2005, the refining capacity of the USA was reduced by the effects of Hurricane Katrina. In September 2005, Sir Richard Branson announced his plan to build an oil refinery to counteract the escalating fuel costs with which his Virgin Atlantic airline has had to contend.

top10 **OIL-CONSUMING** COUNTRIES

	COUNTRY	CONSUMPTION, 2004 (TONNES)
1	USA	937,600,000
2	China	308,600,000
3	Japan	241,500,000
4	Russia	128,500,000
5	Germany	123,600,000
6	India	119,300,000
7	South Korea	104,800,000
8	Canada	99,600,000
9	France	94,000,000
10	Italy	89,500,000
	World total	*3,767,100,000*
	UK	*80,800,000*

Source: BP Statistical Review of World Energy 2005

the10 COUNTRIES WITH **LONGEST** OIL PIPELINES

COUNTRY
TOTAL PIPELINE LENGTH* KM / MILES

1 USA
244,620 / 151,999

2 Russia
89,310 / 55,494

10 Kazakhstan
10,158 / 6,311

9 Brazil
10,308 / 6,405

8 UK
10,894 / 6,769

7 India
11,180 / 6,946

6 Iran
16,064 / 9,981

* Oil + petroleum products   Source: Central Intelligence Agency, 'The World Factbook 2005'

↑ Strategic supply *The pipeline from the Iraq oilfield of Kirkuk carries oil to Ceyhan, Turkey.*

top10 COUNTRIES WITH THE **GREATEST** OIL RESERVES

	COUNTRY	2004 RESERVES (TONNES)
1	Saudi Arabia	36,100,000,000
2	Iran	18,200,000,000
3	Iraq	15,500,000,000
4	Kuwait	13,600,000,000
5	United Arab Emirates	13,000,000,000
6	Venezuela	11,100,000,000
7	Russia	9,900,000,000
8	Kazakhstan	5,400,000,000
9	Libya	5,100,000,000
10	Nigeria	4,800,000,000
	UK	*600,000,000*

Source: BP Statistical Review of World Energy 2005

top10 **OIL-PRODUCING** COUNTRIES

	COUNTRY	PRODUCTION, 2004 (TONNES)
1	Saudi Arabia	505,900,000
2	Russia	458,700,000
3	USA	329,800,000
4	Iran	202,600,000
5	Mexico	190,700,000
6	China	174,500,000
7	Venezuela	153,500,000
8	Norway	149,900,000
9	Canada	147,600,000
10	United Arab Emirates	125,800,000
	World total	*3,867,900,000*
	UK	*95,400,000*

Source: BP Statistical Review of World Energy 2005

top10 OIL **IMPORTERS**, 2004

	COUNTRY	NET OIL IMPORTS (MILLION BARRELS PER DAY)*
1	USA	12.1
2	Japan	5.3
3	China	2.9
4	Germany	2.4
5	South Korea	2.2
6	France	1.9
7	Italy	1.7
8	Spain	1.6
9	India	1.5
10	Taiwan	1.0

* One barrel = 159 litres; weight depends on oil type

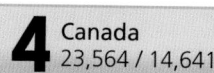

3 Mexico
38,350 / 23,829

5 China
17,758 / 11,034

4 Canada
23,564 / 14,641

Energy & the Environment

top10 MOST ENVIRONMENTALLY FRIENDLY COUNTRIES

	COUNTRY	ESI RANKING*
1	Finland	75.1
2	Norway	73.4
3	Uruguay	71.8
4	Sweden	71.7
5	Iceland	70.8
6	Canada	64.4
7	Switzerland	63.7
8	Guyana	62.9
9	= Argentina	62.7
	= Austria	62.7
	UK	*50.2*

* Based on calculations of 20 key indicators in five categories: environmental systems, environmental stresses, human vulnerability to environmental risks, a society's institutional capacity to respond to environmental threats and a nation's stewardship of the shared resources of the global commons

Source: World Economic Forum, '2005 Environmental Sustainability Index'

⊕ Burning issue
The industrial and domestic output of greenhouse gases is one of the most important items on the world's agenda for a sustainable future.

the10 LEAST ENVIRONMENTALLY FRIENDLY COUNTRIES

	COUNTRY	ESI RANKING
1	North Korea	29.2
2	Taiwan	32.7
3	Turkmenistan	33.1
4	Iraq	33.6
5	Uzbekistan	34.4
6	Haiti	34.8
7	Sudan	35.9
8	Trinidad and Tobago	36.3
9	Kuwait	36.6
10	Yemen	37.3

Source: World Economic Forum, '2005 Environmental Sustainability Index'

top10 COUNTRIES WITH MOST NUCLEAR REACTORS

	COUNTRY	REACTORS
1	USA	104
2	France	59
3	Japan	54
4	Russia	30
5	UK	27
6	Germany	19
7	South Korea	18
8	Canada	16
9	India	14
10	Ukraine	13

Source: International Atomic Energy Agency

top10 CARBON DIOXIDE-EMITTING COUNTRIES

	COUNTRY	CO_2 EMISSIONS PER CAPITA, 2003 (TONNES OF CO_2)
1	Qatar	45.73
2	United Arab Emirates	44.11
3	Bahrain	30.89
4	Singapore	27.89
5	Trinidad and Tobago	24.92
6	Luxembourg	24.28
7	Kuwait	23.17
8	USA	19.95
9	Australia	19.10
10	Canada	19.05
	World average	*3.98*
	UK	*9.53*

Source: Energy Information Administration

CO_2 emissions derive from three principal sources – fossil fuel burning, cement manufacturing and gas flaring – as well as various industrial processes. In the past 60 years, increasing industrialization in many countries has resulted in huge increases in carbon output, a trend that most countries are now actively attempting to reverse, with some degree of success among the former leaders in this Top 10, although the USA remains the worst offender in total, with over 5.9 billion tonnes released in 2003.

top10 ELECTRICITY-CONSUMING COUNTRIES

	COUNTRY	CONSUMPTION KW/HR, 2003
1	USA	4,054,000,000,000
2	China	1,907,000,000,000
3	Japan	1,038,000,000,000
4	Russia	914,000,000,000
5	India	633,000,000,000
6	Germany	594,000,000,000
7	Canada	587,000,000,000
8	France	562,000,000,000
9	UK	396,000,000,000
10	Brazil	365,000,000,000
	World total	*16,661,000,000,000*

top10 COAL-CONSUMING COUNTRIES

	COUNTRY	CONSUMPTION, 2004 (TONNES OF OIL EQUIVALENT)
1	China	956,900,000
2	USA	564,300,000
3	India	204,800,000
4	Japan	120,800,000
5	Russia	105,900,000
6	South Africa	94,500,000
7	Germany	85,700,000
8	Poland	57,700,000
9	Australia	54,400,000
10	South Korea	53,100,000
	World total	*2,778,200,000*
	UK	*39,400,000*

Source: 'BP Statistical Review of World Energy 2005'

top10 ALTERNATIVE POWER*-PRODUCING COUNTRIES

	COUNTRY	PRODUCTION KW/HR, 2003
1	USA	93,530,000,000
2	Germany	31,400,000,000
3	Japan	27,850,000,000
4	Spain	16,270,000,000
5	Brazil	16,240,000,000
6	Italy	11,330,000,000
7	Finland	10,120,000,000
8	Philippines	9,420,000,000
9	Canada	8,540,000,000
10	Denmark	7,950,000,000
	World	*310,100,000,000*
	UK	*7,130,000,000*

* Includes biomass, geothermal, solar and wind electric power

Source: Energy Information Administration

top10 ENVIRONMENTAL CONCERNS IN THE UK

	CONCERN	PERCENTAGE OF PEOPLE CONCERNED*
1	Disposal of hazardous waste	66
2	Effects of livestock methods (BSE, etc)	59
3	Pollution of lakes, rivers and seas	55
4	= Pollution of bathing waters and beaches	52
	= Traffic exhaust fumes	52
6	Loss of plants and animals in the UK	50
7	Depletion of the ozone layer	49
8	Tropical forest destruction	48
9	= Global warming/climate change	46
	= Loss of trees and hedgerows	46

* Survey respondents who said they were 'very worried'

Source: Department of the Environment, Farming and Rural Affairs, 'Survey of Public Attitudes to Quality of Life and to the Environment'

Communications

top10 COUNTRIES SENDING AND RECEIVING THE **MOST LETTERS** (DOMESTIC)

COUNTRY	ITEMS OF MAIL HANDLED, 2004
1 USA	194,000,000,000
2 Japan	24,923,245,000
3 Germany	21,744,000,000
4 UK	21,030,000,000
5 France	17,571,000,000
6 Canada	10,714,615,000*
7 India	8,747,400,000#
8 China	8,235,030,000
9 Brazil	7,957,580,000
10 Italy	6,574,465,610
World total	*429,869,376,225*

* Estimate
# 2003

Source: Universal Postal Union

top10 COUNTRIES WITH THE **MOST POSTAL STAFF**

COUNTRY	FULL-TIME POSTAL STAFF, 2004
1 USA	707,485
2 China	401,000
3 Germany	379,828
4 Russia	309,962
5 India*	262,752
6 France	230,046
7 Great Britain	150,370
8 Italy	147,354
9 Japan	114,158
10 Brazil	107,836
World total	*3,964,642*

* 2003

Source: Universal Postal Union

the10 FIRST CITIES AND COUNTRIES TO ISSUE **POSTAGE STAMPS**

CITY / COUNTRY	STAMPS ISSUED
1 Great Britain	May 1840
2 New York City, USA	Feb 1842
3 Zurich, Switzerland	Mar 1843
4 Brazil	Aug 1843
5 Geneva, Switzerland	Oct 1843
6 Basle, Switzerland	Jul 1845
7 USA	Jul 1847
8 Mauritius	Sep 1847
9 Bermuda	Unknown 1848
10 France	Jan 1849

The first adhesive postage stamps issued in the UK were the Penny Blacks that went on sale on 1 May 1840. The first issued in the USA were designed for local delivery (as authorized by an 1836 Act of Congress) and produced by the City Despatch Post, New York City, inaugurated on 15 February 1842, and later that year incorporated into the US Post Office Department. After a further Act in 1847, the rest of the United States followed suit and the Post Office Department issued its first national stamps: a 5-cent Benjamin Franklin stamp and a 10-cent George Washington stamp, both of which first went on sale in New York City on 1 July 1847. By the time they were withdrawn, 3,712,200 and 891,000, respectively, had been issued.

AMAZING FACT

The First Airmail

The first-ever airmail letter was sent on 7 January 1785 by William Franklin, the son of US statesman Benjamin Franklin, to his son William Temple Franklin. It was carried in a balloon piloted by French balloonist Jean-Piere Blanchard and American doctor John Jeffries, from Dover, UK to the Felmores Forest, France. The letter is now in the collection of the American Philosophical Society.

top10 COMPUTER COUNTRIES

COUNTRY	COMPUTERS, 2004
1 USA	223,810,000
2 Japan	69,200,000
3 China	52,990,000
4 Germany	46,300,000
5 UK	35,890,000
6 France	29,410,000
7 South Korea	26,200,000
8 Italy	22,650,000
9 Canada	22,390,000
10 Brazil	19,350,000
World total	*822,150,000*

Source: Computer Industry Almanac Inc.

top10 COUNTRIES WITH THE MOST INTERNET USERS

COUNTRY	EST. NO. OF INTERNET USERS, 2005
1 USA	203,576,811
2 China	103,000,000
3 Japan	78,050,000
4 Germany	47,127,725
5 India	39,200,000
6 UK	37,800,000
7 South Korea	32,570,000
8 Italy	28,870,000
9 France	25,614,899
10 Brazil	22,320,000
World total	*972,828,001*

Source: Internet World Stats

top10 MOBILE PHONE COUNTRIES

COUNTRY	MOBILE SUBSCRIBERS PER 100
1 Luxembourg	138.17
2 Hong Kong	118.77
3 Sweden	108.47
4 Italy	108.19
5 Czech Republic	105.64
6 Israel	105.25
7 Norway	103.60
8 UK	102.16
9 Slovenia	100.51
10 Taiwan	100.31
World average	*27.61*

Source: International Telecommunications Union, 'World Telecommunication/ICT Development Report 2006'

This is the ratio of mobile phone subscriptions to population – Taiwan, for example, has just over 100 phones per 100 people. For countries showing an even higher average 'teledensity', these figures may include people who have taken out new subscriptions but have not cancelled their old ones, so the original numbers are still counted in the statistics.

top10 COUNTRIES WITH THE MOST TELEPHONES

COUNTRY	TELEPHONE LINES PER 100	TOTAL, 2004
1 China	23.98	311,756,000
2 USA	60.60	177,947,000
3 Japan	46.00	58,788,000
4 Germany	66.15	54,574,000
5 India	4.07	43,960,000
6 Brazil	23.46	42,382,000
7 Russia	27.47	36,616,000
8 France	56.04	33,870,200
9 UK	56.35	33,700,000
10 South Korea	55.31	26,595,100
World	*18.89*	*1,203,247,200*

Source: International Telecommunications Union, 'World Telecommunication/ICT Development Report 2006'

Of the world's telephone lines, Asia has 538,981,500, Europe 327,580,000, the Americas 295,306,500, Africa 25,925,000 and Oceania 13,773,000. In developing countries, mobile phones have replaced non-existent, defunct or inefficent fixed lines, enabling their telephone systems rapidly to adopt 21st-century technology.

TRANSPORT & TOURISM

Land Speed

the10 **FIRST HOLDERS** OF THE LAND SPEED RECORD

DRIVER / CAR	LOCATION	DATE	SPEED KM/H	MPH
1 Gaston de Chasseloup-Laubat, Jeantaud	Achères, France	18 Dec 1898	62.78	39.24
2 Camille Jenatzy, Jenatzy	Achères, France	17 Jan 1899	66.27	41.42
3 Gaston de Chasseloup-Laubat, Jeantaud	Achères, France	17 Jan 1899	69.90	43.69
4 Camille Jenatzy, Jenatzy	Achères, France	27 Jan 1899	79.37	49.92
5 Gaston de Chasseloup-Laubat, Jeantaud	Achères, France	4 Mar 1899	92.16	57.60
6 Camille Jenatzy, Jenatzy	Achères, France	29 Apr 1899	105.26	65.79
7 Leon Serpollet, Serpollet	Nice, France	13 Apr 1902	120.09	75.06
8 William Vanderbilt, Mors	Albis, France	5 Aug 1902	121.72	76.08
9 Henri Fournier, Mors	Dourdan, France	5 Nov 1902	122.56	76.60
10 M. Augières, Mors	Dourdan, France	17 Nov 1902	123.40	77.13

The official Land Speed Record was set and broken five times within a year. The first six holders were rival racers Comte Gaston de Chasseloup-Laubat (France) and Camille Jenatzy (Belgium). The trial, held under the aegis of the Automobile Club de France over a 2-km (1.2-mile) course at Achères, near Paris, was open to any vehicle – both the Jeantaud and the Jenatzy (nicknamed La Jamais Contente/'Never Satisfied') were electrically powered. Leon Serpollet, the first driver to beat them, drove a steam-powered car. US millionaire William Vanderbilt was the first to hold the record driving a petrol-engined vehicle.

the10 **LATEST HOLDERS** OF THE LAND SPEED RECORD

DRIVER / CAR	DATE	SPEED KM/H	MPH
1 Andy Green (UK), ThrustSSC*	15 Oct 1997	1,227.99	763.04
2 Richard Noble (UK), Thrust2*	4 Oct 1983	1,013.47	633.47
3 Gary Gabelich (USA), The Blue Flame	23 Oct 1970	995.85	622.41
4 Craig Breedlove (USA), Spirit of America – Sonic 1	15 Nov 1965	960.96	600.60
5 Art Arfons (USA), Green Monster	7 Nov 1965	922.48	576.55
6 Craig Breedlove (USA), Spirit of America – Sonic 1	2 Nov 1965	888.76	555.48
7 Art Arfons (USA), Green Monster	27 Oct 1964	858.73	536.71
8 Craig Breedlove (USA), Spirit of America	15 Oct 1964	842.04	526.28
9 Craig Breedlove (USA), Spirit of America	13 Oct 1964	749.95	468.72
10 Art Arfons (USA), Green Monster	5 Oct 1964	694.43	434.02

* Location: Black Rock Desert, Nevada, USA; all other speeds were achieved at Bonneville Salt Flats, Utah, USA

Having gained the Land Speed Record on 23 August 1939, British driver John Cobb broke it again on 16 September 1947, when he achieved a land speed of 630.72 km/h (394.20 mph) in his Railton Mobil Special, at Bonneville Salt Flats, Utah, USA. Cobb was killed in 1952 in an attempt on the water speed record, but his land record stood until 1963, since when it has been successively broken and now stands at over double its pre-war figure.

⊕ The speed of sound
RAF pilot Andy Green (b. 1962) smashed the Land Speed Record in ThrustSSC, to become the first to break the sound barrier on land, achieving Mach 1.016.

⊙ The first ton
Belgian racer Camille Jenatzy (1868–1913) celebrates breaking the Land Speed Record. He did so on three occasions, becoming the first driver to exceed 100 km/h in his bullet-shaped electric vehicle La Jamais Contente.

Water & Air Speed

⬅ Water power
With Dave Villwock at the controls, hydroplane Miss Budweiser established a new water speed record for a propeller-driven craft.

Since 1928 water speed records have been under the control of the Union Internationale du Yachting Automobile (later Union Internationale Motonautique) and take place over a kilometre course, averaging the speed of runs in both directions. All these record-holders were propeller-driven craft, but since the 1950s, jet-powered boats, which skim over the surface of the water, have achieved consistently faster speeds, with Ken Warby's Spirit of Australia setting the jet record of 511.11 km/h (317.58 mph) on Blowering Dam, New South Wales, Australia, on 8 October 1978.

the10 **FIRST HOLDERS** OF THE WATER SPEED RECORD

DRIVER / BOAT / LOCATION	DATE	SPEED KM/H	MPH
1 George Wood (USA), Miss America VII, Detroit River, Michigan, USA	4 Sep 1928	149.408	92.838
2 Gar Wood (USA), Miss America VII, Indian Creek, Florida, USA	23 Mar 1929	149.867	93.123
3 Henry Segrave (UK), Miss England II, Lake Windermere, UK	13 Jun 1930	158.938	98.760
4 Gar Wood, Miss America IX, Indian Creek, Florida, USA	20 Mar 1931	164.565	102.256
5 Kaye Don (UK), Miss England II, Tigre, Parana River, Argentina	2 Apr 1931	166.551	103.490
6 Kaye Don, Miss England II, Lake Garda, Italy	9 Jul 1931	177.387	110.223
7 Gar Wood, Miss America IX, Indian Creek, Florida, USA	5 Feb 1932	179.783	111.712
8 Kaye Don, Miss England III, Loch Lomond, Scotland	18 Jul 1932	192.816	119.810
9 Gar Wood, Miss America X, Revier Canal, Detroit, Michigan, USA	20 Sep 1932	201.023	124.910
10 Malcolm Campbell (UK), Blue Bird K3, Lake Maggiore, Switzerland	1 Sep 1937	203.292	126.320

the10 **LATEST HOLDERS** OF THE WATER SPEED RECORD

DRIVER / BOAT / LOCATION	DATE	SPEED KM/H	MPH
1 Dave Villwock, Miss Budweiser, Lake Oroville, California, USA	13 Mar 2004	354.849	220.493
2 Russ Wicks, Miss Freei, Lake Washington, USA	15 Jun 2000	330.711	205.494
3 Roy Duby, Miss US1, Lake Guntersville, Alabama, USA	17 Apr 1962	322.543	200.419
4 Bill Muncey, Miss Thriftaway, Lake Washington, USA	16 Feb 1960	308.996	192.001
5 Jack Regas, Hawaii Kai III, Lake Washington, USA	30 Nov 1957	301.956	187.627
6 Art Asbury, Miss Supertest II, Lake Ontario, Canada	1 Nov 1957	296.988	184.540
7 Stanley Sayres, Slo-Mo-Shun IV, Lake Washington, USA	7 Jul 1952	287.263	178.497
8 Stanley Sayres, Slo-Mo-Shun IV, Lake Washington, USA	26 Jun 1950	258.015	160.323
9 Malcolm Campbell, Bluebird K4, Coniston Water, UK	19 Aug 1939	228.108	141.740
10 Malcolm Campbell, Bluebird K3, Hallwiler See, Switzerland	17 Aug 1938	210.679	130.910

↑ Fastest flight
An X-15 travelling faster than a bullet.

top10 **FASTEST** X-15 FLIGHTS

	PILOT	FLIGHT NO.	DATE	MACH*	SPEED KM/H	MPH
1	William J. Knight	188	3 Oct 1967	6.70	7,274	4,520
2	William J. Knight	175	18 Nov 1966	6.33	6,857	4,261
3	Joseph A. Walker	59	27 Jun 1962	5.92	6,606	4,105
4	Robert M. White	45	9 Nov 1961	6.04	6,589	4,094
5	Robert A. Rushworth	97	5 Dec 1963	6.06	6,466	4,018
6	Neil A. Armstrong	64	26 Jul 1962	5.74	6,420	3,989
7	John B. McKay	137	22 Jun 1965	5.64	6,388	3,938
8	Robert A. Rushworth	89	18 Jul 1963	5.63	6,317	3,925
9	Joseph A. Walker	86	25 Jun 1963	5.51	6,294	3,911
10	William H. Dana	189	4 Oct 1967	5.53	6,293	3,910

* Mach No. varies with altitude – the list is ranked on actual speed

↑ *Pilot William J. Knight and X-15A-2.*

Although some were achieved almost 50 years ago, the speeds attained by the rocket-powered X-15 and X-15A-2 aircraft in a programme of 199 flights in the period 1959–68 remain the greatest ever attained by piloted vehicles in the Earth's atmosphere. They were air-launched by being released from B-52 bombers, and thus do not qualify for the official air speed record, for which aircraft must take off and land under their own power. The X-15s attained progressively greater speeds, ultimately more than double that of the now long-standing conventional air speed record, and set an unofficial altitude record (during Flight No. 91 on 22 August 1963, when Joseph A. Walker piloted an X-15 to 107,960 m/354,200 ft – some 108 km/67 miles high).

top10 FASTEST **PRE-JET AIR SPEED** RECORDS

	PILOT / COUNTRY	LOCATION	AIRCRAFT	DATE	SPEED KM/H	MPH
1	Fritz Wendel, Germany	Augsburg, Germany	Messerschmitt Me209 V1	26 Apr 1939	755.138	469.221
2	Hans Dieterle, Germany	Orianenburg, Germany	Heinkel He100 V8	30 Mar 1939	746.606	463.919
3	Francesco Agello, Italy	Desenzano, Italy	Macchi MC72	23 Oct 1934	709.209	440.682
4	Francesco Agello, Italy	Desenzano, Italy	Macchi MC72	10 Apr 1933	682.078	423.824
5	George H. Stainforth, UK	Lee-on-Solent, UK	Supermarine S6B	29 Sep 1931	665.798	407.494
6	Mario de Bernardi, Italy	Venice, Italy	Macchi M52bis	30 Mar 1928	512.776	318.624
7	Mario de Bernardi, Italy	Venice, Italy	Macchi M52	4 Nov 1927	479.290	297.817
8	Florentin Bonnet, France	Istres, France	Bernard V2	11 Dec 1924	448.133	278.457
9	Alford J. Williams, USA	Mineola, New York, USA	Curtiss R2C-1	4 Nov 1923	429.025	266.584
10	Harold J. Brow, USA	Mineola, New York, USA	Curtiss R2C-1	2 Nov 1923	417.590	259.478

All these aircraft were powered by conventional internal combustion engines. No.1 was the last piston-driven aircraft to gain the official air-speed record (approved by the Féderation Aéronautique Internationale), all subsequent record-holders being jets.

Road Works

top10 BESTSELLING CARS OF ALL TIME

	MANUFACTURER / MODEL	YEARS IN PRODUCTION	EST. NO. MADE*
1	Toyota Corolla	1966–	29,000,000
3	Volkswagen Golf	1974–	>22,000,000
2	Volkswagen Beetle	1937–2003#	21,529,464
4	Lada Riva	1972–97	19,000,000
5	Ford Model T	1908–27	16,536,075
6	Honda Civic	1972–	14,920,000
7	Nissan Sunny/Pulsar	1966–94	13,571,100
8	Honda Accord	1976–	12,520,000
9	Ford Escort/Orion	1967–2000	12,000,000
10	Chevy Impala/Caprice	1959–	11,509,165

* To 1 January 2003, except where otherwise indicated
\# Produced in Mexico 1978–2003

top10 MOTOR VEHICLE-OWNING COUNTRIES

	COUNTRY	CARS	COMMERCIAL VEHICLES	TOTAL
1	USA	128,714,022	87,968,915	216,682,937
2	Japan	53,300,000	19,985,000	73,285,000
3	Germany	44,383,323	3,592,054	47,975,377
4	Italy	33,239,029	3,755,552	36,994,581
5	France	28,700,000	5,897,000	34,597,000
6	UK	27,790,025	3,412,086	31,202,111
7	Russia	21,200,000	5,063,000	26,263,000
8	Spain	18,150,880	4,161,104	22,311,984
9	Brazil	15,800,000	4,045,000	19,845,000
10	Canada	17,964,798	728,545	17,783,343
	World total	*561,686,927*	*202,218,380*	*767,905,307*

Source: 'Ward's Motor Vehicle Facts & Figures 2003'

As the total number of vehicles on the world's roads has increased, the average ratio of people to cars has fallen from 23 in 1960 to 10.6 per car. In the USA there are 2.2 and in the UK 2.1 people per car, but in some countries the ratio is very high: in China it stands as 294 per car and in Myanmar 6,780 people for every car! About two-thirds of the world's vehicles are in the Top 10 countries.

⊙ *Beetlemania*

The bodies of Beetles on the Volkswagen production line, 1960. Launched in pre-war Germany and a byword for reliability, the Beetle became one of the bestselling and most iconic cars of all time. Its distinctive shape was little altered during its unrivalled 66-year manufacturing lifespan.

top10 CAR **PRODUCERS**

	COUNTRY	CAR PRODUCTION, 2004*
1	Japan	8,720,385
2	Germany	5,192,101
3	USA	4,229,625
4	France	3,220,329
5	South Korea	3,122,600
6	Spain	2,402,103
7	China	2,316,262
8	Brazil	1,756,166
9	UK	1,646,881
10	Canada	1,335,464

* Provisional figures

Source: OICA Correspondents Survey

top10 CARS **IN THE UK**, 2005

	MODEL	SALES, 2004
1	Ford Focus	145,010
2	Vauxhall Astra	108,461
3	Vauxhall Corsa	89,463
4	Renault Mégane	87,093
5	Ford Fiesta	83,803
6	Volkswagen Golf	67,749
7	Peugeot 206	67,450
8	Ford Mondeo	57,589
9	Renault Clio	56,538
10	BMW 3 series	44,844

Source: Society of Motor Manufacturers and Traders Ltd

top10 CAR **MANUFACTURERS**

	COMPANY / COUNTRY	CAR PRODUCTION, 2004*
1	General Motors (USA)	8,112,000
2	Ford (USA)	6,526,000
3	Toyota (Japan)	6,241,000
4	Renault-Nissan (France/Japan)	5,328,000
5	Volkswagen group (Germany)	5,024,000
6	DaimlerChrysler (Germany)	4,238,000
7	PSA Peugeot Citröen (France)	3,310,000
8	Honda (Japan)	2,923,000
9	Hyundai (South Korea)	2,697,000
10	Fiat (Italy)	2,078,000

* Including light commercial vehicles

top10 LONGEST **ROAD TUNNELS**

	TUNNEL / LOCATION	YEAR COMPLETED	LENGTH M	FT
1	Laerdal, Norway	2000	24,510	80,413
2	Zhongnanshan, China	2007*	18,040	59,186
3	St Gotthard, Switzerland	1980	16,918	55,505
4	Arlberg, Austria	1978	13,972	45,850
5	Hsuehshan, Taiwan	2005	12,900	42,323
6	Fréjus, France/Italy	1980	12,895	42,306
7	Mont-Blanc, France/Italy	1965	11,611	38,094
8	Gudvangen, Norway	1991	11,428	37,493
9	Folgefonn, Norway	2001	11,100	36,417
10	Kan-Etsu II (southbound), Japan	1990	11,010	36,122

* Under construction – scheduled completion date

Nos. 1, 3, 4 and 7 have all held the record as 'world's longest road tunnel'. Previous record-holders include the 5,854-m (19,206-ft) Grand San Bernardo (Italy-Switzerland, 1964), the 5,133-m (16,841-ft) Alfonos XIII or Viella (Spain, 1948), the 3,237-m (10,620-ft) Queensway (Mersey) Tunnel (Liverpool to Birkenhead, UK, 1934) and the 3,186-m (10,453-ft) Col de Tende (France-Italy, 1882), originally built as a rail tunnel and converted in 1928.

Track Records

top10 FASTEST RAIL JOURNEYS

JOURNEY* / COUNTRY	TRAIN	DISTANCE		SPEED	
		KM	MILES	KM/H	MPH
1 Lyon-St Exupéry to Aix-en-Provence, France	TGV 6171	289.6	179.9	263.3	163.6
2 Hiroshima to Kokura, Japan	15 Nozomi	192.0	119.3	261.8	162.7
3 Frankfurt Flughafen to Siegburg/Bonn, Germany	17 ICE trains	144.0	89.5	233.5	145.1
4 Brussels Midi to Marseilles-St Charles, Belgium/France	ThalysSoleil	1,054.0	654.9	233.4	145.0
5 Madrid Atocha to Cuidad Atocha, Spain	6 AVE trains	170.7	106.1	204.8	127.3
6 Falköping to Katrineholm, Sweden	X2000 438	209.7	130.3	190.6	118.4
7 Seol to Taejeon, North Korea	5 KTX trains	155.0	96.3	189.8	117.9
8 Stevenage to Grantham, UK	1 IC255	125.3	77.9	181.1	112.5
9 Roma (Rome) Termini to Firenze (Florence) SMN, Italy	Eurostar 9458	261.0	162.2	166.6	103.5
10 Wilmington to Baltimore, USA	13 Acela Expresses	110.1	68.4	165.1	102.6

* Fastest journey for each country; all those in the Top 10 have other equally or similarly fast services

Source: 'Railway Gazette International', 2005 World Speed Survey

➲ *Bullet train*

Japan's Shinkansen bullet trains have been in service for over 40 years. Capable of speeds of up to 300 km/h (186 mph), they have long held the world record for the fastest scheduled rail service.

the10 FIRST COUNTRIES WITH RAILWAYS

COUNTRY	FIRST RAILWAY ESTABLISHED
1 UK	27 Sep 1825
2 France	7 Nov 1829
3 USA	24 May 1830
4 Ireland	17 Dec 1834
5 Belgium	5 May 1835
6 Germany	7 Dec 1835
7 Canada	21 Jul 1836
8 Russia	30 Oct 1837
9 Austria	6 Jan 1838
10 Netherlands	24 Sep 1839

The Stockton & Darlington Railway in the UK inaugurated the world's first steam railway service. In their early years some of the countries listed here offered only limited services over short distances, but their opening dates mark the generally accepted beginning of each country's steam railway system.

top10 LONGEST RAIL NETWORKS

COUNTRY	TOTAL RAIL LENGTH	
	KM	MILES
1 USA	227,736	141,508
2 Russia	87,157	54,156
3 China	71,898	44,675
4 India	63,230	39,280
5 Australia	54,439	33,826
6 Canada	48,683	30,250
7 Germany	46,142	28,671
8 Argentina	34,091	21,183
9 France	29,519	18,342
10 Brazil	29,412	18,275
World	*1,115,205*	*692,956*
UK	*17,274*	*10,733*

Source: Central Intelligence Agency, 'The World Factbook 2005'

The USA's rail mileage has declined considerably since its 1916 peak of 408,773 km (254,000 miles).

top10 OLDEST UNDERGROUND RAILWAY SYSTEMS

CITY / COUNTRY	OPENED
1 London, UK	1863
2 Budapest, Hungary	1896
3 Glasgow, UK	1896
4 Boston, USA	1897
5 Paris, France	1900
6 Berlin, Germany	1902
7 New York, USA	1904
8 Philadelphia, USA	1907
9 Hamburg, Germany	1912
10 Buenos Aires, Argentina	1913

Source: Tony Pattison, Centre for Environmental Initiatives Researcher

London and the world's first underground system, a section of the Metropolitan Railway from Paddington to Farringdon Street, with specially adapted steam trains, was opened on 10 January 1863.

top10 LONGEST **UNDERGROUND RAILWAY** NETWORKS

	CITY / COUNTRY	OPENED	STATIONS	TOTAL TRACK LENGTH KM	MILES
1	London, UK	1863	267	392	244
2	New York, USA	1904	468	371	231
3	Moscow, Russia	1935	160	262	163
4	Tokyo, Japan*	1927	241	256	160
5	Paris, France#	1900	297	202	126
6	Mexico City, Mexico	1969	175	201	125
7	San Francisco, USA	1972	42	200	124
8	Chicago, USA	1943	140	173	107
9	Madrid, Spain	1919	201	171	106
10	Washington, USA	1976	83	166	104

* Includes Toei, Eidan lines
# Metro and RER

Source: Tony Pattison, Centre for Environmental Initiatives Researcher

When its current expansion programme is completed, the Seoul Metropolitan Subway, South Korea, one of the world's busiest, will also be the third longest.

top10 LONGEST **RAIL TUNNELS**

	TUNNEL / COUNTRY	YEAR COMPLETED	LENGTH M	FT
1	AlpTransit Gotthard, Switzerland	2010*	57,072	187,244
2	Seikan, Japan	1988	53,850	176,673
3	Channel Tunnel, France/England	1994	50,450	165,518
4	Moscow Metro (Serpukhovsko-Timiryazevskaya line), Russia	1983	38,900	127,625
5	Guadarrama, Spain	2007*	28,377	97,100
6	London Underground (East Finchley/ Morden, Northern Line), UK	1939	27,840	91,339
7	Hakkouda, Japan	2013*	26,455	86,795
8	Iwate, Japan	2013*	25,810	84,678
9	Iiyama, Japan	2013*	22,225	72,917
10	Dai-Shimizu, Japan	1982	22,221	72,904

* Under construction – scheduled completion date

The AlpTransit Gotthard, proposed in 1947 and begun in 1998 following a referendum of the Swiss electorate, will be the world's longest, as the original 15,000-m (49,213-ft) Gotthard tunnel was when completed in 1882. Trains will travel at 250 km/h (155 mph).

Water Ways

↑ Slow boats in China
Barge traffic makes its leisurely progress on China's ancient Grand Canal.

* Canals and navigable rivers
# Excluding Great Lakes
† Of all countries for which data available

Source: Central Intelligence Agency, 'The World Factbook 2005'

top10 LONGEST SHIP CANALS

CANAL / COUNTRY	OPENED	LENGTH KM	M
1 Grand Canal, China	AD 283*	1,795	1,114
2 Erie Canal, USA	1825	584	363
3 Göta Canal, Sweden	1832	386	240
4 St Lawrence Seaway, Canada/USA	1959	290	180
5 Canal du Midi, France	1692	240	149
6 Main-Danube, Germany	1992	171	106
7 Suez, Egypt	1869	162	101
8 Albert, Belgium	1939	130	81
9 Moscow (formerly Moscow-Volga), Russia	1937	129	80
10 Volga-Don, Russia	1952	101	63

* Extended from 605–10 and rebuilt between 1958–72

Connecting Hang Zhou in the south to Beijing in the north, China's Grand Canal was largely built by manual labour alone, long before the invention of the mechanized digging used in the construction of the other major artificial waterways. The Panama Canal, opened in 1914 (82 km/51 miles), just fails to find a place in the Top 10.

top10 LARGEST OIL TANKERS*

TANKER	YEAR BUILT	OPERATOR'S COUNTRY	DEAD-WEIGHT TONNAGE#
1 = TI Africa	2002	Belgium	441,893
= TI Asia	2002	USA	441,893
= TI Europe	2002	Belgium	441,893
4 TI Oceania	2003	USA	441,585
5 Marine Pacific	1979	USA	404,536
6 Enterprise	1981	Hong Kong	360,700
7 Nisa	1983	Saudi Arabia	322,912
8 Settebello	1983	Brazil	322,446
9 Aries Voyager	2006	Greece	320,870
10 Andromeda Voyager	2006	Greece	320,472

* As at Apr 2006
# Total weight of the vessel, including its cargo, crew, passengers and supplies

Source: Lloyd's Register-Fairplay Ltd. www.lrfairplay.com

Once the world's largest tanker, the 485.45-m (1,504-ft), 564,764-ton *Knock Nevis* (formerly *Happy Giant*, *Seawise Giant* and *Jahre Viking*) was damaged during the Iran-Iraq War. In 2004 it was adapted for use in Qatar as a floating storage and offloading unit.

⬆ Queen of the oceans
At her launch the Queen Mary 2 *became the largest passenger ship of all time. In 2006 she lost her crown to the* Freedom of the Seas.

top10 BUSIEST PORTS

	PORT / COUNTRY	CONTAINER TRAFFIC, 2003 TEU*
1	Hong Kong, China	20,499,000
2	Singapore, Singapore	18,411,000
3	Shanghai, China	11,280,000
4	Shenzhen, China	10,615,000
5	Busan, South Korea	10,408,000
6	Kaohsiung, Taiwan	8,843,000
7	Los Angeles, USA	7,149,000
8	Rotterdam, Netherlands	7,107,000
9	Hamburg, Germany	6,138,000
10	Antwerp, Belgium	5,445,000

* Twenty-foot Equivalent Units

Source: American Association of Port Authorities

A 'Twenty-Foot Equivalent Unit' (a container measuring 20 ft long x 8 ft wide x 8.5 ft high) is a standard measurement used in quantifying container traffic, in which Hong Kong is the world leader, although Singapore is the largest in terms of total weight handled, with over 347 million tonnes in 2003, compared with Hong Kong's 207 million.

top10 LARGEST CRUISE SHIPS

	SHIP	ENTERED SERVICE	COUNTRY BUILT	PASSENGER CAPACITY	GROSS TONNAGE
1	Freedom of the Seas	2006	Finland	4,370	158,000
2	Queen Mary 2	2004	France	3,090	148,528
3 =	Mariner of the Seas	2004	Finland	3,840	138,279
=	Navigator of the Seas	2003	Finland	3,840	138,279
5	Explorer of the Seas	2000	Finland	3,840	137,308
6 =	Adventure of the Seas	2001	Finland	3,838	137,276
=	Voyager of the Seas	1999	Finland	3,838	137,276
8	Crown Princess	2006	Italy	3,800	117,477
9 =	Diamond Princess	2004	Japan	3,100	115,875
=	Sapphire Princess	2004	Japan	3,100	115,875

Source: Lloyd's Register-Fairplay Ltd

top10 LARGEST YACHTS

	YACHT	OWNER / COUNTRY	BUILT/ REFITTED	LENGTH M	FT	IN
1	Al Salamah	King Fahd, Saudi Arabia	1999	139.8	456	10
2	Rising Sun	Larry Ellison, USA	2004	138.4	452	8
3	Octopus	Paul Allen, USA	2003	126.1	414	0
4	Savarona	Kahraman Sadikoglu, Turkey (charter)	1931/1992	124.3	408	0
5	Alexander	Latsis family, Greece	1976/1986	122.0	400	2
6	Turama	Latsis family, Greece	1990/2004	116.9	381	9
7	Atlantis II	Niarchos family, Greece	1981	115.6	379	7
8	Pelorus	Roman Abramovich, Russia	2003	114.9	377	3
9	Le Grand Bleu	Roman Abramovich, Russia	2000	112.7	370	0
10	Lady Moura	Nasser al-Rashid, Saudi Arabia	1990	104.8	344	0

Source: 'Power & Motoryacht, 2005'

Marine Transport Disasters

the 10 **LARGEST** PASSENGER SHIPS EVER SUNK

SHIP / LOCATION	DATE	TONNAGE
1 Titanic* Off Newfoundland	14 Apr 1912	46,328
2 Lusitania Off Ireland	7 May 1915	31,550
3 Andrea Doria Off US coast	25 Jul 1956	29,083
4 Angelina Pacific	24 Sep 1979	24,377
5 Lakonia Atlantic	23 Dec 1963	20,314
6 Mikhail Lermontov Off New Zealand	16 Feb 1986	20,027
7 Rasa Sayang Kynosoura, Greece	27 Aug 1980	18,739
8 Bianca C. Off Grenada	22 Oct 1961	18,427
9 Georges Philppar* Off Cape Guardafui	19 May 1931	17,539
10 Admiral Nakhimov Odessa/Batumi	31 Aug 1986	17,053

* Sunk on maiden voyage

This list excludes liners used as troop carriers and lost as a result of military conflict and vessels that were damaged or keeled over, but did not actually sink, such as the 83,763-ton *Seawise University* (formerly *Queen Elizabeth*), which caught fire and partly sank in Hong Kong harbour on 9 January 1972.

↑ *Sinking the unsinkable*
The tragic circumstances surrounding the sinking of the supposedly unsinkable Titanic *on her maiden voyage, the then worst-ever loss of life and the retelling of the story in many books and films have made it the most famous of all marine disasters.*

the 10 WORST PASSENGER **FERRY DISASTERS**

FERRY / LOCATION / DATE	APPROX. NO.KILLED
1 Doña Paz, Philippines, 21 Dec 1987	up to 3,000
2 MV Joola, Gambia, 26 Sep 2003	over 1,863
3 Neptune, Haiti, 17 Feb 1992	1,800
4 Toya Maru, Japan, 26 Sep 1954	1,172
5 Al Salaam Boccaccio 98, Red Sea, 2 Feb 2006	1,018
6 Don Juan, Philippines, 22 Apr 1980	over 1,000
7 Estonia, Baltic Sea, 28 Sep 1994	909
8 Samia, Bangladesh, 25 May 1986	600
9 Tampomas II, Indonesia, 27 Jan 1981	580
10 MV Bukoba, Lake Victoria, Tanzania, 21 May 1996	549

The *Doña Paz* sank in the Tabias Strait, Philippines, after the ferry was struck by the oil tanker MV *Vector*. The loss of life may have been much higher than the official figure (some authorities suggested figures between 4,341 and 4,386) due to overcrowding, but there was no accurate record of the numbers who actually boarded. Chaotic scenes often follow such incidents – as when the families of passengers on the *Al Salaam Boccaccio 98* rioted in Safaga, Egypt, further confusing the reporting of the disaster.

the10 WORST **MARINE DISASTERS**

LOCATION / DATE / INCIDENT   APPROX. NO. KILLED

1 Off Gdansk, Poland, 30 Jan 1945   up to 7,800
The German liner *Wilhelm Gustloff*, laden with refugees, was torpedoed by a Soviet submarine, S-13. The precise death toll remains uncertain, but with recent research suggesting a total of 10,582 on board, it could be over the estimated figure of 7,800.

2 Off Cape Rixhöft (Rozeewie), Poland, 16 Apr 1945   6,800
A German ship *Goya*, carrying evacuees from Gdansk, was torpedoed in the Baltic.

3 Off Yingkow, China, 3 Dec 1948   over 6,000
The boilers of an unidentified Chinese troopship carrying Nationalist soldiers from Manchuria exploded, detonating its ammunition.

4 Off Sumatra, 18 Sep 1944   5,620
The Japanese ship *Junyo Maru*, carrying Dutch, British, American and Australian prisoners of war and Javanese slave labourers, was torpedoed by British submarine HMS *Tradewind*.

5 En route for Okinawa, 29 Jun 1944   5,400
Japanese troop transport *Toyama Maru* was torpedoed by American submarine USS *Sturgeon*, with just 600 survivors of the 6,000 on board.

6 Lübeck, Germany, 3 May 1945   5,000
The German ship *Cap Arcona*, carrying concentration camp survivors, was bombed and sunk by British Typhoon fighter-bombers.

7 Off British coast, Aug to Oct 1588   4,000
Military conflict and storms combined to destroy the Spanish Armada.

8 Off Stolpmünde (Ustka), Poland, 10 Feb 1945   3,500
German war-wounded and refugees were lost when the *General Steuben* was torpedoed by the same Russian submarine that had sunk the *Wilhelm Gustloff* 10 days earlier.

9 Off St Nazaire, France, 17 Jun 1940   over 3,000
The British ship *Lancastria*, carrying troops and French refugees, sank after a dive-bombing attack by Luftwaffe aircraft.

10 Tabias Strait, Philippines, 21 Dec 1987   up to 3,000
The ferry *Doña Paz* was struck by oil tanker MV *Vector*. The *Doña Paz* was so overcrowded that a death toll of 4,341, claimed by some sources, may be possible.

Recent re-assessments of the death tolls in some of the World War II marine disasters means that the most famous marine disaster of all – the *Titanic* – no longer ranks in the Top 10. However, the *Titanic* tragedy remains one of the worst-ever peacetime disasters, along with such notable incidents as that involving the *General Slocum*, an excursion liner that caught fire in the port of New York on 15 June 1904 with the loss of 1,021 lives.

the10 WORST **SUBMARINE DISASTERS***

SUBMARINE / LOCATION / DATE / INCIDENT   NO. KILLED

1 Surcourf, Gulf of Mexico, 18 Feb 1942   159
A French submarine, accidentally rammed by a US merchant ship, the USS *Thomson Lykes*.

2 Thresher, North Atlantic, 10 Apr 1963   129
A three-year-old US nuclear submarine, worth $45,000,000, sank.

3 Kursk (K-141), Barents Sea, 12 Aug 2000   118
A Russian nuclear submarine sank following an unspecified accident during a military exercise, with the loss of all hands. It was raised on 8 Oct 2001.

4 I-12, Central Pacific, c. 15 Jan 1945   114
A Japanese submarine, sank in unknown circumstances.

5 I-174, Central Pacific, c. 12 Apr 1944   107
A Japanese submarine, sank in unknown circumstances.

6 I-26, Off Leyte, Philippines, Oct 1944   105
A Japanese submarine, sank, possibly as a result of US depth-bombing.

7 I-169, Truk, Micronesia, 4 Apr 1944   103
A Japanese submarine flooded and sank while under attack in harbour.

8 I-22, off the Solomon Islands, c. 4 Oct 1942   100
A Japanese submarine sank.

9 = Thetis, Liverpool Bay, UK, 1 Jun 1939   99
A British submarine sank during trials, with civilians on board. (*Thetis* was later salvaged and renamed *Thunderbolt*; on 13 March 1943 she was sunk by an Italian ship with the loss of 63 lives.)

= Seawolf, off Morotai, Indonesia, 3 Oct 1944   99
A US submarine, sunk in error by USS *Rowell*.

= Scorpion, South-west of the Azores, North Atlantic, 21 May 1968   99
A US nuclear submarine, sank after being struck by one of its own torpedos; the wreck was located on 31 October 1968.

* Excluding those as a result of military action

The loss of the *Thresher* is the worst-ever accident involving a nuclear submarine. It sank while undertaking tests off the US coast, and after an exhaustive search was eventually located by the bathyscaphe *Trieste*. It found the remains of the submarine scattered over the ocean floor at a depth of 2,560 m (8,400 ft). The cause of the disaster, if it was ever established, remains a military secret. The loss of the *Kursk* is the most recent of several tragedies affecting the former Soviet fleet: an unidentified vessel was lost with some 90 hands in 1968 and another with a similar number in 1983.

High Fliers

top10 COUNTRIES WITH THE MOST AIRPORTS

	COUNTRY	AIRPORTS (2005 EST.)
1	USA	14,857
2	Brazil	4,136
3	Russia	2,586
4	Mexico	1,833
5	Argentina	1,334
6	Canada	1,326
7	Bolivia	1,065
8	Colombia	980
9	Paraguay	878
10	South Africa	728
	World total	*49,973*

Source: CIA, 'The World Factbook 2005'

top10 AIRLINES WITH THE MOST PASSENGERS

	AIRLINE / COUNTRY	PASSENGERS CARRIED, 2004*
1	American Airlines, USA	91,570,000
2	Delta Air Lines, USA	86,783,000
3	United Airlines, USA	71,236,000
4	Northwest Airlines, USA	56,429,000
5	Japan Airlines, Japan	51,736,000
6	Lufthansa, Germany	48,268,000
7	All Nippon Airways, Japan	46,450,000
8	Air France, France	45,393,000
9	US Airways, USA	42,400,000
10	Continental Airlines, USA	40,548,000

* Total of international and domestic

Source: International Air Transport Association

top10 LARGEST AIRSHIPS EVER BUILT

	AIRSHIP	COUNTRY	YEAR	VOLUME CU M	VOLUME CU FT	LENGTH M	LENGTH FT
1 =	Hindenburg	Germany	1936	200,000	7,062,934	245	804
=	Graf Zeppelin II	Germany	1938	200,000	7,062,934	245	804
3 =	Akron	USA	1931	184,060	6,500,000	239	785
=	Macon	USA	1933	184,060	6,500,000	239	785
5	R101	UK	1930	155,744	5,500,000	237	777
6	Graf Zeppelin	Germany	1928	105,000	3,708,040	237	776
7	L72	Germany	1920	68,500	2,419,055	226	743
8	R100	UK	1929	155,744	5,500,000	216	709
9	R38	UK*	1921	77,136	2,724,000	213	699
10	L70 and L71	Germany	1918	62,200	2,418,700	212	694

* UK-built, but sold to US Navy

the10 FIRST PEOPLE TO PILOT HEAVIER-THAN-AIR AIRCRAFT

	PILOT / DATES / NATIONALITY	AIRCRAFT	APPROX. DISTANCE (M)	DATE*
1	Orville Wright (1871–1948, USA)	Wright Flyer I	37	17 Dec 1903
2	Wilbur Wright (1867–1912, USA)	Wright Flyer I	53	17 Dec 1903
3	Jacob Christian Hansen Ellehammer (1871–1946, Denmark)	Ellehammer	42	12 Sep 1906
4	Alberto Santos-Dumont (1873–1932, Brazil)	No. 14-bis	60	23 Oct 1906
5	Charles Voisin (1882–1912, France)	Voisin-Delagrange I	60	30 Mar 1907
6	Robert Esnault-Pelterie (1881–1957, France)	REP No.1	100	10 Oct 1907
7	Henri Farman (1874–1958, UK, later France)	Voisin-Farman I-bis	712	26 Oct 1907
8	Ferdinand Léon Delagrange (1873–1910, France)	Voisin-Delagrange I	100	5 Nov 1907
9	Comte Henri de La Vaulx (1870–1930, France)	Antoinette	70	19 Nov 1907
10	Alfred de Pischoff (1882–1922, Hungary)	Anzani	50–100	12 Dec 1907

* Of first flight only: most fliers listed flew on subsequent occasions and broke their first-time records

🔻 *The Wright stuff*
Wilbur Wright watches as his brother Orville becomes the first to fly a powered aircraft. The flight lasted 12 seconds, covering 37 m (120 ft).

⬆ *Giant of the skies*
Fully laden, the Russian Antonov An-225 Mriya, the world's largest powered aircraft, weighs 600 tonnes.

the10 FIRST COUNTRIES TO HAVE BALLOON FLIGHTS*

COUNTRY	DATE

1 France — 21 Nov 1783
The Montgolfier brothers, Joseph and Etienne, tested their first unmanned hot-air balloon in the French town of Annonay on 5 June 1783. On 21 November 1783 François Laurent, Marquis d'Arlandes and Jean-François Pilâtre de Rozier took off from the Bois de Boulogne, Paris, in a Montgolfier hot-air balloon. This first-ever manned flight covered a distance of about 9 km (5.5 miles) in 23 minutes, landing safely near Gentilly.

2 Italy — 25 Feb 1784
The Chevalier Paolo Andreani and the brothers Augustino and Carlo Giuseppi Gerli (the builders of the balloon) made the first-ever flight outside France, at Moncucco near Milan, Italy.

3 Austria — 6 Jul 1784
Johann Georg Stuwer made the first Austrian flight from the Prater, Vienna.

4 Scotland — 27 Aug 1784
James Tytler (known as 'Balloon Tytler'), a doctor and newspaper editor, took off from Comely Gardens, Edinburgh, in a hot-air balloon, achieving an altitude of 107 m (350 ft) in a 0.8-km (1/2-mile) hop in a home-made balloon.

5 England — 15 Sep 1784
Watched by a crowd of 200,000, Italian balloonist Vincenzo Lunardi ascended from the Artillery Company Ground, Moorfields, London, flying to Standon near Ware in Hertfordshire. On 4 October 1784 James Sadler flew a Montgolfier balloon at Oxford, thereby becoming the first English-born pilot.

6 Ireland — 19 Jan 1785
Although there are earlier claims, it is likely that Richard Crosbie's hydrogen balloon flight from Ranelagh Gardens, Dublin, was the first in Ireland.

7 Holland — 11 Jul 1785
French balloon pioneer Jean-Pierre Blanchard took off from The Hague in a hydrogen balloon.

8 Germany — 3 Oct 1785
Blanchard made the first flight in Germany from Frankfurt.

9 Belgium — 20 Oct 1785
Blanchard flew his hydrogen balloon from Ghent.

10 Switzerland — 5 May 1788
Blanchard flew from Basel. As well as flights from other European cities, Blanchard made the first in the USA, from Philadelphia, on 9 January 1793, watched by George Washington – as well as future Presidents John Adams, Thomas Jefferson and James Monroe.

* Several of the balloonists also made subsequent flights, but in each instance only their first flights are included

➲ *The first to fly*
With Pilâtre de Rozier and the Marquis d'Arlandes on board, the Montgolfier hot-air balloon takes off, launching France as the pioneer of world aviation.

top10 LONGEST WINGSPAN AIRCRAFT

AIRCRAFT	WINGSPAN M	FT	IN
1 H-4 Hercules 'Spruce Goose'	97.5	320	0
2 Antonov An-225 Cossack	88.4	290	0
3 Airbus A380F	79.8	261	8
4 Antonov An-124 Condor	73.3	240	6
5 Convair B-36 Peacemaker	70.1	230	0
6 Lockheed C-5 Galaxy	67.3	222	9
7 Boeing 777-300ER	64.8	212	7
8 Boeing 747	64.4	211	5
9 Airbus A340-600	63.5	208	2
10 Boeing 777	60.9	199	11

Air Transport Disasters

the10 FIRST AIRCRAFT **FATALITIES**

VICTIM / NATIONALITY / LOCATION	DATE
1 Lt Thomas Etholen Selfridge, American, Fort Myer, USA	17 Sep 1908
2 Eugène Lefèbvre, French, Juvisy, France	7 Sep 1909
3 Ferdinand Ferber, French, Boulogne, France	22 Sep 1909
4 Antonio Fernandez, Spanish, Nice, France	6 Dec 1909
5 Aindan de Zoseley, Hungarian, Budapest, Hungary	2 Jan 1910
6 Léon Delagrange, French, Croix d'Hins, France	4 Jan 1910
7 Hubert Le Blon, French, San Sebastián, Spain	2 Apr 1910
8 Hauvette Michelin, French, Lyons, France	13 May 1910
9 Thaddeus Robl, German, Stettin, Germany	18 Jun 1910
10 Charles Louis Wachter, French, Rheims, France	3 Jul 1910

Following the Wright Brothers' first flights in 1903, the first four years of powered flying remained surprisingly accident-free and it was not until 1908 that anyone was killed in an aeroplane. On 17 September at Fort Myer, Virginia, Orville Wright was demonstrating his *Flyer* to the US Army with Lt Thomas Etholen Selfridge as a passenger when it crash-landed (from a height of just 23 m/75 ft), injuring Wright and killing Lt Selfridge. On 12 July 1910 the 11th fatal accident and the first involving a British citizen occurred when the Hon Charles Stewart Rolls (the Rolls of Rolls-Royce) crashed a Wright *Flyer* during an air show at Bournemouth.

the10 WORST AIR DISASTERS **IN THE UK**

LOCATION / DATE / INCIDENT	NO. KILLED
1 Lockerbie, Scotland, 21 Dec 1988 Pan Am Flight 103 from London Heathrow to New York exploded in mid-air as a result of a terrorist bomb, killing 243 passengers, 16 crew and 11 on the ground in the UK's worst-ever air disaster.	270
2 Staines, Middlesex, 18 Jun 1972 A British European Airways Trident crashed after take-off.	118
3 Siginstone, Glamorgan, 12 Mar 1950 An Avro Tudor V carrying Welsh rugby fans from Belfast inexplicably crashed while attempting to land at Llandow; three survived, one dying later in the worst air crash in the world up to this date.	81
4 Stockport, Cheshire, 4 Jun 1967 A British Midland Argonaut airliner carrying holidaymakers returning from Majorca crashed en route to Manchester Airport killing all but 12 on board.	72
5 Freckelton, Lancashire, 23 Aug 1944 A US Air Force B-24 crashed onto a school after being struck by lightning, killing 10 USAF personnel on board, 38 children, two teachers and other civilians on the ground.	61
6 Manchester Airport, 22 Aug 1985 A British Airtours Boeing 737 caught fire on the ground.	55
7 Near Gatwick Airport, 5 Jan 1969 An Ariana Afghan Airlines Boeing 727 crash-landed; the deaths included two on the ground.	50
8 M1 motorway, Kegworth, 8 Jan 1989 A British Midland Boeing 737-400 attempting to land without engine power crashed on the motorway embankment.	47
9 = Isle of Wight, 15 Nov 1957 Following an engine fire, an Aquila Airlines Solent flying boat G-AKNU crashed in Chessel Down quarry.	45
= Off Sumburgh, Shetland Islands, 6 Nov 1986 A Boeing 234 Chinook helicopter ferrying oil-rig workers ditched in the sea, making it the worst-ever civilian helicopter accident; two passengers were rescued by coastguards.	45

the10 WORST **AIR DISASTERS**

LOCATION / DATE / INCIDENT   NO. KILLED

1 New York, USA, 11 Sep 2001   c.1,622
Following a hijacking by terrorists, an American Airlines Boeing 767 was deliberately flown into the North Tower of the World Trade Center, killing all 81 passengers (including five hijackers), 11 crew on board and an estimated 1,530 on the ground, both as a direct result of the crash and the subsequent fire and collapse of the building, which also killed 479 rescue workers.

2 New York, USA, 11 Sep 2001   c.677
As part of the coordinated attack, hijackers commandeered a second Boeing 747 and crashed it into the South Tower of the World Trade Center, killing all 56 passengers and 9 crew on board and approximately 612 on the ground.

3 Tenerife, Canary Islands, 27 Mar 1977   583
Two Boeing 747s (PanAm and KLM, carrying 380 passengers and 16 crew and 234 passengers and 14 crew, respectively) collided and caught fire on the runway of Los Rodeos airport after the pilots received incorrect control-tower instructions. A total of 61 escaped.

4 Mt Ogura, Japan, 12 Aug 1985   520
A JAL Boeing 747 on an internal flight from Tokyo to Osaka crashed, killing all but four of the 509 passengers and all 15 crew on board.

5 Charkhi Dadri, India, 12 Nov 1996   349
Soon after taking off from New Delhi's Indira Gandhi International Airport, a Saudi Arabian Airlines Boeing 747 collided with a Kazakh Airlines Ilyushin IL-76 cargo aircraft on its descent and exploded, killing all 312 (289 passengers and 23 crew) on the Boeing and all 37 (27 passengers and 10 crew) on the Ilyushin in the world's worst mid-air crash.

LOCATION / DATE / INCIDENT   NO. KILLED

6 Paris, France, 3 Mar 1974   346
Immediately after take-off for London, a Turkish Airlines DC-10 suffered an explosive decompression when a door burst open and crashed at Ermenonville, north of Paris, killing all 335 passengers, including many England rugby supporters, and its crew of 11.

7 Off the Irish coast, 23 Jun 1985   329
An Air India Boeing 747 on a flight from Vancouver to Delhi exploded in mid-air, probably as a result of a terrorist bomb, killing all 307 passengers and 22 crew.

8 Riyadh, Saudi Arabia, 19 Aug 1980   301
Following an emergency landing a Saudia (Saudi Arabian) Airlines Lockheed TriStar caught fire. The crew were unable to open the doors and all 287 passengers and 14 crew died from smoke inhalation.

9 Off the Iranian coast, 3 Jul 1988   290
An Iran Air A300 airbus was shot down in error by a missile fired by the USS *Vincennes*, which mistook it for an Iranian fighter aircraft. All 274 passengers and 16 crew were killed.

10 Sirach Mountain, Iran, 19 Feb 2003   275
An Ilyushin 76 flying from Zahedan to Kerman crashed into the mountain in poor weather. It was carrying 257 Revolutionary Guards and a crew of 18, none of whom survived.

�) *Collision course*
The aftermath of the worst-ever mid-air collision at Charkhi Dadri, India. There were no survivors after a cargo aircraft mistakenly descended into the path of an airliner. Both crashed in flames onto uninhabited farmland.

World Tourism

top10 TOURIST DESTINATIONS OF **UK** **RESIDENTS**

COUNTRY	OVERSEAS VISITORS, 2004
1 Spain	12,202,000
2 France	7,429,000
3 USA	2,622,000
4 Greece	2,461,000
5 Italy	2,134,000
6 Ireland	1,626,000
7 Portugal	1,501,000
8 Netherlands	1,118,000
9 Turkey	986,000
10 Belgium	776,000
Total all countries	*42,912,000*

Source: Travel Trends 2004

top10 TOURIST **DESTINATIONS**

COUNTRY	INTERNATIONAL VISITORS, 2004
1 France	75,100,000
2 Spain	53,600,000
3 USA	46,100,000
4 China*	41,800,000
5 Italy	37,100,000
6 UK	27,800,000
7 Mexico	20,600,000
8 Germany	20,100,000
9 Austria	19,400,000
10 Canada	19,200,000
World total	*763,000,000*

* Hong Kong separately enumerated: 21.8 million visitors in 2004

Source: World Tourism Organization

top10 TOURIST **EARNING COUNTRIES** *

COUNTRY	INTERNATIONAL TOURISM RECEIPTS, 2004 ($)
1 USA	74,500,000,000
2 Spain	45,200,000,000
3 France	40,800,000,000
4 Italy	35,700,000,000
5 Germany	27,700,000,000
6 UK	27,300,000,000
7 China	25,700,000,000
8 Turkey	15,900,000,000
9 Austria	15,400,000,000
10 Australia	13,000,000,000
World total	*623,000,000,000*

* Countries earning the most from tourism

Source: World Tourism Organization

top10 **OLDEST** AMUSEMENT PARKS*

PARK / LOCATION	YEAR FOUNDED
1 Bakken, Klampenborg, Denmark	1583
2 The Prater, Vienna, Austria	1766
3 Blackgang Chine Cliff Top Theme Park, Ventnor, Isle of Wight, UK	1842
4 Tivoli Gardens, Copenhagen, Denmark	1843
5 Lake Compounce Amusement Park, Bristol, Connecticut, USA	1846
6 Hanayashiki, Tokyo, Japan	1853
7 Grand Pier, Teignmouth, UK	1865
8 Blackpool Central Pier, Blackpool, UK	1868
9 Cedar Point, Sandusky, Ohio, USA	1870
10 Clacton Pier, Clacton, UK	1871

* In same location

Source: National Amusement Park Historical Association

top10 **TOURIST ATTRACTIONS** IN THE UK*

ATTRACTION / LOCATION	VISITORS, 2005
1 Blackpool Pleasure Beach, Blackpool	5,970,000
2 British Airways London Eye, London	3,250,000
3 Tower of London, London	1,931,093
4 Kew Gardens, London	1,514,276
5 Edinburgh Castle	1,187,342
6 The Eden Project, Cornwall	1,177,189
7 British Library, London	1,113,114
8 Chester Zoo	1,089,257
9 Canterbury Cathedral	1,054,886
10 Westminster Abbey, London	997,382

* Excluding museums and art galleries (see page 101)

Source: Association of Leading Visitor Attractions (ALVA)

top10 TOURISM **SPENDING COUNTRIES***

COUNTRY	INTERNATIONAL TOURISM EXPENDITURE, 2004 ($)
1 Germany	71,000,000,000
2 USA	65,600,000,000
3 UK	55,900,000,000
4 Japan	38,100,000,000
5 France	28,600,000,000
6 Italy	20,500,000,000
7 Netherlands	16,500,000,000
8 Canada	16,000,000,000
9 Russia	15,700,000,000
10 China	15,200,000,000#
World total	623,000,000,000

* Countries spending the most on tourism
# 2003 data

Source: World Tourism Organization

top10 COUNTRIES WITH THE **BIGGEST INCREASE** IN TOURISM

COUNTRY	% INCREASE, 2003–04
1 Malaysia	48.5
2 Taiwan	31.2
3 Kenya	30.7
4 Guam	27.5
5 China	26.7
6 Turkey	26.1
7 Lebanon	25.8
8 Ukraine	24.9
9 Uruguay	23.7
10 India	23.6
UK	12.3

Source: World Tourism Organization

top10 COUNTRIES OF **ORIGIN OF TOURISTS** TO THE UK

COUNTRY	OVERSEAS VISITORS, 2004
1 USA	1,521,000
2 France	1,116,000
3 Germany	1,050,000
4 Ireland	570,000
5 Italy	501,000
6 Netherlands	479,000
7 Spain	460,000
8 Belgium	378,000
9 Australia	307,000
10 Norway	237,000
Total	9,275,000

Source: Travel Trends 2004

⊙ East meets West
The Tivoli Taj Mahal opened on 15 August 1843. One of many attractions in Tivoli Gardens, Copenhagen, Denmark, it is also one of the world's oldest amusement parks.

➲ Head of the list
The USA easily tops the world list for receipts from tourism, but its own nationals are outspent by Germans.

SPORT

Summer Olympics

SPORTS CONTESTED AT THE MOST OLYMPIC GAMES*

	SPORT	YEARS	APPEARANCES
1	=Fencing	1896–2004	26
	=Gymnastics	1896–2004	26
	=Swimming	1896–2004	26
	=Track & Field	1896–2004	26
5	=Cycling	1896–1900, 1906–2004	25
	=Wrestling	1896, 1904–2004	25
	=Rowing	1900–2004	25
8	=Shooting	1896–1900, 1906–24, 1932–2004	24
	=Sailing#	1900, 1906–2004	24
	=Soccer	1900–28, 1936–2004	24

* Summer Olympics 1896–2004, including the 1906 Intercalated Games
# Formerly Yachting

Other than wartime interruptions in 1916, 1940 and 1944, the Summer Games have been held every four years since 1896. The Intercalated Games were held in 1906. It was intended that they would take place in Athens midway between those in other countries (in this instance, St Louis in 1904 and Rome in 1908), but the 1906 event was never repeated and records set and medals awarded in it are often disregarded.

top10 **MOST MEDALS WON** AT ONE OLYMPIC GAMES*

	NATION	YEAR	GOLD	MEDALS SILVER	BRONZE	TOTAL
1	USA	1904	79	84	82	245
2	USSR	1980	80	69	46	195
3	USA	1984	83	61	30	174
4	UK	1908	54	46	38	138
5	USSR	1988	55	31	46	132
6	East Germany#	1980	47	37	42	126
7	USSR	1976	49	41	35	125
8	Unified Team	1992	45	38	29	112
9	USA#	1992	37	34	37	108
10	USA	1968	45	28	34	107

* Summer Olympics 1896–2004, including the 1906 Intercalated Games
# Not the leading medal-winning nation at that Games

Following the collapse of the Soviet Union, the Unified Team (or 'EUN' – Equipe Unifée) was a short-lived confederation of athletes from the old USSR member countries other than the Baltic states. Some competed under this banner at the 1992 Winter Olympic Games in Albertville and all participated at the 1992 Summer Games at Barcelona, where it led the medals table. Since then, the respective countries have competed separately.

top10 GOLD MEDAL-WINNING COUNTRIES AT THE **SUMMER OLYMPICS***

	COUNTRY	GOLDS
1	USA	907
2	USSR/Russia/Unified Team	525
3	Germany/West Germany	228
4	France	199
5	= Italy	189
	= UK	189
7	East Germany	159
8	Hungary	158
9	Sweden	140
10	Australia	119

* Summer Olympics 1896–2004, including the 1906 Intercalated Games

top10 **MOST OLYMPIC MEDALS** (WOMEN)*

	ATHLETE / COUNTRY	SPORT	YEARS	GOLD	MEDALS SILVER	BRONZE	TOTAL
1	Larissa Latynina, USSR	Gymnastics	1956–64	9	5	4	18
2	=Birgit Fischer, Germany/East Germany	Canoeing/Kayaking	1980–2004	8	4	0	12
	=Jenny Thompson, USA	Swimming	1992–2004	8	3	1	12
4	Vera Cáslavská, Czechoslovakia	Gymnastics	1960–68	7	4	0	11
5	=Agnes Keleti, Hungary	Gymnastics	1952–56	5	3	2	10
	=Polina Astakhova, USSR	Gymnastics	1956–64	5	2	3	10
7	=Lyudmila Tourischeva, USSR	Gymnastics	1968–76	4	3	2	9
	=Nadia Comaneci, Romania	Gymnastics	1976–80	5	3	1	9
	=Dara Torres, USA	Swimming	1984–2000	4	1	4	9
10	=Sofia Muratova, USSR	Gymnastics	1956–60	2	2	4	8
	=Dawn Fraser, Australia	Swimming	1956–64	4	4	0	8
	=Shirley Babashoff, USA	Swimming	1972–76	2	6	0	8
	=Kornelia Ender, East Germany	Swimming	1972–76	4	4	0	8
	=Inge de Bruijn, Netherlands	Swimming	2000–04	4	2	2	8

* Up to and including 2004 Games

top10 UK **GOLD MEDAL-WINNING** SPORTS*

	SPORT	GOLDS
1	Track & Field	54
2	Sailing#	24
3	Rowing	22
4	Swimming & Diving	18
5	Lawn Tennis	17
6	Shooting	14
7	Boxing	13
8	Cycling	12
9	Equestrianism	6
10 =	Hockey	3
=	Polo	3
=	Soccer	3
=	Wrestling	3

* All events up to and including the 2004 Sydney Games, including discontinued events and the 1906 Intercalated Games in Athens
\# Formerly Yachting

⬅ **Vaulting to victory**
Russian gymnast Alexei Nemov (b. 1976) has won a total of 12 Olympic medals, including four golds, in every gymnastics event except rings.

top10 **MOST OLYMPIC MEDALS** (MEN)*

	ATHLETE / COUNTRY	SPORT	YEARS	GOLD	SILVER	BRONZE	TOTAL
1	Nikolai Andrianov, USSR	Gymnastics	1972–80	7	5	3	15
2 =	Edoardo Mangiarotti, Italy	Fencing	1936–60	6	5	2	13
=	Takashi Ono, Japan	Gymnastics	1952–64	5	4	4	13
=	Boris Shakhlin, USSR	Gymnastics	1956–64	7	4	2	13
5 =	Paavo Nurmi, Finland	Track & Field	1920–28	9	3	0	12
=	Sawao Kato, Japan	Gymnastics	1968–76	8	3	1	12
=	Alexei Nemov, Russia	Gymnastics	1996–2000	4	2	6	12
8 =	Carl Osburn, USA	Shooting	1912–24	5	4	2	11
=	Viktor Chukarin, USSR	Gymnastics	1952–56	7	3	1	11
=	Mark Spitz, USA	Swimming	1968–72	9	1	1	11
=	Matt Biondi#, USA	Swimming	1984–92	8	2	1	11

* Up to and including 2004 Games
\# Biondi's total includes one gold medal as preliminary member of a gold medal-winning relay team

top10 **MEDAL-WINNING COUNTRIES** NEVER TO HAVE WON A GOLD MEDAL*

	COUNTRY	GOLD	SILVER	BRONZE	TOTAL
1	Mongolia	0	5	10	15
2	Philippines	0	2	7	9
3 =	Bohemia	0	1	5	6
=	Puerto Rico	0	1	5	6
5 =	Ghana	0	1	3	4
=	Lebanon	0	2	2	4
=	Moldova	0	2	2	4
=	Namibia	0	4	0	4
9 =	Iceland	0	1	2	3
=	Malaysia	0	1	2	3

* Summer Olympics 1896–2004, including the 1906 Intercalated Games

Winter Olympics

top10 **MEDAL-WINNING** COUNTRIES AT THE WINTER OLYMPICS*

	COUNTRY	GOLD	MEDALS SILVER	BRONZE	TOTAL
1	USSR/Unified Team/Russia	122	89	86	297
2	Norway	96	102	84	282
3	USA	78	81	59	218
4	Germany/West Germany	76	78	57	211
5	Austria	50	64	71	185
6	Finland	42	57	52	151
7	Sweden	46	32	44	122
8	East Germany	39	37	35	118
9	Switzerland	37	37	43	117
10	Canada	38	38	44	111

* Up to and including the 2006 Turin Games; includes medals won at figure skating and ice hockey included in the Summer games prior to the launch of the Winter Olympics in 1924

top10 **MEDAL-WINNING COUNTRIES** AT THE 2006 TURIN WINTER OLYMPICS

	COUNTRY	GOLD	MEDALS SILVER	BRONZE	TOTAL
1	Germany	11	12	6	29
2	USA	9	9	7	25
3	Canada	7	10	7	24
4	Austria	9	7	7	23
5	Russia	8	6	8	22
6	Norway	2	8	9	19
7	= Sweden	7	2	5	14
	= Switzerland	5	4	5	14
9	= China	2	4	5	11
	= Italy	5	0	6	11
	= Korea	6	3	2	11

The United Kingdom won just one silver medal and finished in joint 21st place.

top10 OLYMPIC **ICE-HOCKEY** COUNTRIES*

	COUNTRY	GOLD	MEDALS SILVER	BRONZE	TOTAL
1	Canada	9	5	2	16
2	USA	3	8	2	13
3	Soviet Union/Unified Team/Russia	8	2	2	12
4	Sweden	2	3	5	10
5	Czechoslovakia	0	4	4	8
6	Finland	0	2	3	5
7	= Czech Republic	1	0	1	2
	= Germany/West Germany	0	0	2	2
	= Switzerland	0	0	2	2
	= UK	1	0	1	2

* Up to and including the 2006 Turin Games

➲ *Olympic victory*
Italian cross-country skier Stefania Belmondo won medals at four consecutive Winter Olympics, with golds in the 30-km event in 1992 and 15 km in 2002. As a local Olympian, she was chosen to light the Olympic flame at the 2006 Games in Turin.

top10 **MEN'S MEDAL WINNERS** AT THE WINTER OLYMPICS*

ATHLETE / COUNTRY	EVENT	GOLD	SILVER	BRONZE	TOTAL
1 Bjorn Dählie, Norway	Cross Country	8	4	0	12
2 = Ole Einar Bjoerndalen, Norway	Biathlon	5	3	1	9
= Sixten Jernberg, Sweden	Cross Country	4	3	2	9
4 = Kjetil André Aamodt, Norway	Alpine Skiing	4	2	2	8
= Sven Fischer, Germany	Biathlon	4	2	2	8
= Ricco Gross, Germany	Biathlon	4	3	1	8
7 = Ivar Ballangrud, Norway	Speed Skating	4	2	1	7
= Veikko Hakulinen, Finland	Cross Country	3	3	1	7
= Eero Mäntyranta, Finland	Cross Country	3	2	2	7
= Bogdan Musiol, Germany/East Germany	Bobsled	1	5	1	7
= Clas Thunberg, Finland	Speed Skating	5	1	1	7

(MEDALS column headings span GOLD / SILVER / BRONZE / TOTAL)

* All events up to and including the 2006 Turin Games

top10 **WOMEN'S MEDAL WINNERS** AT THE WINTER OLYMPICS*

ATHLETE / COUNTRY	EVENT	GOLD	SILVER	BRONZE	TOTAL
1 = Stefania Belmondo, Italy	Cross Country	2	3	5	10
= Raisa Smetanina, USSR/Unified Team	Cross Country	4	5	1	10
3 = Uschi Disl, Germany	Biathlon	2	4	3	9
= Lyubov Egorova, Unified Team/Russia	Cross Country	6	3	0	9
= Claudia Pechstein, Germany	Speed Skating	5	2	2	9
6 = Karin Kania (née Enke), East Germany	Speed Skating	3	4	1	8
= Galina Kulakova, USSR	Cross Country	4	2	2	8
= Gunda Neimann-Stirnemann, Germany	Speed Skating	3	4	1	8
9 = Andrea Ehrig (née Mitscherlich, formerly Schöne), East Germany	Speed Skating	1	5	1	7
= Marja-Liisa Kirvesniemi (née Hämäläinen), Finland	Cross Country	3	0	4	7
= Larissa Lazutina, Unified Team/Russia	Cross Country	5	1	1	7
= Elena Valbe, Unified Team/Russia	Cross Country	3	0	4	7

(MEDALS column headings span GOLD / SILVER / BRONZE / TOTAL)

* All events up to and including the 2006 Turin Gamesy

⊕ Downhill champion
Kjetil André Aamodt is the leading Alpine skiing medal-winner, with victories in the Winter Olympic Games of 1992, 1994, 2002 and 2006, including four golds – a record for any Alpine competitor.

Until Stefania Belmondo equalled her tally in 2002, Russian Nordic skier Raisa Smetanina (b.1952) stood alone as the only woman ever to win 10 Winter Olympic medals. All were gained in five consecutive Games – from 1976, when she won her first gold, to 1992, when she achieved her last, at the age of 40 (becoming the oldest woman ever to win a Winter Olympic gold medal).

Athletics

top10 FASTEST WINNING TIMES IN THE **LONDON MARATHON (WOMEN)**

	RUNNER / COUNTRY	YEAR*	TIME HR/MIN/SEC
1	Paula Radcliffe, UK	2003	2:15:25
2	Paula Radcliffe, UK	2005	2:17:42
3	Paula Radcliffe, UK	2002	2:18:56
4	Deena Kastor, USA	2006	2:19:36
5	Ingrid Kristiansen, Norway	1985	2:21:06
6	Margaret Okoy, Kenya	2004	2:22:35
7	Ingrid Kristiansen, Norway	1987	2:22:48
8	Joyce Chepchumba, Kenya	1999	2:23:22
9	Derartu Tul, Ethiopia	2001	2:23:57
10	Ingrid Kristiansen, Norway	1984	2:24:26

* Up to and including 2006

top10 FASTEST WINNING TIMES IN THE **LONDON MARATHON (MEN)**

	RUNNER / COUNTRY	YEAR*	TIME HR/MIN/SEC
1	Khalid Khannouchi, USA	2002	2:05:38
2	Evans Rutto, Kenya	2004	2:06:18
3	Antonio Pinto, Portugal	2000	2:06:36
4	Felix Limo, Kenya	2006	2:06:39
5	Abdelkader El Mouaziz, Morocco	2001	2:07:11
6	Martin Lel, Kenya	2005	2:07:26
7	Antonio Pinto, Portugal	1997	2:07:55
8	Gezahegne Abera, Ethiopia	2003	2:07:56
9 =	Abel Anton, Spain	1998	2:07:57
=	Abdelkader El Mouaziz, Morocco	1999	2:07:57

* Up to and including 2006

◉ **In the long run**
Marathons have been run worldwide since they were introduced in the first modern Olympics in 1896.

The first London Marathon was run in March 1981, the idea of former Olympic steeplechaser Chris Brasher after he competed in the 1979 New York City Marathon.

top10 **LONGEST-STANDING WOMEN'S** OUTDOOR ATHLETICS WORLD RECORDS*

	EVENT	TIME/DISTANCE	SET BY / COUNTRY#	DATE
1	800 metres	1 min 53.28 secs	Jarmila Kratochvílová, Czechoslovakia	26 Jul 1983
2 =	400 metres	47.60 secs	Marita Koch, East Germany	6 Oct 1985
=	4x100 metres relay	41.37 secs	East Germany	6 Oct 1985
4	Shot	22.63 metres	Natalya Lisovskay, USSR	7 Jun 1987
5	High jump	2.09 metres	Stefka Kostadinova, Bulgaria	30 Aug 1987
6	Long jump	7.52 metres	Galina Chistyakova, USSR	11 Jun 1988
7	Discus	76.80 metres	Gabriele Reinsch, East Germany	9 Jul 1988
8	100 metres	10.49 secs	Florence Griffith Joyner, USA	16 Jul 1988
9	100 metres hurdles	12.21 secs	Yordanka Donkova, Bulgaria	20 Aug 1988
10	Heptathlon	7,291 points	Jackie Joyner-Kersee, USA	24 Sep 1988

* In recognized Olympic events only; as at 17 December 2005
# At the time of setting the record

Source: International Association of Athletics Federations (IAAF)

top10 **FASTEST MEN** OVER 100 METRES

	ATHLETE / COUNTRY	YEAR	TIME (SECS)
1	Asafa Powell, Jamaica	2005	9.77
2	Maurice Greene, USA	1999	9.79
3	=Donovan Bailey, Canada	1999	9.84
	=Bruny Surin, Canada	1999	9.84
5	=Leroy Burrell, USA	1994	9.85
	=Justin Gatlin, USA	2004	9.85
7	=Carl Lewis, USA	1991	9.86
	=Frank Fredericks, Namibia	1996	9.86
	=Ato Boldon, Trinidad	1998	9.86
	=Francis Obikwelu, Portugal	2004	9.86

Source: IAAF

A special prestige attaches to the holder of the men's 100-metre record, since he is considered the 'fastest man in the world', but the race has been beset by controversy in recent years: records of 9.79 and 9.83 seconds set by Ben Johnson (Canada) were disallowed after he was found guilty of using banned substances and, on 13 December 2005, US athlete Tim Montgomery's record of 9.78 seconds, set in Paris on 14 September 2002, was deleted from the record books for the same reason.

top10 **LONGEST-STANDING MEN'S** OUTDOOR ATHLETICS WORLD RECORDS*

	EVENT	TIME/DISTANCE	SET BY / COUNTRY[#]	DATE
1	Discus	74.08 metres	Jürgen Schult, East Germany	6 Jun 1986
2	Hammer	86.74 metres	Yuriy Sedykh, USSR	30 Aug 1986
3	Shot	23.12 metres	Randy Barnes, USA	20 May 1990
4	Long jump	8.95 metres	Mike Powell, USA	30 Aug 1991
5	400 metres hurdles	46.78 secs	Kevin Young, USA	6 Aug 1992
6	4x100 metres relay	37.40 secs	United States[†]	8 Aug 1992
7	High jump	2.45 metres	Javier Sotomayor, Cuba	27 Jul 1993
8	110 metres hurdles	12.91 secs	Colin Jackson, UK ☆	20 Aug 1993
9	20 kilometre walk	1 hour 17 mins 25 secs	Bernardo Segura, Mexico	7 May 1994
10	Pole vault	6.14 metres	Sergey Bubka, Ukraine	31 Jul 1994

* In recognized Olympic events only; as at 17 December 2005
# At the time of setting the record
† Record equalled, again by USA, on 21 August 1993
☆ Record equalled by Liu Xiang, China, in 2004

Source: IAAF

The longest-standing of all athletics records as recognized by the IAAF is the 4x1,500 metres relay (although not often run) by the West German team in Cologne on 17 August 1977, when they set a new best time of 14 minutes 38.8 seconds.

→ Fastest man on earth
Asafa Powell set a new 100-m record in Athens on 14 June 2005.

Boxing

the10 FIRST MEN TO WIN WORLD TITLES AT THREE DIFFERENT WEIGHTS

	BOXER / COUNTRY	WEIGHTS / YEARS
1	Bob Fitzsimmons, UK	Middle 1891, Heavy 1897, Light-heavy 1903
2	Tony Canzoneri, USA	Feather* 1927, Light 1930, Junior-welter 1931
3	Barney Ross, USA	Light 1933, Junior-welter 1933, Welter 1934
4	Henry Armstrong, USA	Feather 1937, Welter 1938, Light 1938
5	Wilfred Benitez, USA	Junior-welter 1976, Welter 1979, Junior-middle 1981
6	Alexis Arguello, Nicaragua	Feather 1974, Junior-light 1978, Light 1981
7	Roberto Duran, Panama	Light 1972, Welter 1980, Junior-middle 1983
8	Wilfredo Gomez, Puerto Rico	Junior-feather 1977, Feather 1984, Junior-light 1985
9	Thomas Hearns, USA	Welter 1980, Junior-middle 1982, Light-heavy 1987
10	Sugar Ray Leonard, USA	Welter 1979, Junior-middle 1981, Middle 1987

* New York version of the title

Emile Griffith (b.1938; US Virgin Islands) and Terry McGovern (1880–1918; USA) were claimants to the junior-middle and lightweight crowns, respectively, and would have appeared in this list, but most records do not accept the claims as being for the world title. On 29 October 1987 Thomas Hearns beat Juan Roldan of Argentina in Las Vegas for the WBC middleweight crown, to become the first man to win titles at four different weights. In 1988 Sugar Ray Leonard went on to win both his fourth and fifth world titles.

top10 MOST WINS IN WORLD HEAVYWEIGHT TITLE FIGHTS*

	BOXER / COUNTRY[#]	BOUTS	WINS
1	Joe Louis	27	26
2	Muhammad Ali / Cassius Clay	25	22
3	Larry Holmes	25	21
4	Lennox Lewis, UK	22	17
5	= Tommy Burns, Canada	13	12
	= Mike Tyson	16	12
7	= Joe Frazier	11	10
	= Evander Holyfield	16	10
	= Jack Johnson	11	10
10	Ezzard Charles	13	9

* As at 1 January 2006
[#] All USA unless otherwise stated

This list also represents the *Top 10 Most World Heavyweight Title Bouts* with the exception of Floyd Patterson (USA), who would be in at 9th with 12 fights.

top10 HEAVIEST CHAMPIONSHIP FIGHTS*

	FIGHTERS[#] / WEIGHT (LB)	DATE	COMBINED WEIGHT	
			KG	LB
1	Nikolai Valuev (324) v John Ruiz (237³/₄)	17 Dec 2005	254.8	562
2	Vitaly Klitschko (250) v Danny Williams (270)	11 Dec 2004	235.9	520
3	Lennox Lewis (256¹/₂) v Vitaly Klitschko (248)	21 Jun 2003	228.8	505
4	Lennox Lewis (247) v Michael Grant (250)	29 Apr 2000	225.4	497
5	Lennox Lewis (249) v David Tua (245)	11 Nov 2000	224.1	494
6	Hasim Rahman (238) v Lennox Lewis (253¹/₂)	22 Apr 2001	222.9	492
7	Primo Carnera (259¹/₂) v Paulino Uzcudun (229¹/₄)	22 Oct 1933	221.7	489
8	= Lennox Lewis (251) v Oliver McCall (237)	2 Jul 1997	221.4	488
	= Lennox Lewis (244) v Andrew Golota (244)	14 Oct 1997	221.4	488
10	= Riddick Bowe (243) v Michael Dokes (244)	6 Feb 1993	220.9	487
	= Lennox Lewis (250) v Francois Botha (237)	15 Jul 2000	220.9	487
	= John Ruiz (241) v Hasim Rahman (246)	13 Dec 2003	220.9	487

* As at 1 January 2006
[#] Winner first

Known as 'The Beast from The East', Russian Nikolai Valuev is not only the heaviest world heavyweight champion but, at 2.13 m (7 ft), is also the tallest. He is unbeaten in 44 fights.

↺ **Russian giant**
WBA heavyweight champion Nikolai Valuev (b.1972) won his title from John Ruiz, despite fighting with one hand, his other having been injured.

the10 LATEST UNDISPUTED* WORLD HEAVYWEIGHT CHAMPIONS[#]

BOXER	DATE LAST HELD UNIFIED TITLE
1 Lennox Lewis, UK	29 Apr 2000
2 Riddick Bowe	14 Dec 1992
3 Evander Holyfield	13 Nov 1992
4 James 'Buster' Douglas	25 Oct 1990
5 Mike Tyson	10 Feb 1990
6 Leon Spinks	18 Mar 1978
7 Muhammad Ali	15 Feb 1978
8 George Foreman	30 Oct 1974
9 Joe Frazier	22 Jan 1973
10 Muhammad Ali	29 Apr 1967

* The term 'undisputed' refers to a boxer who has won all three recognized titles (WBA, WBC, IBF) in his weight class

[#] As at 1 January 2006, as recognized by the three main bodies at the time: WBA – World Boxing Association, WBC – World Boxing Council, IBF – International Boxing Federation; with the exception of Lennox Lewis, all those listed are from the USA

⬆ Tyson v Lewis
In his 2002 defence of his world title, British heavyweight Lennox Lewis (right) won with a knockout in the 8th round.

the10 FIRST BRITISH-BORN WORLD CHAMPIONS

BOXER	BIRTHPLACE	WEIGHT AT WHICH FIRST TITLE WON	FIRST TITLE WON
1 Ike Weir	Belfast	Featherweight	1889
2 Bob Fitzsimmons	Helston, Cornwall	Middleweight	1891
3 Joe Bowker	Salford	Bantamweight	1904
4 Freddie Welsh	Pontypridd	Lightweight	1914
5 Ted 'Kid' Lewis	London	Welterweight	1915
6 Jimmy Wilde	Tylorstown, Wales	Flyweight	1916
7 Jack 'Kid' Berg	London	Light-welterweight	1930
8 Jackie Brown	Manchester	Flyweight	1932
9 Benny Lynch	Clydesdale	Flyweight	1935
10 Peter Kane	Golborne, nr Warrington	Flyweight	1938

Although British-born Bob Fitzsimmons (1863–1917) fought for New Zealand, he went on to win world titles at three weights including heavyweight; he is the only British-born boxer to win the sport's premier title. Some sources regard Weir's assertion to be the first world featherweight champion as dubious because he claimed the title following an 80-round draw with Frank Murphy (England) at Kouts, Indiana, on 31 March 1889.

Basketball

top10 POINTS SCORERS IN THE NBA*

	PLAYER	POINTS
1	Kareem Abdul-Jabbar	38,387
2	Karl Malone	36,928
3	Michael Jordan	32,292
4	Wilt Chamberlain	31,419
5	Moses Malone	27,409
6	Elvin Hayes	27,313
7	Hakeem Olajuwon	26,946
8	Oscar Robertson	26,710
9	Dominique Wilkins	26,668
10	John Havlicek	26,395

* As at the end of the 2004–05 season

top10 MOST FIELD GOALS MADE IN THE NBA*

	PLAYER	FIELD GOALS ATTEMPTED	FIELD GOALS MADE
1	Kareem Abdul-Jabbar	28,307	15,837
2	Karl Malone	26,210	13,528
3	Wilt Chamberlain	23,497	12,681
4	Michael Jordan	24,537	12,192
5	Elvin Hayes	24,272	10,976
6	Hakeem Olajuwon	20,991	10,749
7	Alex English	21,036	10,659
8	John Havlicek	23,930	10,513
9	Dominique Wilkins	21,589	9,963
10	Patrick Ewing	19,241	9,702

* As at the end of the 2004–05 season

Source: National Basketball Association

top10 MOST POINTS IN A SINGLE NBA GAME*

	PLAYER	MATCH	DATE	POINTS
1	Wilt Chamberlain	Philadelphia Warriors v New York Knicks	2 Mar 1962	100
2	Kobe Bryant	Los Angeles Lakers v Toronto Raptors	22 Jan 2006	81
3	Wilt Chamberlain	Philadelphia Warriors v Los Angeles Lakers#	8 Dec 1961	78
4 =	Wilt Chamberlain	Philadelphia Warriors v Chicago Packers	13 Jan 1962	73
=	Wilt Chamberlain	San Francisco Warriors v New York Knicks	16 Nov 1962	73
=	David Thompson	Denver Nuggets v Detroit Pistons	9 Apr 1978	73
7	Wilt Chamberlain	San Francisco Warriors v Los Angeles Lakers	3 Nov 1962	72
8 =	Elgin Baylor	Los Angeles Lakers v New York Knicks	15 Nov 1960	71
=	David Robinson	San Antonio Spurs v Los Angeles Clippers	24 Apr 1994	71
10	Wilt Chamberlain	San Francisco Warriors v Syracuse Nationals	10 Mar 1963	70

* As at the end of the 2004–05 season
# Triple overtime game

top10 MOST GAMES PLAYED IN THE NBA*

	PLAYER	MATCHES
1	Robert Parish	1,611
2	Kareem Abdul-Jabbar	1,560
3	John Stockton	1,504
4	Karl Malone	1,476
5	Kevin Willis	1,419
6	Reggie Miller	1,389
7	Moses Malone	1,329
8	Buck Williams	1,307
9	Elvin Hayes	1,303
10	Mark Jackson	1,296

* As at the end of the 2004–05 season

If American Basketball Association appearances were included, Moses Malone's two seasons with the ABA would move him up to fifth place with 1,455 games played, while Artis Gilmore would be in eighth place with 1,329 games.

the10 LATEST **NBA CHAMPIONS**

	WINNERS	SCORE	SEASON
1	San Antonio Spurs	4–3	2004–05
2	Detroit Pistons	4–1	2003–04
3	San Antonio Spurs	4–2	2002–03
4	Los Angeles Lakers	4–0	2001–02
5	Los Angeles Lakers	4–1	2000–01
6	Los Angeles Lakers	4–2	1999–00
7	San Antonio Spurs	4–1	1998–99
8	Chicago Bulls	4–2	1997–98
9	Chicago Bulls	4–2	1996–97
10	Chicago Bulls	4–2	1995–96

Source: National Basketball Association

➔ NBA champions
Bolton Celtics enter their 60th season as the holders of the most NBA championship titles, with 16 from 1957 to 1986.

top10 **SCORING AVERAGES** IN AN NBA CAREER*

	PLAYER	AVERAGE POINTS PER GAME
1	Michael Jordan	30.12
2	Wilt Chamberlain	30.07
3	Allen Iverson#	27.44
4	Elgin Baylor	27.36
5	Jerry West	27.03
6	Shaquille O'Neal	26.74
7	Bob Pettit	26.36
8	George Gervin	26.18
9	Oscar Robertson	25.68
10	Karl Malone	25.02

* As at the end of the 2004–05 season
# Active in 2004–05

top10 TEAMS WITH THE **MOST NBA TITLES***

	TEAM	TITLES
1	Boston Celtics	16
2	Minneapolis/ Los Angeles Lakers#	14
3	Chicago Bulls	6
4	= Detroit Pistons	3
	= Philadelphia/ Golden State Warriors#	3
	= San Antonio Spurs	3
	= Syracuse Nationals/ Philadelphia 76ers#	3
8	= Baltimore/Washington Bullets#	2
	= Houston Rockets	2
	= New York Knicks	2

* As at the end of 2004–05 season
# Teams separated by / indicate change of franchise and have won the championship under both names

Source: National Basketball Association

the10 COACHES WITH THE **MOST WINS** IN THE NBA*

	COACH	YEARS	REGULAR SEASON WINS
1	Lenny Wilkens	31	1,315
2	Don Nelson#	26	1,190
3	Pat Riley	21	1,110
4	Larry Brown#	22	987
5	Bill Fitch	25	944
6	Jerry Sloan#	20	943
7	Red Auerbach	20	938
8	Dick Motta	25	935
9	Jack Ramsay	21	864
10	Phil Jackson#	14	832

* As at the end of the 2004–05 season
# Active in 2004–05

American Football

⬆ **Football stars** The Dallas Cowboys are one of the most successful teams in the National Football League.

top10 **MOST SUCCESSFUL** SUPER BOWL TEAMS*

	TEAM	WINS	LOSSES	APPEARANCES
1	Dallas Cowboys	5	3	8
2	= Denver Broncos	2	4	6
	= Pittsburgh Steelers	5	1	6
4	= Miami Dolphins	2	3	5
	= New England Patriots	3	2	5
	= Oakland/Los Angeles Raiders	3	2	5
	= San Francisco 49ers	5	0	5
	= Washington Redskins	3	2	5
9	= Buffalo Bills	0	4	4
	= Green Bay Packers	3	1	4
	= Minnesota Vikings	0	4	4

* Based on appearances up to and including Superbowl XL, 2006

top10 **MOST POINTS** IN A REGULAR NFL SEASON*

	PLAYER / TEAM	SEASON	POINTS
1	Paul Hornung, Green Bay Packers	1960	176
2	Shaun Alexander, Seattle Seahawks	2005	169
3	Gary Anderson, Minnnesota Vikings	1998	164
4	Jeff Wilkins, St. Louis Rams	2003	163
5	Priest Holmes, Kansas City Chiefs	2003	162
6	Mark Moseley, Washington Redskins	1983	161
7	Marshall Faulk, St. Louis Rams	2000	160
8	Mike Vanderjagt, Indianapolis Colts	2003	157
9	Gino Cappelletti, Boston Patriots	1964	155
10	Emmitt Smith, Dallas Cowboys	1995	150

* Up to and including 2005

top10 BIGGEST WINNING MARGINS IN THE SUPER BOWL

	WINNERS	RUNNERS-UP	YEAR	SCORE	MARGIN
1	San Francisco 49ers	Denver Broncos	1990	55–10	45
2	Chicago Bears	New England Patriots	1986	46–10	36
3	Dallas Cowboys	Buffalo Bills	1993	52–17	35
4	Washington Redskins	Denver Broncos	1988	42–10	32
5	Los Angeles Raiders	Washington Redskins	1984	38–9	29
6 =	Baltimore Ravens	New York Giants	2001	34–7	27
=	Tampa Bay Buccaneers	Oakland Raiders	2003	48–21	27
8	Green Bay Packers	Kansas City Chiefs	1967	35–10	25
9	San Francisco 49ers	San Diego Chargers	1995	49–26	23
10	San Francisco 49ers	Miami Dolphins	1985	38–16	22

Source: National Football League

The closest Super Bowl was in 1991 when the New York Giants beat the Buffalo Bills 20–19. Scott Norwood missed a 47-yard field goal eight seconds from the end of time to deprive the Bills of their first-ever Super Bowl win. It was the Giants' second win.

top10 MOST TOUCHDOWNS IN AN NFL CAREER*

	PLAYER	TOUCHDOWNS	YEARS
1	Jerry Rice	208	1985–2004
2	Emmitt Smith	175	1995–2004
3	Marcus Allen	145	1982–97
4	Marshall Faulk#	136	1994–
5	Cris Carter	131	1987–2002
6	Jim Brown	126	1957–65
7	Walter Payton	125	1975–87
8	John Riggins	116	1971–85
9	Lenny Moore	113	1956–67
10	Marvin Harrison#	110	1996–

* Regular seasons only, up to and including 2005
# Active in 2005

top10 PLAYERS WITH THE MOST NFL CAREER POINTS*

	PLAYER	POINTS
1	Gary Anderson	2,434
2	Morten Andersen	2,358
3	George Blanda	2,002
4	Norm Johnson	1,736
5	Nick Lowery	1,711
6	Jan Stenerud	1,699
7	John Carney#	1,634
8 =	Eddie Murray	1,594
=	Matt Stover#	1,594
10	Al Del Greco	1,584

* Regular season only up to and including the 2005 season
# Still active during 2005–06 season

Source: National Football League

Born in 1959, Gary Anderson started his career with the Steelers in 1982 before two seasons with Philadelphia in 1995–96. He had a year with the 49ers in 1997, moving on to the Minnesota Vikings in 1998 and then to the Tennessee Titans in 2003. He broke George Blanda's points record in 2000. Anderson came out of retirement in 2003 and again in 2004.

top10 AVERAGE HOME ATTENDANCES IN THE NFL, 2005*

	TEAM / AGGREGATE	AVERAGE
1	Washington Redskins 716,999	89,624
2	New York Giants 628,519	78,564
3	Kansas City Chiefs 623,325	77,915
4	New York Jets 619,958	77,494
5	Denver Broncos 608,790	76,098
6	Carolina Panthers 587,700	73,462
7	Cleveland Browns 578,330	72,291
8	Miami Dolphins 575,256	71,907
9	Buffalo Bills 575,248	71,906
10	Atlanta Falcons 565,106	70,638

* Regular season only

top10 NFL COACHES WITH THE MOST WINS*

	COACH	GAMES WON
1	Don Shula	347
2	George Halas	324
3	Tom Landry	270
4	Curly Lambeau	229
5	Chuck Noll	209
6	Dan Reeves	201
7	Chuck Knox	193
8	Marty Schottenheimer#	191
9	Bill Parcells#	174
10	Paul Brown	170

* Regular and post-season games, up to and including the 2005–06 season
# Active in the 2005–06 season

Source: National Football League

International Soccer

top10 MOST SUCCESSFUL TEAMS IN EUROPE*

	CLUB / COUNTRY	CHAMPIONS' LEAGUE	UEFA CUP	CUP-WINNERS CUP	TOTAL
1	Real Madrid, Spain	9	2	0	11
2	= Barcelona, Spain	1	3	4	8
	= Liverpool, England	5	3	0	8
	= AC Milan, Italy	6	0	2	8
5	= Ajax, Netherlands	4	1	1	6
	= Bayern Munich, Germany	4	1	1	6
	= Juventus, Italy	2	3	1	6
8	Inter Milan, Italy	2	3	0	5
9	Valencia, Spain	0	3	1	4
10	= Anderlecht, Belgium	0	1	2	3
	= Manchester United, England	2	0	1	3
	= Parma, Italy	0	2	1	3
	= Porto, Portugal	2	1	0	3
	= Tottenham Hotspur, England	0	2	1	3

* Based on wins in the Champions League/Cup, UEFA Cup/Fairs Cup and Cup-winners Cup, up to and including 2004–05

top10 MOST DOMESTIC LEAGUE TITLES*

	CLUB	COUNTRY	TITLES
1	Glasgow Rangers	Scotland	51
2	Linfield	Northern Ireland	45
3	Glasgow Celtic	Scotland	39
4	Olympiakos	Greece	33
5	Rapid Vienna#	Austria	32
6	Benfica	Portugal	31
7	CSKA Sofia	Bulgaria	30
8	= Ajax Amsterdam	Netherlands	29
	= Real Madrid	Spain	29
10	= Ferencvaros	Hungary	28
	= Juventus	Italy	28

* Amongst UEFA affiliated countries as at the end of the 2004–05 season
# Total includes one war-time German League title

The best totals for the other leading European nations are: England – Liverpool, 18; Germany – Bayern Munich, 19; France – Saint Etienne, 10; and Belgium – Anderlecht, 27.

⊙ Top transfer for Zidane
Three times winner of the FIFA World Player of the Year title, Zinedine Zidane (b.1972) became the world's most expensive player when he moved to his present club, Real Madrid, in 2001.

top10 WORLD **TRANSFERS***

PLAYER / NATIONALITY	FROM	TO	YEAR	FEE (£)
1 Zinedine Zidane, France	Juventus, Italy	Real Madrid, Spain	2001	47,700,000
2 Luis Figo, Portugal	Barcelona, Spain	Real Madrid, Spain	2000	37,400,000
3 Hernan Crespo, Italy	Parma, Italy	Lazio, Italy	2000	35,700,000
4 Gianluigi Buffon, Italy	Parma, Italy	Juventus, Italy	2001	33,000,000
5 Christian Vieri, Italy	Lazio, Italy	Inter Milan, Italy	1999	31,000,000
6 Rio Ferdinand, England	Leeds United, England	Manchester United, England	2002	29,100,000
7 Gaizka Mendieta, Spain	Valencia, Spain	Lazio, Italy	2001	28,900,000
8 Ronaldo, Brazil	Inter Milan, Italy	Real Madrid, Spain	2002	28,490,000
9 Juan Sebastian Veron, Argentina	Lazio, Italy	Manchester United, England	2001	28,100,000
10 Rui Costa, Portugal	Fiorentina, Italy	AC Milan, Italy	2001	28,000,000

* As at 1 January 2006

The world's first £100,000 player was Omar Sivori when he moved to Juventus (Italy) from River Plate (Argentina) in 1957; the world's first £1,000,000 player was Giuseppe Savoldi when he moved from Bologna (Italy) to Napoli (Italy) in 1975; the world's first £10,000,000 player was Gianluigi Lentini when he moved from Torino (Italy) to AC Milan (Italy) in June 1992; and the first to be transferred for £20,000,000 was the Brazilian Denilson, when he moved from Sao Paolo (Brazil) to Real Betis (Spain) in 1998.

top10 **BIGGEST WINS** IN MAJOR INTERNATIONAL TOURNAMENTS*

	WINNERS / LOSERS	TOURNAMENT	SCORE
1	Australia v American Samoa	2002 World Cup Qualifier	31–0
2	Australia v Tonga	2002 World Cup Qualifier	22–0
3	Kuwait v Bhutan	2000 Asian Championship Qualifier	20–0
4 =	China v Guam	2000 Asian Championship Qualifier	19–0
=	Iran v Guam	2002 World Cup Qualifier	19–0
6	Tahiti v American Samoa	2000 Oceania Championship Qualifier	18–0
7 =	China v Maldives	1992 Olympic Games Qualifier	17–0
=	Iran v Maldives	1998 World Cup Qualifier	17–0
=	Australia v Cook Islands	2000 Oceania Championship	17–0
10 =	Denmark v France	1908 Olympic Games	17–1
=	Australia v Cook Islands	1998 Oceania Championship	16–0
=	Tajikistan v Guam	2002 World Cup Qualifier	16–0
=	South Korea v Nepal	2004 Asian Championship Qualifier	16–0

* As at 1 January 2006

The record wins for other major tournaments are: Copa America: Argentina v Ecuador, 1942, 12–0; European Championship: Spain v Malta, 1984, 12–1; British Championship: England v Ireland, 1899, 13–2. The record for women's football is 21–0 achieved on four occasions, all in World Cup qualifying matches: 1997 Japan v Guam; 1998 Canada v Puerto Rico; 1998 New Zealand v Samoa; and 1998 Australia v Western Samoa. These last two matches were on the same date: 9 October 1998.

top10 **MOST MATCHES PLAYED** IN THE FINAL STAGES OF THE WORLD CUP*

	COUNTRY	TOURNAMENTS	MATCHES
1	Brazil	17	87
2	Germany/West Germany	15	85
3	Italy	15	70
4	Argentina	13	60
5	England	11	50
6	Spain	11	45
7	France	11	44
8	Mexico	12	41
9	Uruguay	10	40
10	Sweden	9	39

* Up to and including the 2002 event

Football

the10 FIRST ENGLAND PLAYERS SENT OFF IN FULL INTERNATIONALS

	PLAYER	OPPONENTS	TOURNAMENT	YEAR
1	Allan Mullery	Yugoslavia	European Championships	1968
2	Alan Ball	Poland	World Cup Qualifier	1973
3	Trevor Cherry	Argentina	Friendly	1977
4	Ray Wilkins	Mexico	World Cup Finals	1986
5	David Beckham	Argentina	World Cup Finals	1998
6	Paul Ince	Sweden	European Championships Qualifier	1998
7	Paul Scholes	Sweden	European Championships Qualifier	1999
8	David Batty	Poland	European Championships Qualifier	1999
9	Alan Smith	Macedonia	European Championships Qualifier	2002
10	David Beckham	Austria	World Cup Qualifier	2005

Of the 10 instances, the 2005 sending off of David Beckham was the only one in which England went on to win the game with 10 men. Following Mullery's dismissal, England lost the semi-final 1-0.

top10 PREMIERSHIP APPEARANCES

	PLAYER	CLUB(S)	APPEARANCES*
1	Gary Speed	Leeds United, Everton, Newcastle United, Bolton Wanderers	470
2	Alan Shearer	Blackburn Rovers, Newcastle United	430
3	David James	Liverpool, Aston Villa, West Ham United, Manchester City	423
4 =	Ryan Giggs	Manchester United	421
=	Gareth Southgate	Crystal Palace, Aston Villa, Middlesbrough	421
6	Teddy Sheringham	Nottingham Forest, Tottenham Hotspur, Manchester United, Portsmouth, West Ham United	388
7	Andy Cole	Newcastle United, Manchester United, Blackburn Rovers, Fulham, Manchester City	386
8	Sol Campbell	Tottenham Hotspur, Arsenal	385
9 =	Nigel Martyn	Crystal Palace, Leeds United, Everton	372
=	Ray Parlour	Arsenal, Middlebrough	372

* As at 26 January 2006

the10 CLUBS WITH THE MOST BRITISH TITLES

	TEAM	LEAGUE TITLES*	FA CUP	LEAGUE CUP	TOTAL
1	Glasgow Rangers	51	31	24	106
2	Glasgow Celtic	39	33	12	84
3	Liverpool	18	6	7	31
4	Manchester United	15	11	1	27
5	Arsenal	13	10	2	25
6	Aston Villa	7	7	5	19
7	Aberdeen	4	7	5	16
8 =	Everton	9	5	0	14
=	Heart of Midlothian	4	6	4	14
10	Tottenham Hotspur	2	8	3	13

* Top Flight only; to the end of the 2004–05 season

top10 CLUBS WITH THE LONGEST CONTINUOUS SPELLS IN THE 'TOP FLIGHT'*

	CLUB	LAST SEASON OUT OF TOP FLIGHT	CONTINUOUS SEASONS
1	Arsenal	1914–15	80
2	Everton	1953–54	52
3	Liverpool	1961–62	44
4	Manchester United	1974–75	31
5	Tottenham Hotspur	1977–78	28
6	Aston Villa	1987–88	18
7	Chelsea	1988–89	17
8	Newcastle United	1991–92	14
9	Middlesbrough	1997–98	8
10	Charlton Athletic	1999–2000	6

* The old 1st division or, since 1992–93, the Premiership; as at the start of the 2005–06 season

Coventry City ended 34 years in the 'top flight' in 2001, when they were relegated from the Premier League.

top10 PREMIERSHIP **GOALSCORERS***

	PLAYERS	CLUB(S)	GOALS
1	Alan Shearer	Blackburn Rovers, Newcastle United	254
2	Andy Cole	Newcastle United, Manchester United, Blackburn Rovers, Fulham, Manchester City	184
3	Robbie Fowler	Liverpool, Leeds United, Manchester City	154
4	Thierry Henry	Arsenal	150
5	Les Ferdinand	Queens Park Rangers, Newcastle United, Tottenham Hotspur, West Ham United, Leicester City, Bolton Wanderers	149
6	Teddy Sheringham	Nottingham Forest, Tottenham Hotspur, Manchester United, Portsmouth, West Ham United	143
7	Michael Owen	Liverpool, Newcastle United	125
8	Dwight Yorke	Aston Villa, Manchester United, Blackburn Rovers, Birmingham City	122
9	Jimmy Floyd Hasselbaink	Leeds United, Chelsea, Middlesbrough	120
10	Ian Wright	Arsenal, West Ham United	113

* As at 26 January 2006

top10 CLUBS WITH THE **MOST ENGLISH FA CUP WINS***

	TEAM	FIRST WIN	LAST WIN	TOTAL
1	Manchester United	1909	2004	11
2	Arsenal	1930	2005	10
3	Tottenham Hotspur	1901	1991	8
4	Aston Villa	1887	1957	7
5	= Blackburn Rovers	1884	1928	6
	= Newcastle United	1910	1955	6
	= Liverpool	1965	2001	6
8	= The Wanderers	1872	1878	5
	= West Bromwich Albion	1888	1968	5
	= Everton	1906	1995	5

* Up to and including 2005

top10 **TRANSFER FEES** BETWEEN ENGLISH CLUBS*

	PLAYER	FROM	TO	YEAR	FEE (£)
1	Rio Ferdinand	Leeds United	Manchester United	2002	29,100,000
2	Wayne Rooney	Everton	Manchester United	2004	27,000,000
3	Shaun Wright-Phillips	Manchester City	Chelsea	2005	21,000,000
4	Rio Ferdinand	West Ham United	Leeds United	2000	18,000,000
5	Damien Duff	Blackburn Rovers	Chelsea	2003	17,000,000
6	Alan Shearer	Blackburn Rovers	Newcastle United	1996	15,000,000
7	Louis Saha	Fulham	Manchester United	2004	12,820,000
8	Dwight Yorke	Aston Villa	Manchester United	1998	12,600,000
9	Juan Sebastian Veron	Manchester United	Chelsea	2003	12,500,000
10	= Emile Heskey	Leicester City	Liverpool	2000	11,000,000
	= Robbie Fowler	Liverpool	Leeds United	2001	11,000,000
	= Frank Lampard	West Ham United	Chelsea	2001	11,000,000

* As at 26 January 2006

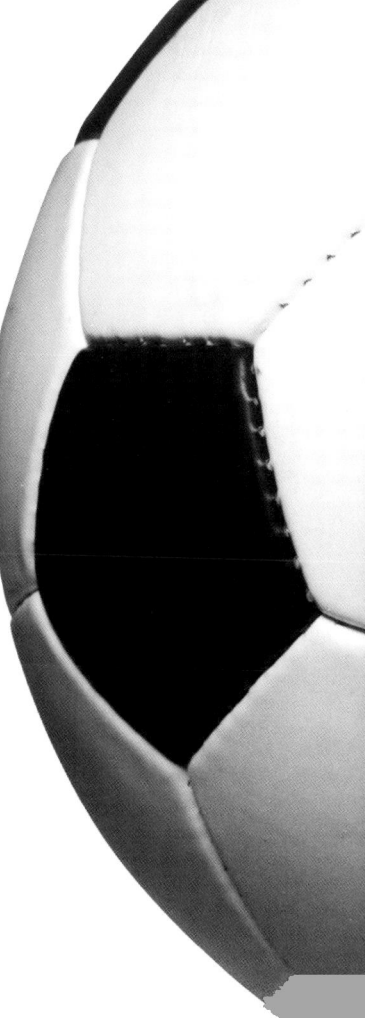

The first £100 transfer fee dates from 1892, when Aston Villa bought Willie Groves from West Bromwich and the first four-figure fee from 1905, when Middlesbrough paid Sunderland £1,000 for Alf Common. When Jimmy Greaves signed for Spurs from Milan in 1961, the fee was £99,999, to avoid his having to carry the burden of being 'Britain's first £100,000 footballer', a title given a year later when Manchester United acquired Denis Law for that sum. In 1979 Trevor Francis became Britain's first £1 million player.

Rugby

the10 LATEST WINNERS OF RUGBY LEAGUE'S MAN OF STEEL AWARD*

	PLAYER	CLUB	YEAR
1	Jamie Lyon	St Helens	2005
2	Andy Farrell	Wigan Warriors	2004
3	Jamie Peacock	Bradford Bulls	2003
4	Paul Sculthorpe	St Helens	2002
5	Paul Sculthorpe	St Helens	2001
6	Sean Long	St Helens	2000
7	Adrian Vowles	Castleford Tigers	1999
8	Iestyn Harris	Leeds Rhinos	1998
9	James Lowes	Bradford Bulls	1997
10	Andy Farrell	Wigan Warriors	1996

* Awarded to the Player of the Year in the British Super League; up to and including 2005

The Man of Steel Award was inaugurated in 1977 and honours the outstandng player in Britain, as voted by members of the Rugby League press; they also present other awards, such as Young Player of the Year. Winners are not necessarily the leading try-scorers or winning captains, nor are they always British: recent winners Jamie Lyon and Adrian Vowles are both Australian, as is 1986's Man of Steel Gavin Miller, while in 1992 New Zealand's Dean Bell won it.

top10 RUGBY LEAGUE CHALLENGE CUP TEAMS

	TEAM	YEARS*	WINS
1	Wigan/Wigan Warriors	1924–2002	17
2	Leeds/Leeds Rhinos	1910–99	12
3	St Helens	1956–2004	9
4	Widnes	1930–84	7
5	= Huddersfield	1913–53	6
	= Bradford/Bradford Northern/Bulls	1906–2003	6
7	= Halifax	1903–87	5
	= Warrington	1905–74	5
9	= Wakefield Trinity	1909–63	4
	= Castleford/Castleford Tigers	1935–86	4

* Of first and last wins

The first Challenge Cup final, then called the Northern Union Cup, was held at Headingley, Leeds, on 24 April 1897, with Batley the first winners, beating St Helens 10-3 in front of a crowd of 13,492. When Wigan were eliminated by Salford in 1996, it ended Wigan's eight-year run without defeat in the Challenge Cup.

the10 MOST CAPPED ENGLAND RUGBY UNION PLAYERS*

	PLAYER	YEARS	CAPS
1	Jason Leonard	1990–2004	114
2	Rory Underwood	1984–96	85
3	Martin Johnson	1993–2003	84
4	Lawrence Dallaglio	1995–2004	73
5	Will Carling	1988–97	72
	= Matt Dawson	1995–2005	72
7	= Rob Andrew	1985–97	71
	= Richard Hill	1997–2004	71
9	Neil Back	1994–2003	66
10	Jeremy Guscott	1989–99	65

* As at 28 December 2005

top10 POINTS-SCORERS IN RUGBY UNION MAJOR INTERNATIONALS

	PLAYER / COUNTRY	YEARS	POINTS*
1	Neil Jenkins, Wales/British Lions	1991–2002	1,090
2	Diego Dominguez, Italy/Argentina	1989–2003	1,010
3	Andrew Mehrtens, New Zealand	1995–2004	967
4	Michael Lynagh, Australia	1984–95	911
5	Jonny Wilkinson, England/British Lions	1998–2005	884
6	Matthew Burke, Australia	1993–2004	878
7	Gavin Hastings, Scotland/British Lions	1986–95	733
8	Grant Fox, New Zealand	1985–93	645
9	Nicky Little, Fiji	1976–2004	592
10	Hugo Porta, Argentina	1971–90	590

* As at 28 December 2005

AMAZING FACT

Rugby Kicks Off

Although it is widely claimed that William Webb Ellis invented rugby in 1823 at Rugby School when he picked up a football and ran with it, the sport almost certainly developed from earlier, boisterous forms of football. The first rules were drawn up in 1848 and the Rugby Football Union formed by Edwin Ash in 1871 when the laws of the game were codified, with the number of players reduced from 20 to 15 in 1876. Rugby League dates from 1895 when 22 northern teams broke away from the RFU to form the Northern Union.

top10 MOST POINTS IN A WORLD CUP CAREER*

	PLAYER	COUNTRY	YEARS	POINTS
1	Gavin Hastings	Scotland	1987–95	227
2	Michael Lynagh	Australia	1987–95	195
3	Jonny Wilkinson	England	1999–2003	182
4	Grant Fox	New Zealand	1987–91	170
5	Andrew Mehrtens	New Zealand	1995–99	163
6	Gonzalo Quesada	Argentina	1995–99	135
7	Matt Burke	Australia	1995–99	125
8	Thierry Lacroix	France	1991–95	124
9	Gareth Rees	Canada	1987–99	120
10	Frederic Michalak	France	2003	103

* Up to and including the 2003 tournament

top10 POINTS IN ONE RUGBY WORLD CUP

	PLAYER	COUNTRY	YEAR*	POINTS
1	Grant Fox	New Zealand	1987	126
2	Jonny Wilkinson	England	2003	113
3	Thierry Lacroix	France	1995	112
4	Gavin Hastings	Scotland	1995	104
5	Frederic Michalak	France	2003	103
6	Gonzalo Quesada	Argentina	1999	102
7	Matt Burke	Australia	1999	101
8	Elton Flatley	Australia	2003	100
9	Janni de Beer	South Africa	1999	97
10	Andrew Mehrtens	New Zealand	1995	84

* Up to and including the 2003 World Cup

top10 TRY-SCORERS IN RUGBY UNION TEST MATCHES

	PLAYER / COUNTRY	TESTS	CAREER	TRIES*
1	David Campese, Australia	101	1982–96	64
2	Rory Underwood, England/British Lions*	91(6)	1984–96	50(1)
3	Daisuke Ohata, Japan	50	1997–2005	49
4	Christian Cullen, New Zealand	58	1996–2002	46
5	Jeff Wilson, New Zealand	60	1993–2001	44
6	Doug Howlett, New Zealand	50	2000–05	41
7	= Serge Blanco, France	93	1980–91	38
	= Joost van der Westhuizen, South Africa	89	1993–2003	38
9	Jonah Lomu, New Zealand	63	1994–2002	37
	= Tana Umaga, New Zealand	73	1997–2005	37

* As at 26 December 2005
* Figures in brackets indicate appearances and tries for the British Lions

Australian winger David Campese (b.1962) was originally a Rugby League player, but switched to Union, gaining his first cap and scoring his first try in an international at the age of 19 on 14 August 1982 in a match against New Zealand. On 23 October 1996 he played his 100th international to become the first southern hemisphere player to reach this milestone. His 64 tries, seven penalties, eight conversions and two drop goals contributed to a career Test points total of 315.

top10 MOST TRIES IN A SUPER LEAGUE REGULAR SEASON*

	PLAYER	CLUB	YEAR	TRIES
1	Danny McGuire	Leeds Rhinos	2004	29
2	Paul Newlove	St Helens	1996	28
3	Kris Radlinski	Wigan Warriors	2001	27
4	= Matt Daylight	Gateshead Thunder	1999	25
	= Toa Kohe-Love	Warrington Wolves	1999	25
	= Darren Albert	St Helens	2005	25
	= Lesley Vainikolo	Bradford	2005	25
8	= Jason Robinson	Wigan	1996	24
	= Anthony Sullivan	St Helens	1999	24
	= Dennis Moran	London Broncos	2003	24
	= Keith Senior	Leeds	2005	24

* Up to and including 2005

Danny McGuire (b.1982) played his first season for Leeds Rhinos in 2002, represented England the following year and, in 2004, became the Super League's leading scorer, as well as being named Player of the Year by the Rugby League Writers Association. The Rugby Super League is technically a pan-European league of the 132 leading clubs. In reality it is synonymous with British Rugby League, with the additon (from the 2006 season) of French team Les Catalans of Perpignan.

Cricket

top10 BIGGEST WINS BY ENGLAND IN TEST CRICKET†

	OPPONENTS	YEAR	GROUND	MARGIN
1	Australia	1938	The Oval	Innings and 579 runs
2	India	1974	Lord's	Innings and 285 runs
3	Bangladesh	2005	Lord's	Innings and 261 runs
4	West Indies	1957	The Oval	Innings and 237 runs
5	Australia	1891–92	Adelaide Oval	Innings and 230 runs
6	Australia	1911–12	Melbourne Cricket Ground	Innings and 225 runs
7	Australia	1886	The Oval	Innings and 217 runs
8	New Zealand	1962–63	Eden Park	Innings and 215 runs
9	Zimbabwe	2000	Lord's	Innings and 209 runs
10	India	1952	Old Trafford	Innings and 207 runs

† As at 27 March 2006

England's record margin was achieved in the 5th Test on 20–24 August 1938. Len Hutton batted for over 11 hours to set a then-record of 364, including 35 fours, while Maurice Leyland contributed 187 and Joseph Hardstaff 169 to England's total of 903 for 7 declared. This was the first time in Test history that the 900 mark was crossed; it took almost 60 years for it to be surpassed by Sri Lanka's 952 against India in 1997.

top10 RUN-MAKERS FOR ENGLAND IN TEST CRICKET†

	BATSMAN	MATCHES	RUNS
1	Graham Gooch	118	8,900
2	Alec Stewart	133	8,463
3	David Gower	117	8,231
4	Geoff Boycott	108	8,114
5	Michael Atherton	115	7,728
6	Colin Cowdrey	114	7,624
7	Walter Hammond	85	7,249
8	Len Hutton	79	6,971
9	Ken Barrington	82	6,806
10	Graham Thorpe	100	6,744

† As at 27 March 2006

Graham Gooch (b.1953) not only gained this record-breaking Test total but added it to a tally of 44,846 First-class runs, with a further 4,290 in one-day internationals and 22,211 in List A one-day matches.

top10 MOST FIRST CLASS RUNS†

	BATSMAN	YEARS	TOTAL INNINGS	HIGHEST SCORE*	RUNS
1	Jack Hobbs	1905–34	1,325	365#	61,760
2	Frank Woolley	1906–38	1,530	305#	58,959
3	Patsy Hendren	1907–37	1,300	301#	57,611
4	Philip Mead	1905–36	1,340	280#	55,061
5	W.G. Grace	1865–1908	1,478	344	54,211
6	Herbert Sutcliffe	1919–45	1,098	313	50,670
7	Walter Hammond	1920–51	1,005	336	50,551
8	Geoff Boycott	1962–86	1,014	261#	48,426
9	Tom Graveney	1948–72	1,223	258	47,793
10	Graham Gooch	1973–2000	990	333	44,846

† As at 27 March 2006
# Not out

Sir John Berry 'Jack' Hobbs (1882–1963) was known as 'The Master', perhaps unsurprisingly. He achieved his record total in a First-class career of almost 30 years during which he also scored a record 199 centuries, over half of them after his 40th birthday. Hobbs was *Wisden* Cricketer of the Year in 1909 and again in 1926. He was knighted in 1953 and was numbered by *Wisden* as one of the top five cricketers of the 20th century.

top10 MOST RUNS IN TEST CRICKET†

	BATSMAN / COUNTRY	YEARS	MATCHES	RUNS
1	Brian Lara, West Indies	1990–	123	11,211
2	Allan Border, Australia	1978–94	156	11,174
3	Steve Waugh, Australia	1965–2004	168	10,927
4	Sachin Tendulkar, India	1989–	132	10,469
5	Sunil Gavaskar, India	1971–87	125	10,122
6	Graham Gooch, England	1975–95	118	8,900
7	Javed Miandad, Pakistan	1976–93	124	8,832
8	Viv Richards, West Indies	1975–91	121	8,540
9	Alec Stewart, England	1990–2003	133	8,463
10	David Gower, England	1978–92	117	8,231

† As at 27 March 2006

Brian Lara (b.1969) holds the current record for highest individual First-class innings with 501 not out at Edgbaston, UK, in 1994, the only quintuple century ever achieved, as well as the highest in Test cricket. His 400 not out against England at St John's, Antigua and Barbuda, in 2004, is the only quadruple century in Test cricket. In 2005 in Adelaide, Australia, he overtook Allan Border's record 11,174 runs to become Test cricket's most prolific scorer.

top10 **WICKET–TAKERS** IN A FIRST–CLASS CAREER[†]

	BOWLER	CAREER	WICKETS
1	Wilf Rhodes	1898–1930	4,187
2	Alfred 'Titch' Freeman	1914–36	3,776
3	Charlie Parker	1903–35	3,278
4	Jack Hearne	1888–1923	3,061
5	Tom Goddard	1922–52	2,979
6	W.G. Grace	1865–1908	2,876
7	Alex Kennedy	1907–36	2,874
8	Derek Shackleton	1948–69	2,857
9	Tony Lock	1946–71	2,844
10	Fred Titmus	1949–82	2,830

† As at 27 March 2006

top10 WICKET-TAKERS IN **TEST CRICKET**[†]

	BOWLER / COUNTRY	YEARS	MATCHES	WICKETS
1	Shane Warne, Australia	1992–	136	662
2	Muttiah Muralitharan, Sri Lanka	1992–	101	600
3	Glenn McGrath, Australia	1993–	119	542
4	Courtney Walsh, West Indies	1984–2001	132	519
5	Anil Kumble, India	1990–	106	510
6	Kapil Dev, India	1978–94	131	434
7	Richard Hadlee, New Zealand	1973–90	86	431
8	Wasim Akram, Pakistan	1985–2002	104	414
9	Curtly Ambrose, West Indies	1988–2000	98	405
10	Ian Botham, England	1977–92	102	383

† As at 27 March 2006

top10 **WICKETS** FOR ENGLAND IN TEST CRICKET[†]

	BOWLER	MATCHES	WICKETS
1	Ian Botham	102	383
2	Bob Willis	90	325
3	Fred Trueman	67	307
4	Derek Underwood	86	297
5	Brian Statham	70	252
6	Alec Bedser	51	236
7	Andrew Caddick	62	234
8	Darren Gough	58	229
9	Jon Snow	49	202
10	Matthew Hoggard	51	197

† As at 27 March 2006

Tennis

top10 MOST CAREER TOURNAMENT WINS – MEN

	PLAYER / COUNTRY	WINS*
1	Jimmy Connors, USA	109
2	Ivan Lendl, Czechoslovakia/USA	94
3	John McEnroe, USA	77
4	Pete Sampras, USA	64
5	= Bjorn Borg, Sweden	62
	= Guillermo Vilas, Argentina	62
7	Andre Agassi, USA	60
8	Ilie Nastase, Romania	57
9	Boris Becker, Germany	49
10	Rod Laver, Australia	47

* As at 1 January 2006

➲ *Singles-minded*
In a 20-year career span Martina Navratilova competed in 380 singles tournaments, winning 167 titles. This record and her nine Wimbledon wins remain unbeaten.

top10 MOST CAREER TOURNAMENT WINS – WOMEN

	PLAYER / COUNTRY	WINS*
1	Martina Navratilova, Czechoslovakia/USA	167
2	Chris Evert-Lloyd, USA	154
3	Steffi Graf, Germany	107
4	Margaret Court (née Smith), Australia	92
5	Evonne Cawley (née Goolagong), Australia	68
6	Billie Jean King (née Moffitt), USA	67
7	Virginia Wade, UK	55
8	Monica Seles, Yugoslavia/USA	53
9	Lindsay Davenport, USA	51
10	Martina Hingis, Switzerland	40

* As at 1 January 2006

top10 MOST MEN'S GRAND SLAM SINGLES TITLES*

	PLAYER / COUNTRY	A	F	W	US	TOTAL
1	Pete Sampras, USA	2	0	7	5	14
2	Roy Emerson, Australia	6	2	2	2	12
3	= Bjorn Borg, Sweden	0	6	5	0	11
	= Rod Laver, Australia	3	2	4	2	11
5	Bill Tilden, USA	0	0	3	7	10
6	= Andre Agassi, USA	4	1	1	2	8
	= Jimmy Connors, USA	1	0	2	5	8
	= Ivan Lendl, Czechoslovakia/USA	2	3	0	3	8
	= Fred Perry, UK	1	1	3	3	8
	= Ken Rosewall, Australia	4	2	0	2	8

A – Australian Open, F – French Open, W – Wimbledon, US – US Open

* Up to and including 2005

top10 MOST WOMEN'S GRAND SLAM SINGLES TITLES

	PLAYER / COUNTRY	YEARS	A	F	W	US	TOTAL
1	Margaret Court (née Smith), Australia	1960–73	11	5	3	5	24
2	Steffi Graf, Germany	1987–99	4	6	7	5	22
3	Helen Wills-Moody, USA	1923–38	0	4	8	7	19
4	= Chris Evert-Lloyd, USA	1974–86	2	7	3	6	18
	= Martina Navratilova, Czechoslovakia/USA	1978–90	3	2	9	4	18
6	Billie Jean King (née Moffitt), USA	1966–75	1	1	6	4	12
7	= Maureen Connolly, USA	1951–54	1	2	3	3	9
	= Monica Seles, Yugoslavia/USA	1990–96	4	3	0	2	9
9	= Molla Mallory (née Bjurstedt), USA	1915–26	0	0	0	8	8
	= Suzanne Lenglen, France	1919–26	0	2	6	0	8

A – Australian Open, F – French Open, W – Wimbledon, US – US Open

* Up to and including 2005

top10 MOST **WOMEN'S GRAND SLAM TITLES***

	PLAYER / COUNTRY#	YEARS	SINGLES	DOUBLES	MIXED	TOTAL
1	Margaret Court (née Smith), Australia)	1960–75	24	19	19	62
2	Martina Navratilova, Czechoslovakia/USA	1974–2003	18	32	9	59
3	Bille Jean King (née Moffitt), USA	1961–80	12	16	11	39
4	Margaret Du Pont, USA	1941–62	6	21	10	37
5 =	Louise Brough, USA	1942–57	6	21	8	35
=	Doris Hart, USA	1948–55	6	14	15	35
7	Helen Wills-Moody, USA	1922–38	19	9	3	31
8	Elizabeth Ryan, USA	1914–34	0	17	9	26
9	Suzanne Lenglen, France	1919–26	12	8	5	25
10 =	Pam Shriver, USA	1981–91	0	22	1	23
=	Steffi Graf, Germany	1987–99	22	1	0	23

* Up to and including 2005

top10 MOST **WOMEN'S SINGLES TITLES** AT WIMBLEDON

	PLAYER / COUNTRY	YEARS*	WINS
1	Martina Navratilova, Czechoslovakia/USA	1978–90	9
2	Helen Wills–Moody, USA	1927–38	8
3 =	Dorothea Chambers (née Douglass), UK	1903–14	7
=	Steffi Graf, Germany	1988–1996	7
5 =	Blanche Hillyward (née Bingley), UK	1886–1900	6
=	Suzanne Lenglen, France	1919–25	6
=	Billie Jean King (née Moffitt), USA	1966–75	6
8 =	Lottie Dod, UK	1887–93	5
=	Charlotte Sterry (née Cooper), UK	1895–1908	5
10	Louise Brough, USA	1948–55	4

* Of first and last win; up to and including 2005

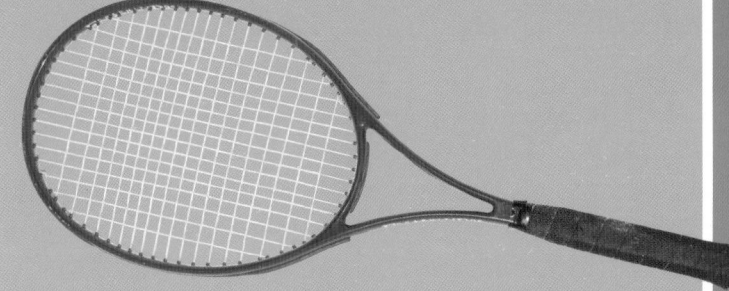

top10 MOST MEN'S **GRAND SLAM TITLES***

	PLAYER / COUNTRY#	YEARS	SINGLES	DOUBLES	MIXED	TOTAL
1	Roy Emerson	1959–71	12	16	0	28
2	John Newcombe	1964–76	7	17	1	25
3	Todd Woodbridge	1990–2004	0	16	7	23
4	Frank Sedgman	1948–52	5	9	8	22
5	Bill Tilden, USA	1913–30	10	6	5	21
6	Rod Laver	1959–71	11	6	3	20
7 =	John Bromwich	1938–50	2	13	4	19
=	Neale Fraser	1957–62	3	11	5	19
9 =	Jean Borotra, France	1925–36	4	9	5	18
=	Ken Rosewall	1953–72	8	9	1	18

* Up to and including 2005
# Australia unless otherwise stated

top10 MOST **MEN'S SINGLES TITLES** AT WIMBLEDON

	PLAYER / COUNTRY	YEARS*	WINS
1 =	Willie Renshaw, UK	1881–89	7
=	Pete Sampras, USA	1993–2000	7
3 =	Laurence Doherty, UK	1902–06	5
=	Bjorn Borg, Sweden	1976–80	5
5 =	Reginald Doherty, UK	1897–1900	4
=	Tony Wilding, New Zealand	1910–13	4
=	Rod Laver, Australia	1961–69	4
8 =	Wilfred Baddeley, UK	1891–95	3
=	Arthur Gore, UK	1901–09	3
=	Bill Tilden, USA	1920–30	3
=	Fred Perry, UK	1934–36	3
=	John Newcombe, Australia	1967–71	3
=	John McEnroe, USA	1981–84	3
=	Boris Becker, Germany	1985–89	3
=	Roger Federer, Switzerland	2003–05	3

* Of first and last win; up to and including 2005

Golf

⬆ **Tiger economy**
The career earnings of Tiger Woods are unmatched in the history of professional golf.

top10 CAREER **MONEY WINNERS (MEN)***

	PLAYER / COUNTRY#	WINNINGS ($)
1	Tiger Woods	57,940,144
2	Vijay Singh, Fiji	46,407,643
3	Phil Mickelson	36,167,360
4	Davis Love III	32,817,075
5	Ernie Els, South Africa	26,552,751
6	Jim Furyk	25,175,800
7	David Toms	24,953,728
8	Justin Leonard	20,720,563
9	Nick Price, Zimbabwe	20,395,519
10	Kenny Perry	19,766,233

* On the US PGA Tour as at 26 March 2006
# All from the USA unless otherwise stated

Source: PGA Tour

top10 CAREER **MONEY WINNERS (WOMEN)***

	PLAYER / COUNTRY	WINNINGS ($)
1	Annika Sörenstam, Sweden	18,512,764
2	Karrie Webb, Australia	10,748,665
3	Juli Inkster, USA	9,954,470
4	Meg Mallon, USA	8,767,439
5	Beth Daniel, USA	8,503,533
6	Rosie Jones, USA	8,306,013
7	Se Ri Pak, Korea	8,087,834
8	Betsy King, USA	7,637,621
9	Laura Davies, UK	7,352,195
10	Dottie Pepper, USA	6,827,284

* On the LPGA Tour, as at 20 March 2006

Source: LPGA

top10 **BIGGEST WINNING MARGINS** IN MEN'S MAJORS

	PLAYER / COUNTRY	YEAR	TOURNAMENT	VENUE	WINNING MARGIN
1	Tiger Woods, USA	2000	US Open	Pebble Beach	15
2	Tom Morris Sr, UK	1862	British Open	Prestwick	13
3	= Tom Morris Jr, UK	1870	British Open	Prestwick	12
	= Tiger Woods, USA	1997	US Masters	Augusta	12
5	Willie Smith, USA	1899	US Open	Baltimore	11
6	= Jim Barnes, USA	1921	US Open	Columbia	9
	= Jack Nicklaus, USA	1965	US Masters	Augusta	9
8	= J.H. Taylor, UK	1900	British Open	St Andrews	8
	= James Braid, UK	1908	British Open	Prestwick	8
	= J.H.Taylor, UK	1913	British Open	Hoylake	8
	= Ray Floyd, USA	1976	US Masters	Augusta	8
	= Tiger Woods, USA	2000	British Open	St Andrews	8

The biggest winning margin in the other Major – the US PGA Championship – was in 1980 when Jack Nicklaus won by seven strokes from Andy Bean at Oak Hill.

top10 **LOWEST 4-ROUND** WINNING TOTALS IN MEN'S MAJORS

	PLAYER / COUNTRY / VENUE	YEAR	TOURNAMENT	SCORE
1	David Toms, USA Atlanta	2001	US PGA	265
2	= Greg Norman, Australia Royal St George's	1993	British Open	267
	= Steve Elkington, Australia Riviera	1995	US PGA	267
4	= Tom Watson, USA Turnberry	1977	British Open	268
	= Nick Price, Zimbabwe Turnberry	1994	British Open	268
6	= Nick Price, Zimbabwe Southern Hills	1994	US PGA	269
	= Davis Love III, USA Winged Foot	1997	US PGA	269
	= Tiger Woods, USA St Andrews	2000	British Open	269
9	= Nick Faldo, UK St Andrews	1990	British Open	270
	= Tiger Woods, USA Augusta	1997	Masters	270
	= Tiger Woods, USA Valhalla	2000	US PGA	270

David Toms' record-breaking total – 15 under par – at Atlanta was made up with rounds of 66-65-65-69. In addition to this win, he has won 12 events on the PGA Tour.

↑ **World No.1**
In 2006 Sweden's Annika Sörenstam was ranked first among women golfers.

top10 PLAYERS TO WIN THE **MOST PROFESSIONAL MAJORS** IN A CAREER*

	PLAYER / COUNTRY#	YEARS	BRITISH OPEN	US OPEN	MASTERS	PGA	TOTAL
1	Jack Nicklaus	1962–86	3	4	6	5	18
2	Walter Hagen	1924–29	4	2	0	5	11
3	Tiger Woods	1997–2005	2	2	4	2	10
4	= Ben Hogan	1946–53	1	4	2	2	9
	= Gary Player, South Africa	1959–78	3	1	3	2	9
6	Tom Watson	1975–83	5	1	2	0	8
7	= Harry Vardon, UK	1896–1914	6	1	0	0	7
	= Gene Sarazen	1922–35	1	2	1	3	7
	= Bobby Jones	1923–30	3	4	0	0	7
	= Sam Snead	1942–54	1	0	3	3	7
	= Arnold Palmer	1958–64	2	1	4	0	7

* Up to and including 2005
# All from USA unless otherwise indicated

top10 MOST **WOMEN'S MAJORS**

	PLAYER / COUNTRY*	YEARS#	MAJORS
1	Patty Berg	1937–58	15
2	Mickey Wright	1958–66	13
3	Louise Suggs	1946–59	11
4	= Babe Zaharias	1940–54	9
	= Annika Sörenstam, Sweden	1999–2005	9
6	Betsy Rawls	1951–69	8
7	Juli Inkster	1984–2002	7
8	= Kathy Whitworth	1965–75	6
	= Pat Bradley	1980–86	6
	= Patty Sheehan	1983–96	6
	= Betsy King	1987–97	6
	= Karrie Webb, Australia	1999–2002	6

* All from USA unless otherwise stated
# Of first and last wins

Water Sports

top10 **OLYMPIC SAILING*** COUNTRIES#

	COUNTRY	GOLD	MEDALS SILVER	BRONZE	TOTAL
1	USA	18	22	18	58
2	UK	23	14	10	47
3	France	16	11	14	41
4	Sweden	9	12	11	32
5	Norway	17	11	3	31
6	= Denmark	11	8	6	25
	= Netherlands	7	9	9	25
8	Germany/West Germany	6	6	7	19
9	Australia	5	3	8	16
10	= New Zealand	6	4	5	15
	= Spain	10	4	1	15
	= USSR/Unified Team/Russia	4	6	5	15

* Previously Olympic yachting
# Up to and including the 2004 Games

⊙ Sailing to victory

The success of 2003 America's Cup-winning yacht Alinghi was all the more remarkable as it was owned by a group from Switzerland, a landlocked country, although its crew was multinational – and was skippered by Russell Couts, previously a member of the winning New Zealand crew.

the10 **LATEST WINNERS** OF THE AMERICA'S CUP

	WINNER	SKIPPER	COUNTRY	YEAR
1	Alinghi	Russell Couts	Switzerland	2003
2	New Zealand	Russell Couts	New Zealand	2000
3	Black Magic I	Russell Couts	New Zealand	1995
4	America[3]	Bill Koch	USA	1992
5	Stars and Stripes	Dennis Conner	USA	1988
6	Stars and Stripes	Dennis Conner	USA	1987
7	Australia II*	John Bertrand	Australia	1983
8	Freedom	Dennis Conner	USA	1980
9	Courageous	Ted Turner	USA	1977
10	Courageous	Ted Hood	USA	1974

* The first non-American winner of the race since it was inaugurated in 1851

top10 **OLYMPIC ROWING** COUNTRIES*

	COUNTRY	GOLD	MEDALS SILVER	BRONZE	TOTAL
1	United States	30	30	21	81
2	Germany/West Germany	27	19	20	66
3	East Germany	33	7	8	48
4	UK	21	18	8	47
5	USSR/Unified Team/Russia	13	20	13	46
6	Italy	14	13	10	37
7	Canada	8	13	13	34
8	France	6	14	13	33
9	Romania	15	10	7	32
10	Australia	8	9	12	29

* Men and women, up to and including 2004

⊙ Sheer skill
Multiple record-holder Emma Sheers from Australia is the current water-ski World Champion in slalom and jump events.

top10 FASTEST WINNING TIMES IN THE OXFORD-CAMBRIDGE BOAT RACE*

	WINNER	YEAR	TIME MIN:SEC
1	Cambridge	1998	16:19
2	Cambridge	1999	16:41
3	Oxford	2005	16:42
4	Oxford	1984	16:45
5	Oxford	1976	16:50
6	Oxford	2002	16:54
7	Cambridge	1996	16:58
8	Oxford	1991	16:59
9	Cambridge	1993	17:00
10	Oxford	1985	17:11

* Putney to Mortlake course, up to and including 2005

The first Boat Race was on 10 June 1829. Oxford won easily in 14 minutes and three seconds; both crews weighed in at 11 st 1 lb 12 oz (70.8 kg) average. The race is now held over 6,779 metres (4 miles 374 yards) from Putney to Mortlake.

top10 WATERSKIERS WITH THE MOST WORLD CUP WINS*

	SKIER / COUNTRY	M/F*	SLALOM	JUMP	TOTAL
1	Andy Mapple, UK	M	31	–	31
2	= Jaret Llewellyn, Canada	M	–	18	18
	= Emma Sheers, Australia	F	2	16	18
4	= Kristi Johnson (née Overton), USA	F	13	–	13
	= Toni Neville, Australia	F	3	10	13
6	= Wade Cox, USA	M	10	–	10
	= Freddy Krueger, USA	M	–	10	10
8	Bruce Neville, Australia	M	–	9	9
9	Scot Ellis, USA	M	–	7	7
10	= Susi Graham, Canada	F	6	–	6
	= Carl Roberge, USA	M	1	5	6

* Up to and including 2005
* Male/female

Waterskiing was invented in 1922 by 18-year-old Ralph W. Samuelson of Lake City, Minnesota, USA. The first international governing body, the World Water Ski Union, was established in 1946 in Geneva, Switzerland. Its successor, the International Water Ski Federation, organized the Water Ski World Cup, from 1996.

top10 LONGEST STANDING SWIMMING WORLD RECORDS*

	SWIMMER / COUNTRY / EVENT	TIME MIN:SEC	DATE SET
1	Janet Evans, USA 1500 metres freestyle (W)	15:52.10	26 Mar 1988
2	Janet Evans, USA 400 metres freestyle (W)	4:03.85	22 Sep 1988
3	Janet Evans, USA 800 metres freestyle (W)	8:16.22	20 Aug 1989
4	Kristini Egerszegi, Hungary 200 metres backstroke (W)	2:06.62	25 Aug 1991
5	Yanyan Wu, China 200 metres individual medley (W)	2:09.72	17 Oct 1997
6	Alexsandr Popov, Russia 50 metres freestyle (M)	0:21.64	16 Jun 2000
7	Anna-Karin Kammerling, Sweden 50 metres butterfly (W)	0:25.57	30 Jul 2000
8	Yana Klochkova, Ukraine 400 metres individual medley (W)	4:33.59	16 Sep 2000
9	Inge de Bruijn, Netherlands 100 metres butterfly (W)	0:56.61	17 Sep 2000
10	Pieter van den Hoogenband, Netherlands, 100 metres freestyle (M)	0:47.84	19 Sep 2000

* Long course records as at 1 January 2006; (W) = women (M) = men

Winter Sports

	SNOWBOARDER / COUNTRY	YEARS	GOLD	SILVER	BRONZE	TOTAL
1	Nicolas Huet, France	1999–2005	2	1	2	5
2	=Mike Jacoby, USA	1996–97	1	2	–	3
	=Helmut Pramstaller, Austria	1996–97	1	–	2	3
	=Jasey-Jay Anderson, Canada	2001–05	3	–	–	3
	=Antti Autti, Finland	2003–05	2	–	1	3
6	=Bernd Kroschewski, Germany	1997	1	–	1	2
	=Markus Hurme, Finland	1997–2001	–	1	1	2
	=Anton Pogue, USA	1997–2001	–	–	2	2
	=Markus Ebner, Germany	1999–2001	1	1	–	2
	=Stefan Kaltschuetz, Austria	1999–2001	–	1	1	2
	=Mathieu Bozzetto, France	1999–2003	–	2	–	2
	=Dejan Kosir, Slovenia	2001–03	1	1	–	2
	=Kim Christiansen, Norway	2001–05	1	–	1	2
	=Simon Schoch, Switzerland	2003	–	1	1	2
	=Seth Wescott, USA	2003–05	1	1	–	2

Source: Fédération Internationale de Ski (FIS)

	SKATER / COUNTRY	MEN	WOMEN	PAIRS	DANCE	TOTAL
1	=Sonja Henie, Norway	0	10	0	0	10
	=Irina Rodnina, USSR	0	0	10	0	10
	=Ulrich Salchow, Sweden	10	0	0	0	10
4	=Herma Planck (née Szabo), Austria	0	5	2	0	7
	=Karl Schafer, Austria	7	0	0	0	7
6	=Aleksandr Gorshkov, USSR	0	0	6	0	6
	=Lyudmila Pakhomova, USSR	0	0	0	6	6
	=Aleksandr Zaitsev, USSR	0	0	6	0	6
9	=Dick Button, USA	5	0	0	0	5
	=Carol Heiss, USA	0	5	0	0	5
	=Michelle Kwan, USA	0	5	0	0	5

* Up to and including the 2005 World Championships

⬅ Canadian snow man
Snowboarder Jasey-Jay Anderson was first in the Parallel GS and Parallel Slalom events at the 2005 FIS Snowboarding Championship at Whistler in his native Canada.

top10 WOMEN'S ALPINE SKIING WORLD CUP TITLES

SKIER / COUNTRY	O	D	GS	SG	S	C	TOTAL
1 Annemarie Moser-Pröll, Austria	6	7	3	0	0	1	17
2 Vreni Schneider, Switzerland	3	0	5	0	6	0	14
3 Katja Seizinger, Germany	2	4	0	5	0	0	11
4 Renate Götschl, Austria	1	4	0	2	0	3	10
5 Erika Hess, Switzerland	2	0	1	0	5	1	9
6 = Michela Figini, Switzerland	2	4	1	1	0	0	8
= Hanni Wenzel, Liechtenstein	2	0	2	0	1	3	8
8 Maria Walliser, Switzerland	2	2	1	1	0	1	7
9 = Janika Kostelic, Croatia	2	0	0	0	2	2	6
= Carole Merle, France	0	0	2	4	0	0	6
= Lisa-Marie Morerord, Switzerland	1	0	3	0	2	0	6
= Anita Wachter, Austria	1	0	2	0	0	3	6

Heading: TITLES

* Up to and including the 2004–05 season

O = Overall; D = Downhill; GS = Giant Slalom; SG = Super Giant Slalom; S = Slalom; C = Combined

Annemarie Moser-Pröll (b.1953) gained her tally of titles at the Alpine skiing World Championship events during the 1970s. She also won silver medals at the 1972 Winter Olympics and gold at the 1980 Games.

top10 MEN'S ALPINE SKIING WORLD CUP TITLES*

SKIER / COUNTRY	O	D	GS	SG	S	C	TOTAL
1 Ingemar Stenmark, Sweden	3	0	8	0	8	0	19
2 = Marc Girardelli, Luxembourg	5	2	1	0	3	4	15
= Pirmin Zurbriggen, Switzerland	4	2	3	4	0	2	15
4 Hermann Maier, Austria	4	2	3	5	0	0	14
5 = Phil Mahre, USA	3	0	2	0	1	3	9
= Alberto Tomba, Italy	1	0	4	0	4	0	9
7 Gustavo Thoeni, Italy	4	0	2	0	2	0	8
8 = Kjetil André Aamodt, Norway	1	0	1	1	1	3	7
= Stephan Ebergarter, Austria	2	3	0	2	0	0	7
10 Jean-Claude Killy, France	2	1	2	0	1	0	6

Heading: TITLES

* Up to and including the 2004–05 season

O = Overall; D = Downhill; GS = Giant Slalom; SG = Super Giant Slalom; S = Slalom; C = Combined

The World Cup was launched in the 1966–67 season, under the auspices of the Fédération Internationale de Ski (FIS), and is a winter-long series of races with champions in five categories, as well as an overall champion.

Motor Sports

top10 DRIVERS WITH THE MOST FORMULA ONE WINS*

	DRIVER / COUNTRY	YEARS	WINS
1	Michael Schumacher, Germany	1992–2005	84
2	Alain Prost, France	1981–93	51
3	Ayrton Senna, Brazil	1985–93	41
4	Nigel Mansell, UK	1985–94	31
5	Jackie Stewart, UK	1965–73	27
6 =	Jim Clark, UK	1962–68	25
=	Niki Lauda, Austria	1974–85	25
8	Juan Manuel Fangio, Argentina	1950–57	24
9	Nelson Piquet, Brazil	1980–91	23
10	Damon Hill, UK	1993–98	22

* Up to and including the 2005 season

top10 MANUFACTURERS WITH THE MOST FORMULA ONE WINS*

	MANUFACTURER	FIRST WIN / DRIVER	WINS
1	Ferrari#	1951 British GP (José Froilán González)	183
2	McLaren#	1968 Belgian GP (Bruce McLaren)	148
3	Williams#	1977 British GP (Clay Regazzoni)	113
4	Lotus	1960 Monaco GP (Stirling Moss)	79
5	Brabham	1964 French GP (Dan Gurney)	35
6	Benetton	1986 Mexican GP (Gerhard Berger)	27
7	Renault#	1979 French GP (Jean-Pierre Jabouille)	25
8	Tyrrell	1971 Spanish GP (Jackie Stewart)	23
9	BRM	1959 Dutch GP (Jo Bonnier)	17
10	Cooper	1958 Argentina GP (Stirling Moss)	16

* Up to and including the 2005 season
# Raced in 2005

top10 MOST RALLY WINS*

	DRIVER / COUNTRY	WINS
1	Carlos Sainz, Spain#	26
2	Colin McRae, UK#	25
3	Tommi Makinen, Finland	24
4	Juha Kankkunen, Finland	23
5 =	Didier Auriol, France	20
=	Sebastien Loeb, France#	20
7	Markku Alen, Finland	19
8 =	Marcus Gronholm, Finland#	18
=	Hannu Mikkola, Finland	18
10	Massimo Biasion, Italy	17

* Up to and including the 2005 season
# Active in 2005

Source: FIM World Rally Championship

⊙ Winning formula
His remarkable tally of 84 Formula One Grand Prix wins places third youngest World Champion Michael Schumacher (b. 1969) far ahead of his closest rivals.

top10 YOUNGEST FORMULA ONE WORLD CHAMPIONS

	DRIVER / COUNTRY	YEAR	AGE YEARS	DAYS
1	Fernando Alonso, Spain	2005	24	59
2	Emerson Fittipaldi, Brazil	1972	25	273
3	Michael Schumacher, Germany	1994	25	315
4	Jacques Villeneuve, Canada	1997	26	200
5	Niki Lauda, Austria	1975	26	201
6	Jim Clark, UK	1963	27	187
7	Jochen Rindt, Austria	1970	28	168
8	Ayrton Senna, Brazil	1988	28	223
9	James Hunt, UK	1976	29	55
10	Nelson Piquet, Brazil	1981	29	60

top10 MOST **BRITISH GRAND PRIX WINS** *

DRIVER / COUNTRY	YEARS	WINS
1 = Jim Clark, UK	1962–65, 1967	5
= Alain Prost, France	1983, 1985, 1989–90, 1993	5
3 Nigel Mansell, UK	1986–87, 1991–92	4
4 = Jack Brabham, Australia	1959–60, 1966	3
= Niki Lauda, Austria	1976, 1982, 1984	3
= Michael Schumacher, Germany	1998, 2002, 2004	3
7 = José Froilán González, Argentina	1951, 1954	2
= Alberto Ascari, Italy	1952–53	2
= Stirling Moss, UK	1955, 1957#	2
= Jackie Stewart, UK	1969, 1971	2
= Emerson Fittipaldi, Brazil	1972, 1975	2
= Jacques Villeneuve, Canada	1996–97	2
= David Coulthard (UK)	1999–2000	2

* Up to and including the 2005 race
# Shared win with Tony Brooks

The British Grand Prix was first raced at Brooklands in 1926, but the wins list count only from 1950 when the World Championship started. That year's British Grand Prix at Silverstone (13 May 1950) was the first-ever race in the World Championships.

top10 MOST **GRAND PRIX WINS BY BRITISH DRIVERS** *

DRIVER	FIRST GRAND PRIX WIN / CAR	RACE WINS
1 Nigel Mansell	1985 European (Williams)	31
2 Jackie Stewart	1965 Italian (BRM)	27
3 Jim Clark	1962 Belgian (Lotus)	25
4 Damon Hill	1993 Hungarian (Williams)	22
5 Stirling Moss	1955 British (Mercedes-Benz)	16#
6 Graham Hill	1962 Dutch (BRM)	14
7 David Coulthard	1995 Portuguese (Williams)	13
8 James Hunt	1975 Dutch (Hesketh)	10
9 = John Surtees	1963 German (Ferrari)	6
= Tony Brooks	1957 British (Vanwall)	6#

* Up to and including the 2005 season
# Including shared win

the10 **LEAST SUCCESSFUL** FORMULA ONE DRIVERS *

DRIVER / COUNTRY	YEARS	STARTS
1 Andrea De Cesaris, Italy	1980–94	208
2 Martin Brundle, UK	1984–96	158
3 Derek Warwick, UK	1981–93	147
4 Jean Pierre Jarier, France	1971–83	134
5 Eddie Cheever, USA	1978–89	132
6 Pierluigi Martini, Italy	1985–95	118
7 Philippe Alliot, France	1984–94	110
8 Mika Salo, Finland	1994–2002	109
9 Jos Verstappen, Netherlands	1994–2003	107
10 Jenson Button, UK	2000–05	100

* Based on number of starts without a win up to and including the 2005 season

Motorcycling

top10 COUNTRIES WITH THE MOST SOLO MOTORCYCLING WORLD TITLES*

	COUNTRY	TITLES
1	Italy	72
2	UK	43
3	Spain	28
4 =	Germany/West Germany	16
=	USA	16
6	Australia	9
7 =	Southern Rhodesia	8
=	Switzerland	8
9	Japan	7
10	South Africa	5

* As at the end of the 2005 season

← **Winner's flag**
Italian rider Valentino Rossi (b.1979) won seven World Championships between 1997 and 2005, five of them consecutive.

top10 RIDERS WITH THE MOST SOLO MOTORCYCLING WORLD TITLES*

	RIDER / COUNTRY	500/MOTOGP	350CC	250CC	125CC	80/50CC	TOTAL
1	Giacomo Agostini, Italy	8	7	–	–	–	15
2	Angel Nieto, Spain	–	–	–	7	6	13
3 =	Mike Hailwood, UK	4	2	3	–	–	9
=	Carlo Ubbiali, Italy	–	–	3	6	–	9
5 =	Phil Read, UK	2	–	4	1	–	7
=	Valentino Rossi, Italy	5	–	1	1	–	7
=	John Surtees, UK	4	3	–	–	–	7
8 =	Geoff Duke, UK	4	2	–	–	–	6
=	Jim Redman, Southern Rhodesia	–	4	2	–	–	6
10 =	Mick Doohan, Australia	5	–	–	–	–	5
=	Anton Mang, West Germany	–	2	3	–	–	5

* As at the end of the 2005 season

top10 RIDERS WITH THE MOST MOTO CROSS WORLD TITLES*

	RIDER / COUNTRY	500CC	250CC	125CC	TOTAL
1	Stefan Everts, Belgium	2	6	1	9
2	Joel Robert, Belgium	–	6	–	6
3 =	Roger de Coster, Belgium	5	–	–	5
=	Eric Geboers, Belgium	2	1	2	5
=	Georges Jobe, Belgium	3	2	–	5
=	Joel Smets, Belgium	5	–	–	5
7 =	Harry Everts, Belgium	–	1	3	4
=	Torsten Hallman, Sweden	–	4	–	4
=	Heikki Mikkola, Finland	3	1	–	4
10 =	Greg Albertyn, South Africa	–	2	1	3
=	Alessio Chiodi, Italy	–	–	3	3
=	Paul Friedrich, East Germany	3	–	–	3
=	Andre Malherbe, Belgium	3	–	–	3
=	Guennady Moisseev, USSR	–	3	–	3
=	Gaston Rahier, Belgium	–	–	3	3
=	David Thorpe, UK	3	–	–	3

* FIM World titles 1957–2005

top10 RIDERS WITH THE MOST **SUPERBIKE** RACE WINS*

	RIDER / COUNTRY	WINS
1	Carl Fogarty, UK	59
2 =	Troy Corser, Australia	31
=	Colin Edwards, USA	31
4	Doug Polen, USA	27
5	Raymand Roche, France	23
6	Troy Bayliss, Australia	22
7	Noriyuki Haga, Japan	19
8	Pier Francesco Chili, Italy	17
9 =	Giancarlo Falappa, Italy	16
=	Neil Hodgson, UK	16

* Since the start of Superbike racing in 1988 to the end of the 2005 season

➔ Fogarty's firsts
Up to his retirement in 2000, British rider Carl Fogarty (b.1966) established a commanding lead with 59 Superbike victories.

top10 RIDERS WITH THE MOST **SPEEDWAY** WORLD TITLES*

	RIDER / COUNTRY	YEARS	TITLES
1	Ivan Mauger, New Zealand	1968–79	6
2 =	Ove Fundin, Sweden	1956–67	5
=	Tony Rickardsson, Sweden	1994–2002	5
4 =	Barry Briggs, New Zealand	1957–66	4
=	Hans Nielsen, Denmark	1986–95	4
6 =	Ole Olsen, Denmark	1971–78	3
=	Erik Gundersen, Denmark	1984–88	3
8 =	Fred Williams, UK	1950–53	2
=	Jack Young, Australia	1951–52	2
=	Ronnie Moore, New Zealand	1954–59	2
=	Peter Craven, UK	1955–62	2
=	Bruce Penhall, USA	1981–82	2
=	Greg Hancock, USA	1992–97	2

* Up to and including 2005

Up to 1995 the world title was decided by a series of qualifying heats with the final being a single-night event. Since 1995 it has been a season-long series of Grand Prix events with points tallied up throughout the season ultimately deciding the champion.

top10 MOST **ISLE OF MAN TT WINS**

	RIDER#	YEARS	WINS
1	Joey Dunlop	1977–2000	26
2	Mike Hailwood	1961–79	14
3 =	Steve Hislop	1987–94	11
=	Dave Molyneux	1989–2005	11
=	Phillip McCallen (Ireland)	1992–97	11
6 =	Stanley Woods	1923–39	10
=	Giacomo Agostini (Italy)	1966–72	10
=	Rob Fisher	1994–2002	10
9 =	Siegfried Schauzu (West Germany)	1967–75	9
=	Mick Boddice	1983–91	9
=	David Jefferies	1999–2002	9

* As at end of 2005 season
# All riders from the UK unless otherwise stated

Motorcycle racing began on the Isle of Man when a 20-mph speed limit was imposed on British roads. The Auto-Cycle Club (now Auto-Cycle Union) launched the first TT (Tourist Trophy) meeting on 28 May 1907. Since 1911, the event has featured Senior and Junior races over a 60.6-km (37.75-mile) course.

Cycling

top10 MOST WINS IN THE **TOUR DE FRANCE***

	RIDER / COUNTRY	YEARS	WINS
1	Lance Armstrong, USA	1999–2005	7
2	= Jacques Anquetil, France	1957–64	5
	= Eddy Merckx, Belgium	1969–74	5
	= Bernard Hinault, France	1978–85	5
	= Miguel Induráin, Spain	1991–95	5
6	= Philippe Thys, Belgium	1913–20	3
	= Louison Bobet, France	1953–55	3
	= Greg LeMond, USA	1986–90	3
9	= Lucien Petit-Breton, France	1907–08	2
	= Firmin Lambot, Belgium	1919–22	2
	= Ottavio Bottecchia, Italy	1924–25	2
	= Nicolas Frantz, Luxembourg	1927–28	2
	= André Leducq, France	1930–32	2
	= Antonin Magne, France	1931–34	2
	= Sylvère Maes, Belgium	1936–39	2
	= Gino Bartali, Italy	1938–48	2
	= Fausto Coppi, Italy	1949–52	2
	= Bernard Thévenet, France	1975–77	2
	= Laurent Fignon, France	1983–84	2

* Up to and including 2005

top10 RIDERS WITH MOST WINS IN THE **THREE MAJOR TOURS***

	NAME / COUNTRY	TOUR	GIRO	VUELTA	YEARS	TOTAL
1	Eddy Merckx, Belguim	5	5	1	1968–74	11
2	Bernard Hinault, France	5	3	2	1978–85	10
3	Jacques Anquetil, France	5	2	1	1957–64	8
4	= Fausto Coppi, Italy	2	5	0	1940–53	7
	= Miguel Induráin, Spain	5	2	0	1991–95	7
	= Lance Armstrong, USA	7	0	0	1999–2005	7
7	= Alfredo Binda, Italy	0	5	0	1925–33	5
	= Gino Bartali, Italy	2	3	0	1938–48	5
	= Felice Gimondi, Italy	1	3	1	1965–76	5
10	= Tony Rominger, Switzerland	0	1	3	1992–95	4
	= Roberto Heras, Spain	0	0	4	2000–05	4

* Up to and including 2005

The three major tours are: Tour de France, launched in 1903, won by Maurice Garin, France; Tour of Italy (Giro d'Italia) first contested in 1909, won by Luigi Ganna, Italy; and Tour of Spain (Vuelta de España), first held in 1935, won by Gustave Deloor, Belgium.

⬇ *Seven wonders*
American cyclist Lance Armstrong (b.1971) overcame serious illness to become the most successful Tour de France competitor of all time, with seven consecutive victories between 1999 and 2005.

top10 COUNTRIES WITH MOST **TOUR DE FRANCE WINNERS**

	COUNTRY	WINS
1	France	36
2	Belgium	18
3	USA	10
4	Italy	9
5	Spain	8
6	Luxembourg	4
7	= Netherlands	2
	= Switzerland	2
9	= Denmark	1
	= Germany	1
	= Ireland	1

* Up to and including 2005

top10 **OLYMPIC CYCLING** NATIONS*

	COUNTRY	GOLD MEDALS
1	France	39
2	Italy	36
3	Germany/West Germany	16
4	USSR/Russia	15
5	Holland	14
6	= Australia	13
	= USA	13
8	UK	12
9	= Belgium	6
	= Denmark	6
	= East Germany	6

* All events up to and including the 2004 Athens Games, including discontinued events and the 1906 Intercalated Games

AMAZING FACT

A Bicycle Race For Two

Now discontinued as an Olympic event, a men's 2,000-m (6,560-ft) tandem race was competed from 1906 to 1972. British riders John Matthews and Arthur Rushen won gold in 1906, with German brothers Bruno and Max Götz gaining silver.

top10 WINNERS OF **CYCLING CLASSICS***

	RIDER / NATIONALITY	YEARS	MSR	TL	TF	LBL	PR	TOTAL
1	Eddy Merckx, Belgium	1966–76	7	2	2	5	3	19
2	Roger de Vlaeminck, Belgium	1970–79	3	2	1	1	4	11
3	= Constante Girardengo, Italy	1918–26	6	3	–	–	–	9
	= Fausto Coppi, Italy	1946–54	3	5	–	–	1	9
	= Sean Kelly, Ireland	1984–92	2	3	–	2	2	9
6	= Rik Van Looy, Belgium	1958–65	1	1	2	1	3	8
7	Gino Bartalli, Italy	1939–50	4	3	–	–	–	7
8	= Henri Pelissier, France	1911–21	1	3	–	–	2	6
	= Alfredo Binda, Italy	1925–31	2	4	–	–	–	6
	= Francesco Moser, Italy	1975–84	1	2	–	–	3	6
	= Moreno Argentin, Italy	1985–91	–	1	1	4	–	6
	= Johan Museeuw, Belgium	1993–2002	–	–	3	–	3	6

* Up to and including 2005

After the three major Tours, the Classics are the most prestigious of all cycling races. All Classics are single day races and since 2005 have formed part of the UCI (Union Cycliste Internationale) Pro Tour. The top five, often regarded as the toughest of the Classics, are known as the Monuments. They are:

(i) Milan-San Remo (MSR) – raced each spring, it was first held in 1907 and is the longest of all Classics at nearly 300 km (186 miles).

(ii) Tour of Lombardy (TL) – held in October and first raced as the Milan-Milan race in 1905.

(iii) Tour of Flanders (TF) – held early April each year, it was first staged in 1913.

(iv) Liége-Bastogne-Liége (LBL) – is the oldest of all current Classics, first held for amateurs in 1892 and since 1894 for professionals.

(v) Paris-Roubaix (PR) – held since 1896 and known as the Hell of the North.

Only three riders have won all five Monuments: Roger De Vlaeminck, Rik Van Looy and Eddy Merckx, all of whom were Belgian.

top10 **OLDEST** CYCLING CLASSIC RACES AND TOUR

	RACE	FIRST HELD
1	Liège-Bastogne-Liège	1892
2	Paris-Brussels	1893
3	Paris-Roubaix	1896
4	Paris-Tours	1896
5	Tour de France	1903
6	Tour of Lombardy	1905
7	Milan-San Remo	1907
8	Tour of Italy	1909
9	Tour of Flanders	1913
10	Championship of Zurich	1914

The Bordeaux-Paris race was the first of the major cycling races and was, until its demise in 1988, the oldest of all Classics. Regarded as the 'Derby of Road Racing', the Bordeaux-Paris race lasted for around 16 hours, starting in darkness in the early hours of the morning. The first race in 1891 was won by Britain's George Pilkington Mills. Originally for amateurs, it became a professional race and remained so until its last staging in 1988.

Skateboarding

top10 **SKATEBOARDERS** WITH THE MOST GOLD MEDALS IN THE X GAMES

	SKATER / COUNTRY	YEARS	BIG AIR	STREET/PARK	VERT	TOTAL*
1	Tony Hawk, USA	1995–2003	–	–	9	9
2	Andy Macdonald, USA	1996–2002	–	–	8	8
3	Bucky Lasek, USA	1999–2004	–	–	6	6
4	Rodil de Araujo Jr, Brazil	1996–2002	–	5	–	5
5	Bob Burnquist, Brazil	2000–05	–	–	4	4
6 =	Chris Senn, USA	1995–99	–	3	–	3
=	Eric Koston, Thailand	2000–03	–	–	3	3
=	Pierre-Luc Gagnon, Canada	2002–05	–	–	3	3
9	Paul Rodriguez, USA	2004–05	–	2	–	2
10 =	Matt Dove, USA	2001	–	–	1	1
=	Kerry Getz, USA	2001	–	1	–	1
=	Ryan Sheckler, USA	2003	–	1	–	1
=	Sandro Dias, Brazil	2004	–	–	1	1
=	Chad Muska, USA	2004	–	1	–	1
=	Danny Way, USA	2005	1	–	–	1

* Medals won in X Games 1–11 and 2003 X Games Global; includes doubles and best trick

◄ *Flyin' Ryan*
Ryan Sheckler became the world's youngest professional skateboarder at 13, going on to win numerous competitions.

top10 **VERT SKATEBOARDERS** WITH THE MOST MEDALS IN THE X GAMES

	SKATER / COUNTRY	YEARS	BRONZE	MEDALS SILVER	GOLD	TOTAL*
1	Tony Hawk, USA	1995–2003	3	2	9	14#
2	Andy Macdonald, USA	1996–2003	2	3	8	13†
3 =	Bucky Lasek, USA	1998–2004	–	4	6	10
=	Bob Burnquist, Brazil	1998–2005	3	3	4	10
5 =	Rune Glifberg, Denmark	1995–2004	6	2	–	8
=	Pierre-Luc Gagnon, Canada	2002–05	1	4	3	8
7 =	Neal Hendrix, USA	1995–2003	2	2	–	4
=	Mike Crum, USA	1999–2003	2	2	–	4
=	Sandro Dias, Brazil	2002–05	1	2	1	4
10	Colin McKay, Canada	2000–05	1	2	–	3

* Includes doubles and best trick
# Also won a silver medal for Street in 1995
† Also won two silver medals for Street 1997–78

the10 LATEST **STREET/PARK SKATEBOARDING** CHAMPIONS AT THE X GAMES

YEAR	SKATER / COUNTRY
2005	Paul Rodriguez, USA
2004	Paul Rodriguez, USA
2003	Eric Koston (street), USA
2003	Ryan Sheckler (park), USA
2002	Rodil de Araujo Jr (street), Brazil
2002	Rodil de Araujo Jr (park), Brazil
2001	Kerry Getz, USA
2000	Eric Koston, USA
1999	Chris Senn, USA
1998	Rodil de Araujo Jr, Brazil

top10 STREET SKATERS, 2005 (MALE)

SKATER / COUNTRY	WCS WORLD RANKING POINTS, 2005
1 Ryan Sheckler, USA	3,725
2 Ronnie Creager, USA	3,650
3 Jereme Rogers, USA	3,100
4 Greg Lutzka, USA	2,650
5 Austen Seaholm, USA	1,750
6 Dayne Brummet, USA	1,700
7 Daisuke Mochizuki, Japan	1,675
8 Rick McCrank, Canada	1,450
9 Mike Peterson, USA	1,400
10 Kyle Berard, USA	1,165

Source: World Cup Skateboarding (WCS)

Ranking is arrived at by adding the points from a skater's four best results at North American WCS Points Events (Lake Forest, Toronto, Vancouver, Philadelphia) together with their best three results from WCS Points Events in Europe, Australia, South America and Asia. Skaters must take part in the World Championships in Münster, Germany, to win the No.1 ranking.

● *P-Rod's double X*
Paul Rodriguez (nickname 'P-Rod') won consecutive victories in the X Games.

top10 STREET SKATERS, 2005 (FEMALE)

SKATER / COUNTRY	WCS WORLD RANKING POINTS, 2005*
1 Vanessa Torres, USA	3,350
2 Lauren Perkins, USA	3,200
3 Lyn-Z Adams Hawkins, USA	2,200
4 Lacey Baker, USA	2,150
5 = Amy Caron, USA	2,000
= Elissa Steamer, USA	2,000
7 Sophie Poppe, Belgium	1,550
8 Elizabeth Nitu, USA	1,350
9 Georgina Matthews, New Zealand	1,250
10 Anne-Sophie Julien, France	1,100

* Total of points won in the Gallaz Skate Jam, World Championships Germany, Slam City Jam and West 49 Canadian Open

Source: World Cup Skateboarding (WCS)

top10 VERT SKATERS, 2005 (MALE)

SKATER / COUNTRY	WCS WORLD RANKING POINTS, 2005
1 Sandro Dias, Brazil	4,600
2 Rodrigo Menezes, Brazil	3,200
3 Neal Hendrix, USA	3,175
4 Bob Burnquist, Brazil	2,650
5 Trevor Ward, Australia	2,325
6 Otavio Neto, Brazil	2,100
7 Macelo Kosake, Brazil	1,750
8 Mathias Ringstrom, Sweden	1,600
9 Lincoln Ueda, Brazil	1,425
10 Max Dufour, Canada	1,300

Source: World Cup Skateboarding (WCS)

top10 VERT SKATERS, 2005 (FEMALE)

SKATER / COUNTRY	WCS WORLD RANKING POINTS, 2005*
1 Cara-Beth Burnside, USA	3,000
2 Mimi Knoop, USA	2,400
3 Karen Jones, Brazil	1,700
4 Jen O'Brien, USA	1,650
5 = Tina Neff, Germany	1,550
= Apryl Woodcock, USA	1,550
7 Holly Lyons, USA	1,450
8 Rebecca Aimee Davis, UK	1,400
9 Nicole Zuck, USA	650
10 Mandy Esch, USA	600

* Total of points won in the Slam City Jam, World Championships Germany, X Games and West Beach Games Soul Bowl

Source: World Cup Skateboarding (WCS)

Horse Sports

top10 NATIONAL HUNT WINS IN A SEASON*

	JOCKEY	YEARS	WINS
1	Tony McCoy	2001–02	289
2	Tony McCoy	2002–03	256
3	Tony McCoy	1997–98	253
4	Tony McCoy	1999–2000	245
5	Peter Scudamore	1988–89	221
6	Tony McCoy	2003–04	209
7	Tony McCoy	2004–05	200
8	Richard Dunwoody	1993–94	197
9	Tony McCoy	2000–01	191
10	Tony McCoy	1996–97	190

* Based on wins by champion jockeys up to and including the 2004–05 season

top10 JOCKEYS IN THE BREEDERS' CUP*

	JOCKEY	YEARS	WINS
1	Jerry Bailey	1991–2005	15
2	Pat Day	1984–2001	12
3	Mike Smith	1992–2002	10
4	Chris McCarron	1985–2001	9
5	Gary Stevens	1990–2000	8
6 =	Eddie Delahoussaye	1984–93	7
=	Laffit Pincay Jr	1985–93	7
=	José Santos	1986–2002	7
=	Pat Valenzuela	1986–2003	7
10 =	Corey Nakatani	1996–2004	6
=	John Velazquez	1998–2004	6

* Up to and including 2005

Source: The Breeders' Cup

top10 COUNTRIES WITH THE MOST OLYMPIC SHOW-JUMPING MEDALS*

	COUNTRY	GOLD	SILVER	BRONZE	TOTAL
1	Germany/West Germany	13	3	7	23
2	USA	4	8	3	15
3	France	5	4	5	14
4	Italy	3	5	5	13
5	UK	1	3	5	9
6	Sweden	3	1	3	7
7 =	Belgium	1	2	3	6
=	Switzerland	1	3	2	6
9 =	Mexico	2	1	2	5
=	Netherlands	2	3	0	5

* Up to and including the 2004 Olympics

top10 JOCKEYS IN THE ENGLISH CLASSICS*

	JOCKEY	YEARS#	1,000 GUINEAS	2,000 GUINEAS	DERBY	OAKS	ST LEGER	WINS
1	Lester Piggott	1954–92	2	5	9	6	8	30
2	Frank Buckle	1792–1827	6	5	5	9	2	27
3	Jem Robinson	1817–48	5	9	6	2	2	24
4	Fred Archer	1874–86	2	4	5	4	6	21
5 =	Bill Scott	1821–46	0	3	4	3	9	19
=	Jack Watts	1883–97	4	2	4	4	5	19
7	Willie Carson	1972–94	2	4	4	4	3	17
8 =	John Day	1826–41	5	4	0	5	2	16
=	George Fordham	1859–83	7	3	1	5	0	16
10	Joe Childs	1912–33	2	2	3	4	4	15

* Up to and including 2005
# Of first and last wins

top10 MOST OLYMPIC DRESSAGE MEDALS*

	COUNTRY	GOLD	SILVER	BRONZE	TOTAL
1	Germany/West Germany	18	9	8	35
2	Sweden	7	5	7	19
3	Switzerland	3	6	4	13
4 =	France	3	5	2	10
=	USSR/Russia	4	3	3	10
6 =	Netherlands	2	4	2	8
=	USA	0	1	7	8
8	Denmark	0	3	0	3
9 =	Austria	1	0	1	2
=	Spain	0	1	1	2

* Up to and including the 2004 Olympics

the10 **FASTEST WINNING TIMES** OF THE PRIX DE L'ARC DE TRIOMPHE*

	HORSE	JOCKEY	YEAR	TIME MIN/SEC
1	Peintre Célèbre	Olivier Peslier	1997	2:24.60
2	Bago	Thierry Gillet	2004	2:25.00
3	Sinndar	Johnny Murtagh	2000	2:25.80
4	Trempolino	Pat Eddery	1987	2:26.30
5	Marienbard	Frankie Dettori	2002	2:26.70
6	Tony Bin	John Reid	1988	2:27.30
7	Hurricane Run	Kieren Fallon	2005	2:27.40
8	Dancing Brave	Pat Eddery	1986	2:27.70
9	Detroit	Pat Eddery	1980	2:28.00
10	All Along	Walter Swinburn	1983	2:28.10

* Up to and including 2005

Held every October at the Longchamp racecource in the Bois de Boulogne, Paris. The first Prix de l'Arc de Triomphe was in 1920, to celebrate the Allies' victory in World War I. Raced over 2,400 metres (about 1 mile 4 furlongs), the race is for horses of three years of age and upwards.

top10 JOCKEYS IN A **FLAT RACING SEASON***

	JOCKEY	YEARS	WINS
1	Gordon Richards	1947	269
2	Gordon Richards	1949	261
3	Gordon Richards	1933	259
4	Fred Archer	1885	246
5	Fred Archer	1884	241
6	Frankie Dettori	1994	233
7	Fred Archer	1883	232
8	Gordon Richards	1952	231
9	Fred Archer	1878	229
10	Gordon Richards	1951	227

In the pink
US jockey Jerry Bailey gallops to his record 15th Breeders' Cup victory.

* Up to and including the 2005 season

Gordon Richards rode over 200 winners in a season 12 times, while Archer did so on eight occasions. The only other men to reach double centuries are Tommy Loates (1893), Pat Eddery (1990), Michael Roberts (1992) and Kieren Fallon (1997, 1998, 1999 and 2003).

Stadium Stats

top10 **BIGGEST** STADIUMS*

	STADIUM	LOCATION	YEAR OPENED	OFFICIAL CAPACITY
1	Strahov Stadium	Prague, Czech Republic	1926	250,000
2	May Day Stadium	Pyöngyang, North Korea	1989	150,000
3	Saltlake Stadium	Calcutta, India	1984	120,000
4	Estádio Azteca	Mexico City, Mexico	1966	114,465
5	Michigan Stadium	Ann Arbor, Michigan, USA	1927	107,501
6	Beaver Stadium	Penn State University, Pennsylvania, USA	1960	107,282
7	Neyland Stadium	Knoxville, Tennessee, USA	1921	104,079
8	Jornalista Mário Filho#	Rio de Janeiro, Brazil	1950	103,045
9	Ohio Stadium	Colombus, Ohio, USA	1922	101,568
10	National Stadium Bukit Jalil	Kuala Lumpur, Malaysia	1998	100,200

* Excluding speedway and motor racing circuits and horse racing tracks
# Formerly the Maracana Stadium

The Strahov Stadium, a wooden structure built in 1926 and since much modified, covers a total area of 6.3 sq km (2.4 sq miles).

⊙ *Political arena*
The 16-arched May Day Stadium, North Korea, has a floor area of 207,000 sq m (2,228,125 sq ft). It is used for both sporting events and political parades in which there can be as many as 100,000 people on the pitch.

top10 BIGGEST SOCCER **STADIUMS IN SCOTLAND**

	GROUND / HOME TEAM	OFFICIAL CAPACITY, 2005–06
1	Celtic Park Celtic	60,506
2	Hampden Park Queen's Park/ Scotland	52,046
3	Ibrox Stadium Rangers	50,444
4	Pittodrie Aberdeen	22,199
5	Rugby Park Kilmarnock	18,128
6	Tynecastle Park Heart of Midlothian	17,702
7	Easter Road Hibernian	17,400
8	Tannadice Park Dundee United	14,209
9	Fir Park Motherwell	13,742
10	East End Park Dunfermline	12,509

the10 BIGGEST SOCCER STADIUMS IN ENGLAND

GROUND / HOME TEAM	OFFICIAL CAPACITY, 2005
1 Old Trafford Manchester United	68,936
2 St James' Park Newcastle United	52,387
3 City of Manchester Stadium Manchester City	48,500
4 Stadium of Light Sunderland	48,300
5 Anfield Liverpool	45,522
6 Villa Park Aston Villa	43,300
7 Stamford Bridge Chelsea	42,449
8 Elland Road Leeds United	40,242
9 Goodison Park Everton	40,103
10 Hillsborough Sheffield Wednesday	39,859

Manchester United are expanding their Old Trafford capacity to 75,000 in 2006 and Arsenal (currently 11th on the list with their Highbury Stadium holding 38,500) will be moving into a new ground, The Emirates Stadium, with a 60,000 capacity, also in 2006. Leeds United's Elland Road ground had the biggest capacity for any club outside the Premiership in 2005–06.

the10 BIGGEST STADIUMS TO **HOST MATCHES** IN WORLD CUP 2006

STADIUM	LOCATION	HOME TEAM	OFFICIAL CAPACITY
1 Olympic Stadium	Berlin	Hertha Berlin	74,220
2 Alliaqnz Arena	Munich	Bayern Munich	66,016
3 Westfaloenstadion	Dortmund	Borussia Dortmund	65,982
4 Arena Aufschalke	Gelsenkirchen	Schalke 04	53,804
5 Gottlieb-Daimler Stadion	Stuttgart	Vfb Stuttgart	53,200
6 AOL Arena	Hamburg	Hamburg SV	51,055
7 Waldstadion	Frankfurt	Intracht Frankfurt	48,132
8 Rhine Energy Stadium	Cologne	1.FC Cologne	46,120
9 AWD Arena	Hannover	Hannover 96	44,652
10 Zentralstadion	Leipzig	FC Sachsen Leipzig	44,199

top10 **MOST WATCHED** PROFESSIONAL SPORTING LEAGUES

	LEAGUE	SPORT	COUNTRY	SEASON	AVERAGE*
1	National Football League	American Football	USA	2005	67,463
2	Bundesliga 1	Soccer	Germany	2004–05	37,771
3	Australian Football League	Australian Rules	Australia	2004	35,703
4	FA Premier League	Soccer	England	2004–05	33,893
5	Major League Baseball	Baseball	USA/Canada	2005	30,970
6	La Liga	Soccer	Spain	2004–05	28,401
7	Canadian Football League	Canadian Football	Canada	2004	27,303
8	Serie A	Soccer	Italy	2004–05	25,805
9	Ligue 1	Soccer	France	2004–05	21,392
10 =	J-League 1	Soccer	Japan	2004	18,965
=	NFL Europe	American Football	Europe	2005	18,965

* Average attendance during latest season

Further Information

THE UNIVERSE & THE EARTH

Asteroids
http://neo.jpl.nasa.gov/
NASA's Near Earth Object Program

Astronautics
http://www.astronautix.com/
Spaceflight news and reference

Comets
http://www.cometography.com/
Comet catalogue and descriptions

Islands
http://islands.unep.ch/isldir.htm
Information on the world's islands

NASA
http://www.nasa.gov/home/index.html
The main website for the US space programme

Oceans
http://www.oceansatlas.org/index.jsp
The UN's resource on oceanographic issues

Planets
http://www.nineplanets.org/
A multimedia tour of the Solar System

Mountains
http://peaklist.org/
Lists of the world's tallest mountains

Space
http://www.space.com/
Reports on events in space exploration

Waterfalls
http://www.world-waterfalls.com/
Data on the world's tallest and largest waterfalls.

LIFE ON EARTH

Animals
http://animaldiversity.ummz.umich.edu/site/index.html
A wealth of animal data

Birds
http://www.bsc-eoc.org/avibase/avibase.jsp
A database on the world's birds

Conservation
http://iucn.org/
The leading nature conservation site

Endangered
http://www.cites.org/
Lists of endangered species of flora and fauna

Environment
http://www.unep.ch/
The UN's Earthwatch and other programmes

Fish
http://www.fishbase.org/home.htm
Global information on fishes

Food and Agriculture Organization
http://www.fao.org/
Statistics from the UN's FAO website

Forests, UK
http://www.forestry.gov.uk/
The website of the Forestry Commission

Insects
http://ufbir.ifas.ufl.edu/
The University of Florida Book of Insect Records

Sharks
http://www.flmnh.ufl.edu/fish/Sharks/sharks.htm
Extensive shark research and attack reports

THE HUMAN WORLD

Crime, international
http://www.interpol.int/
Interpol's crime statistics

Crime, UK
http://www.homeoffice.gov.uk/
Home Office crime and prison population figures

Death penalty
http://web.amnesty.org/pages/deathpenalty-statistics-eng
Facts ands statistics from Amnesty International

Leaders
http://www.terra.es/personal2/monolith/home.htm
Facts about world leaders since 1945

Parliaments
http://www.ipu.org/
Women in parliaments, etc from the Inter-Parliamentary Union

Population and names
http://www.statistics.gov.uk/
The UK in figures and naming trends for the UK population

Religions
http://www.worldchristiandatabase.org/wcd/
World religion data

Royalty
http://www.royal.gov.uk/
The official site of the British Monarchy, with histories

Rulers
http://rulers.org/
A database of the world's rulers and political leaders

World Health Organization
http://www.who.int/en/
World health information and advice

TOWN & COUNTRY

Countries
http://www.theodora.com/wfb/
Country data, rankings, etc

Country and city populations
http://www.citypopulation.de/cities.html
A searchable guide to the world's countries and major cities

Country data
http://www.odci.gov/cia/publications/factbook/
The CIA World Factbook

Country population
http://www.un.org/esa/population/unpop.htm
The UN's worldwide data on population issues

Development
http://www.worldbank.org/
World development and other statistics

Population
http://www.census.gov/
US and international population statistics

Population issues
http://www.un.org/esa/population/unpop.htm
The UN's Population Division

Refugees
http://www.unhcr.org/
UNHCR, the UN Refugee Agency

Skyscrapers
http://www.emporis.com/en/bu/sk/
The Emporis database of high-rise buildings

Tunnels
http://home.no.net/lotsberg/
A database of the world's tunnels

CULTURE

The Art Newspaper
http://www.theartnewspaper.com/
News and views on the art world

The Bookseller
http://www.thebookseller.com/
The organ of the British book trade

The British Library
http://www.bl.uk/
The route to the catalogues and exhibitions in the national library

Education
http://www.dfes.gov.uk/statistics/
Official statistics relating to education in the UK

Languages of the world
http://www.ethnologue.com/
The world's 6,912 living languages

Languages online
http://global-reach.biz/globstats/index.php3
Facts and figures on online languages

Library loans
http://www.plr.uk.com/
The UK's most-borrowed books

The Man Booker Prize
http://www.themanbookerprize.com/
Britain's most prestigious literary prize

Museums & galleries
http://www.24hourmuseum.org.uk/
A guide to exhibitions and events at the UK

UNESCO
http://www.unesco.org/
Comparative international statistics on education and culture

MUSIC

All Music Guide
http://www.allmusic.com/
A comprehensive guide to all genres of music

Billboard
http://www.billboard.com/
US music news and charts data

The Brit Awards
http://www.brits.co.uk/
The official website for the popular music awards

The British Phonographic Industry Ltd
http://www.bpi.co.uk/
Searchable database of gold discs and other certified awards

Grammy Awards
http://www.naras.org/
The official site for the famous US music awards

Launch
http://uk.launch.yahoo.com/index.html
UK music charts and news from Yahoo

MTV
http://www.mtv.co.uk/
The online site for the MTV UK music channel

New Musical Express
http://www.nme.com/
The online version of the popular music magazine

Official UK Charts Company
http://www.theofficialcharts.com/
Weekly and historical music charts

VH1
http://www.vh1.com/
Online UK music news

STAGE & SCREEN

Academy Awards
http://www.oscars.org/academyawards/
The official "Oscars" website

BBC
http://www.bbc.co.uk/
Gateway to BBC TV and radio, with a powerful Internet search engine

Empire Online
http://www.empireonline.co.uk/
The website of the UK film magazine

Film Distributors' Association
http://www.launchingfilms.com/
Trade site for UK film releases and statistics

Golden Globe Awards
http://www.hfpa.org/
Hollywood Foreign Press Association's Golden Globes site

Internet Movie Database
http://www.imdb.com/
The best of the publicly accessible film websites; IMDbPro is available to subscribers

London Theatre Guide
http://www.londontheatre.co.uk/
A comprehensive guide to West End theatre productions

Screen Daily
http://www.screendaily.com/
Daily news from the film world at the website of UK weekly Screen International

Variety
http://www.variety.com/
Extensive entertainment information (extra features available to subscribers)

Yahoo! Movies
http://uk.movies.yahoo.com/
Charts plus features, trailers and links to the latest film UK releases

COMMERCIAL WORLD

The Economist
http://www.economist.com/
Global economic and political news

Energy
http://www.bp.com/
The BP Statistical Review of World Energy

Environmental Sustainability Index
http://sedac.ciesin.columbia.edu/es/esi/
Data on the planet's future

Forbes magazine
http://www.forbes.com/
'Rich lists' and other rankings

Gold
http://www.gold.org/
The website of the World Gold Council

International Labour Organization
http://www.ilo.org/
Facts and figures on the world's workers

Organisation for Economic Co-operation and Development
http://www.oecd.org/home/
World economic and social statistics

Telecommunications
http://www.itu.int
Worldwide telecommunications statistics

United Nations Development Programme
http://www.undp.org/
Country GDPs and other development data

The World Bank
http://www.worldbank.org/
World trade and labour statistics

TRANSPORT & TOURISM

Air disasters
http://www.airdisaster.com/
Reports on aviation disasters

Airports
http://www.airports.org/
Airports Council International's world coverage

Association of Leading Visitor Attractions
http://www.alva.org.uk/
Information on the UK's top tourist attractions

Car manufacture
http://www.oica.net/
The International Organization of Motor Vehicle Manufacturers' website

Metros
http://www.lrta.org/world/worldind.html
The world's light railways and tram systems

Railways
http://www.railwaygazette.com/
The world's railway business in depth from Railway Gazette International

Shipwrecks
http://www.shipwreckregistry.com/
A database of the world's lost ships

Tourism
http://www.staruk.org.uk/
UK tourism stats from Star UK

Tourism Offices Worldwide Directory
http://www.towd.com/
Tourism offices around the world

World Tourism Organisation
http://www.world-tourism.org/
The world's top tourism organization

SPORT

Athletics
www.britishathletics.info/
British athletics news and rankings

Cricket
http://www.cricinfo.com/
Cricinfo, launched in 1993, since merged with the online version of Wisden

FIFA
http://www.fifa.com
The official website of FIFA, the world governing body of soccer

Football
www.football-league.co.uk
The official site of the Football League

Formula One
http://www.formula1.com/
The official F1 website

Olympics
www.olympic.org/uk/games/index_uk.asp
The official Olympics website

Premier League
http://www.premierleague.com
The official web site of soccer's Premier League

Rugby
http://www.itsrugby.com/
Comprehensive rugby site

Skateboarding
http://www.wcsk8.com/
Results, biographies, etc from World Cup Skateboarding

Skiing
http://www.fis-ski.com/
Fédèration Internationales de Ski, the world governing body of skiing and snowboarding

Index

Acknowledgements

Special research: Ian Morrison (sport);
Dafydd Rees (US data and Music)

Alexander Ash
Caroline Ash
Nicholas Ash
Peter Bond
Richard Braddish
Thomas Brinkhoff
Richard Chapman
Stanley Coren
Christopher Forbes
Russell E. Gough
Robert Grant
Angela Hayes
Richard Hurley
Larry Kilman
Aylla Macphail
Chris Mead
Sylvia Morris
Roberto Ortiz de Zarate
Tony Pattison
Christiaan Rees
Robert Senior
Lucy T. Verma

Academy of Motion Picture Arts and Sciences
– Oscar statuette is the registered trademark
and copyrighted property of the Academy of
Motion Picture Arts and Sciences
Advertising Age
Airports Council International
Air Transport Users Council
American Association of Port Authorities
Amnesty International
Amusement Business
Argos Insurance Services
The Art Newspaper
Association of Leading Visitor Attractions
Audit Bureau of Circulations Ltd
BBC
BBC Radio 1
Billboard
Box Office Mojo
BP Statistical Review of World Energy 2004
The Breeders' Cup
British Academy of Film and Television Awards
The BRIT Awards
British Council
British Film Institute
British Library
British Phonographic Industry
British Video Association
Business Week
Cameron Mackintosh Ltd
Central Intelligence Agency
Checkout
Christie's
Classic FM

Comité Interprofessionnel du Vin de
Champagne
Commission for Distilled Spirits
Computer Industry Almanac
Cremation Society of Great Britain
CricInfo
Criminal Statistics England & Wales
De Beers
Deloitte
Department for Environment, Food and Rural
Affairs
Earth Impact Database
The Economist
Encyclopedia of Insects
Energy Information Administration
Entertainment and Leisure Software Publishers
Association
Ethnologue
Euromonitor
Europa
Family Business Magazine
Fédération Internationale de Football
Association
Fédération Internationale de Motorcyclisme
Fédération Internationale de Ski
Feline Advisory Bureau/Felix
Food and Agriculture Organization of the
United Nations
Forbes
Forestry Commission
Gold Fields Mineral Services
Governing Council of the Cat Fancy
HM Treasury
Home Office
Interbrand
Interflora
International Air Transport Association
International Association of Athletics
Federations
International Centre for Prison Studies
International Civil Aviation Organization
International Game Fish Association
The International Institute for Strategic
Studies, *The Military Balance 2005–2006*
International Intellectual Property Alliance
International Labour Organization
International Monetary Fund
International Obesity Task Force
International Olympic Committee
International Shark Attack File/American
Elasmobranch Society/Florida Museum of
Natural History
International Telecommunication Union
International Union for Conservation of
Nature and Natural Resources
Internet Movie Database
Internet World Stats
Joint United Nations Programme on HIV/AIDS
(UNAIDS)
The Kennel Club
Ladies Professional Golf Association

Lloyds Register-Fairplay Ltd
London Marathon
LTB Gordonsart/Art Sales Index
Meteorological Office
MRIB
Music Information Database
National Aeronautics and Space
Administration (NASA), USA
National Amusement Park Historical
Association
National Basketball Association (USA)
National Football League (USA)
AC Nielsen
Nielsen BookScan
Office for National Statistics
The Official UK Charts Company
Organisation for Economic Co-operation and
Development
Organisation Internationale des Constructeurs
d'Automobiles
Periodical Publishers Association
Population Reference Bureau
Power & Motoryacht
Professional Golfers' Association
Railway Gazette International
Royal Astronomical Society
Royal Opera House, Covent Garden
Screen Digest
Screen International
Shakespeare Centre
Society of Motor Manufacturers and Traders
Ltd
Sotheby's
Sport England (formerly Sports Council)
Stockholm International Peace Research
Institute
Stores
Suttons Seeds
Travel Trends
UK Mammals
United Nations
United Nations Children's Fund
United Nations Educational, Scientific and
Cultural Organization
United Nations Population Division
Universal Postal Union
US Census Bureau
US Committee for Refugees and Immigrants
US Geological Survey
Variety
Ward's Motor Vehicle Facts & Figures
World Association of Newspapers
World Bank
World Cup Skateboarding
World Economic Forum
World Gold Council
World Health Organization
World Nuclear Association
World of Learning
World Tourism Organization

Picture Credits

The publishers would like to thank the following sources for their kind permission to reproduce the photographs and illustrations in this book.

(Abbreviations key: t = top, b = bottom, r = right, l = left, c = centre)

Antonov ASTC: 199t.

Christie's Images Ltd: 102-103, 104, 105, 106.

Corbis: 14r Bettmann, 16-17t Rick Doyle, 17 Dean Conger, 18 Peter Guttman, 19t Pablo Corral V, 21t Warren Morgan, 21b Free Agents Limited, 25 Douglas Peebles, 28 Jim Zuckerman, 31 Bryn Colton/Assignments Photographers, 32-33 Bettmann, 33r Cath Mullen/Frank Lane Picture Agency, 35 Bob Gomel, 37 Pierre Holtz/Reuters, 38b, 39 Jeffrey L. Rotman, 40l Robert Dowling, 40r Lawrence Manning, 44l Darrell Gulin, 44r Frans Lanting, 45 Joe McDonald, 54t LWA-Dann Tardif, 57 Kevin Dodge, 61 Gianni Giansanti, 62 Tim Graham, 63l Patrick Ward, 63r Stephane Cardinale/People Avenue, 64t Richard Olivier, 67 Fat Chance Productions, 68 Hulton-Deutsch Collection, 69 t&b Bettmann, 70, 71t Hulton-Deutsch Collection, 71b, 72 Baldev, 78 Rafiqur Rahman/Reuters, 80l Abaed Omar Qusini/Reuters, 81r Saeed Ali Achakzai/Reuters, 82 David Zimmerman, 83t Tom Wagner/CORBIS SABA, 83b Bettmann, 86 Lake County Museum, NY, 87 Massimo Listri, 89 Jean-Philippe Arles/Reuters, 94b Chris Andrews Publications/CORBIS, 95 Alessia Pierdomenico/Reuters, 97t Helen King, 98l Ron Watts, 99 Steve Raymer, 100-101c Nik Wheeler, 103b Hulton-Deutsch Collection, 107 Reuters, 110t Seth Wenig/Reuters, 111 Bettmann, 112t Hans Klaus Techt/epa, 119 Michael Mulvey/Dallas Morning News, 120t Andrew Gombert/epa, 123r Elizabeth Kreutz/NewSport, 124 Bo Zaunders, 127 Micheline Pelletier/CORBIS SYGMA, 130 Bettmann, 131 Rupert Horrox, 136-137c Stewart Tilger, 139 Hamshere Keith/CORBIS SYGMA, 149b Warner Bros/ZUMA, 154 Christies Images Ltd, 155 Tobias Schwarz/Reuters, 157 Walt Disney Pictures/Pixar Animation/Bureau L.A.Collections, 158l G. Schuster/zefa, 158-159r Lester Lefkowitz, 163 Carlo Cortes IV/Reuters, 166 Lou Dematteis, 167 Jean-Pierre Amet/Bel Ombra, 169 Ming Ming/Reuters/, 175t Jose Fuste Raga, 176 Charles O'Rear, 179 Ed Kashi, 180-181 Skyscan, 188 Neil Rabinowitz, 190t Derek Trask, 195 Christian Charisius/Reuters, 196t Bettmann, 198b Bettmann, 199b Bettmann, 200 V.Velengurin/R.P.G./CORBIS SYGMA, 201 CORBIS SYGMA, 204l Bob Krist, 207 Reuters, 210l John Gress/Reuters, 211r John Kolesidis/Reuters, 212b Tobias Schwarz/Reuters, 213 Reuters, 216 Icon SMI, 218b Victor Fraile/Reuters, 222-223 Le Segretain Pascal/CORBIS SYGMA, 225 Mike Finn-Kelcey/Reuters, 226t Michael Kim, 228t Michael Fiala/Reuters, 229 Marc Serota/Reuters, 230 Reuters, 234-235 Giampiero Sposito/Reuters, 236b Victor Fraile/Reuters, 238 Reuters, 240 Lucy Nicholson/Reuters, 241 Lucy Nicholson/Reuters, 242t Ina Fassbender/Reuters, 244b KCNA/epa.

Empics: 215 Steven Senne/AP, 237b Steve Etherington.

Frank Lane Picture Agency: 16 Norbert Wu/Minden Pictures.

Getty Images: 24 Jim Sugar, 58t Frans Lemmens, 73 AFP, 77 Robert Harding World Imagery, 114 Donald Kravitz, 117 Scott Gries, 186-187r, 187b, 190b, 192-193r AFP, 194 Yann Layma, 208 Menahem Kahana/AFP, 209 Javier Soriano/AFP, 224 The Image Bank, 231, 232 Joe Klamar/AFP, 243.

Ivan Hissey: 22-23, 28-29, 32-33b, 45b, 48, 86t, 88, 142, 178t, 178-179b, 206-207.

i-Stock: 19b, 22, 23t, 38t, 41, 42, 43, 48, 49, 50, 51, 52, 53l, 54, 55, 56, 58b, 59, 60, 61b, 64b, 66, 76, 79, 80-81, 84, 92, 93, 94t, 96, 97c, 98r, 100-101, 102l, 110b, 112-113, 116b, 118, 120b, 122, 125, 132t, 135b, 142, 146b, 147t, 148b, 149t, 150, 152, 156, 162, 164, 165, 166-167, 168, 170, 171, 172, 173, 174, 175, 177, 178, 182, 183, 186l, 191, 192l, 197, 198t, 204r, 210-211c, 212t, 214, 217, 218-219t, 219, 221, 226b, 227, 228b, 236t, 237t, 239, 242b, 244-245t, 245b.

Kobal Collection: 126 Miramax, 132b Columbia/Goldcrest, 133t Universal/Wing Nut Films, 135t Lucasfilm/20th Century Fox, 140 Dreamworks Pictures, 141 Nickelodeon Movies, 143 Warner Bros, 144 Columbia/Michaels, Darren, 145 Warner Bros, 146t 20th Century Fox/Dreamworks/ILM (Industrial Light & Magic), 147b 20th Century Fox/Appleby, David, 148t Miramax, 151 Lions gate/Sebastian, Lorey, 153 Warner Brothers.

NASA: 10t, 11t, 11ac, 11bc, 11b, 12c, 12r, 12l, 14l, 15, 189t, 189b.

NHPA: 36 Joe Blossom.

David Penrose: 23b.

Rex Features: 121 Richard Young.

Science Photo Library: 10b Mark Garlick, 53r Russell Kightley.

South African Astronomical Observatory: 13.

United International Pictures: 136b.

Publisher's Acknowledgements
Cover design: 'Ome Design.

Packager's Acknowledgements
Palazzo Editions would like to thank Richard Constable and Robert Wallster for their design contributions, and Ivan Hissey for the specially commissioned illustrations.